READING FOR
THE PLOT

READING FOR THE PLOT

Design and Intention

in Narrative

PETER BROOKS

VINTAGE BOOKS
A DIVISION OF RANDOM HOUSE
NEW YORK

Portions of a number of these chapters have been
previously published, in different form, in the following periodicals: *Comparative Literature, Diacritics, New
Literary History, New York Literary Forum, Novel: A
Forum on Fiction, PMLA,* and *Yale French Studies.*

Library of Congress Cataloging in Publication Data

Brooks, Peter.
Reading for the plot.

Bibliography: p.
Includes index.
1. Fiction—Technique.   2. Plots (Drama, novel, etc.)
3. Narration (Rhetoric)   I. Title.
[PN3378.B76   1985]   808.3   84-40516
ISBN 0-394-72909-9 (pbk.)

Manufactured in the United States of America

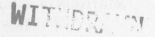

To the memory of
PAUL DE MAN
EXTRAORDINARY COLLEAGUE,
TEACHER, AND FRIEND

*Are not our lives too short for that full utterance
which through all our stammerings is of course
our only and abiding intention?*
Joseph Conrad, LORD JIM

CONTENTS

PREFACE

This is a book about plots and plotting, about how stories come to
be ordered in significant form, and also about our desire and need
for such orderings. Plot as I conceive it is the design and intention
of narrative, what shapes a story and gives it a certain direction or
intent of meaning. We might think of plot as the logic or perhaps
the syntax of a certain kind of discourse, one that develops its
propositions only through temporal sequence and progression.
Narrative is one of the large categories or systems of understanding
that we use in our negotiations with reality, specifically, in the case
of narrative, with the problem of temporality: man's time-boundedness, his consciousness of existence within the limits of mortality.
And plot is the principal ordering force of those meanings that we
try to wrest from human temporality. Plot is so basic to our experience of reading, and indeed to our very articulation of experience in general, that criticism has often passed it over in silence,
as too obvious to bear discussion. Yet the obvious can often be the
most interesting, as well as the most difficult, to talk about.

Our common sense of plot—our capacity to recognize its common
forms and their characteristics—derives from many sources, including no doubt the stories of our childhood. Most of all, perhaps,
it has been molded by the great nineteenth-century narrative tradition that, in history, philosophy, and a host of other fields as well
as literature, conceived certain kinds of knowledge and truth to be
inherently narrative, understandable (and expoundable) only bv

way of sequence, in a temporal unfolding. In this golden age of narrative, authors and their public apparently shared the conviction that plots were a viable and a necessary way of organizing and interpreting the world, and that in working out and working through plots, as writers and readers, they were engaged in a prime, irreducible act of understanding how human life acquires meaning. Narrative as a dominant mode of representation and explanation comes to the fore—speaking in large generalization—with the advent of Romanticism and its predominantly historical imagination: the making and the interpretation of narrative plots assumes a centrality and importance in literature, and in life, that they did not have earlier no doubt because of a large movement of human societies out from under the mantle of sacred myth into the modern world where men and institutions are more and more defined by their shape in time. In our own century, we have become more suspicious of plots, more acutely aware of their artifice, their arbitrary relation to time and chance, though we no doubt still depend on elements of plotting, however ironized or parodied, more than we realize.

Mainly, then, this is a book about plots of the dominant modern narrative tradition; I make no claim to covering all the varieties of plot—and the refusals of plot—that would need discussion were this a survey. Most of my examples are taken from nineteenth-century novels and from those twentieth-century narratives that, however complicating and even subversive of the tradition, maintain a vital relation to it. And my very premises for the study of plot largely derive from this tradition: that is, I have looked for the ways in which the narrative texts themselves appear to represent and reflect on their plots. Most viable works of literature tell us something about how they are to be read, guide us toward the conditions of their interpretation. The novels of the great tradition all offer models for understanding their use of plots and their relation to plot as a model of understanding. Hence my discussions of specific plots and of the concept of plot tend both to start and to finish with what the narrative texts themselves suggest about the role of plot in shaping texts and, by extension, lives.

Even more than with plot, no doubt, I shall be concerned with plotting: with the activity of shaping, with the dynamic aspect of narrative—that which makes a plot "move forward," and makes us read forward, seeking in the unfolding of the narrative a line of intention and a portent of design that hold the promise of progress toward meaning. My interest in the dynamics of narrative, and in plotting as a human activity, entails an attempt to move beyond strict allegiance to the various formalisms that have dominated the study of narrative in recent decades, including the substantial body of structuralist work on narrative, of the type that the French, with a nice sense of neologism, have baptized "narratology," meaning the organized and coherent analysis of narrative structures and discourse. I have learned much from narratology, and I owe a general debt to the tendency of structuralist thought as a whole to see literature as one part of a wider range of man's signifying practices, the way he reshapes his world through the use of signs and fictions. The models of analysis proposed by narratologists— derived in most instances from linguistic theory—have often been boldly illuminating, showing up basic patterns and systematic re- lations neglected in the more interpretive Anglo-American critical tradition. But for my purposes, narratological models are exces- sively static and limiting. Whatever its larger ambitions, narratology has in practice been too exclusively concerned with the identifi- cation of minimal narrative units and paradigmatic structures; it has too much neglected the temporal dynamics that shape narra- tives in our reading of them, the play of desire in time that makes us turn pages and strive toward narrative ends. Narratology has, of course, properly been conceived as a branch of poetics, seeking to delineate the types of narrative, their conventions, and the for- mal conditions of the meanings they generate; whereas I am more concerned with how narratives work on us, as readers, to create models of understanding, and with why we need and want such shaping orders.

My study, then, while ever resting its case on the careful reading of texts, intends to take its stand beyond pure formalism, attempt- ing to talk of the dynamics of temporality and reading, of the motor forces that drive the text forward, of the desires that connect narrative ends and beginnings, and make of the textual middle a highly charged field of force. "*Form* fascinates when we no longer have the force to understand force from within itself," Jacques Derrida has written in criticism of the formalist imagination of structuralism. I am not certain that we can ever "understand" force (nor does Derrida claim to), but it ought to be possible to recognize its place in narrative, and to find ways of talking about our experience of reading narrative as a dynamic operation, consuming and shaping time as the medium of certain meanings that depend on energy as well as form.

My interest in loosening the grip of formalism has taken me to psychoanalysis, particularly to the work of Freud himself, which presents a dynamic model of psychic processes and thus may offer the promise of a model pertinent to the dynamics of texts. Psychoanalysis, after all, is a primarily narrative art, concerned with the recovery of the past through the dynamics of memory and desire. And Freud's own project was much more closely concerned with the use and the understanding of signs, especially narrative signs, than has usually been acknowledged, as the rereading of Freud proposed by Jacques Lacan can help us to see. It is not that I am interested in the psychoanalytic study of authors, or readers, or fictional characters, which have been the usual objects of attention for psychoanalytically informed literary criticism. Rather, I want to see the text itself as a system of internal energies and tensions, compulsions, resistances, and desires.

Ultimately, we may dream of a convergence of psychoanalysis and literary criticism because we sense that there ought to be a correspondence between literary and psychic dynamics, since we constitute ourselves in part through our fictions within the constraints of a transindividual symbolic order, that of signs, including, pre-eminently, language itself. Through study of the work accomplished by fictions we may be able to reconnect literary criticism to human concern. In our attempt to move beyond strict formalism—while not losing sight of what formalism has taught us—psychoanalysis promises, and requires, that in addition to linguistic paradigms and the rules of the sign-system, we engage the dynamic of memory and the history of desire as they work to shape the creation of meaning within time. My aim here is in some measure to make good on the claim—put forward by Susan Sontag some years ago—that rather than theories of interpretation we need an "erotics" of art.

The plot of my own argument in this study will make loops and detours in the pursuit of its subject. I have attempted to interweave textual readings with discussion of the speculative and theoretical issues that such readings both provoke and illustrate. My wish to study models of plots and plotting as they are proposed by narrative texts themselves has dictated working closely with selected texts while also seeking to extrapolate from them to larger problems. This approach cannot make a claim to full coverage of the topic; it aims rather to suggest new ways of conceiving it. Also, the textual grounding of such an approach means that I at times pursue issues in interpretation of the individual texts that may appear to lead us rather far from the main line of argument, yet, I hope, always to return to that line with enhanced understanding. The model of plot for my own argument may be something like Pascal's in his *Pensées*: a "digression on each point in order to reach the center."

The chapters that follow in fact tend to alternate readings of specific texts with more speculative excursions into Freud (though here, too, concentrating on his texts rather than on any overall system) and into the general dynamics of narrative. The first chapter makes a gradual approach to the novels that will be my main concern through discussion of some general points about narrative, seeking to define some ways of thinking about the place of plot in narrative, formulating preliminary hypotheses about its functioning, and taking on as necessary what other analysts of narrative have said about these questions. Chapter 2 then confronts the nebulous but fundamental question of desire in and for narrative, mainly by way of some seminal novels by Balzac. Chapter 3 addresses what I see as a crucial early nineteenth-century novel, Stendhal's *Le Rouge et le noir*, by way of the problems in paternity, generational conflict, and transmission worked through by its plot. By the time we reach Chapter 4, I have accumulated enough examples and general issues to propose a model, derived from a reading of Freud's *Beyond the Pleasure Principle*, that provides a suggestive, but by no means exclusive, template for analysis. Chapter 5 turns to testing this model against a specific "highly plotted" novel, Dickens's *Great Expectations*. The concerns of Chapter 6 are quite different: it explores the popular novel, using as example Eugène Sue's *Les Mystères de Paris*, its themes and its readership, asking what such an instance of the "consumption" of plot can tell us about the need for plot. Chapter 7 then makes a necessary encounter with a stumbling block, Flaubert, whose dissent from and subversion of traditional modes of plotting both illuminate the great tradition of narrative and announce its future transformations. With Chapter 8, we begin to move beyond narrative to narrating, to questions of telling and listening and the "transferential" model of plot and reading that they imply. Chapter 9 studies these issues in a specific fictional text, Conrad's *Heart of Darkness*; whereas in Chapter 10 one of Freud's case histories, that of the "Wolf Man," becomes the testing ground for the models and methods so far developed. Chapter 11 uses a problematic and challenging "modernist" work, Faulkner's *Absalom, Absalom!*, to discuss the tenuous status and continuing importance of plots and plotting. Hence Chapters 1, 4, and 8 offer the main theoretical armature of my argument, while Chapters 3, 5, 7, 9, and 11 provide its main "readings" of novelistic texts; Chapters 2, 6, and 10 are highly mixed breeds. The Conclusion, finally, suggests what has happened to plotting in our time, and returns to Freud, specifically to the model of the psychoanalytic transference, as a way to illuminate our subject.

Parts of a number of these chapters have been published in earlier versions in several periodicals: *PMLA*, *Yale French Studies*, *New Literary History*, *New York Literary Forum*, *Novel*, *Poétique*, *Diacritics*, *Comparative Literature*. I wish to thank the editors of these journals, both for the hospitality of their pages and for permission to reuse the material. In all cases, the earlier versions have been substantially revised and expanded.

I am grateful also to a large number of people in various universities who, by the invitation to lecture from my work in progress, forced progress to occur—made me put ideas on paper and then through questions and challenges helped me to clarify them. Let me mention in particular Janet Beizer, Jules Brody, Ralph Cohen, Michael Fried, Jane Gallop, Richard Klein, Stephen Nichols, Burton Pike, Richard Sennett, and Anthony Vidler. But the study also owes debts that cannot be more specifically or individually acknowledged to colleagues and students at Cornell, Johns Hopkins, Harvard, Dartmouth, Princeton, Bryn Mawr, Brown, University of Virginia, Rutgers, University of Pittsburgh, New York University, Miami University of Ohio, Ohio State University, University of Texas at Austin, as well as the Institute for Architecture and Urban Studies in New York and the Humanities Institute, Santa Cruz, California. Philip Lewis read the whole manuscript with his customary critical acumen. I wish I had more often had a ready answer to his pertinent queries.

I was the beneficiary of an American Council of Learned Societies Fellowship in 1979, which gave me a semester's free time for research and especially the opportunity to explore the material of Chapter 6 in Paris; travel grants from the American Philosophical Society and the Griswold Faculty Research Fund, Yale University, in 1978; and a National Endowment for the Humanities Summer Stipend in 1980, which permitted an uninterrupted period for further research. I am most sincerely grateful to these organizations for their support of a project whose progress must have appeared inordinately slow.

More than anything else I have written, this book derives directly from my teaching, in particular a National Endowment for the Humanities Summer Seminar offered in 1976, which provided the initial impetus for thinking about many of these questions, and summer courses taught at the University of Texas Summer Institute in Literature in 1978 and 1979, as well as a number of graduate seminars at Yale and an undergraduate course on "Narrative Forms"—one of the introductory courses of The Literature Major—which I taught for a number of years. Students in all of these courses have not only taught me much, they have also, by their very presence, their assent or resistance, given shape to my thought and language. Moreover, in "Narrative Forms" I had the benefit of teaching in cooperation with an exceptionally talented group of colleagues to whom I no doubt owe more than I would even wish to acknowledge: to Andrea Bertolini, Barbara Guetti, Joseph Halpern, Barbara Johnson, David Marshall, J. Hillis Miller, Walter Reed. Another sometime colleague of that course, David A. Miller, has over the years been the most loyal of critics and friends.

It counts as a special pleasure to acknowledge all that I owe to the friendship of Michael Holquist, who more than anyone else first started me thinking about the questions discussed in this book, and who over the gaps of space and time has ever maintained the dialogue.

I have been fortunate to have had for many years the efficient and elegant aid provided by Sheila M. Brewer. And for this book I have had the very great fortune of finding in Carol Brown Janeway a wholly sympathetic editor. Finally, Margaret, Preston, Catherine, and Nathaniel don't expect thanks but deserve them.

READING FOR
THE PLOT

I

Reading for the Plot

I

Our lives are ceaselessly intertwined with narrative, with the stories that we tell and hear told, those we dream or imagine or would like to tell, all of which are reworked in that story of our own lives that we narrate to ourselves in an episodic, sometimes semi-conscious, but virtually uninterrupted monologue. We live immersed in narrative, recounting and reassessing the meaning of our past actions, anticipating the outcome of our future projects, situating ourselves at the intersection of several stories not yet completed. The narrative impulse is as old as our oldest literature: myth and folktale appear to be stories we recount in order to explain and understand where no other form of explanation will work. The desire and the competence to tell stories also reach back to an early stage in the individual's development, to about the age of three, when a child begins to show the ability to put together a narrative in coherent fashion and especially the capacity to recognize narratives, to judge their well-formedness. Children quickly become virtual Aristotelians, insisting upon any storyteller's observation of the "rules," upon proper beginnings, middles, and particularly ends. Narrative may be a special ability or competence that we learn, a certain subset of the general language code which, when mastered, allows us to summarize and retransmit narratives in other words and other languages, to transfer them into other media, while remaining recognizably faithful to the original narrative structure and message.

Narrative in fact seems to hold a special place among literary forms—as something more than a conventional "genre"—because of its potential for summary and retransmission: the fact that we can still recognize "the story" even when its medium has been considerably changed. This characteristic of narrative has led some theorists to suppose that it is itself a language, with its own code and its own rules for forming messages from the code, a hypothesis that probably does not hold up to inspection because narrative appears always to depend on some other language code in the creation of its meanings. But it does need to be considered as an operation important to all of our lives. When we "tell a story," there tends to be a shift in the register of our voices, enclosing and setting off the narrative almost in the manner of the traditional "once upon a time" and "they lived happily ever after": narrative demarcates, encloses, establishes limits, orders. And if it may be an impossibly speculative task to say what narrative itself is, it may be useful and valuable to think about the kinds of ordering it uses and creates, about the figures of design it makes. Here, I think, we can find our most useful object of attention in what has for centuries gone by the name of plot.

"Reading for the plot," we learned somewhere in the course of our schooling, is a low form of activity. Modern criticism, especially in its Anglo-American branches, has tended to take its valuations from study of the lyric, and when it has discussed narrative has emphasized questions of "point of view," "tone," "symbol," "spatial form," or "psychology." The texture of narrative has been considered most interesting insofar as it approached the density of poetry. Plot has been disdained as the element of narrative that least sets off and defines high art—indeed, plot is that which especially characterizes popular mass-consumption literature: plot is why we read *Jaws*, but not Henry James. And yet, one must in good logic argue that plot is somehow prior to those elements most discussed by most critics, since it is the very organizing line, the thread of design, that makes narrative possible because finite and comprehensible.

Aristotle, of course, recognized the logical priority of plot, and a recent critical tradition, starting with the Russian Formalists and coming up to the French and American "narratologists," has revived a quasi-Aristotelian sense of plot. When E. M. Forster, in the once influential *Aspects of the Novel*, asserts that Aristotle's emphasis on plot was mistaken, that our interest is not in the "imitation of an action" but rather in the "secret life which each of us lives privately," he surely begs the question, for if "secret lives" are to be narratable, they must in some sense be plotted, display a design and logic.[1]

There are evidently a number of different ways one might go about discussing the concept of plot and its function in the range of narrative forms. Plot is, first of all, a constant of all written and oral narrative, in that a narrative without at least a minimal plot would be incomprehensible. Plot is the principle of interconnectedness and intention which we cannot do without in moving through the discrete elements—incidents, episodes, actions—of a narrative: even such loosely articulated forms as the picaresque novel display devices of interconnectedness, structural repetitions that allow us to construct a whole; and we can make sense of such dense and seemingly chaotic texts as dreams because we use interpretive categories that enable us to reconstruct intentions and connections, to replot the dream as narrative. It would, then, be perfectly plausible to undertake a typology of plot and its elements from the *Iliad* and the *Odyssey* onward to the new novel and the "metafictions" of our time.[2] Yet it seems clear also that there have been some historical moments at which plot has assumed a greater importance than at others, moments in which cultures have seemed to develop an unquenchable thirst for plots and to seek the expression of central individual and collective meanings through narrative design. From sometime in the mid-eighteenth century through to the mid-twentieth century, Western societies appear to have felt an extraordinary need or desire for plots, whether in fiction, history, philosophy, or any of the social sciences, which in fact largely came into being with the Enlightenment and Romanticism. As Voltaire announced and then the Romantics confirmed, history replaces theology as the key discourse and central imagination in that historical explanation becomes nearly a necessary factor of any thought about human society: the question of what we are typically must pass through the question of where we are, which in turn is interpreted to mean, how did we get to be there? Not only history but historiography, the philosophy of history, philology, mythography, diachronic linguistics, anthropology, archaeology, and evolutionary biology all establish their claim as fields of inquiry, and all respond to the need for an explanatory narrative that seeks its authority in a return to origins and the tracing of a coherent story forward from origin to present.

The enormous narrative production of the nineteenth century may suggest an anxiety at the loss of providential plots: the plotting of the individual or social or institutional life story takes on new urgency when one no longer can look to a sacred masterplot that organizes and explains the world. The emergence of narrative plot as a dominant mode of ordering and explanation may belong to the large process of secularization, dating from the Renaissance and gathering force during the Enlightenment, which marks a falling-away from those revealed plots—the Chosen People, Redemption, the Second Coming—that appeared to subsume transitory human time to the timeless. In the last two books of *Paradise Lost*, Milton's angel Michael is able to present a full panorama of human history to Adam, concluding in redemption and a timeless future of bliss; and Adam responds:

How soon hath thy prediction, Seer Blest,
Measur'd this transient World, the Race of time,
Till time stand fixt: beyond is all abyss,
Eternity, whose end no eye can reach. (Book 12, lines 553–56)

By the end of the Enlightenment, there is no longer any consensus on this prediction, and no cultural cohesion around a point of fixity which allows thought and vision so to transfix time. And this may explain the nineteenth century's obsession with questions of origin, evolution, progress, genealogy, its foregrounding of the historical narrative as par excellence the necessary mode of explanation and understanding.[3]

We still live today in the age of narrative plots, consuming avidly Harlequin romances and television serials and daily comic strips, creating and demanding narrative in the presentation of persons and news events and sports contests. For all the widely publicized nonnarrative or antinarrative forms of thought that are supposed to characterize our times, from complementarity and uncertainty in physics to the synchronic analyses of structuralism, we remain more determined by narrative than we might wish to believe. And yet, we know that with the advent of Modernism came an era of suspicion toward plot, engendered perhaps by an overelaboration of and overdependence on plots in the nineteenth century. If we cannot do without plots, we nonetheless feel uneasy about them, and feel obliged to show up their arbitrariness, to parody their mechanisms while admitting our dependence on them. Until such a time as we cease to exchange understandings in the form of stories, we will need to remain dependent on the logic we use to shape and to understand stories, which is to say, dependent on plot. A reflection on plot as the syntax of a certain way of speaking our understanding of the world may tell us something about how and why we have come to stake so many of the central concerns of our society, and of our lives, on narrative.

II

These sweeping generalizations will bear more careful consideration later on. It is important at this point to consider more closely just how we intend to speak of plot, how we intend to work with it, to make it an operative analytic and critical tool in the study of narrative. I want to urge a conception of plot as something in the nature of the logic of narrative discourse, the organizing dynamic of a specific mode of human understanding. This pursuit will in a moment take us into the discussion of narrative by a number of critics (of the type recently baptized narratologists), but perhaps the best way to begin is through a brief exercise in an old and thoroughly discredited form, the plot summary, in this case of a very old story. Here, then, is the summary of a story from the Grimm brothers, known in their version as "All-Kinds-of-Fur":[4]

A dying queen makes her husband promise that he will remarry only with a woman as beautiful as she, with the same golden hair. He promises, and she dies. Time passes, and he is urged by his councilors to remarry. He looks for the dead queen's equal, but finds no one; until, years later, his eyes light on his daughter, who looks just like her mother, with the same golden hair. He will marry her, though his councilors say he must not. Pressed to answer, the daughter makes her consent contingent on the performance of three apparently impossible tasks: he must give her three dresses, one as golden as the sun, one as silvery as the moon, the third as glittering as all the stars, plus a cloak made of a thousand different furs. The king, in fact, succeeds in providing these and insists on the marriage. The daughter then flees, blackens her face and hands, covers herself with the cloak of furs, and hides in the woods, where she is captured as a strange animal by the king of another country. She goes to work as a scullery maid in his kitchens, but on three successive occasions she appears at the king's parties clothed in one of her three splendid dresses and dances with him; and three times she cooks the king's pudding and leaves in the bottom of the dish one of the tokens she has brought from home (a golden ring, a golden spinning wheel, a golden reel). On the third repetition, the king slips the ring on her finger while they are dancing, and when she returns to the kitchen, in her haste she does not blacken one hand entirely. The king searches her out, notices the white finger and its ring, seizes her hand, strips off the fur cloak to reveal the dress underneath, and the golden hair, and claims her in marriage.

What have we witnessed and understood here? How have we moved from one desire that we, like the king's councilors, know to be prohibited, to a legitimate desire whose consummation marks the end of the tale? And what is the meaning of the process lying between beginning and end—a treble testing, with the supplemental requirement of the cloak; flight and disguise (using the cloak to become subhuman, almost a beast); then a sort of striptease revelation, also treble, using the three dresses provided by the father and the three golden objects brought from home (tokens, perhaps, of the mother), followed by recognition? How have we crossed from one kingdom to another through those woods which, we must infer, border on both of them? We cannot really answer such questions, yet we would probably all agree that the middle of the tale offers a kind of minimum satisfactory process that works through the problem of desire gone wrong and brings it to its cure. It is a process in which the overly eroticized object—the daughter become object of desire to the father—loses all erotic and feminine attributes, becomes unavailable to desire, then slowly, through repetition by three (which is perhaps the minimum repetition to suggest series and process), reveals her nature as erotic object again but now in a situation where the erotic is permitted and fitting. The tale is characterized by that laconic chasteness which Walter Benjamin found characteristic of the great oral stories, a refusal of psychological explanation and motivation.[5] It matter-of-factly takes on the central issues of culture—incest, the need for exogamy—without commentary. Like a number of the Grimms' tales, it seems to ask the question, Why do girls grow up, leave their homes and their fathers, and marry other men? It answers the question without explanation, through description of what needs to happen, the process set in motion, when normal forms are threatened, go awry: as in "Hawthorn Blossom" (the Grimms' version of "Sleeping Beauty"), we are given a kind of counter-example, the working-out of an antidote. The tale appears as the species of explanation that we give when explanation, in the logical and discursive sense, seems impossible or impertinent. It thus transmits a kind of wisdom that itself concerns transmission: how we pass on what we know about how life goes forward.

Folktale and myth may be seen to show narrative as a form of thinking, a way of reasoning about a situation. As Claude Lévi-Strauss has argued, the Oedipus myth may be "about" the unsolvable problem of man's origins—born from the earth or from parents?—a "chicken or egg" problem that finds its mythic "solution" in a story about generational confusion: Oedipus violates the de-

marcations of generations, becomes the "impossible" combination
of son/husband, father/brother, and so on, subverting (and thus
perhaps reinforcing) both cultural distinctions and categories of
thought. It is the ordering of the inexplicable and impossible situation as narrative that somehow mediates and forcefully connects
its discrete elements, so that we accept the necessity of what cannot
logically be discoursed of. Yet I don't think we do justice to our
experience of "All-Kinds-of-Fur" or the Oedipus myth in reducing
their narratives—as Lévi-Strauss suggests all mythic narratives can
be reduced—to their "atemporal matrix structure," a set of basic
cultural antinomies that the narrative mediates.[6] Nor can we, to be
sure, analyze these narratives simply as a pure succession of events
or happenings. We need to recognize, for instance, that there is a
dynamic logic at work in the transformations wrought between the
start and the finish of "All-Kinds-of-Fur," a logic which makes sense
of succession and time, and which insists that mediation of the
problem posed at the outset takes time: that the meaning dealt with
by narrative, and thus perhaps narrative's raison d'être, is of and
in time. Plot as it interests me is not a matter of typology or of
fixed structures, but rather a structuring operation peculiar to those
messages that are developed through temporal succession, the in-
strumental logic of a specific mode of human understanding. Plot,
let us say in preliminary definition, is the logic and dynamic of
narrative, and narrative itself a form of understanding and
explanation.

Such a conception of plot seems to be at least compatible with
Aristotle's understanding of *mythos,* the term from the *Poetics* that
is normally translated as "plot." It is Aristotle's claim that plot (*mythos*) and action (*praxis*) are logically prior to the other parts of
dramatic fictions, including character (*ethos*). *Mythos* is defined as
"the combination of the incidents, or things done in the story," and
Aristotle argues that of all the parts of the story, this is the most
important. It is worth quoting his claim once more:

Tragedy is essentially an imitation not of persons but of action
and life, of happiness and misery. All human happiness or

misery takes the form of action; the end for which we live is a certain kind of activity, not a quality. Character gives us qualities, but it is in our actions—what we do—that we are happy or the reverse. In a play accordingly they do not act in order to portray the Characters; they include the Characters for the sake of the action. So that it is the action in it, i.e. its Fable or Plot, that is the end and purpose of the tragedy; and the end is everywhere the chief thing.[7]

Later in the same paragraph he reiterates, using an analogy that may prove helpful to thinking about plot: "We maintain, therefore, that the first essential, the life and soul, so to speak, of Tragedy is Plot; and that the Characters come second—compare the parallel in painting, where the most beautiful colours laid on without order will not give one the same pleasure as a simple black-and-white sketch of a portrait." Plot, then, is conceived to be the outline or armature of the story, that which supports and organizes the rest. From such a view, Aristotle proceeds to derive three consequences. First, the action imitated by the tragedy must be complete in itself. This in turn means that it must have a beginning, a middle, and an end—a point wholly obvious but one that will prove to have interesting effects in its applications. Finally, just as in the visual arts a whole must be of a size that can be taken in by the eye, so a plot must be "of a length to be taken in by the memory." This is important, since memory—as much in reading a novel as in seeing a play—is the key faculty in the capacity to perceive relations of beginnings, middles, and ends through time, the shaping power of narrative.

But our English term "plot" has its own semantic range, one that is interestingly broad and possibly instructive. The *Oxford English Dictionary* gives seven definitions, essentially, which the *American Heritage Dictionary* helpfully reduces to four categories:

1. (a) A small piece of ground, generally used for a specific purpose. (b) A measured area of land; lot.
2. A ground plan, as for a building; chart; diagram.

3. The series of events consisting of an outline of the action of a narrative or drama.
4. A secret plan to accomplish a hostile or illegal purpose; scheme.

There may be a subterranean logic connecting these heterogeneous meanings. Common to the original sense of the word is the idea of boundedness, demarcation, the drawing of lines to mark off and order. This easily extends to the chart or diagram of the demarcated area, which in turn modulates to the outline of the literary work. From the organized space, plot becomes the organizing line, demarcating and diagramming that which was previously undifferentiated. We might think here of the geometrical expression, plotting points, or curves, on a graph by means of coordinates, as a way of locating something, perhaps oneself. The fourth sense of the word, the scheme or conspiracy, seems to have come into English through the contaminating influence of the French *complot*, and became widely known at the time of the Gunpowder Plot. I would suggest that in modern literature this sense of plot nearly always attaches itself to the others: the organizing line of plot is more often than not some scheme or machination, a concerted plan for the accomplishment of some purpose which goes against the ostensible and dominant legalities of the fictional world, the realization of a blocked and resisted desire. Plots are not simply organizing structures, they are also intentional structures, goal-oriented and forward-moving.

Plot as we need and want the term is hence an embracing concept for the design and intention of narrative, a structure for those meanings that are developed through temporal succession, or perhaps better: a structuring operation elicited by, and made necessary by, those meanings that develop through succession and time. A further analysis of the question is suggested here by a distinction urged by the Russian Formalists, that between *fabula* and *sjužet*. *Fabula* is defined as the order of events referred to by the narrative, whereas *sjužet* is the order of events presented in the narrative discourse. The distinction is one that takes on evident analytic force when one is talking about a Conrad or a Faulkner, whose dislocations of normal chronology are radical and significant, but it is no less important in thinking about apparently more straightforward narratives, since any narrative presents a selection and an ordering of material. We must, however, recognize that the apparent priority of *fabula* to *sjužet* is in the nature of a mimetic illusion, in that the *fabula*—"what really happened"—is in fact a mental construction that the reader derives from the *sjužet*, which is all that he ever directly knows. This differing status of the two terms by no means invalidates the distinction itself, which is central to our thinking about narrative and necessary to its analysis since it allows us to juxtapose two modes of order and in the juxtaposing to see how ordering takes place. In the wake of the Russian Formalists, French structural analysts of narrative proposed their own pairs of terms, predominantly *histoire* (corresponding to *fabula*) and *récit*, or else *discours* (corresponding to *sjužet*). English usage has been more unsettled. "Story" and "plot" would seem to be generally acceptable renderings in most circumstances, though a structural and semiotic analysis will find advantages in the less semantically charged formulation "story" and "discourse."[8]

"Plot" in fact seems to me to cut across the *fabula/sjužet* distinction in that to speak of plot is to consider both story elements and their ordering. Plot could be thought of as the interpretive activity elicited by the distinction between *sjužet* and *fabula*, the way we *use* the one against the other. To keep our terms straight without sacrificing the advantages of the semantic range of "plot," let us say that we can generally understand plot to be an aspect of *sjužet* in that it belongs to the narrative discourse, as its active shaping force, but that it makes sense (as indeed *sjužet* itself principally makes sense) as it is used to reflect on *fabula*, as our understanding of story. Plot is thus the dynamic shaping force of the narrative discourse. I find confirmation for such a view in Paul Ricoeur's definition of plot as "the intelligible whole that governs a succession of events in any story." Ricoeur continues, using the terms "events" and "story" rather than *fabula* and *sjužet*: "This provisory definition immediately shows the plot's connecting function between an event or events and the story. A story is *made out of* events to the extent that plot *makes* events *into* a story. The plot, therefore, places us at the crossing point of temporality and narrativity. . . ."[9] Ricoeur's emphasis on the constructive role of plot, its active, shaping function, offers a useful corrective to the structural narratologists' neglect of the dynamics of narrative and points us toward the reader's vital role in the understanding of plot.

The Russian Formalists presented what one might call a "constructivist" view of literature, calling attention to the material and the means of its making, showing how a given work is put together. "Device" is one of their favorite terms—a term for demonstrating the technical use of a given motif or incident or theme. Typical is Boris Tomachevsky's well-known illustration of the technical sense of "motivation": if a character in a play hammers a nail into the wall in Act I, then he or another character will have to hang himself from it in Act III. The work of Tomachevsky, Victor Shklovsky, Boris Eichenbaum is invaluable to the student of narrative since it so often cuts through thematic material to show the constructed armature that supports it.[10] Perhaps the instance of the Russian Formalists' work most compelling for our purposes is their effort to isolate and identify the minimal units of narrative, and then to formulate the principles of their combination and interconnection. In particular, Vladimir Propp's *The Morphology of the Folktale* merits attention as an early and impressive example of what can be done to formalize and codify the study of narrative.

Faced with the mass of material collected by folklorists and the inadequacy of attempts to order it through thematic groupings or patterns of derivation, Propp began with a gesture similar to that of Ferdinand de Saussure at the inception of modern linguistics, bracketing questions of origin and derivation and reference in order to find the principles of a morphology of a given body of material. Taking some one hundred tales classified by folklorists as fairy tales, he sought to provide a description of the fairy tale according to its component parts, the relation of these parts to one another and to the tale as a whole, and hence the basis for a comparison among tales. Propp claims that the essential morphological

components are function and sequence. One identifies the functions by breaking down the tale into elements defined not by theme
or character but rather according to the actions performed: function is "an act of character, defined from the point of view of its
significance for the course of the action."[11] Functions will thus
appear in the analysis as labels for kinds of action, such as "interdiction," "testing," "acquisition of the magical agent," and so on;
whereas sequence will concern the order of the functions, the logic
of their consecution. As a result of his study, Propp with a certain
bravado puts forward four theses concerning the fairy tale:

1. The functions are stable, constant elements whoever carries
   them out.
2. The number of functions is limited (there are just thirty-
   one in the Russian fairy tale).
3. The sequence of functions is always identical (not all are
   present in every tale, but the sequence of those present is
   invariable).
4. All fairy tales are of one type in regard to their structure.

Whatever the validity of Propp's theses, the concept of function,
and the "functionalist" view of narrative structure it implies, stresses
in a useful way the role of verbs of action as the armature of
narrative, their logic and articulation and sequence. Propp suggests
an approach to the analysis of narrative actions by giving precedence to *mythos* over *ethos*, indeed by abstracting plot structure from
the persons who carry it out. Characters for Propp are essentially
agents of the action; he reduces them to seven "dramatis personae,"
defined by the "spheres of influence" of the actions they perform:
the Villain, the Donor, the Helper, the Princess and her Father
(who together function as a single agent), the Dispatcher, the Hero,
and the False Hero. The names that an individual tale will assign
to these agents—and the way it may combine or divide them—are
relatively unimportant, as are their attributes and motivations. What
counts is their role as vehicles of the action, their placement and
appearance in order to make sure that the Hero is dispatched, for

instance, or that he is presented with false claims that he must expose and overcome. Propp's analysis clearly is limited by the relatively simple and formulaic nature of the narratives he discusses. Yet something like the concept of "function" may be necessary in any discussion of plot, in that it gives us a way to think about what happens in narrative from the point of view of its significance to the course of the action as a whole, the articulation of narrative as a structure of actions.

Propp's insistence on sequence and function results in a "syntagmatic" analysis, that is, one concerned with the combination of units along a horizontal axis, as in a sentence. Within French structuralism, there has rather been a strong emphasis on the "paradigmatic," an attention to the vertical axis which represents the grammar and lexicon of narrative, the elements and sets of relations which an individual narrative must call upon and activate.[12] Lévi-Strauss's interest in the "atemporal matrix structure" of narrative, the basic set of relationships which underlies and generates any given mythic narrative, is an example. So is the work of the semiotician A. J. Greimas, who takes Propp's analysis and, in the spirit of Lévi-Strauss, tries to reformulate the seven "dramatis personae" in the form of a matrix structure, a set of symmetrical oppositions which defines a kind of field of force. Greimas offers a taxonomy whose inherent tensions generate the production of narrative. It looks like this:

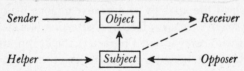

Without giving a full exposition of what Greimas calls his *modèle actantiel*—the dramatis personae have been rebaptized *actants*, emphasizing their quality of agency—one can see that the tale is conceived as a set of vectors, where the Hero's (the Subject's) search for the Object (the Princess, for instance) is helped or hindered, while the Object of the search itself (herself) is sent, or given, or put in the way of being obtained. The dotted line between Subject and Receiver indicates that very often these two coincide: the Hero is working for himself.[13]

The language used by Greimas—especially Subject and Object, but also Sender (*Destinateur*) and Receiver (*Destinataire*)—indicate that he is working also under the influence of a linguistic model, so central to structuralist thought in general. The work of Propp and other Russian Formalists has proved susceptible of a reformulation by way of the linguistic model, by structuralists concerned to provide a general poetics of narrative (or "narratology"), that is, the conditions of meaning, the grammar and the syntax of narrative forms. Tzvetan Todorov (who more than anyone else introduced the ideas of the Russian Formalists into French structuralism) works, for instance, from the postulate of a "universal grammar" of narrative.[14] Starting from a general analogy of narrative to a sentence writ large, Todorov postulates that the basic unit of narrative (like Propp's function) is a clause, while the agents are proper nouns, semantically void until predicated. The predicate terms are verbs (actions) and adjectives (states of being). His analysis proceeds largely with the study of verbs, the most important component of narrative, which have status (positive or negative), mood (imperative, optative, declarative, etc.), aspect (indicative, subjunctive), voice (passive or active). Clauses combine in different manners to form sequences, and complete narrative sequences are recognizable from their accomplishment of a transformation of the initial verb, now changed in status, mood, aspect, or by an added auxiliary verb.

Todorov best represents the linguistic model, applied to narrative analysis, in its most developed form. But such work is no doubt less valuable as a systematic model for analysis than as a suggestive metaphor, alerting us to the important analogies between parts of speech and parts of narrative, encouraging us to think about narrative as system, with something that approximates a grammar and rules of ordering that approximate a syntax. Perhaps the most challenging work to come out of narratology has used the linguistic model in somewhat playful ways, accepting it as a necessary basis for thought but opening up its implications in an engagement with the reading of texts. What I have most in mind here is Roland

Barthes's *S/Z*, a book that combines some of the rigors of structuralist analysis, in its patient tracing of five codes through a tale
broken down into 561 *lexias*, with interspersed speculative excur-
suses on narrative and its reading.[15]

If we ask more specifically where in *S/Z* we find a notion ap-
proximating "plot," I think the answer must be: in some combination of Barthes's two irreversible codes—those that must be decoded
successively, moving in one direction—the *proairetic* and the *hermeneutic*, that is: the code of actions ("Voice of the Empirical") and
the code of enigmas and answers ("Voice of Truth"). The proairetic
concerns the logic of actions, how their completion can be derived
from their initiation, how they form sequences. The limit-case of
a purely proairetic narrative would be approached by the picaresque tale, or the novel of pure adventure: narratives that give
precedence to the happening. The hermeneutic code concerns rather
the questions and answers that structure a story, their suspense,
partial unveiling, temporary blockage, eventual resolution, with the
resulting creation of a "dilatory space"—the space of suspense—
which we work through toward what is felt to be, in classical narrative, the revelation of meaning that occurs when the narrative
sentence reaches full predication. The clearest and purest example
of the hermeneutic would no doubt be the detective story, in that
everything in the story's structure, and its temporality, depends on
the resolution of enigma. Plot, then, might best be thought of as
an "overcoding" of the proairetic by the hermeneutic, the latter
structuring the discrete elements of the former into larger interpretive wholes, working out their play of meaning and significance. If we interpret the hermeneutic to be a general gnomic code,
concerned not narrowly with enigma and its resolution but broadly
with our understanding of how actions come to be semiotically
structured, through an interrogation of their point, their goal, their
import, we find that Barthes contributes to our conception of plot
as part of the dynamics of reading.

What may be most significant about *S/Z* is its break away from
the somewhat rigid notion of structure to the more fluid and dynamic notion of structuration. The text is seen as a texture or

weaving of codes (using the etymological sense of "text") ⟨
reader organizes and sorts out only in provisional ways, ⟨
never can master it completely, indeed is himself in part "u⟩ ⟨⟩
in his effort to unravel the text. The source of the codes is in what
Barthes calls the *déjà-lu*, the already read (and the already written),
in the writer's and the reader's experience of other literature, in a
whole set of intertextual interlockings. In other words, structures,
functions, sequences, plot, the possibility of following a narrative
and making sense of it, belong to the reader's literary competence,
his training as a reader of narrative.[16] The reader is in this view
himself virtually a text, a composite of all that he has read, or heard
read, or imagined as written. Plot, as the interplay of two of Barthes's
codes, thus comes to appear one central way in which we as readers
make sense, first of the text, and then, using the text as an interpretive model, of life. Plot—I continue to extrapolate from
Barthes—is an interpretive structuring operation elicited, and ne-
cessitated, by those texts that we identify as narrative, where we
know the meanings are developed over temporal succession in a
suspense of final predication. As Barthes writes in an earlier essay
("Introduction to the Structural Analysis of Narrative"), what animates us as readers of narrative is *la passion du sens*, which I would
want to translate as both the passion *for* meaning and the passion
of meaning: the active quest of the reader for those shaping ends
that, terminating the dynamic process of reading, promise to bestow
meaning and significance on the beginning and the middle.[17]

But what Barthes discusses less well is the relation of the sense-
making operations of reading to codes outside the text, to the
structuring of "reality" by textual systems. He tends to dismiss the
referential or cultural code ("Voice of Science") as a "babble" con-
veying a society's received opinions and stereotypes. In particular,
he does not pursue the questions of temporality raised by the irreversible nature of the proairetic and the hermeneutic codes. In
the "Introduction to the Structural Analysis of Narrative," Barthes
claims that time in narrative belongs only to the referent (to the
fabula) and has nothing to do with the narrative discourse. And
even in *S/Z*, which shows a diminished subservience to the para-

digmatic model, Barthes's allegiances to the "writeable text" (*texte scriptible*: that which allows and requires the greatest constructive effort by the reader) and to the practice of "new new novelists" make him tend to disparage his irreversible codes as belonging to an outmoded ideology, and to reserve his greatest admiration for the symbolic ("Voice of the Text"), which allows one to enter the text anywhere and to play with its stagings of language itself.

Some correction of perspective is provided by Gérard Genette in *Narrative Discourse*, which along with the work of Todorov and Barthes constitutes the most significant contribution of the French structuralist tradition to thinking about narrative. In his careful and subtle study of the relationships among story, plot, and narrating, Genette pays close attention to the functioning of the infinitely variable gearbox that links the told to the ways of its telling, and how the narrative discourse—his principal example is Proust's *A la recherche du temps perdu*—works to subvert, replay, or even pervert the normal passages of time.[18] Noting the inescapable linearity of the linguistic signifier, Genette faces most directly the paradox of form and temporality when he points out that narrative as we commonly know it—as a book, for instance—is literally a spatial form, an object, but that its realization depends on its being gone through in sequence and succession, and that it thus metonymically "borrows" a temporality from the time of its reading: what he calls a "pseudo-time" of the text.[19]

Genette thus offers a kind of minimalist solution to the question of structure and temporality, and dissents in part from the structural narratologists' excessive emphasis on the paradigmatic, their failure to engage the movement and dynamic of narrative. Genette's solution may be too cautious. For not only does the reading of narrative take time; the time it takes, to get from beginning to end—particularly in those instances of narrative that most define our sense of the mode, nineteenth-century novels—is very much part of our sense of the narrative, what it has accomplished, what it means. Lyric poetry, we feel, strives toward an ideal simultaneity of meaning, encouraging us to read backward as well as forward (through rhyme and repetition, for instance), to grasp the whole in one visual and auditory image; and expository argument, while it can have a narrative, generally seeks to suppress its force in favor of an atemporal structure of understanding; whereas narrative stories depend on meanings delayed, partially filled in, stretched out. Unlike philosophical syllogisms, narratives ("All-Kinds-of-Fur," for example) are temporal syllogisms, concerning the connective processes of time. It is, I think, no accident that most of the great examples of narrative are long and can occupy our reading time over days or weeks or more: if we think of the effects of serialization (which, monthly, weekly, or even daily, was the medium of publication for many of the great nineteenth-century novels) we can perhaps grasp more nearly how time in the representing is felt to be a necessary analogue of time represented. As Rousseau contends in the preface to *La Nouvelle Héloïse*, a novel that in so many ways announces the nineteenth-century tradition, to understand his characters one must know them both young and old, and know them through the process of aging and change that lies in between, a process worked out over a stretch of pages.[20] And Proust's narrator says much the same thing at the end of *Le Temps retrouvé*, where—in the shadow of impending death—he resolves to dedicate himself to the creation of a novel that will, of necessity, have "the shape of time."[21]

Plot as a logic of narrative would hence seem to be analogous to the syntax of meanings that are temporally unfolded and recovered, meanings that cannot otherwise be created or understood. Genette's study of narrative discourse in reference to Proust leads him to note that one can tell a story without any reference to the place of its telling, the location from which it is proffered, but that one cannot tell a story without indications of the time of telling in relation to the told: the use of verb tenses, and their relation one to another, necessarily gives us a certain temporal place in relation to the story. Genette calls this discrepancy in the situation of time and place a "dissymmetry" of the language code itself, "the deep causes of which escape us."[22] While Genette's point is valid and important in the context of linguistics and the philosophy of language, one might note that commonsensically the deep causes are evident to the point of banality, if also rather grim: that is, man is ambulatory, but he is mortal. Temporality is a problem, and an irreducible factor of any narrative statement, in a way that location is not: "All-Kinds-of-Fur" can be articulated from anywhere, but it needs to observe the sequence of tenses and the succession of events. It is my simple conviction, then, that narrative has something to do with time-boundedness, and that plot is the internal logic of the discourse of mortality.

Walter Benjamin has made this point in the simplest and most extreme way, in claiming that what we seek in narrative fictions is that knowledge of death which is denied to us in our own lives: the death that writes *finis* to the life and therefore confers on it its meaning. "Death," says Benjamin, "is the sanction of everything that the storyteller can tell."[23] Benjamin thus advances the ultimate argument for the necessary retrospectivity of narrative: that only the end can finally determine meaning, close the sentence as a signifying totality. Many of the most suggestive analysts of narrative have shared this conviction that the end writes the beginning and shapes the middle: Propp, for instance, and Frank Kermode, and Jean-Paul Sartre, in his distinction between living and telling, argued in *La Nausée*, where in telling everything is transformed by the structuring presence of the end to come, and narrative in fact proceeds "in the reverse"; or, as Sartre puts it in respect to autobiographical narration in *Les Mots*, in order to tell his story in terms of the meaning it would acquire only at the end, "I became my own obituary."[24] These are arguments to which we will need to return in more detail. We should here note that opposed to this view stand other analysts, such as Claude Bremond, or Jean Pouillon, who many years ago argued (as a Sartrean attempting to rescue narrative from the constraints Sartre found in it) that the preterite tense used classically in the novel is decoded by the reader as a kind of present, that of an action and a significance being forged before his eyes, in his hands, so to speak.[25] It is to my mind an interesting and not wholly resolvable question how much, and in what ways, we in reading image the pastness of the action presented, in most cases, in verbs in the past tense. If on the one hand we realize the action progressively, segment by segment, as a kind of present in terms of our experience of it—the present of an argument, as in my summary of "All-Kinds-of-Fur"—do we not do so precisely in anticipation of its larger hermeneutic structuring by conclusions? We are frustrated by narrative interminable, even if we know that any termination is artificial, and that the imposition of ending may lead to that resistance to the end which Freud found in his patients and which is an important novelistic dynamic in such writers as Stendhal and Gide.[26] If the past is to be read as present, it is a curious present that we know to be past in relation to a future we know to be already in place, already in wait for us to reach it. Perhaps we would do best to speak of the *anticipation of retrospection* as our chief tool in making sense of narrative, the master trope of its strange logic. We have no doubt forgone eternal narrative ends, and even traditional nineteenth-century ends are subject to self-conscious endgames, yet still we read in a spirit of confidence, and also a state of dependence, that what remains to be read will restructure the provisional meanings of the already read.

III

I shall now bring this discussion of how we might talk about narrative plot to bear on two brief texts, the first of them located at the hermeneutic end of the spectrum—if we may use Barthes's two codes as "poles" of narrative language for the moment—the other at the proairetic. The first is thus necessarily a detective story, Sir Arthur Conan Doyle's "The Musgrave Ritual," the history of one of Sherlock Holmes's early cases—prior to Watson's arrival on the scene—which Holmes will recount to Watson to satisfy his curiosity concerning the contents of a small wooden box, to wit: "a crumpled piece of paper, an old-fashioned brass key, a peg of wood with a ball of string attached to it, and three rusty old discs of metal."[27] The crumpled paper is a copy of the questions and answers of the ritual referred to in the title, the ritual recited by each male Musgrave at his coming of age. It has been the object of the indiscreet attention of Reginald Musgrave's butler, Brunton, who has been dismissed for his prying—then has disappeared, and shortly after him, the maid Rachel Howells, whom he loved and then jilted, whose footprints led to the edge of the lake, from which the county police recovered a linen bag containing "a mass of old rusted and discolored metal and several dull-colored pieces of pebble or glass." Now all these separate enigmas must—as is ever the case in Holmes's working hypothesis—be related as part of the same "chain of events." Holmes needs, he says, "to devise some common thread upon which they might all hang": precisely the interpretive thread of plot.

The key must lie in the ritual itself, which Musgrave considers "rather an absurd business," a text with no meaning other than its consecration as ritual, as rite of passage. Holmes believes otherwise, and he does so because the other curious outsider, Brunton, has done so. The solution of the case consists in taking the apparently meaningless metaphor of the ritual—seen by the Musgraves simply to stand for the antiquity of their house and the continuity of their line—and unpacking it as metonymy.[28] The central part of the tale displays a problem in trigonometry in action, as Holmes interprets the indications of the ritual as directions for laying out a path on the ground, following the shadow of the elm when the sun is over the oak, pacing off measurements, and so forth: he literally plots out on the lawn the points to which the ritual, read as directions for plotting points, refers him, thus realizing the geometrical sense of plotting and the archaic sense of plot as a bounded area of ground. In the process, he repeats the plotting-out already accomplished by Brunton: when he thrusts a peg into the ground, he finds with "exultation" that within two inches of it a depression marks where Brunton has set his peg. The work of detection in this story makes particularly clear a condition of all classic detective fiction, that the detective repeat, go over again, the ground that has been covered by his predecessor, the criminal. Tzvetan Todorov has noted that the work of detection that we witness in the detective story, which is *in praesentia* for the reader, exists to reveal, to realize the story of the crime, which is *in absentia* yet also the important narrative since it bears the meaning.[29] Todorov identifies the two orders of story, inquest and crime, as *sjužet* and *fabula*. He thus makes the detective story the narrative of narratives, its classical structure a laying-bare of the structure of all narrative in that it dramatizes the role of *sjužet* and *fabula* and the nature of their relation. Plot, I would add, once more appears as the active process of *sjužet* working on *fabula*, the dynamic of its interpretive ordering.

Furthermore, in repeating the steps of the criminal-predecessor, Holmes is literalizing an act that all narrative claims to perform, since narrative ever, and inevitably—if only because of its use of the preterite—presents itself as a repetition and rehearsal (which the French language, of course, makes the same thing) of what has already happened. This need not mean that it did in fact happen— we are not concerned with verification—and one can perfectly well reverse the proposition to say that the claim to repeat in fact produces the event presented as prior: the story is after all a construction made by the reader, and the detective, from the implications of the narrative discourse, which is all he ever knows. What is important, whatever our decision about priority here, is the constructive, semiotic role of repetition: the function of plot as the active repetition and reworking of story in and by discourse.

Within the conventions of the detective story—and of many other narratives as well—repetition results in both detection and apprehension of the original plotmaker, the criminal: in this case Brunton, whom Holmes finally finds asphyxiated in a crypt in the cellar, into which he has descended for the treasure, and into which he has been sealed by the fiery Welsh maid Rachel Howells. Nonetheless, this solution, finding the *fabula* and its instigator, involves a considerable measure of hypothetical construction, since Brunton is dead and Rachel Howells has fled: verification of the *fabula* lies in its plausibility, its fitting the needs of explanation. And as soon as this level of the *fabula*—the story of the crime—has been constructed, it produces a further level, as Holmes and Musgrave re-examine the contents of the bag that Howells presumably threw into the lake, and Holmes identifies the dull pieces of metal and glass as the gold and jewels of the crown of the Stuarts. He thus at last designates the meaning of the ritual, which we had been content, for the duration of the inquest, to consider merely a trigonometric puzzle, a guide to plotting, and which at the last is restored to its meaning as rite of passage—but in a more nearly world-historical sense, since it was intended as a mnemonic aid to the Cavalier party, to enable the next Charles to recover the crown of his fathers once he had been restored to the throne. Watson says to Holmes at the start of the tale, "These relics have a history, then?" And Holmes replies, "So much so that they *are* history" (p. 445). Between "having a history" and "being history," we move to a deeper level of *fabula*, and the spatio-temporal realization of the story witnessed as Holmes plots out his points on the lawn at the last opens up a vast temporal, historical recess, another story, the history of regicide and restoration, which is brought to light only because of the attempted usurpation of the servant Brunton. As Holmes says at the end, the ritual, the secret of its meaning lost, was passed down from father to son, "until at last it came within reach of a man who tore its secret out of it and lost his life in the venture" (p. 458). Earlier we were told that Brunton was a "school-master out of place" when he entered service with the Musgraves, which may confirm our feeling that usurpation is the act of an intellectual alert to the explosive creative potential of stories. Usurpation is an infraction of order, an attempted change of place, pre-eminently what it takes to incite narrative into existence: to pull Holmes from his lethargy—described at the start of the tale, as he lies about with his violin and his books, "hardly moving save from the sofa to the table"—and to begin the plotted life.

What I most wish to stress, in this reading of "The Musgrave Ritual" as an allegory of plot, is how the incomprehensible meta-phor of transmission must be unpacked as a metonymy, literally by plotting its cryptic indications out on the lawn. Narrative is this acting out of the implications of metaphor. In its unpacking, the original metaphor is enacted both spatially (the ground plan es-tablished by Holmes) and temporally (as we follow Holmes in his pacings and measurements). If the plotting of a solution leads to a place—the crypt with Brunton's body—this opens up temporal constructions—the drama played out between Brunton and Rachel Howells—which redirect attention to the object of Brunton's search, which then in turn opens up a new temporal recess, onto history. If we take metaphor as the paradigmatic axis that marks a synthetic grasp or presentation of a situation, the terminal points of the narrative offer a blinded metaphor of transmission (the ritual as "absurd business") and an enlightened metaphor of transmission (the ritual as part of the history of English monarchy): beginning and end offer a good example of Todorov's "narrative transformation," where start and finish stand in the relation—itself metaphorical—of "the same-but-different."[30] Todorov, however, says little about the dynamic processes of the transformation. What lies between the two related poles is the enactment of the first metaphor as metonymy—and then, a hypothetical and mental enactment of the results thus obtained—in order to establish the second, more fully semiotic metaphor. We start with an inactive, "collapsed" metaphor and work through to a reactivated, transactive one, a metaphor with its difference restored through metonymic process. The structure is quite similar to that of "All-Kinds-of-Fur," where we had an initial collapse of the tension necessary to metaphor in the oversameness of threatened incest, followed by the compensatory overdifferentiation of the daughter become (disguised as) beast, resolved in the same-but-different of legitimate erotic union. In "The Musgrave Ritual," we are made to witness in much greater detail the concerted discourse of the transformation, which is no doubt necessary to the detective story, where what is at stake is a gain in knowledge, a self-conscious creation of meaning. But in every case of narrative, it seems fair to say, there must be enactment in order to produce transformation: the plotting-out of initial givens (the ritual, the impasse of misdirected desire) so that their uses may be transformed. Plot, once again, is the active interpretive work of discourse on story.

One could perhaps claim also that the result aimed at by plotting is in some large sense ever the same: the restoration of the possibility of transmission, a goal achieved by the successful transformations of both "All-Kinds-of-Fur" and "The Musgrave Ritual." The nineteenth-century novel in particular will play out repeatedly and at length the problem of transmission, staging over and over again the relations of fathers to sons (and also daughters to mothers, aunts, madwomen, and others), asking where an inheritable wisdom is to be found and how its transmission is to be acted toward. If in Benjamin's thesis, to which I alluded earlier, "Death is the sanction of everything that the storyteller can tell," it is because it is at the moment of death that life becomes *transmissible*. The translations of narrative, its slidings-across in the transformatory process of its plot, its movements forward that recover markings from the past in the play of anticipation and retrospection, lead to a final situation where the claim to understanding is incorporate with the claim to transmissibility. One could find some of the most telling illustrations of this claim in the nineteenth century's frequent use of the framed tale which, dramatizing the relations of tellers and listeners, narrators and narratees, regularly enacts the problematic of transmission, looking for the sign of recognition and the promise to carry on, revealing, too, a deep anxiety about the possibility of transmission, as in Marlow's words to his auditors in *Heart of Darkness*: "Do you see the story? Do you see anything?" Here again are questions that will demand fuller discussion later on.

One further lesson drawn from our reading of Sherlock Holmes's reading of the Musgrave ritual needs consideration here. In an essay called "Story and Discourse in the Analysis of Narrative," Jonathan Culler has argued that we need to recognize that narrative proceeds according to a "double logic," in that at certain problematic moments story events seem to be produced by the requirements of the narrative discourse, its needs of meaning, rather than vice-versa, as we normally assume.[31] In other words, the apparently normal claim that *fabula* precedes *sjužet*, which is a reworking of the givens of *fabula*, must be reversed at problematic, challenging moments of narrative, to show that *fabula* is rather produced by the requirements of *sjužet*: that something must have happened because of the results that we know—that, as Cynthia Chase puts it about Daniel Deronda's Jewishness, "his origin is the effect of its effects."[32] Culler cautions critics against the assumption that these two perspectives can be synthesized without contradiction. The "contradiction" has, I think, been visible and a worry to some of

the most perceptive analysts of narrative, and to novelists themselves, for some time: one can read a number of Henry James's
discussions in the Prefaces as concerned with how the artificer
hides, or glosses over, the contradiction; and Sartre's reflections
on how the finalities of telling transform the told—eventually furnishing a basis for his rejection of the novel—touch on the same
problem.

Yet I am not satisfied to see the "contradiction" as a literary aporia
triumphantly detected by criticism and left at that. The irreconcilability of the "two logics" points to the peculiar work of understanding that narrative is called upon to perform, and to the
paralogical status of its "solutions." Let me restate the problem in
this way: prior events, causes, are so only retrospectively, in a reading back from the end. In this sense, the metaphoric work of eventual totalization determines the meaning and status of the metonymic
work of sequence—though it must also be claimed that the metonymies of the middle produced, gave birth to, the final metaphor.
The contradiction may be in the very nature of narrative, which
not only uses but *is* a double logic. The detective story, as a kind
of dime-store modern version of "wisdom literature," is useful in
displaying the double logic most overtly, using the plot of the inquest to find, or construct, a story of the crime which will offer
just those features necessary to the thematic coherence we call a
solution, while claiming, of course, that the solution has been made
necessary by the crime. To quote Holmes at the end of another of
his cases, that of "The Naval Treaty": "The principal difficulty in
your case . . . lay in the fact of there being too much evidence. What
was vital was overlaid and hidden by what was irrelevant. Of all
the facts which were presented to us we had to pick just those which
we deemed to be essential, and then piece them together in their
order so as to reconstruct this very remarkable chain of events." [33]
Here we have a clear *ars poetica*, of the detective and of the novelist,
and of the plotting of narrative as an example of the mental operation described by Wallace Stevens as "The poem of the mind in
the act of finding / What will suffice."

It would be my further claim that narrative's nature as a contradictious double logic tells us something about why we have and need narrative, and how the need to plot meanings is itself productive of narrative. We may explore this proposition by way of a text that appears wholly other from the detective fiction I have been discussing—appears closer to the proairetic pole of narrative, loosely stringing together units of action and incident, and indeed often explicitly alluding to its hero in terms of picaresque models. The text is Rousseau's *Confessions*, and I shall use as my example from it the notorious episode that closes Book Two, the story of the stolen ribbon. Rousseau has been serving as a lackey in the household of Mme de Vercellis, and feeling that he (quite like the Musgraves' butler Brunton) is out of his place, misplaced, and therefore ever on the lookout for some special mark of favor that would indicate that Mme de Vercellis knows he is destined for better things. But she dies without any recognition of Rousseau, and without any legacy. In the ensuing liquidation of her household, Rousseau steals a little pink and silver ribbon, which is found in his room. Asked where he got it, he lies and says that Marion, a young peasant girl serving as a cook, gave it to him. Confronted with Marion, who calmly denies the allegation, Rousseau persists in his account, which leads Marion to exclaim, "You are making me very unhappy, but I wouldn't want to be in your place." [34] In doubt as to the truth, the Comte de la Roque (Mme de Vercellis's heir) dismisses them both. Rousseau now goes on to image the probable future scenario of Marion's life: dismissed under the shadow of accusation, penniless, without recommendation or protection, what could become of her? Rousseau sketches with hypothetical certainty a career that would make her "worse than myself," that is, presumably, a prostitute. This cruel memory has continued to trouble him so that in his insomnias the figure of Marion comes to reproach him with the crime, as if it had been committed only yesterday, but he has never been able to bring himself to make a clean breast of it, even to his closest friend. In fact, the desire to deliver himself of the weight of this particular crime, he then tells us, contributed greatly to his decision to write his confessions.

The facts of the case and its consequences have thus far been presented by Rousseau the narrator in what he claims the reader cannot deny to be an open and straightforward confession. Now, starting a new paragraph, he argues that he would not be faithful to the object of his book if he did not inform the reader as well of his inner feelings during the episode, of his *dispositions intérieures*, and if he feared to excuse himself in what accords with the truth. He had no intention of harming Marion. Curiously, it was his friendship for her that caused the accusation. She was present in his thoughts, and he excused himself by way of the first object that occurred to him: "je m'excusai sur le premier objet qui s'offrit." This apparently gratuitous and aberrant choice of person to serve as victim—unsettling in its suggestion of random vectors of plot— then receives something closer to a motivation when Rousseau explains that he accused Marion of doing what he wanted to do: of having given him the ribbon since he intended to give it to her. Thus his *amitié* for Marion appears to partake of love, and he can imagine being the recipient of what he wanted to give, which allows of a further reversal when the love-offering is poisoned in its source: love veers to sadism. What prevents Rousseau from owning up and straightening out this tangled ribbon is not the fear of punishment but the fear of shame: "I only saw the horror of being recognized, publicly declared, with myself present, thief, liar, false accuser." As so often in the *Confessions*, it is the fear of judgment from the outside, judgment by those who cannot see the *dispositions intérieures*, that appears to motivate both bad behavior and the confession that such behavior necessitates: the fear of being judged as in a place where he does not belong produces both lies and confessions. Repeatedly we have incidents where Rousseau, the wandering musician for instance, tells his fictive story to putative benefactors, only to have to retell the true story as confession. Here, Rousseau ends the account of the stolen ribbon with the statement that he will never speak of the matter again: a resolve which he will then break in the fourth reverie of the *Rêveries d'un promeneur solitaire*.

Juxtaposed in the episode of the stolen ribbon as presented in the *Confessions* we have a straightforward account of narrative events, presented in their chronological order; a subsequent narrative of inner feelings and motives standing in stark contradiction to the narrative of events; a hallucinatory narrative of the hypothetical future of the other persona of the episode, Marion; and a narrative of the generation of the text of the *Confessions*, since the need to tell this story—or these stories—claims genetic force. Is there any way we can order these four elements in a logical discourse? Apparently not, since the very point of the discrepancy between the narrative of actions and narrative of internal dispositions is their fundamental lack of congruence, the inability of either ever fully to coincide with or explain the other. One could no doubt discover a motive of connection between the two through a psychoanalytic discourse: Rousseau provides a key for so doing when he introduces his desire for Marion into the scenario and suggests that somehow this desire produced effects opposite from what he intended, the subject and object of desire changed places, and love became sadistic. All this could be reconceptualized by way of Freud, most pertinently through the concept of denial, denegation. But to bring such a psychoanalytic discourse to bear would in fact be—given the nature of Freud's analyses of the problem—to add another layer of narrative, however illuminating, to those Rousseau has already piled up. It would not offer an escape from narrative.

Rousseau's narrative layerings suggest a failure to find a single answer to the question of where his proper *place* is, what his publicly declared name, rank, and character are to be. Always out of place, never coincident with his inner self in the eyes of others—and thus in his behavior—he is always going back over the traces of conduct and interior disposition, not to reconcile them—which is impossible—but to confess their irreconcilability, which generates Marion's future story and Rousseau's future confessions. In other words, the only ordering or solution to the problem in understanding Rousseau has set up here is more narrative. No analytic moral logic will give the answer to the question, why did I behave that way? as it will not answer the question, how can I be in my proper place? nor indeed the question subtending these, who am I? Questions such as these cannot be addressed—as they might have been earlier in Rousseau's century—by a *portrait moral*, a kind of analytic topography of a person. The question of identity, claims Rousseau—and this is what makes him at least symbolically the *incipit* of modern narrative—can be thought only in narrative terms, in the effort to tell a whole life, to plot its meaning by going back over it to record its perpetual flight forward, its slippage from the fixity of definition. To understand me, Rousseau says more than once in the *Confessions*, most impressively at the close of Book Four, the reader must follow me at every moment of my existence; and it will be up to the reader, not Rousseau, to assemble the elements of the narrative and determine what they mean. Thus what Rousseau must fear, in writing his *Confessions*, is not saying too much or speaking lies, but failing to say everything. In claiming the need to *tout dire*, Rousseau makes explicit that the contradictions encountered in the attempt to understand and present the self in all its truth provide a powerful narrative machine. Any time one goes over a moment of the past, the machine can be relied on to produce more narrative—not only differing stories of the past, but future scenarios and narratives of writing itself. There is simply no end to narrative on this model, since there is no "solution" to the "crime."[35] The narrative plotting in its entirety is the solution, and since that entirety has no endpoint for the writing—as opposed to the biological—self, Rousseau is reduced to requesting the reader's permission to *make* an end here: "Qu'il me soit permis de n'en reparler jamais."

There are many other contrivances of finality and endstop in the *Confessions*: conversion, fall (from childhood, from grace, into authorship, into publicity, etc.), and even simulacra of death, since Rousseau more than once reports himself to have become "no better than a dead man," whose afterlife must then begin anew. There is a repeated insistence on special experiences and unique moments that open and close epochs in Rousseau's life, as if in an attempt to demarcate and stabilize the passage of life and time. As Sartre claimed, in order to narrate one's life one must become one's own obituary. Rousseau writes so many obituaries he finally subverts the necrological form: he is ever reborn, not so much through a Protean change in shape (on the contrary, while claiming multiple beginnings and ends, he also asserts that he has never changed) but more like Antaeus, by repeatedly touching ground with a vision of the essential Jean-Jacques. The ultimate finality becomes the book itself, which is presented in its completed form once only, on the very first page of the *Confessions*, precisely in a future scenario of reading and judgment: "Let the trumpet of the Last Judgment sound when it will; I shall come forward with this book in my hand to present myself before the Sovereign Judge. I shall say aloud: here is what I have done, what I have thought, what I was. . . . Eternal Being, gather around me the numberless crowd of my fellow men: let them hear my confessions. . . ." To imagine one's self-composed obituary read at the Judgment Day constitutes the farthest reach in the anticipation of retrospective narrative understanding. It is one that all narratives no doubt would wish to make: all narrative posits, if not the Sovereign Judge, at least a Sherlock Holmes capable of going back over the ground, and thereby realizing the meaning of the cipher left by a life. Narrative thus seems ever to imagine in advance the act of its transmission, the moment of reading and understanding that it cannot itself ever know, since this act always comes after the writing, in a posthumous moment.

Our example from the "proairetic" end of the narrative spectrum has turned out to be fully as "hermeneutic" as the detective story. This should cause us no surprise, since any narrative, from the very simplest, is hermeneutic in intention, claiming to retrace event in order to make it available to consciousness. In their work on oral narratives produced by inner-city adolescents, the sociolinguists William Labov and Joshua Waletsky have stressed that stories always appear to have a moment of "evaluation": a moment at which the narrator calls attention to the point of what he is telling, and its importance, makes an appeal to the significance he has wrested from experience through his narrative shaping of it.[36] More sophisticated narrative fictions tend to embed fictive readers within the text, and to stage efforts at decipherment and interpretation, as, notably, in much of the late work of Henry James, or in Proust, or Faulkner, or (a particularly curious instance) Flaubert's *Bouvard et Pécuchet*. Perhaps of greater interest than the concept of plot, especially when we address highly plotted narratives, is that of plotting, the moments where we seize the active work of structuring revealed or dramatized in the text. A nice example for me has always been the scene in Michelangelo Antonioni's film *Blow-Up* (adapted from a story by Julio Cortázar) in which the photographer-protagonist attempts to reconstruct what has occurred earlier in the day in a London park through the enlargement of the photographs he took in the park—and then enlargements of parts of his enlargements—and the arrangement of his photographs in an intentional sequence. What starts him on the reconstruction is the gaze of the girl in the photographs, the direction in which her eyes look: the gaze appears to seek an object, and by following its direction—and its intention—he discovers, shaded and barely visible, a face in the shrubbery and the glinting barrel of a pistol. Then by following the direction of the pistol barrel—its aim or intention—he locates the zone of shadow under a tree which may represent a corpse, that of a man whom the girl was leading toward the shrubbery, perhaps toward a trap. In this scene of reconstruction, finding the right sequence of events, putting together the revelatory plot, depends on uncovering that "line of sight," that aim and intention, that will show how incidents link together. And finding, or inventing, the plot that seems to lie hidden in the shadows of the park and in the grainy darkness of the photographs could alone give meaning to the events, which, while recorded through the veracious and revealing "objective" lens of the camera, remain unavailable to interpretation so long as they are not plotted.

If I emphasize plotting even more than plot, it is because the participle best suggests the dynamic aspect of narrative that most interests me: that which moves us forward as readers of the narrative text, that which makes us—like the heroes of the text often, and certainly like their authors—want and need plotting, seeking through the narrative text as it unfurls before us a precipitation of shape and meaning, some simulacrum of understanding of how meaning can be construed over and through time. I am convinced that the study of narrative needs to move beyond the various formalist criticisms that have predominated in our time: formalisms that have taught us much, but which ultimately—as the later work of Barthes recognized—cannot deal with the dynamics of texts as actualized in the reading process. My own interests—as will become progressively clearer as one moves through this volume—have more and more taken me to psychoanalysis and especially to the text of Freud: since psychoanalysis presents a dynamic model of psychic processes, it offers the hope of a model pertinent to the dynamics of texts. The validity of this approach can, of course, be tested only in the doing, in the readings for plots that will follow.

As I suggested in the preface, we look to a convergence of psycho-analysis and literary criticism because we sense that there ought to be a correspondence between literary and psychic dynamics, since to an important degree we define and construct our sense of self through our fictions, within the constraints of a transindividual symbolic order. In the attempt to go beyond pure formalism—while never discarding its lessons—psychoanalysis promises, and requires, that in addition to such usual narratological preoccupa-tions as function, sequence, and paradigm, we engage the dynamic of memory and the history of desire as they work to shape the recovery of meaning within time. Beyond formalism, Susan Sontag argued some years ago, we need an erotics of art.[37] What follows may be conceived as a contribution to that erotics, or, more soberly, a reading of our compulsions to read.

2

Narrative Desire

Plot as we have defined it is the organizing line and intention of narrative, thus perhaps best conceived as an activity, a structuring operation elicited in the reader trying to make sense of those meanings that develop only through textual and temporal succession. Plot in this view belongs to the reader's "competence," and in his "performance"—the reading of narrative—it animates the sense-making process: it is a key component of that "passion of (for) meaning" that, Barthes says, lights us afire when we read. We can, then, conceive of the reading of plot as a form of desire that carries us forward, onward, through the text. Narratives both tell of desire—typically present some story of desire—and arouse and make use of desire as dynamic of signification. Desire is in this view like Freud's notion of Eros, a force including sexual desire but larger and more polymorphous, which (he writes in *Beyond the Pleasure Principle*) seeks "to combine organic substances into ever greater unities."[1] Desire as Eros, desire in its plastic and totalizing function, appears to me central to our experience of reading narrative, and if in what follows I evoke Freud—and, as a gloss on Freud, Jacques Lacan—it is because I find in Freud's work the best model for a "textual erotics." I am aware that "desire" is a concept too broad, too fundamental, almost too banal to be defined. Yet perhaps it can be described: we can say something about the forms that it takes in narrative, how it represents itself, the dynamic it generates.

Desire is always there at the start of a narrative, often in a state of initial arousal, often having reached a state of intensity such that movement must be created, action undertaken, change begun. The *Iliad* opens with Agamemnon and Achilles locked in passionate quarrel over the girl Briseis, and the *Odyssey* with Odysseus, detained on Calypso's island, expressing the longing of his *nostos*, the drive to return home. To cite an explicitly erotic instance, Jean Genet's *Notre-Dame des fleurs* opens on an act of masturbation, and the narrative and its persons are called forth as what is needed for the phantasies of desire. One could no doubt analyze the opening paragraph of most novels and emerge in each case with the image of a desire taking on shape, beginning to seek its objects, beginning to develop a textual energetics. A rock-bottom paradigm of the dynamic of desire can be found in one of the very earliest novels in the Western tradition, *Lazarillo de Tormes* (1554), where all of the hero's tricks and dodges are directed initially at staying alive: Lazaro, the ragged, homeless *pícaro*, must use his wits, his human ingenuity, to avoid the ever-present threat of starvation. Each chapter develops as a set of tricks and stratagems devised to overcome a specific form of the threat, and thus literally to enable life, and narrative, to go forward: the most telling illustration may be the second chapter, where Lazaro must simulate the actions of a mouse and a snake to work his way into his master the priest's locked bread chest. The resistance to desire in this novel is simply, and brutally, total deprivation of what sustains life; while the traditional comic structure—in theater and then in novel—presents the resistance of an older generation of "blocking figures" to the plotting of the younger generation, seeking erotic union.[2] As in a great many folktales—the example of "Jack the Giant Killer" and its permutations comes to mind—the specifically human faculty of ingenuity and trickery, the capacity to use the mind to devise schemes to overcome superior force, becomes a basic dynamic of plot. If the giants of folktale are always stupid, it is because they stand opposed to human wit, which is seen as a capacity for leverage on the world, precisely that which overcomes inert obstacles, sets change in motion, reformulates the real.

By the nineteenth century, the *pícaro*'s scheming to stay alive has typically taken a more elaborated and socially defined form: it has become ambition. It may in fact be a defining characteristic of the modern novel (as of bourgeois society) that it takes aspiration, getting ahead, seriously, rather than simply as the object of satire (which was the case in much earlier, more aristocratically determined literature), and thus it makes ambition the vehicle and emblem of Eros, that which totalizes the world as possession and progress. Ambition provides not only a typical novelistic theme, but also a dominant dynamic of plot: a force that drives the protagonist forward, assuring that no incident or action is final or closed in itself until such a moment as the ends of ambition have been clarified, through success or else renunciation. Somewhat in the manner of the traditional sequence of functions in the folktale analyzed by Propp, ambition provides an armature of plot which the reader recognizes, and which constitutes the very "readability" of the narrative text, what enables the reader to go about the construction of the text's specific meanings. Ambition is inherently totalizing, figuring the self's tendency to appropriation and aggrandizement, moving forward through the encompassment of more, striving to have, to do, and to be more. The ambitious hero thus stands as a figure of the reader's efforts to construct meanings in ever-larger wholes, to totalize his experience of human existence in time, to grasp past, present, and future in a significant shape. This description, of course, most obviously concerns male plots of ambition. The female plot is not unrelated, but it takes a more complex stance toward ambition, the formation of an inner drive toward the assertion of selfhood in resistance to the overt and violating male plots of ambition, a counter-dynamic which, from the prototype *Clarissa* on to *Jane Eyre* and *To the Lighthouse*, is only superficially passive, and in fact a reinterpretation of the vectors of plot.[3]

The ambitious heroes of the nineteenth-century novel—those of Balzac, for instance—may regularly be conceived as "desiring machines" whose presence in the text creates and sustains narrative movement through the forward march of desire, projecting the self onto the world through scenarios of desire imagined and then

acted upon. Etymology may suggest that the self creates a circle—
an *ambitus*—or aureola around itself, mainly in front of itself, attempting ever to move forward to the circumference of that circle
and to widen it, to cast the nets of the self ever further. A most
obvious example would be Eugène de Rastignac, hero of Balzac's
Le Père Goriot, who, as the action of that novel begins, has just
returned from his first soirée in Parisian high society and has discovered the uses of ambition:

> To be young, to have a thirst for society, to be hungry for a
> woman, and to see two houses open to oneself! to place one's
> foot in the Faubourg Saint-Germain with the Vicomtesse de
> Beauséant, and one's knee in the Chaussée d'Antin, with the
> Comtesse de Restaud! to plunge with one's glance into the
> salons of Paris all in a line, and to believe oneself a handsome
> enough young man to find there aid and protection in the
> heart of a woman! to feel oneself ambitious enough to give a
> proud stamp of the foot to the tightrope on which one must
> walk with the assurance that the acrobat won't fall, and to have
> found the best of balancing poles in a charming woman![4]

The disarming directness, even crudity, of the quotation suggests
how Rastignac is conceived as a bundle of desires which need only
be given a field for their exercise—the topography of which is
suggested in the quotation—for the narrative to move forward.

The novel will indeed unfold as an anatomy of human desire,
where the introduction of the professional master-plotter, Vautrin,
will serve explicitly to theorize desire and the logical consequences
of its full enactment. In a world so charged with desire, the central
drama becomes—as in the Christian arch-drama—one of temptation. If Rastignac is able to resist the specific terms of Vautrin's
plot, which offers the dowered maiden as the direct consequence
of murder—a temptation that makes *too* clear a certain logic of
desire—it is because he has found a more nuanced system for the
realization of ambition in the conjunction of erotic and financial
power represented by another woman, Delphine de Nucingen. Ras-

tignac negotiates a path between the absolutes of plot expounded by his two would-be fathers, Vautrin and Goriot. It is sign and condition of his success that he gives absolute allegiance to neither and goes beyond both, escaping the constraints of paternity, moving forward with the hyperbolic rapidity typical of Balzacian narratives of ambition, accelerating toward a goal that here is represented in the famous final scene in which the hero, from his vantage point on the rise of Père-Lachaise cemetery, can view the *beaux quartiers* of Paris as ready for his possession: a world charged with meaning and possibility because it is charged, like the glance that takes visionary possession of it, with desire. In other cases (for instance, in the career of Lucien de Rubempré, across the two novels *Illusions perdues* and *Splendeurs et misères des courtisanes*) the narrative of ambition accelerates to the overheating and loss of energy of the desiring machine, indeed sometimes to its explosion.

But to characterize desire as a machine may be inadequate. As Michel Serres has argued, the eighteenth century's preoccupation with the machine, as a system for the transmission of forces outside itself, gives way in the nineteenth century to fascination with the motor, containing its source of movement within itself, built on the three principles of difference (of temperature), reservoir (of fuel), and circulation.[5] The self-contained motor, working through combustion—typically, the steam engine—also corresponds to the emerging conception of human desire. If with La Mettrie in the eighteenth century we had *l'homme machine*, by the time of Freud we have moved to *l'homme moteur*.

Freud's thought was from the outset marked by a physicalist-energetic conception and vocabulary (often a source of embarrassment to his epigones) which came from his training in the "Helmholtz School" of medicine, as he learned it in the physiological laboratory of his master, Ernst Brücke. Brücke's *Lectures on Physiology*—I quote here from Ernest Jones's summary—taught that organisms were "systems of atoms, moved by forces, according to the principle of conservation of energy . . . popularized by Helmholtz. The sum of forces (motive forces and potential forces) remains constant in every isolated system. The real causes are

symbolized in sciences by the word 'force' . . . and this applies as
well to the organism man."[6] Freud, we know, had recourse, sequen-
tially and then simultaneously, to three conceptual descriptions
of mental life: the topographical, the economic, and the dynamic.
The economic could also be called the energetic, since it involves
investments, movements, and discharges of energies, derived from
physics and especially from thermodynamics. The dynamic model
derives psychic processes from the interplay of forces, which are
originally drives (or as the unfortunate standard English translation
would have it, instincts). The unconscious is the place of drives or
instincts in conflict, a basic dualism whence comes its permanent
driving force, which in turn activates the counteractive force of
repression. The motor force of the drive or instinct is described in
one of the key metapsychological essays of 1915, "Instincts and
Their Vicissitudes":

> By the pressure [*Drang*] of an instinct we understand its motor
> factor, the amount of force or the measure of the demand for
> work which it represents. The characteristic of exercising pres-
> sure is common to all instincts; it is in fact their very essence.
> Every instinct is a piece of activity. . . .[7]

Here, as so often in Freud, we have a psychic motor or steam
engine, with the instinctual providing a reservoir of fuel and the
driving power whose differential forms are then represented through
energetic exchanges.

Freud's way, in this as in so much else, was prepared not only
by the scientists but also by the poets and novelists of the nineteenth
century. Stendhal, for instance, returns again and again to the
concept of "energy," a characteristic he finds lacking, indeed repressed, in French society of the Restoration period, and which he
seeks in the hero of plebeian origins (Julien Sorel) or of Italian
nationality (Fabrice del Dongo) and finds most of all in the intensely
passionate amoral heroines of the Italian Renaissance who are the
main actors of the *Chroniques italiennes*.[8] Following Stendhal, many
writers seized upon the engines and motors of nascent industrialism

as central thematic and symbolic forces in their work. An early paradigm appears in the first paragraph of Balzac's *Illusions perdues*, a novel that begins by evoking the coming to France of the mechanical Stanhope press, these "devouring presses," the narrator calls them, which in turn will be supplanted by the steam-driven press, producing an enormous new demand for cheap paper that will drive David Séchard to the monomaniac obsession of the inventor, and to his ultimate exploitation by a new breed of industrial printers—and creating also the possibility of modern mass journalism, which will be the medium of the brief triumph and dismal failure of Lucien de Rubempré. In fact, the very production of the novel *Illusions perdues*, and more acutely its sequel, *Splendeurs et misères des courtisanes*, was caught up in the dynamic of the new journalism, as Balzac sought, unsuccessfully, to publish in the new medium of the *roman-feuilleton*, the novel published in installments in the mass-circulation daily newspaper. The devouring presses chewed up paper, ideas, and would-be poets, powering the way to what the critic Sainte-Beuve contemptuously labeled an "industrial literature."

Like Rastignac, Lucien de Rubempré is a bundle of appetencies that will motivate and animate the plot of his novels. But *Illusions perdues* appears at its outset to lay bare not only the desiring subject, but also the general dynamic subsuming and even controlling all specific forms of human desire, the very motor force of its plot. The thematic cluster of Lucien the poet, printing, and journalism makes particularly evident the intimate relations of desire, narrative, and the dynamics of plot. Through the key experience of journalism, the novel will set up a system of potentially unlimited energetic transformations and exchanges, a system where money, erotic desire, and language become interchangeable factors in an overheated circuit of power and signification. Subjacent to the circulatory system of signs, financial and linguistic, is indeed what might be called a libidinal economy, which in Balzac's world may always be the ultimate system of energies.[9] Balzac apparently believed (it was one of his father's articles of faith) that man is endowed with a limited quantity of vital energy, in essence sexual potency, which he could either prudently conserve or else exorbitantly expend: the *Comédie humaine* reposes on a basic typology of the conservers and the spenders. Lucien falls into dissipation; constantly satisfied by the ravishing Coralie, the "mainspring of his will" is "softened," his motor cools, eventually running down to the entropy of suicide—from which he will be saved by the intervention of the most highly charged motor of the *Comédie humaine*, the master-plotter Vautrin.

Vautrin, the all-powerful and demonic surrogate father, may remind us of Lucien's suicide note, where he develops a theory of "family maladies" from the example of a daughter who never married because she was *malade de son père*. Lucien's generalizations from this example allow us to see all of France as sick by way of the father, suffering from a general malady of paternity which, for Balzac the monarchist and reactionary, has much to do with the killing of the one legitimate father in the regicide of 1793. The version of the "family romance" advanced by Lucien is illustrated throughout the *Comédie humaine* as a struggle of energetic but powerless young talent against the repressive gerontocracy of the Restoration. Corresponding to a France sick by way of the father stands the action of the devouring presses, the movement toward mass journalism, publicity, democracy, the reign of public opinion: everything that for Balzac constituted the very antithesis of legitimate authority. The motor of the presses comes to represent an inevitable historical dynamic. It represents as well the dynamic of the modern narrative text, itself inevitably historical, caught in an irreversible and ever-accelerating process of change, a plot of energy and devourment which Balzac, as a dissenter from his time, perceives with particular clarity even as his own text succumbs to its dynamic.[10] Life in the text of the modern is a nearly thermodynamic process; plot is, most aptly, a steam engine.

One could, of course, accumulate examples. Around the time of *Illusions perdues*, Alfred de Vigny introduced the locomotive into his poem "La Maison du Berger" as an "iron bull," a terrifying "roaring dragon" carrying "tempests" within its "burning belly," charging forward out of control. After representing the locomotive in *Dombey and Son*, Dickens in *Hard Times* created Coketown, with its "vast piles of building full of windows where there was a rattling and a trembling all day long, and where the piston of the steam-engine worked monotonously up and down like the head of an elephant in a state of melancholy madness"—a world driven by the motion of the piston.[11] Flaubert, in *L'Education sentimentale*, arranges to have Frédéric Moreau's declaration of passion to Madame Arnoux interrupted by the crashing and explosive noises of a steam-pump and a variety of other engines during the exemplary episode where Frédéric pursues his love object to Arnoux's factory at Creil, in the new industrial suburbs of Paris. The locomotive itself makes a major appearance here, appropriately enough, in an example of "socialist art" produced by Pellerin following the Revolution of 1848, a painting "representing the Republic, or Progress, or Civilization, in the guise of Jesus Christ driving a locomotive, crossing a virgin forest."[12] The generally anti-industrial and antitechnological attitude of most nineteenth-century poets and novelists is more and more matched by a fascination with engines and forces. Before the Italian futurist chief Marinetti would declare the roaring automobile to be more beautiful than the Victory of Samothrace, the apogee of the industrial engine had been reached in the work of Jules Verne and, especially, Emile Zola.

With Zola, nearly every novel centers on an engine itself or else a social institution that functions as an engine: the locomotive of *La Bête humaine*; the dynamic, expanding pressure chamber of the department store in *Au Bonheur des dames*; the coal mine of *Germinal*, with its steam elevator and underground railway; the alcohol still of *L'Assommoir*. Not only do these in each case provide the thematic core of the novels in which they figure, they also represent the dynamics of the narrative, furnish the motor power by which the plot moves forward. In this sense, Zola's engines—like Balzac's "devouring presses"—are a *mise-en-abyme* of the novel's narrative motor, an explicit statement of the inclusion within the novel of the principle of its movement. Instructive in this regard is what may be Zola's simplest engine, the still of *L'Assommoir*—with its rolls of tubing and its great copper belly heated by an invisible flame, apparently inhabited by demonic forces—which returns with a regular and inexorable cadence in the novel, providing through its uninterrupted trickle of distilled alcohol the very fuel of the narrative and creating finally a level of heat and explosive vapor that make it the motor of the bleak lives it powers to extinction. In *La Bête humaine*, Jacques Lantier's *fêlure*, the hereditary crack through which flows a primordial homicidal impulse, explicitly recalls the locomotive's release of steam from its pistons, and there is in fact a generalized cross-over and metaphorical exchange of properties between Lantier and the engine he drives. The end of this novel, as of others by Zola, offers the apotheosis of the engine beyond human control, as Lantier and his fireman fall to the rails in their death struggle and are severed by the wheels, while the driverless and overheated locomotive accelerates to unimagined speeds, bearing its passengers to certain destruction in derailment and explosion. The erotic and aggressive drives of the human characters ultimately become invested in the industrial engine that subsumes and represents them all, laying bare the dynamic of the narrative text as pure motor force.

Yet Zola's most extraordinary engine is not of industrial manufacture. It is the sexual organ of the courtesan Nana, prime mover of the Parisian social world who by the end of the novel, *Nana*, becomes the very motor principle of production, as her lovers and keepers struggle to satisfy her desires. Thus the industrialist Steiner's steel mills: "There were, out there, in a corner of the provinces, workers black with coal, soaked in sweat, who night and day tensed their muscles and felt their bones crack, to supply Nana's pleasures. She devoured everything, like a great fire...."[13] The apotheosis of Nana's force is most explicit a few pages later when the theater director Mignon visits her sumptuous town house, and can only compare the work it represents to colossal public works he has seen: a "cyclopean" aqueduct near Marseilles, or the new port of Cherbourg. But Nana's work is yet more astonishing because of its engine: "She had done it with something else, with a little stupidity that everyone laughed at, with a bit of her delicate nudity, with this shameful and so powerful nothing, whose force could lift the world; with this all alone, without workers, without machines invented by engineers, she had moved Paris and built herself a fortune where corpses slept.—'In the name of heaven, what a tool!' exclaimed Mignon" (pp. 332–33). In this remarkable passage, Nana's sexual organ, which is nothing, absence, becomes a tool more powerful than all phallic engines, capable of supreme leverage on the world. Eros appears here all the more appropriately as a motor in that its mechanical operation is hidden, and it functions—as the whole imagistic system of the novel has made abundantly clear—through internal combustion. By the end of the chapter from which I have been quoting, Nana's *sexe* will—in the manner of Freud's Eros—claim a kind of mythic status, in a visionary moment where it mounts to the sky and "shines on its supine victims, in the manner of a rising sun which lights up a field of carnage" (p. 335). Here is pure force, the *vis ultima* of the world equally devout to sex and to death.

My interest in these emblematic motors and engines invented by novelists, as by Freud, derives from my dissatisfaction with the various formalisms that have dominated critical thinking about narrative, and from my search for models that would be more adequate to our experience of reading narrative as a dynamic operation—what makes plot move us forward to the end, to put it in simplest terms. As Jacques Derrida once wrote in criticism of Jean Rousset's *Forme et signification*, a book he found typical of a certain structuralist thought, in such work "the geometric or the morphologic is corrected only by a mechanics, never by an energetics." [14] Derrida writes further: "*Form* fascinates when one no longer has the force to understand force from within itself." Like Derrida, I can make no claim to understanding force in itself. But I think we do well to recognize the existence of textual force, and that we can use such a concept to move beyond the static models of much formalism, toward a dynamics of reading and writing. In the motors and engines I have glanced at, including Eros as motor and motor as erotic, we find representations of the dynamics of the narrative text, connecting beginning and end across the middle and making of that middle—what we read *through*—a field of force.

We will come back to the narrative motor in order to conceptualize more fully its workings through explicit study of the model
offered by Freud in *Beyond the Pleasure Principle*. At present, it is
important to pursue the notion of desire as that which is initiatory
of narrative, motivates and energizes its reading, and animates the
combinatory play of sense-making. We need, that is, to come closer
to an understanding of that "passion for (of) meaning" that Barthes
found central to the reading of narrative, to talk about desire not
only as the motor force of plot but as the very motive of narrative.
What follows, then, will in a sense be an exploration of the conjunction of the narrative of desire and the desire of narrative. Here
my text of reference will be Balzac's first major novel, *La Peau de
chagrin*, which appears to me to be an allegory not only of life but
of the telling of the life story.

II

La Peau de chagrin falls into three sections. Part 1, "The Talisman,"
presents Raphaël de Valentin at an acute and apparently penul-
timate point of crisis: he enters a gambling house to hazard his last
coin, loses, decides to end his life by a leap into the Seine, but defers
the act until nightfall. He then wanders into an antique shop, where
he explores the dusty debris of centuries of civilization, meets the
antique dealer, and receives from him the magic talisman, which,
he is told, will realize all his wishes but at the price of diminishing
the length of his life, since each wish realized will shrink the size
of the skin. His first wish is for a flaming orgy, which promptly
arrives. It is toward the end of this night of excess that Raphaël
undertakes to narrate the history of his life to his friend Emile
(who, we later discover, will be fast asleep well before Raphaël
finishes). Part 2, "The Woman Without a Heart," Raphaël's own
first-person narrative, presents a tale of penury and struggle under
severe paternal surveillance—focused particularly in the paternal
interdiction of gambling—followed by studious labor in a Paris
garret, and impossible love for Foedora, the "woman without a
heart," and then initiation into the passionate antitheses of the life

of the gambler and debauchee. Raphaël's narrative of the past in Part 2 brings his life up to the immediate past—what was presented in Part 1—and the gambling away of his last money. At this point in his narrative, recounting the despair and destitution leading to suicide, Raphaël remembers the existence of the talisman he has received and with it the possibility of fortune, which he at once wishes for and immediately thereafter receives, as a lawyer's clerk arrives when the orgiasts have reassembled for breakfast to tell Raphaël he has inherited six million francs. Hereafter begins Part 3, "The Agony," which—leaving Raphaël's narration to return again to impersonal narrative—will tell the story of Raphaël's subsequent existence as an extended death agony: his attempt to live beyond desire in the effort to prolong his life, the impossibility of doing so, and the inevitable shrinking of the skin, to the moment of his convulsive death.

At the dead center of the novel is the moment when Raphaël's act of narration reaches the incident that stood at the outset of the novel—his entrance into the gambling house to play his last twenty-franc piece. Here in the text stand three points of ellipsis (. . .) or "points of suspension," as French would put it, a sign of incompletion, suspension, and change of direction. For they are followed by Raphaël's "suddenly" remembering the forgotten talisman in his pocket. Brusquely exalted, he brandishes the skin and cries: "Now I want to live! . . . I wished for two hundred thousand francs of income, and I will have them." [15] In this exemplary moment, the story of the past catches up with the present, intersects with it, in a formulation of the desire that subtended the story of the past, a desire now brought to full realization. It is as if this novel had taken the desire that in various forms drives most novelistic plots and offered its full satisfaction halfway through the novel. Thus *La Peau de chagrin* violates the usual structure of desire in the novel, which is oriented toward the end, and indeed in one instant lifts all the interdictions—summed up in the figure of the censoring father and the prohibition of gambling—which one would expect the novel to have to struggle with slowly, and not necessarily with total success. The realization of desire appears to be total, the ob-

stacles to fulfillment, including the law of the father, completely
overcome—Raphaël's mother, we note, has been dead since his
childhood, which no doubt providentially removes her from the
scenario of fulfillment—and we may well ask whether we are in a
nineteenth-century novel of Parisian society or rather in a fairy
tale.

But in the manner of so many fairy tales, the realization of desire
comes in sinister forms, destructive of the self. What Raphaël indeed discovers at the moment when his desire opens onto its full
realization is death: "Il voyait la MORT" (p. 209). Desire realized
through the magic skin *is* death, the diminishment of the life span.
Hence realization must also mean the death of desire: as Raphaël
discovers as a consequence of his vision of death, he can no longer
desire: "The world belonged to him, he could do and have everything, and he no longer wanted anything"—"il pouvait tout et ne
voulait plus rien." The only possible preservation of this self whose
most profound desires can be realized by the talisman is in the
renunciation of desiring. Raphaël understands this logic instanta-
neously, and he announces to the assembled guests, congratulating
him on his fortune and demanding his largesse, that he now desires
nothing: "Je ne désire rien." In the midst of the cacophony of vulgar
desires shouted at him by those around the table, Raphaël then
instinctively discovers the next step in the logic, the desire to wish
death upon the others: " 'I almost have the desire to wish the death
of all of you,' replied Valentin, with a deep and somber look at the
guests" (p. 211).

We may find in this sadistic wish further confirmation that what
Raphaël has discovered at the moment when his life's story has
disclosed the possibility of total fulfillment is what lies *beyond* the
pleasure principle, beyond the realization of orgiastic desire: the
death instinct, the drive toward extinction. For sadism, according
to Freud—who had notable difficulties in accounting for this destructive urge until he came to the insights of *Beyond the Pleasure
Principle*—is a displaced example, indeed the only directly observ-
able example that psychoanalysis encounters, of the death instinct
at work.[16] Nearly the whole of Freud's argument in *Beyond the*

Pleasure Principle is allegorized here: in Raphaël's discovery that with the possibility of total realization of desire, the self encounters the impossibility of desiring, because to desire becomes, and can only be, the choice of death of that same self. The talisman concentrates in itself and phantasmatically represents the paradoxical logic of Freud's essay: that Eros is subtended by the death instinct, the drive of living matter to return to the quiescence of the inorganic, a state prior to life.

Thus it is that we find Raphaël in the third part of *La Peau de chagrin* trying to continue to live at the price of life, living a death-within-life in order to preserve life-within-death. He has, we are told, chosen to live chastely in the manner of Origen, by "castrating his imagination" (p. 217), arranging his existence so that he may avoid ever pronouncing an imperative or even an optative. Emblematic of this existence is the specially constructed opera glass he uses at the theater: a lorgnon that deforms the objects on which it focuses, distorts the image, rendering the world ugly, annulling the possibility of desire. The world not charged with desire is thus without beauty. It is also simply an impossibility: Raphaël despite himself is led into the formulation of desires, including the desire for the death of others—in his duel—and he dies convulsively biting his beloved Pauline in the breast, in the final inarticulate gasp of desire.

The problem, as Raphaël early discovers, is one of antiphrasis: "This skin shrinks [*se rétrécit*] when I have a wish . . . it's an antiphrasis . . . desires, you see, should extend" (p. 204). Desire should stretch, extend, and project the self. Figured in Raphaël's words—pronounced, appropriately, at the tail-end of an orgy—is desire as erection, as the tumescence of a self in a state of domination, an imperious and imperial self.[17] Yet this magic skin retracts and shrinks with the realization of desire, in a kind of postcoital quiescence which Freud, too, adduces as an example of the relation between the pleasure principle and the death instinct. The self subjugates through the realization of desire, but that realization diminishes the self, retracts it, until the point where the skin—lying, at the last, in Pauline's hand—shrivels away to nothing. And here the paradox of the self becomes explicitly the paradox of narrative plot as the reader consumes it: diminishing as it realizes itself, leading to an end that is the consummation (as well as the consumption) of its sense-making. If the motor of narrative is desire, totalizing, building ever-larger units of meaning, the ultimate determinants of meaning lie *at the end*, and narrative desire is ultimately, inexorably, desire *for* the end.

Raphaël's telling of his life's story, from childhood to the moment of preparation for death, begins with explicit evocation of the panoramic vision of one's life traditionally attributed to the dying: he speaks of the "lucidity which allows me to embrace in this instant all my life as in one tableau where figures, colors, shadows, light, half-shades are faithfully rendered. . . . Seen from this distance, my life is as if foreshortened [*rétrécie*] by a psychological phenomenon" (p. 120).[18] We find here the necessary postulate of classical narrative which, starting from the end as the moment of significant revelation, embraces and comprehends the past as a panorama leading to realization in the ultimate moment. It is notable that the verb Raphaël uses to describe this effect of synoptic vision is the same as that which he will use to describe the action of the magic skin under the commands of desire: *rétrécir*, to retract, to shrink, to foreshorten. Any narrative plot, in the sense of a significant organization of the life story, necessarily espouses in some form the problematic of the talisman: the realization of the desire for narrative encounters the limits of narrative, that is, the fact that one can tell a life only in terms of its limits or margins. The telling is always *in terms of* the impending end.

"*Vouloir* nous brûle, et *pouvoir* nous détruit" ("Desire sets us afire and power destroys us"), the antique dealer has said to Raphaël in the grand antithesis that describes not only the typical plot of the *Comédie humaine*, but also the very nature of narrative plot, consuming itself as it projects itself forward, retracting as it extends, calling for its end from its beginning. As alternative to the *vouloir/pouvoir* paradox, the antique dealer offers the possibility he calls *savoir*, by which he means vicarious and imaginary enjoyment, "the sublime faculty of making the universe appear in one's head," experiencing pleasure in purely ideal form (p. 87). Can narrative fictions offer this alternative to the logic of desire in life represented by the magic skin? On an initial inspection, and on the thematic level, the answer would seem to be negative: the antique dealer's visionary knowledge—like Frenhofer's imaginary masterpiece in Balzac's *Le Chef d'oeuvre inconnu*—exists only in the realm of the ineffable and the incommensurable. Once there is text, expression, writing, one becomes subject to the processes of desiring and dying. If narrative makes a claim to the recuperation of a *savoir* from the dynamic of *vouloir/pouvoir*, it must, I think, be of a different nature from the antique dealer's: a knowledge that is by definition always retrospective and too late, or perhaps knowledge *of* the too-late—a question to which I shall return.

Raphaël's "discovery" of the talisman and its capacity to realize his formulation of desire in the course of his act of narration, and then the cohabitation of desire with death, requires further thought, and a reformulation. For if Raphaël is apparently telling the story of past desire, it is the telling itself that rediscovers the talisman and its representation of Eros. Do we detect here that the desire of narrating—the desire subtending the act of narration itself—which we thought to be dependent on the story it recapitulates, is in fact an autonomous instance of desire? That is, under Raphaël's explicitly formulated demand for pleasure and fortune may lie that which can never be satisfied by the realization of explicit wishes: the more nearly absolute desire to be heard, recognized, listened to. The desire to tell may be the sole meaning of Raphaël's act of narration. The talisman—this skin inscribed with Arabic writing in the form of an inverted pyramid—offers a metaphor not only of life as desire but also of narration, telling, as another form of desire. We seem to have moved from desire as inhabiting the *récit*, the narrative plot, to desire as the motor of *narration*, the narrating discourse, to use Gérard Genette's further elaboration of the basic *histoire/récit* distinction.[19]

Narrative may first come to life as narration, as the inchoate intent to tell—as when Rousseau discovers in the episode of the stolen ribbon the necessity of narrative as the only way to portray an incoherent self—where telling stories becomes the only viable form of "explanation." It is useful to recall at this point that for much of his narrative, Raphaël has had no listener: Emile has fallen asleep. He wakes up when Raphaël "discovers" the talisman and breaks into loud exclamations. Emile denies having slept, claims that he is still following the story: "Foedora or death, I'm with you" (p. 203)—which indicates that he has in fact taken leave of the story a number of pages back. That Raphaël should be thus talking to the air makes more starkly clear the absolutism of the desire from which narrative as narrating is born: it is in essence the desire to be heard, recognized, understood, which, never wholly satisfied or indeed satisfiable, continues to generate the desire to tell, the effort to enunciate a significant version of the life story in order to captivate a possible listener.

Desire as narrative thematic, desire as narrative motor, and desire as the very intention of narrative language and the act of telling all seem to stand in close interrelation. This interrelation demands further thought, and we might start by returning for a moment to Freud, to a passage in *Beyond the Pleasure Principle* where he encounters Goethe's *Faust*, pre-eminently the representation of man's unquenchable striving. In his study of instinctual drives, Freud sets aside the wishful belief that there might be an "instinct toward perfection at work in human beings," and goes on to suggest how the dynamic that appears to produce forward and upward movement really works:

What appears in a minority of human individuals as an untiring impulsion towards further perfection can easily be understood as a result of the instinctual repression upon which is based all that is most precious in human civilization. The repressed instinct never ceases to strive for complete satisfaction, which would consist in the repetition of a primary experience of satisfaction. No substitutive or reactive formations and no sublimations will suffice to remove the repressed instinct's persisting tension; and it is the difference in amount between the pleasure of satisfaction which is *demanded* and that which is actually *achieved* that provides the driving factor which will permit of no halting at any position attained, but, in the poet's words, *"ungebändigt immer vorwärts dringt"* ["presses ever forward unsubdued"]. (p. 42)

Freud's version of Faustian man is inhabited by a motor whose "driving factor" is the result of tension caused by difference which powers his life's story forward, striving upward to its end.

Here we can introduce another return to Freud, Lacan's interpretation of the concept of desire, desire as born of the difference or split between need and demand: for instance, the infant's need for the breast (for nourishment) and his demand, which is in essence a demand for love from the other (for instance, from the mother). To cite Jean Laplanche and J.-B. Pontalis: "Desire is born from the gap [*l'écart*] between need and demand; it is irreducible to need, for it is not in its principle relation to a real object, independent of the subject, but rather to a phantasy; it is irreducible to demand, in that it seeks to impose itself without taking account of language and the unconscious of the other, and insists upon being absolutely recognized by the other." [20] In this gap, desire comes into being as a perpetual want for (of) a satisfaction that cannot be offered in reality. Desire is inherently unsatisfied and unsatisfiable since it is linked to memory traces and seeks its realization in the hallucinatory reproduction of indestructible signs of infantile satisfaction: it reposes on phantasmatic scenarios of satisfaction. Such unconscious desire becomes, in the later life of the subject, a motor of actions whose significance is blocked from consciousness, since interpretation of its scenarios of fulfillment is not directly accessible to consciousness.

One can now begin to grasp the manner in which desire comes to inhabit the language of narration. In Lacan's interpretation of the Saussurian analysis of the sign, the bar separating signifier from signified (S/s) becomes the bar of repression, indicating the inaccessibility of the true signified (the object of unconscious desire). Discourse hence becomes the interconnection of signifiers one with another in a "signifying chain" where meaning (in the sense of access to the meaning of unconscious desire) does not consist in any single link of the chain, yet through which meaning nonetheless *insists*. The analyst, for instance, hears in the analysand's language the pressure *toward* meaning, which is never pinned down or captured since there is a perpetual sliding or slippage of the signified from under the signifier. Thus it is that language can "mean" something other than what it "says," can suggest intentions of which the subject is not consciously aware. This slippage is particularly characteristic of the metonymic pole of language—the particular tropology of narrative, according to Roman Jakobson. If narrative desire keeps moving us forward, it is because narrative metonymy can never quite speak its name. As Lacan writes, "The enigmas that desire poses to any 'natural philosophy,' its frenzy miming the abyss of the infinite, the intimate collusion in which it envelops the pleasure of knowing and that of dominating with pleasure, belongs to no other derangement of instinct than its being caught on the rails—eternally extended toward the *desire of something else*—of metonymy." [21] Narrative is hence condemned to *saying* other than what it *would mean*, spinning out its movement toward a meaning that would be the end of its movement.

"Ah! if you knew my life," says Raphaël to Emile on the threshold of his account. Yet the "knowledge" of his life then offered—which is supposed to explain what led him to the brink of suicide—in fact reads not as an explanation, as a statement of reasons and their consequences, but as a baffled attempt of desire to come to terms with its objects and its meaning. Raphaël tells essentially the story of loss of the mother, struggle with the tyranny of the father—focused in the prohibition of gambling—followed by emancipation from his father but simultaneous enslavement to his law, now internalized: from the moment his father treats him as a man, he learns of the family's financial ruin and must take upon himself the salvation of its honor. With the death of the father, the Name-of-the-Father—the father as prohibition, law, "morality"—emerges only the stronger, to be submitted to in full abnegation, or else rejected in a total revolt, symbolized by the life of the gambler. In his successive choices—first, the life of monastic study, writing a treatise on the will in the "aerial solitude" of a garret, then the plunge into dissipation, gambling, the life beyond one's means—Raphaël's existence suggests the frenzy of a desire which still is oriented toward unmastered infantile scenarios.

His story comes to focus more and more on Foedora, the "woman without a heart" who gives Part 2 of the novel its title. Foedora represents the problem of desire in that, eminently desirable, she is herself impervious to desire, a smooth surface on which desire cannot take hold. *La Femme sans coeur* could in fact be considered a euphemism, and a displacement or metonymy, for another lack: the lack of sex, the lack of the bodily opening through which Raphaël's desire could find satisfaction. Such an interpretation forcibly presents itself to the reader in the curious and memorable scene in which Raphaël hides behind the curtains in Foedora's bedroom in order to see her undress. This eminently infantile scenario has its explicit motivation in the desire to see if Foedora has any hidden bodily defect that would explain her refusal to give in to erotic desire. When Raphaël sees her naked—yet slightly veiled by her light shift—there is no defect visible, but rather the absence of defect: the all-too-perfect, the marble body of the Medusa. Raphaël encounters here the significance of the absent phallus. Yet since the anatomy of this absence—part of Foedora's female "perfection"—is veiled, itself an inaccessible absence, the sexual difference gives no passage to desire, no means of appropriation of the object. Rather, as in Freud's reading of the Medusa myth, it is the looking subject—the voyeur—who receives the mark of castration.[22]

"Foedora or death," cries Emile, roused from sleep, claiming that he has in fact been listening all along. If he has missed much of the story, he has nonetheless—perhaps in the manner of the analyst's "floating attention"—seized on the central antithesis in which Raphaël has become stuck, the hyperbolic moment of desire which has been prolonged and narrativized, become the narrative conundrum—all the more so in that the antithesis threatens to collapse into an identity, since Foedora *is* death, precisely the death of the desire which in her inaccessibility to desire she represents. What, ultimately, does Raphaël as narrator of his life's story have to tell? The story of the insistence of a desire as persistent as it is incoherent, a desire whose lack of satisfaction gives death as the only alternative, but whose satisfaction also would be death. Here we have figured the contradictory desire of narrative, driving toward the end which would be both its destruction and its meaning, suspended on the metonymic rails which tend toward that end without ever being able quite to say the terminus.

To cite Lacan again, describing the "indestructibility of unconscious desire" in terms that speak specifically to the situation and the motive of narrative, "It is in a memory, comparable to what is called by that name in our modern thinking machines . . . that lies this chain which *insists* on reproducing itself in the transference, and which is that of a dead desire" (p. 518). The paradox of the "dead desire" is of course that it continues very much to live, but in displaced and unrecognized form, as desire that cannot speak its right name—could speak its name only by way of the substitutive condensation of metaphor, as in the magic talisman itself—yet for this very reason continues as a force in the present, driving the discourse of the subject forward in the word-to-word connections of metonymy, extending the desiring subject forward on those "rails" that figure the necessary dynamic of desire, a motor insisting—as narrative ever does—toward the unnamed meaning, the name that could be recaptured only in a recapitulative movement starting from the end. If we ask where and how we find this insistence of past desire most powerfully alive within the signifying chain of narrative, we may want to answer that first and last it lies in the very project of telling, in the insistence, of Rousseau, for example, or of Raphaël, to narrate the story of the past even in the absence of any clear "point" to that story, even, eventually, in the absence of a listener.

The psychoanalyst, as my last quotation from Lacan notes, hears the voice of dead desire most particularly in the transference, in the reproductive workings-through of the life story triggered by the analysand-analyst relation, a possible model of text and reading that will need more thorough exploration later on. What, we may want to ask at this point, should we finally make of the emblem of human existence discovered by Raphaël's effort to tell his life? The talisman may, I suggested, be a metaphor in Lacan's sense: by the play of substitution, a signifier has moved into the place of the signified, under the bar; and understanding the process of this signifier's repression can point the way to access to the signified of unconscious desire. That is, the substitution—the characteristic operation of metaphor—of a present signifier for an absent one can spark an understanding of the meaning of that which is absent. The talisman "stands for" the paroxysm of human desire, laying bare its frenzied contradictions by the very hyperbole of the fulfillment it offers. Furthermore, in the context of Raphaël's life story, the talisman, as the fulfillment of the gambler's every wish, as those loaded dice with which the gambler cannot lose, may speak of the perfect removal of that father whose censoring presence was more and more concentrated in the prohibition of gambling. The talisman operates as a metaphor of parricide, the triumph of the son in the oedipal structure.[23] And yet, since with these loaded dice the winning gambler also always loses—completely—the talisman works also as a metaphor of the father's triumph, castration of the son.

These contradictions of the talisman cannot be resolved. We should rather recognize that the magic skin is an "arabesque," like the squiggly line that Balzac inscribed as epigraph to the novel (and later literal-minded typesetters turned into a snake):

Balzac gave as source for the epigraph Sterne's *Tristram Shandy* (book 6, chapter 40), where Corporal Trim creates the arabesque by brandishing his cane in the air, to represent the free, unfixed life of the bachelor—desire free and unchanneled. Taken in conjunction with the other arabesques of *Tristram Shandy* (book 9, chapter 4) which explicitly designate the unfettered, digressive line of Tristram's narrative, the incessant detours of its plot, Corporal

Trim's gesture as reused by Balzac seems to comment on narrative itself, suggesting the fantastic designs drawn by narrative desire. The arabesque inscribed on the magic skin—its text inscribed in Arabic, in the form of an inverted pyramid—carries the message of desire realized, beginning with the line (as translated in the novel): "If you possess me, you will possess everything," and ending, at the foot of this shrinking, retracting pyramid, with "So be it!": in French, the single word *Soit!* The end of the pyramid, the last word of desire in its hyperbolic satisfaction, offers only the enigma of desire and life itself.

"If only you knew my life," Raphaël has said to Emile, in a phrase that could stand for most tellings of the life's story, where the claim that intelligibility, meaning, understanding depend on a fully predicated narrative sentence, on a narrative totality, never is and never can be realized. Yet the performance of the narrative act is in itself transformatory, predicating the material of the life story in a changed context—subordinating all its verbs to the verb "I tell"—and thus most importantly soliciting the entry of a listener into relation with the story. The narrative act discovers, and makes use of, the intersubjective nature of language itself, medium for the exchange of narrative understandings. Here in the dialogic dynamic of the narrative transference—a topic for later elaboration—we may make our nearest approach to the antique dealer's notion of *savoir*, the knowledge wrested from the doomed dialectic of *vouloir* and *pouvoir*, in the transformatory function of narrating itself.

The paradigm of what I have in mind would be the *Thousand and One Nights*, Balzac's inspiration as he sought to make the magic of an "oriental tale" unfold within the frame of contemporary Paris. In the *Thousand and One Nights*, Shahrazad's storytelling takes a desire that has gone off the rails—the Sultan's desire, derailed by his wife's infidelity, become sadistic and discontinuous, so that the mistress of the night must have her head chopped off in the morning—and cures it by prolonging it, precisely by narrativizing it. Desire becomes reinvested in tellings of and listenings to stories, it is reconstituted as metonymy—over a thousand and one nights—until the Sultan can resume a normal erotic state, marrying

Shahrazad, who thus fulfills her name as "savior of the city." Narration, in this allegory, is seen to be life-giving in that it arouses and sustains desire, ensuring that the terminus it both delays and beckons toward will offer what we might call a lucid repose, desire both come to rest and set in perspective.

Narratives portray the motors of desire that drive and consume their plots, and they also lay bare the nature of narration as a form of human desire: the need to tell as a primary human drive that seeks to seduce and to subjugate the listener, to implicate him in the thrust of a desire that never can quite speak its name—never can quite come to the point—but that insists on speaking over and over again its movement toward that name. For the analyst of narrative, these different yet convergent vectors of desire suggest the need to explore more fully the shaping function of desire, its modeling of the plot, and also the dynamics of exchange and transmission, the roles of tellers and listeners. But prior to pursuing the theoretical questions thus implied, I shall turn to consider in some detail a single novel, attempting to disengage the models of plot and plotting that it appears to propose, and to understand what these have to do with individual biography and collective history.

3

The Novel and the Guillotine, or Fathers and Sons in *Le Rouge et le noir*

Le Rouge et le noir offers an exemplary entry into the nineteenth-century novel, its dynamics, and the interpretive problems these pose. Published a few months after the triumph of the bourgeoisie in the Revolution of 1830—inaugurating an era of expansive capitalism and the acceleration of social change—*Le Rouge et le noir* displays an unprecedented concern with energy—the hero's and the text's—and provides a first decisive representation of man constructing his own life's plot in response to the sociopolitical dynamics of modern history, which both shapes the individual career and plays roulette with its most concerted plans. As Harry Levin has written, with Stendhal we undergo "the rites of initiation into the nineteenth century," and this is so in good part because Stendhal's novels are inescapably pervaded by a historical perspective that provides an interpretive framework for all actions, ambitions, self-conceptions, and desires.[1] Nowhere is the historical problematic more evident than in the question of authority that haunts *Le Rouge et le noir*, not only in the minds of its individual figures but in its very narrative structures. The novel not only represents but also is structured by an underlying warfare of legitimacy and usurpation; it hinges on the fundamental question, To whom does France belong? This question in turn implicates and is implicated in an issue of obsessive importance in all of Stendhal's novels, that of paternity.

Upon reflection, one can see that paternity is a dominant issue within the great tradition of the nineteenth-century novel (extending well into the twentieth century), a principal embodiment of its concern with authority, legitimacy, the conflict of generations, and the transmission of wisdom. Turgenev's title, *Fathers and Sons*, sums up what is at stake in a number of the characteristic major novels of the tradition: not only *Le Rouge et le noir*, but also such novels as Balzac's *Le Père Goriot*, Mary Shelley's *Frankenstein*, Dickens's *Great Expectations*, Dostoevsky's *The Brothers Karamazov*, James's *The Princess Casamassima*, Conrad's *Lord Jim*, Gide's *Les Faux-Monnayeurs*, Joyce's *Ulysses*, Mann's *The Magic Mountain*, Faulkner's *Absalom, Absalom!*, to name only a few of the most important texts that are essentially structured by this conflict. It is characteristic of *Ulysses* as a summa of the nineteenth- and twentieth-century novel that its filial protagonist, Stephen Dedalus, should provide an overt retrospective meditation on the problem:

> Fatherhood, in the sense of conscious begetting, is unknown to man. It is a mystical estate, an apostolic succession, from only begetter to only begotten. On that mystery and not on the madonna which the cunning Italian intellect flung to the mob of Europe the church is founded and founded irremovably because founded, like the world, macro- and microcosm, upon the void. Upon incertitude, upon unlikelihood. *Amor matris*, subjective and objective genitive, may be the only true thing in life. Paternity may be a legal fiction. Who is the father of any son that any son should love him or he any son?[2]

Stephen's theological musing on the "apostolic succession" of fatherhood strikes to the key problem of transmission: the process by which the young protagonist of the nineteenth-century novel discovers his choices of interpretation and action in relation to a number of older figures of wisdom and authority who are rarely biological fathers—a situation that the novel often ensures by making the son an orphan, or by killing off or otherwise occulting the biological father before the text brings to maturity its dominant alternatives.

The son then most often has a choice among possible fathers from whom to inherit, and in the choosing—which may entail a succession of selections and rejections—he plays out his career of initiation into a society and into history, comes to define his own authority in the interpretation and use of social (and textual) codes.

Freud, in his well-known essay "Family Romances," develops the typical scenario based on the child's discovery that *pater semper incertus est*: the phantasy of being an adopted child whose biological parents are more exalted creatures than his actual parents, which is then superseded when the child accepts the actual mother but creates a phantasized, illegitimate father, and bastardizes siblings in favor of his own sole legitimacy. It may be significant, as Roland Barthes notes, that the child appears to "discover" the Oedipus complex and the capacity for constructing coherent narrative at about the same stage in life.[3] The most fully developed narratives of the child become a man all seem to turn on the uncertainty of fatherhood, to use this uncertainty to unfold the romance of authority vested elsewhere, and to test the individual's claim to personal legitimacy within a struggle of different principles of authority. In the nineteenth century, these issues touch every possible register of society, history, and fiction, and nowhere more so than in France, where the continuing struggle of revolution and restoration played itself out in dramatic political upheavals and reversals throughout the century. Particularly during the Restoration, after the fall of Napoleon who seemed to incarnate the triumph of energy and youth over the resistances of age, tradition, and hierarchy, France experienced a relapse into an intense conflict of generations. France was governed by old men who had come of age during the Ancien Régime, Louis XVIII and Charles X (both brothers of Louis XVI), and their ministers. Titles of nobility and certificates of noncollaboration with the Napoleonic regime were necessary to recognition, and the young men of the bourgeoisie (and the people) who had seen the doors of the future open under Napoleon now found them closed. Many of the writers of the period—Stendhal, Balzac, Musset—as well as later historians converge in the diagnosis of a regime and a social structure set in resistance to the real dynamism of the country. The Revolution of 1830 appears in hindsight merely inevitable. In cultural politics, 1830 also appears as an intensely oedipal moment, best symbolized in the famous première of Victor Hugo's *Hernani*, marking the raucous victory of the young Romantics and the forces of movement.[4] And the nineteenth-century novel as a genre seems to be inseparable from the conflict of movement and resistance, revolution and restoration, and from the issues of authority and paternity, which provide not only the matter of the novel but also its structuring force, the dynamic that shapes its plot.

I want now to return from this brief sketch of the issue of paternity and authority to the plot of *Le Rouge et le noir* by way of the novel's end, by way of the guillotine that so abruptly severs Julien Sorel's life and brilliant career, and thereby threatens our efforts to construct a coherent interpretation of the novel. Just before Julien Sorel's end, the narrator tells us, "Jamais cette tête n'avait été aussi poétique qu'au moment où elle allait tomber" ("Never had this head been so poetic as at the moment it was about to fall").[5] The next moment of the text—the next sentence—it is all over, and the narrator is commenting on the style with which the head fell: "Everything took place simply, fittingly, and without any affectation on his part." In an elision typical of Stendhal, the climactic instant of decapitation is absent. We have the vibrations of the fall of the blade of the guillotine, but not the bloody moment. The elision is the more suspect in that it is not clear that Julien's head needed to fall at all. As a traditional and rationalist criticism of Stendhal used to say, Julien's shooting of Mme de Rênal—which entails his decapitation—appears arbitrary, gratuitous, insufficiently motivated. Engaged to marry the pregnant Mathilde de la Mole, adored of her as she is adored of her father, surely Julien the master-plotter, the self-declared disciple of Tartuffe, could have found a way to repair the damage done to his reputation by Mme de Rênal's letter of accusation. Those other critics who try to explain Julien's act on psychological grounds merely rationalize the threat of the irrational, which is not so importantly psychological as "narratological": the scandal of the manner in which Stendhal has shat-

tered his novel and then cut its head off.[6] Still another scandal—
and another elision—emerges in this ending because of the novel's
chronology, which would place Julien's execution well into 1831.
Yet in this novel subtitled "Chronicle of 1830" we have no mention
of the most notable event of the year: the July Revolution. Indeed,
Mme de Rênal in the last pages of the novel proposes to seek
clemency for Julien by pleading with King Charles X, who had
been dethroned for almost a year. The discrepancy is particularly
curious in that the whole of Julien's ideology and career—of revolt,
usurpation, the transgression of class lines—seems to beckon to and
call for revolution. Is the guillotine that executes Julien, the "peasant in revolt" as he has called himself at his trial, a displaced figure
for "les Trois Glorieuses," a revolution notable for having made
no use of the guillotine? Is the catastrophic ending of *Le Rouge et
le noir* a displaced and inverted version of the revolution that should
have been?[7]

Perhaps we have begun to sketch the outlines of a problem in
narrative design and intention, in plot and its legitimating authority
(including history as plot), and in the status of the end on which,
traditionally, the beginning and middle depend for their retrospective meaning. We can come closer to defining the problem with
two statements that Julien makes shortly before the arrival of Mme
de Rênal's accusatory letter. When the Marquis de la Mole has given
him a new name, M. le chevalier Julien Sorel de la Vernaye, and
a commission as lieutenant in the hussars, he reflects, "After all . . .
my novel is finished" (p. 639). Yet the novel—if not his, then whose?—
will continue for another eleven chapters. Shortly after the statement just quoted, Julien receives twenty thousand francs from the
Marquis, with the stipulation that "M. Julien de la Vernaye"—the
Sorel has now been excised—will consider this a gift from his real
(that is, natural, illegitimate) father and will donate some of it to
his legal father, Sorel the carpenter, who took care of him in childhood. Julien wonders if this fiction of the illegitimate aristocratic
father might not be the truth after all: "Might it really be possible,
he said to himself, that I am the natural son of some great noble
exiled in our mountains by the terrible Napoleon? With every mo-

ment this idea seemed less improbable to him ... My hatred for my father would be a proof ... I would no longer be a monster!" (p. 641). The word "monster," as we shall see, evokes a network of references to Julien's moments of self-identification as the plebeian in revolt, the usurper, the hypocrite, the seducer, the Tartuffe, he who, in the manner of all monsters, transgresses and calls into question the normal orders of classification and regulation. But can illegitimacy rescue him from monstrosity, when throughout the novel illegitimacy has appeared the very essence of the monstrous? Can hatred for the legal father be a proof of innocence, that is, of the lack of monstrosity, of the lack of a need to act the hypocrite? If so, have we really all along been reading not a "Chronicle of 1830" but an eighteenth-century novel—by a writer such as Fielding or Marivaux—where the hero is a foundling whose aristocratic origins eventually will out, and will offer a complete retrospective motivation—and absolution—for his desire to rise in the world: usurpation recovered as natural affinity? Legitimized by illegitimacy, Julien's plot could simply be a homecoming, a *nostos*, the least transgressive, the least monstrous of narratives.

Earlier in the novel, M. de Rênal, reflecting on his children's evident preference of Julien to their father, exclaims: "Everything in this century tends to throw opprobrium on *legitimate* authority. Poor France!" (p. 353). The comment explicitly connects political issues of legitimacy and authority with paternity, itself inextricably bound up in the problem of legitimacy and authority. The shape and intention of the novel are tied closely to this network of issues. The way in which the novel poses the questions of authority and legitimacy might be formulated first of all in the queries: What kind of a novel is this? To what models of plot and explanation does it refer us? There occurs a striking example of this problem early in the novel (Book 1, Chapter 9), in the episode of the "portrait in the mattress." Julien has just learned that M. de Rênal and his servants are going to restuff the straw mattresses of the house. He turns to Mme de Rênal and begs her to "save him" by removing from his mattress, before M. de Rênal reaches it, a small cardboard box containing a portrait. And he begs her as well not to look at the portrait in the box; it is his "secret." The narrator, typically cross-cutting from the perceptions of one character to those of another, tells us that Mme de Rênal's nascent love for Julien (of which she is still largely ignorant) gives her the heroic generosity of spirit necessary to perform what she takes to be an act of self-sacrifice, since she assumes that the portrait must be that of the woman Julien loves. Once she has retrieved the box and given it to Julien, she succumbs to the "horrors of jealousy." Cutting back to Julien, we find him burning the box, and we learn that it in fact contains a portrait of Napoleon—*l'usurpateur*, Julien names him here—with lines of admiration scratched on its back by Julien. The misunderstanding between the two characters, where neither perceives what is at stake for the other, cannot be confined to the realm of the personal: they are living in different worlds, indeed in different novels. For Mme de Rênal, the drama has to do with love and jealousy, with amorous rivalry and the possibility of adultery. She thinks she is a character in an eighteenth-century novel of manners, *Les Egarements du coeur et de l'esprit*, perhaps, or (as one of its innocents) *Les Liaisons dangereuses*. Julien, on the contrary, is living in the world of modern narrative—post-Revolutionary, post-Napoleonic—which precisely throws into question the context of "manners" and the novel of manners, subverts its very possibility. Napoleon, the "usurper" in Julien's pertinent epithet, represents a different order of *égarement*, or wandering from the true path: the intrusion of history into society, the reversal of a stable and apparently immutable world, that of the Ancien Régime, which made "manners" as social and as literary code possible and necessary. If, as Julien says a few chapters later, the "fatal memory" of Napoleon will forever prevent young Frenchmen like himself from being happy, the reason is that Napoleon represented the possibility of *la carrière ouverte aux talents*: advancement through merit, the legitimation of class mobility, legalized usurpation. While Julien studies not to appear a disciple of Napoleon, he manages at various times in the novel to resemble first Robespierre, then Danton, both of whom stand behind Napoleon as destroyers of the Ancien Régime who, at the very least, historicized the concept of *le monde*, thus making the novel of manners in the strict definition impossible. The scene of the portrait in the mattress signals the impossibility of the novel of manners as Mme de Rênal understands it: questions of love and interpersonal relations no longer play themselves out in a closed and autonomous sphere. They are menaced by class conflict as historicized in the persistent aftermath of the French Revolution.

In a number of essays and reflections over the years, Stendhal developed an explicit theory of why the Revolution had rendered social comedy—*la comédie de Molière*, in his shorthand—impossible. He explains himself most fully in "La Comédie est impossible en 1836," where he argues that social comedy could work only with a unified audience, sharing the same code of manners and comportment, and agreeing on what was deviant and extravagant in terms of this code. The Revolution, in destroying the society of court and salon, and raising to consciousness the claims of different social classes, shattered the unity of sensibility on which Molière's effects were predicated; at a performance of *Le Bourgeois Gentil-homme* in 1836, half the audience would laugh at the would-be gentleman, Monsieur Jourdain—as was Molière's intention—but the other half would admire and approve him.[8] When social class becomes the basis for political struggle, one man's object of ridicule becomes another man's serious social standard. The demonstration applies as well to the novel (as Stendhal noted in the margins of a copy of *Le Rouge et le noir*):[9] the novel of manners is itself threatened with usurpation, it cannot exclude from its pages something else, something that had best be called politics. Mme de Rênal has no knowledge or understanding of politics, yet she is living in a world where all other questions, including love, eventually are held hostage to the political, and this is true as well for the novel in which she figures.

Politics in *Le Rouge et le noir* is the unassimilable other, which in fact is all too well assimilated since it determines everything: nothing can be thought in isolation from the underlying strife of legitimacy and usurpation that polarizes the system within which all other differences are inscribed and that acts as a necessary (though

I refuse to say ultimate) interpretant to any message formulated
in the novel. A telling illustration of this proposition occurs in
chapter 18 of book 1, which describes the king's visit to Verrières
and which is rich in representations of the movement from red to
black, as Julien first cuts a figure in the mounted Honor Guard
and then dons the cassock to assist the Abbé Chélan in the magnificent *Te Deum* at the chapel of Bray-le-Haut, which so over-
whelms him that in this moment "he would have fought for the
Inquisition, and in good faith." It is in the midst of this religious
spectacular that the narrator treacherously comments, "Such a day
undoes the work of a hundred issues of Jacobin newspapers." The
reader who has been paying attention will understand that this
undoing has been the intent and design of the religious ceremony,
staged and financed by the Marquis de la Mole: it is one more
political gesture in the continuing struggle to say to whom France
belongs.

But if politics is the indelible tracer dye in the social and narrative
codes of the novel, the very force of the political dynamic is matched
by the intensity with which it is repressed. For to admit to the force
of the political is to sanction a process of change, of temporal
slippage and movement forward—of history, in fact—whereas the
codes of the Restoration are all overtly predicated on temporal
analepsis, a re-creation within history of an ahistorical past, a fac-
simile Ancien Régime that rigorously excludes the possibility of
change, of revolution. Hence those who claim to be the legitimate
masters of France cannot allow themselves to mention politics: the
"Charter of the Drawing-Room" in the Hôtel de la Mole prohibits
mockery of God and the Establishment, bans praise of Voltaire,
Rousseau, and the Opposition newspapers, and decrees "especially
that one never talk politics" (p. 457). The result is boredom, for
what has been repressed is what interests everyone most passionately, and indeed ultimately motivates those acts that claim ostensibly to belong to the domain of manners, since manners themselves—
such an act as changing into silk stockings and slippers for dinner—
are political gestures. Politics stands as the great repressed that ever
threatens to break through the bar of repression. Politics, as some-

one calling himself "the author" puts it in a parenthetical debate with another figure called "the publisher," is like a pistol shot in the middle of a concert. Even before Julien's pistol shot shatters the ceremony of the Mass in the church at Verrières, there is a constant threat of irruption of the political into manners, a denuding of the mechanisms governing the relations of power and of persons, an exposure of the dynamic governing history and narrative.

At stake in the play of politics and its repression is, I have suggested, the issue of legitimate authority versus usurpation; and in this opposition we find the matrix of the principal generative and governing structures of the novel. The interrelated questions of authority, legitimacy, and paternity unfold on all levels of the text: in Julien's use of models to conceive and to generate his own narrative, in the problematizing of his origins and his destiny, in the overriding question of who controls the text. To treat only briefly the first of these issues: we know that Julien from his first appearance in the novel moves in a web of bookish models, derived first of all from Las Cases's memoir of Napoleon, the *Memorial de Sainte-Hélène*, the *Bulletins* of the Grande-Armée, and Rousseau's *Confessions*, which are then supplemented by the New Testament, which Julien has simply learned by heart, and by Joseph de Maistre's book on the papacy; to these one could add occasional references to Corneille's *Le Cid* as model of honor, and continuing citation of Molière's *Tartuffe*, another text memorized. The extent to which Julien believes in his texts of reference varies, but so does the meaning of "belief," since he has chosen to be the *hypokrites*, the player of roles. It is significant that the Abbé Pirard will note Julien's complete ignorance of Patristic doctrine: Julien's texts provide individual interpretations of models of behavior but no authoritative tradition of interpretation and conduct.

As a result, Julien continually conceives himself as the hero of his own text, and that text as something to be created, not simply endured. He creates fictions, including fictions of the self, that motivate action.[10] The result is often inauthenticity and error, the choice of comportments dictated by models that are inappropriate.

In Julien's "seduction" of Mme de Rênal, for instance, we are told that his success comes not from efforts to play the role of a consummate Don Juan but from his natural unhappiness at failing to please so beautiful a woman: when he bursts into tears, he achieves a victory his stratagems had failed to win. His sense of "duty" to "an ideal model which he proposed to imitate" indeed nearly spoils what is most attractive to Mme de Rênal, and robs Julien of the pleasure he might have experienced. Yet just when the reader is ready to judge that Julien would do better to abandon models and roles, the narrator turns around and points out that the contrived self-conceptions alone have put Julien in a position where his *naturel* can effect results. In a typically dialectical statement, the narrator tells us: "In a word, what made Julien a superior being was precisely what prevented him from enjoying the pleasure that had come his way" (p. 298).

Julien's fictional scenarios make him not only the actor, the feigning self, but also the stage manager of his own destiny, constantly projecting the self into the future on the basis of hypothetical plots. One of the most striking examples of such hypotheses occurs when, after receiving Mathilde's summons to come to her bedroom at one o'clock in the morning, he imagines a plot—in all senses of the term, including plot as machination, as *complot*—in which he will be seized by Mathilde's brother's valets, bound, gagged, imprisoned, and eventually poisoned. So vivid is this fiction that the narrator tells us: "Moved like a playwright by his own story, Julien was truly afraid when he entered the dining room" (p. 536). Such fictions may even encompass the political, as when Julien immolates his last vestiges of remorse toward the Marquis—the benefactor whose daughter he is about to seduce—by evoking the fate of MM. Fontan and Magalon, political prisoners of the regime: an evocation that is factually accurate but of the most fictive relevance to his own case, as indeed, we may feel, are all his self-identifications as plebeian in revolt and peasant on the rise, since they do not correspond either to our perceptions of his identity or to his own identifications with more glorious models. Because the scenarist of self-conceptions cannot maintain a stable distinction between the self and its fictions, Julien must unceasingly write and rewrite the narrative of a self defined in the dialectic of its past actions and its prospective fictions.

To Julien's generation of his narrative from fictional models we can juxtapose the seriality of those figures of paternity who claim authority in his career. He is set in relationship to a series of ideal or possible fathers, but in a curious manner whereby each father figure claims authority, or has authority conferred on him, at just the moment when he is about to be replaced. The "real," or at least legal, father, Sorel the carpenter, is already well on the way to repudiation when the novel opens; his first replacement, the chirurgien-major who has bequeathed his Legion of Honor to Julien, is dead and his legacy suppressed in the movement from red to black. The paternity of the Abbé Chélan emerges in strong outline only when Julien has left him for the seminary, where the severe Abbé Pirard will eventually address Julien as *filius*. "I was hated by my father from the cradle," Julien will say to Pirard, "this was one of my greatest misfortunes; but I will no longer complain of fortune, I have found another father in you, sir" (p. 444).[11] Yet this moment of overt recognition comes only in Chapter 1 of Book 2, that is, after Julien's translation to Paris and his establishment in the Hôtel de la Mole: precisely the moment when Pirard begins to give way to the Marquis de la Mole, who will complicate the question of paternity and play out its various transformations.

It is at the moment of transition from Pirard's paternity to the Marquis's that the question of Julien's legitimation through illegitimacy is first explicitly raised: the possibility that he might be the natural child of some aristocrat (perhaps hidden in the mountains of Franche-Comté during the Napoleonic wars), which would explain what the Abbé (and later the Marquis) see as his natural nobility. For the Abbé and the Marquis, Julien's natural nobility is something of a scandal in the order of things, one that requires remotivation and authorization through noble blood, be it illegitimately transmitted. If, like the foundling of an eighteenth-century novel or a Molière comedy, Julien were at last to find that he has been fathered by an aristocrat, this discovery would legitimate his

exceptionality, his deviance from the normal condition of the peasant, and show that what was working as hidden design in his destiny
was, as the Abbé puts it, "la force du sang" (p. 441). The strength
of bloodline would rewrite Julien's narrative as satisfactorily motivated, no longer aberrant and deviant, and rescue Julien's transgressive career, and the novel's dynamic, from the political realm
by restoring them to the anodyne of manners.

A curious dialogue between the Abbé and the Marquis, these
two believers in paternal authority and the legitimate order, explicitly formulates for the first time the theory of Julien's illegitimate nobility. The dialogue creates a chiasmus of misunderstanding
concerning the anonymous gift of five hundred francs to Julien,
as each speaker mistakenly infers from the other's words possession
of some secret knowledge about Julien's origins and thus makes
further unfounded inferences. It is through misinterpretation and
the postulation of concealment—of what is "really," so far as we
know, the absence of anything to be concealed—that Julien's noble
illegitimacy begins to achieve textual status, to acquire an authorship based on a gratuitous play of substitutes for the origin. Further
retroactive motivations for the origin then fall into line. The next
step follows from Julien's duel with the Chevalier de Beauvoisis,
who doesn't want it thought that he has taken the field of honor
against a simple secretary to the Marquis: the Chevalier hence lets
it be known that Julien is the natural child of "an intimate friend
of the Marquis de la Mole," and the Marquis then finds it convenient
to lend, as he puts it, "consistency" to this version. He will go on
to furnish Julien with a blue costume in addition to the secretarial
black; wearing the former, he will be the younger son of the old
Duc de Chaulnes (who, I note in passing, comes to be an object of
hatred to Julien, a representation of repressive authority).[12] The
Marquis then authorizes the Abbé Pirard "to keep no longer the
secret" of Julien's birth. The blue costume is followed by the cross
(of the Legion of Honor): the cross that the legitimate son, Norbert
de la Mole, has been demanding in vain for some eighteen months.
This process of seemingly casual ennoblement by way of illegitimacy, motivating and promoting Julien's rise in the world through

a hidden authority, will reach its climax when the recuperated and effaced plebeian makes himself—through Mathilde's pregnancy—into the natural son-in-law, himself continuing the bloodline, and stands on the verge of becoming the legal son-in-law, Mathilde's husband, the Chevalier de la Vernaye.

But I have so far said nothing about another figure of paternal authority in the narrative: the narrator. The relation of the narrator to Julien—and of all Stendhalian narrators to the young protagonists of his novels—is patently paternalistic, a mixture of censure and indulgence; the narrator sets a standard of worldly wisdom that the protagonist must repeatedly violate, yet confesses to a secret admiration for the violation, especially for *l'imprévu*, the unforeseeable, the moments when Julien breaks with the very notion of model and pattern. The narrator constantly judges Julien in relation to his chosen models, measuring his distance from them, noting his failures to understand them, his false attributions of success to them, and the fictionality of the constructions he builds from them. As Victor Brombert has so well pointed out, the Stendhalian narrator typically uses hypothetical grammatical forms, asserting that if only Julien had understood such and such, he would have done so and so, with results different from those to which he condemns himself.[13] To take just one example, which characteristically concerns what did not happen between Julien and Mme de Rênal: "If Mme de Rênal had had the slightest *sang-froid*, she would have complimented him on the reputation he had won, and Julien, with his pride set at ease, would have been gentle and amiable with her, especially since her new dress seemed to him charming" (p. 290). Constantly referring to the worlds of misunderstanding between his characters, the missed chances and might-have-beens, the narrator repeatedly adumbrates other novels, texts of the might-have-been-written. This obtrusive narrator, master of every consciousness in the novel, claims to demonstrate why things necessarily happened the way they did, yet inevitably he suggests the arbitrariness and contingency of every narrative turn of events, how easily it might have been otherwise.

"Paternalism" is of course a highly charged concept for Stendhal—a man who used a hundred different pseudonyms, who in his letters to his sister referred to their father as "the bastard," thereby no doubt indicating his wish to consider himself as illegitimate, and who once remarked that if you notice an old man and a young man together who have nothing to say to each other, you can be certain that they are father and son.[14] Encoded in his novels is always the problem of whether paternity is possible, whether there might be a father and son who could talk to one another. The unfinished *Lucien Leuwen* comes closest to staging a perfect father, yet even he must eventually be rejected: as Lucien says, my father wishes my happiness, but in his own manner.[15] It is a fault inherent to fatherhood that to act toward the son, even with the intent of aiding him in *la chasse du bonheur*, is inevitably to exercise an illegitimate (because *too* legitimate) control, to impose a model that claims authoritative (because authorial) status. All Stendhal's novels record the failure of authoritative paternity in his protagonists' lives, and at the same time demonstrate the narrator's effort to retrieve the failure by being himself the perfect father, he who can maintain the conversation with his son. Yet there comes a point in each novel where the protagonist must slip from under the control of the narrator-father as well.

Julien, it seems, slips from under the control of each of his figures of paternal authority when that control becomes too manifest. The paternal narrator seeks to restrain Julien, to circumscribe him through the deployment of the father's greater worldly wisdom, yet he also admires those moments when Julien kicks at the traces of narratorial control, creates the unforeseen. Julien's slippage from under the exercise of authority—his self-inventing, self-creating quality—typifies the highly metonymic character of the Stendhalian hero, figure of unarrested, unappeasable desire which can never be anchored in a definitive meaning, even retrospectively. The entire narrative mode of Stendhal's novels is in fact markedly metonymic, indeed virtually serial, giving the impression of a perpetual flight forward, a constant self-invention at the moment and of the moment. The Stendhalian novel appears to be a self-inventing artifact. What we know of Stendhal's habits of composition (particularly

from the marginalia to the manuscript of *Lucien Leuwen*) suggests
that he literally invented his fiction from day to day, using only the
most meager of anecdotes as an armature. Each day's writing—or
later, with *La Chartreuse de Parme*, each day's dictation—became an
extrapolation of what the protagonist should become on the basis
of what he had been, and done, the day before. The astonishing
sense of rapidity given by these novels was matched in fact by
rapidity of invention, a refusal of revision and the return backward:
they are the least palimpsestic texts imaginable.[16]

Upon reflection, one sees that Stendhal makes curiously non-
retrospective use of narrative, which, I have argued, is in essence
a retrospective mode, tending toward a finality that offers retrospective illumination of the whole. The Stendhalian protagonist
ever looks ahead, planning the next moment, projecting the self
forward through ambition: creating in front of the self, as it were,
the circle of the *ambitus*, the to-be-realized. Lucien Leuwen repeatedly refers to himself as *un grand peut-être* ("a great perhaps"),
and Julien, too, ever eludes fixed definitions in favor of constant
becoming. The narrator generally seems concerned to judge the
present moment, or at most the moment just past, rather than to
delve into the buried past in search of time lost. Flaubert will epit-
omize the essentially retrospective nature of his own, and no doubt
most, narrative when, in *L'Education sentimentale*, he has Frédéric
Moreau, faced with the portraits of Diane de Poitiers at Fontainebleau, experience *concupiscence rétrospective*, desire oriented toward
an irrecoverable past.[17] Stendhal's novels, in contrast, seem to be
based on *désir prospectif*, desire in and for the future. If, as Georg
Lukács claims, *L'Education sentimentale* typifies the novel's organic
use of time, Stendhalian time is inorganic, momentary, characterized by abruptness and discontinuity.[18] This quality may well appear
paradoxical in a novelist so preoccupied with history, which is necessarily retrospective. Yet it accords with Stendhal's political liberalism, his belief that only the future could reconcile and resolve
the contradictions of the present—and, in the process, create readers capable of understanding his novels. His venture into something
resembling the historical novel, in *La Chartreuse de Parme*, is indeed

accomplished by making the retrospective impulse an object of satire: the powdered wigs of the court of Parma represent Restoration as make-believe, a ridiculous (and doomed) effort to set back the clocks of history. We might say that Stendhal's typical verb tense is the future perfect, that of the will-have-been-accomplished: a tense that allows for the infinite postponement of accomplishment. And this may offer one clue to the need for the arbitrary and absolute *finis* of the guillotine.

Le Rouge et le noir, in its rapid, evasive, unarrestable narrative movement, and in the narrator's games of containment and outmaneuver with the protagonist, ever tends to suggest that things might be otherwise than they are or, perhaps more accurately, that otherwise is how things are but not how they might have been. Curiously, the apparently stable figure of the triangle, which René Girard found to be the basic structure of mediated desire in the novel—where A desires B because B is desired by C—lends itself to this narrative instability and uncontrollability, since the very abstraction of the triangle figure permits a free substitution of persons at its corners.[19] Thus, when Julien is most profoundly unhappy at his inability to make Mathilde love him with any constancy, the novel suddenly opens up its most comic episode, the courtship of the Maréchale de Fervaques according to the formula provided, along with a volume of manuscript love letters, by the absurd Russian Prince Korasoff—an episode that is an exercise in pure, which is to say empty, style. The Russian prescribes that Julien must make love to another lady—any other lady—of Mathilde's society. Julien chooses Mme de Fervaques and manages to make eloquent speeches to her by arranging himself in the drawing room so that he appears to look at her while he is gazing past her to Mathilde, the third point of the triangle. The love letters that he daily copies and delivers are so lacking in specific pertinence to their referents that when he once forgets to make the substitution of "Paris" and "Saint-Cloud" for the "London" and "Richmond" of the original, his oversight makes no appreciable difference. Nor is their addressee of much importance: even after Mme de Fervaques has joined the dialogue and begun to answer him, he continues simply to copy Korasoff's letters. The narrator comments: "Such is the advantage of the grandiloquent style: Mme de Fervaques was not at all astonished by the lack of relationship between his replies and her letters" (p. 613). The grandiloquent style (*style emphatique*) stands for all that Stendhal detested in such Romantic contemporaries as Chateaubriand and Victor Hugo: a grandiose inanity that was the opposite of the penetrating, denuding prose Stendhal had from childhood admired in the *philosophes* and the *Idéologues*. Julien's success in bringing Mathilde to heel is assured when she opens his desk drawer and finds there a pile of Mme de Fervaques's replies in envelopes that he has not even bothered to open. What impresses her most is not simply that he should be the sentimental choice of the grand Mme de Fervaques but that the relation should be void of content—a matter of envelopes rather than of the messages they enclose. When she falls, vanquished, at Julien's feet, her surrender is a tribute to the authority of empty style, style as pure geometry.

The emptiness generates a plenitude, for Julien's courtship of Mme de Fervaques results in Mathilde's sustained passion for Julien and in her pregnancy, a full meaning that assures the continuity that entails all Julien's future successes—title, fortune, new name. When the Marquis, acting through the Abbé Pirard, suggests that Julien offer a gift "to M. Sorel, carpenter in Verrières, who took care of him in childhood" (pp. 640–41), he offers overt and final realization of Julien's primordial wish not to belong to his biological father. The "family romance" has, for once, come true. The elaborate fictions of Julien's legitimation through illegitimacy may correspond to Mathilde's pregnancy from elaborate and empty games of style. The episode of Mme de Fervaques offers a remarkable demonstration of the instability of motivation in relation to result, a figure of the narrative's capacity to generate its significant structures from empty configurations, to institute new, authoritative governing structures in its apparently random flight forward. With Mathilde's pregnancy and Julien's dreams for the future of his son—he never conceives the child *in utero* as anything but a son—the past is made, retrospectively, to take on the dynastic authority that it has always lacked. By transmitting paternity and projecting it into the future, Julien can at last postulate fully the paternity that stands behind him, believe in the illegitimacy that ennobles and legitimates him. Julien by this point belongs to the Restoration, indeed stands as a figure of how restoration is carried out: by using politics to attain a place in a system of manners that then is used to efface politics, pretending that the way things came to be as they are (by revolution and reaction, for instance) does not belong to history, that the place of each thing, and person, in the structure of things is immutable.

We have worked our way back to the end, to the moment where the apparent stability achieved by Julien, his guarantee of a non-political and uneventful future, is catastrophically exploded, shattered by the pistol shot in the church of Verrières, annihilated by the fall of the blade of the guillotine. We need to return here to Julien's tentative belief in his remotivated paternity—a belief expressed in a conditional of probability (translated earlier in this chapter): "Serait-il bien possible . . . que je fusse le fils naturel de quelque grand seigneur exilé dans nos montagnes par le terrible Napoléon? A chaque instant cette idée lui semblait moins improbable"—juxtaposed to its "proof" in his hatred for the legal father—"Ma haine pour mon père serait une preuve"—and the comment that with this realization of the family romance he would no longer be a monster—"Je ne serais plus un monstre" (p. 641)—and also his remark, a few lines earlier, that his novel is over and the merit is his alone: "Après tout, mon roman est fini, et à moi seul tout le mérite." If we can understand how hatred works to guarantee a benign origin, authorizing the political change of place and of class as necessary and nontransgressive, we still need to ask why the novel that claims to be finished continues for another eleven chapters, and why these chapters stage the return of the monster.

The word "monster" is used on a few occasions in the text. It appears to refer in particular to ingratitude, especially toward figures of paternal authority, and also to erotic transgression, usurpation, class conflict and the stance of the "plebeian in revolt," a stance that Julien tends to assume at moments of crisis (for example, upon Mathilde's declaration of love and at his trial) perhaps because it is simplifying and political, a decisive model for action. The monster figures the out-of-place, the unclassifiable, the transgressive, the desiring, the seductive.[20] The letter that Mme de Rênal writes under the dictation of her confessor will provoke catastrophe because it sketches precisely the portrait of Julien as monster: "Poor and avid, it is by means of the most consummate hypocrisy, and by the seduction of a weak and unhappy woman, that this man has sought to make a place for himself and to become something. . . . In conscience, I am forced to think that one of his means to success in a household is to seek to seduce the most notable woman there. Covered by an appearance of disinterestedness and by phrases from novels, his sole and overriding object is to succeed in gaining control of the master of the house and his fortune" (pp. 643–44). The whole letter indeed reads like an outline of *Tartuffe*, the classic story of the usurper who comes to the point of throwing the legitimate masters out of the house:

> C'est à vous d'en sortir, vous qui parlez en maître:
> La maison m'appartient, et je le ferai connaître.
> [It is for you to get out, you who speak as master:
> The house belongs to me, and I shall make it known.]
> (Act 4, scene 7, lines 1557–58)

This portrait of Julien has a certain truth, not only because it offers an interpretation that an unsympathetic reader might well adopt but also because it corresponds to Julien's occasional portrayals of himself as the monster. If we were looking for psychological explanations, could we not say that Julien, in attempting to kill Mme de Rênal, is seeking to kill the monster, to eradicate the person who has preserved and transmitted the monster image of himself? And perhaps he is seeking to assure as well his own eradication by assuming the monster identity—for if he dies, the monster will die with him. Such an explanation gains plausibility when we find that Julien at his trial publicly assumes this identity, calling himself a "peasant who has revolted against the lowness of his condition" (p. 674). In raising this political specter that everyone wants repressed, this potential of monstrous usurpation, Julien, as the Abbé Frilair points out, virtually commits suicide. It is as if he were confessing to a guilt deeper than his crime in order to make sure that full punishment would ensue. And that is one way to lay the monster to rest.

But such an "explanation" seems too easy, too smooth. It covers up and reduces the scandal of the ending, and this strikes me as a mistake, especially since "ending" is a chronic scandal in Stendhal's narratives: *La Chartreuse de Parme* collapses its set so fast that three of the four major characters are done away with in the space of a few sentences, and two important novels, *Lucien Leuwen* and *Lamiel*, never managed to get finished at all. Like his admirer André Gide, Stendhal dislikes concluding.[21] Would it, then, be more productive to think of the Stendhalian ending as a version of what the Russian Formalists called "the laying bare of the device," which here would be the very device of plotting, the need for beginning, middle, and end, which in the laying bare would be shown to be both necessary and arbitrary?

I do not want to use an appeal to what has been called in some recent criticism the *arbitraire du récit*, the gratuitous freedom of narrative, as explanatory in itself. I do, however, want to call attention to a specific and curious intrusion of the arbitrary that we find in the relation between the anecdote that served as source and armature for *Le Rouge et le noir* and the narrative discourse invented on its basis, between the "raw material" of story and its elaborations in Julien's plot. This anecdote is strangely contextualized early in the novel itself, in condensed and displaced form, as a weird indicator of things to come. I am thinking of the moment when Julien, on his way to the Rênal house for the first time, stops in the church of Verrières for a show of prayer, and finds a scrap of newspaper, on which he reads: "Details of the execution and the last moments of Louis Jenrel, executed at Besançon the . . ." The rest of the article is torn off. Turning the scrap over, he reads: "The first step" (p. 240). That Julien also thinks he sees blood on the pavement (it is in fact water from the font, colored by light coming through the crimson curtains) adds to the sense of a foreshadowing which appears somewhat crude in the context of Stendhalian subtlety. We seem to have the intrusion within the novel of the crime, trial, and execution of Antoine Berthet: the story that Stendhal found in *La Gazette des Tribunaux*, and used as outline for his novel—a *fait-divers* covered over by the narrative discourse but only half-accommodated to its new context.[22] That Louis Jenrel is an anagram of Julien Sorel may indicate something about the partially concealed, half-assimilated status of this anecdote in the novel: the anecdote is present in the manner of a statement displaced into a corner of a dream, demanding expansion and relocation in the process of dream interpretation. How do we read the newspaper in the novel?

The ending of the novel appears to mark a new intrusion of newspaper into novel, dictating that Julien must finish in the same manner as the prototype from whom he has so markedly deviated. That is, maybe Julien shoots Mme de Rênal and goes to the guillotine *because* that original monster Antoine Berthet shot Mme Michoud de la Tour and went to the guillotine, and here my "because" does not belong to the domain of source studies or psychological explanation but to narratology, to a perverse logic of narrative. Julien is handed over to the guillotine because the novel is collapsed back into the anecdote, the *fait-divers*, in which it originated and from which it has diverged.[23] This outcome may on the one hand suggest that Julien's plot finally is not his own, to shape as he wills. On the other hand, it may suggest a more general suspicion of narrative invention, which appears to be subject to interference from outside texts—to the uncontrollable intrusion of a newspaper fragment, for example, that at the last constitutes a mortal intertext.

Saying that Julien attempts murder and suffers execution because he must be made to fulfill Berthet's scenario is, of course, critically perverse, but it has the advantage of not concealing the perverse relations of Stendhal's novel to Julien's. The climactic moment of *Le Rouge et le noir* may be an instance of what is known in classical rhetoric as a "metalepsis of the author": assigning to the author's agency an action that should normally have been given an agency in the text, as when one says that Vergil "makes" Dido die in Book 4 of the *Aeneid*, or when Sterne or Diderot invokes the author's power to accomplish (or defer) some event in the narrative.[24] Neither Stendhal nor the narrator so overtly appears to stage-manage events—Julien's fatal act indeed inaugurates a period of diminished narratorial intervention, as we shall see—yet the effect is similar, a denuding of the very act of narrative invention. One cannot get around the problem or the effect by claiming that Julien's narrative fills in the "details" that are torn off from the newspaper story, thus providing a new, fuller motivation for crime and execution, for it is precisely in the details pertaining to the motives for crime and execution that the text radically frustrates us. Re-motivating the text here, to make it a well-behaved, docile narrative, will always require ingenious extrapolation, classically psychological in nature. It may be better to recognize that the *fait-divers* in the novel remains somewhat diverse, resisting assimilation to our usual models of seamless novelistic worlds. Although it may be perverse to read Julien's plot as motivated in its very undoing by Berthet's plot, such a reading at least forces us to face the rhetorical problem of the ending, putting before us the question of Julien's novel—whose end Julien announces before the pistol shot at Verrières—in relation to Stendhal's, with its peculiar leftover, the status of which we need to determine.

We must now knit closer ties between Julien's two remarks, "My novel is finished" and "I would no longer be a monster." We have seen that "monster" alludes to the irrepressible presence of class conflict and politics, which turn on the ultimate questions: Where does legitimate authority lie? Who shall inherit France? "Monster" connotes ambition, mobility, the desire to rise and to change places, to be somewhere one doesn't belong, to become (as by seduction and usurpation) something one cannot be by definition (by birth). The monster is the figure of displacement, transgression, desire, deviance, instability, the figure of Julien's project for himself, of his projective plot. In fact, the monster is conjointly the figure of politics and of plottedness, of politics as plot and plot as politics. Plot itself—narrative design and intention—is the figure of displacement, desire leading to change of position. The plotted narrative is a deviance from or transgression of the normal, a state of abnormality and error, which alone is "narratable." What Julien identifies as his "novel" at the moment he declares it finished is precisely a deviant trajectory that has led him away from the authority of his legal origins, that has deauthorized origins and all other principles of legitimate authority, to the point where he could postulate a new authority in the theory of natural nobility. Yet, since that nobility, that legitimacy through illegitimacy, has been achieved through the deviance and usurpation of a highly political career, it is *ipso facto* tinged with monsterism. Later in the century, novels by Balzac, Hugo, Eugène Sue, Dickens, Dostoevsky, and others will exploit a world of the criminally deviant, as if the underworld of the transgressive and dangerous social elements were the last fund of "narratable" material in an increasingly bland social and literary system. Julien has no connection to the underworld, as yet undiscovered in 1830; yet his plot is already criminally deviant and transgressive, politically usurpatory. Hence what must be punished is not so much any specific act or political stance but rather the fact of having had a plot.

Can we then say that Julien Sorel is handed over to the guillotine because he has had a plot? There must be the guillotine at the end because there has been the novel, that strange excrescence of telling produced by the tissue of living. The telling perpetuates itself through more telling—scenarios for its further development, adumbrations of how it might be told otherwise—and then the simple monstrous anecdote of Antoine Berthet obtrudes again at the end, as Stendhal's reminder (to himself, to us) that to have lived in the divergence of plot, to have lived as the narratable, means somehow to be deviant, hence, in some cosmic narratological court, to be guilty. To frame Julien's novel within his own novel—to continue beyond the end of Julien's novel and take it to pieces—is Stendhal's way of having a plot and punishing it, of writing a novel and then chopping its head off.

The narrative "leftover" that follows Julien's shooting of Mme de Rênal presents a Julien already castrated of the desiring that creates the novelistic plot: no longer interested in ambition, he judges his whole Parisian experience to have been an error; no longer interested in Mathilde and his worldly marriage, he returns to the explicitly maternal embrace of Mme de Rênal.[25] "He never thought of his successes in Paris; he was bored with them" (p. 664). His mode of thought and being here passes beyond the self-conceptualization and the invention of roles necessary to the plotted existence; he rejects the mediating figures essential to the creation of scenarios of desire and displacement: "One dies as one can. . . . What do *others* matter to me?" (p. 667). Not only does Julien appear to renounce his models in these final chapters, he seems also to move beyond the control and guidance of the paternal narrator. There is far less commentary by the narrator in these chapters; indeed his voice nearly falls silent, to leave the stage to Julien's almost uninterrupted monologue. The last four chapters (42–45), following Julien's sentencing, also lack titles and epigraphs, a departure from the rest of the novel that accords with the notable effacement of the narrator's discursiveness and dramatic presence. Julien has simultaneously moved beyond paternal authority and beyond the plotted novel. He is no longer narratable material; his novel has closed shop, and the extranovelistic perspective of its closing chapters serves to underline the disjuncture between plot and life, between Julien's novel and Stendhal's, between authoritative meaning and the subversion of meaning.

It is as if Stendhal had decided to enclose within *Le Rouge et le noir* the scenario for what he liked to refer to, contemptuously, as a "novel for chambermaids." Not that Julien and his plot have much to do with chambermaids, except in his social origin, and also in the offer made to him early in the novel of Mme de Rênal's chambermaid, Elisa, as a suitable wife—an offer whose acceptance would have effectively arrested the plot of ambition, short-circuited the novel. But we may perhaps take the "chambermaid's novel" more generally as the figure of seductive literature. To read a novel—and to write one—means to be caught up in the seductive coils of a deviance: to seduce, of course, is to lead from the straight path, to create deviance and transgression. Stendhal seduces us through

Julien's story, then he denounces the seduction. With the fall of
the blade of the guillotine, he puts an end to the artificiality of the
plotted story.

Something similar, though perhaps inverse, happens to the plotting of history in Stendhal's novel. The Revolution of 1830, as I
mentioned, never manages to get represented in the novel even
though in strict chronology it should; the novel as concert waits in
suspense for this true historical pistol shot, which never comes. Yet
the entire political dynamic of Julien's career tends toward that
revolution: his personal transgression will be played out on the
national theater in 1830—and then again, more savagely, in 1848
and 1871. The whole novel motivates and calls for the Revolution
of 1830, as if it should be the forty-sixth chapter of Book 2, the
one beyond the last. In refusing to furnish us with that extra chapter, Stendhal performs a gesture similar to his dismantling of Julien's novel, suggesting that one cannot finally allow even history
to write an authoritative plot for the novel.

The issue of authority, in all its manifestations, remains unresolved. Julien achieves no final relationship to any of his figures
of paternity. It is indeed Sorel the carpenter who re-emerges in
the place of the father at the end, and Julien attributes to him the
jolly thought that the expectation of a legacy of three or four
hundred louis from his son will make him, like any father, happy
to have that son guillotined. The fathers inherit from the sons. As
for Julien's own paternity, his plan that Mme de Rênal take care
of his son—whom Mathilde will neglect—goes for naught when
Mme de Rênal dies three days after he does. The fate of this son—
if son it be—never is known. The novel rejects not only specific
fathers and authorities but the very model of authority, refusing
to subscribe to paternity as an authorizing figure of novelistic relationships. Ultimately, this refusal may indicate why Stendhal has
to collapse his novels as they near their endings: the figure of the
narrator as father threatens domination, threatens to offer an au-
thorized version. He too must be guillotined.

The question, who shall inherit France? is left unresolved. The
question, who shall inherit from Julien Sorel? is resolved only on

the financial plane; and the victory of Sorel *père* over his son is perhaps an ironic representation of the novelist's ultimate and absolute paternal power to put his creatures to death. But the novel comments further on its close and perverse relation to the guillotine when Julien, in prison, recalls Danton's grammatical musings on the eve of his death: "It's singular, the verb *to guillotine* can't be conjugated in all its tenses; one can say: 'I will be guillotined, you will be guillotined,' but one doesn't say: 'I have been guillotined' " (p. 677). For very good semantic reasons, the verb is grammatically defective: one cannot, in the first person, use it retrospectively. We encounter again, even here at the end, Stendhal's typical prospectivity, his predilection for the future perfect: "I will have been guillotined"—the tense of deferral, the tense that denies retrospective satisfaction. Deferral haunts as well Stendhal's relation to the "happy few" he designated as the inheritors of his message. In *La Vie de Henry Brulard*, he famously inscribes these happy few, his readers, in a future fifty or a hundred years after his time. To do so is to defer the question of readership and to temporalize the spatiality of the dialogue in which readership might be thought to consist. The uncertain reader may then, too late, want to ask of the novel why it should be thus and not otherwise: or, in the words ascribed to Beaumarchais that serve as epigraph to Book 2, chapter 32: "Hélas! pourquoi ces choses et non pas d'autres?"

Le Rouge et le noir, perhaps more acutely than more "normally" plotted novels, makes us aware of both the consonances and the disjunctures of life and its telling, of event and might-have-been, of biological pattern and concerted deviance from it. Julien Sorel's brilliant, brief, transgressive, and truncated career raises in acute form questions about significant ends and their relation to generative structures of narrative. Stendhal's somewhat perverse refusal to end "naturally"—his postponement of conclusion, superseded by the catastrophic eclipse—places us before the problem of standard narrative form, the ways in which we usually understand beginnings, middles, and ends. In particular, his obsessive concern with problems of paternity and authority—on the structural and textual as well as thematic levels—makes us ask why we have fictional biographies, what we expect them to do. *Le Rouge et le noir* solicits our attention and frustrates our expectation because we have some sense of the fitting biographical pattern: one in which sons inherit from fathers and pass on, be it through Stephen Dedalus's "apostolic succession," a wisdom gained, a point of understanding attained. Stendhal's perversity may make us realize that such a patterning is both necessary and suspect, the product of an interpretation motivated by desire, and that we also must acknowledge the work of more negative forces of recurrence and revenge. How we move from beginning to end in a significant way—creating a pattern of transformation in the sequence leading from beginning to end—demands further reflection, and a more fully elaborated model of understanding, which we will find suggested in the most boldly speculative work of Freud.

4

Freud's Masterplot:
A Model for Narrative

Our exploration so far of how plots may work and what may motivate them suggests, if not the need, at least the intellectual desirability of finding a model—a model that would provide a synthetic and comprehensive grasp of the workings of plot, in the most general sense, and of the uses for plot. To meet these requirements, such a model will have to be more dynamic than those most often proposed by the structuralists; it will have to provide ways to think about the movement of plot and its motor force in human desire, its peculiar relation to beginnings and ends, its apparent claim to rescue meaning from temporal flux. As my argument thus far will have indicated, I find the most suggestive indications for the needed model in the work of Freud, since this still offers the most probing inquiry into the dynamics of the psychic life, and hence, by possible extension, of texts. If we turn toward Freud, it is not in the attempt to psychoanalyze authors or readers or characters in narrative, but rather to suggest that by attempting to superimpose psychic functioning on textual functioning, we may discover something about how textual dynamics work and something about their psychic equivalences.

It may be helpful to begin our discussion by recapitulating for a moment, by way of one of the best essays in structuralist narratology, Tzvetan Todorov's "Narrative Transformations." [1] Working toward a greater formalization of the criteria advanced by Victor

Shklovsky and Vladimir Propp for understanding the "wholeness" of a narrative, Todorov elaborates a model of narrative transformation whereby plot—*sjužet, récit*—is constituted in the tension of two formal categories, difference and resemblance. Transformation—a change in a predicate term common to beginning and end—represents a synthesis of difference and resemblance; it is, we might say, the same-but-different. Now, "the same-but-different" is a common (and if inadequate, not altogether false) definition of metaphor. If Aristotle affirmed that the master of metaphor must have an eye for resemblances, modern treatments of the subject have affirmed equally the importance of difference included within the operation of resemblance, the chief value of the metaphor residing in its "tension." Narrative operates as metaphor in its affirmation of resemblance, in that it brings into relation different actions, combines them through perceived similarities (Todorov's common predicate term), appropriates them to a common plot, which implies the rejection of merely contingent (or unassimilable) incident or action. Plot is the structure of action in closed and legible wholes; it thus must *use* metaphor as the trope of its achieved interrelations, and it must *be* metaphoric insofar is it is totalizing. Yet it is equally apparent that the key figure of narrative must in some sense be not metaphor but metonymy: the figure of contiguity and combination, of the syntagmatic relation.[2] The description of narrative needs metonymy as the figure of linkage in the signifying chain: precedence and consequence, the movement from one detail to another, the movement *toward* totalization under the mandate of desire.

The problem with "the same-but-different" as a definition of narrative is the implication of simultaneity and stasis in such a formulation, its implicitly spatial modeling of a temporal form. Todorov, faithful to the lesson of Propp, recognizes the need to consider sequence and succession as well as the paradigmatic matrix; he supplements his definition with the remark: "Rather than a 'coin with two faces,' [transformation] is an operation in two directions: it affirms at once resemblance and difference; it puts time into motion and suspends it, in a single movement; it allows discourse to acquire a meaning without this meaning becoming pure information; in a word, it makes narrative possible and reveals its very definition" (p. 240). The image of a double operation upon time has the value of returning us to the frequently eluded fact that narrative meanings are developed in time, that any narrative partakes more or less of what Proust called "un jeu formidable . . . avec le Temps," and that this game of time is not merely in the world of reference (or in the *fabula*) but also in the narrative, in the *sjužet*, if only because the meanings developed by narrative *take time*: they unfold through the time of reading. If at the end of a narrative we can suspend time in a moment when past and present hold together in a metaphor—which may be that recognition or *anagnorisis* which, said Aristotle, every good plot should bring— that moment does not abolish the movement, the slidings, the mistakes, and partial recognitions of the middle. The "dilatory space" of narrative, as Barthes calls it—the space of retard, postponement, error, and partial revelation—is the place of transformation: where the problems posed to and by initiatory desire are worked out and worked through.

Barthes makes explicit an assumption common to much thought about narrative when he claims that meaning (in the "classical" or "readable" text) resides in full predication, completion of the codes in a "plenitude" of signification, which makes the "passion for meaning" ultimately desire for the end. It is at the end—for Barthes as for Aristotle—that recognition brings its illumination, which then can shed retrospective light. The function of the end, whether considered syntactically (as in Todorov and Barthes) or ethically (as in Aristotle) or as formal or cosmological closure (as by Barbara H. Smith or Frank Kermode), continues to fascinate and to baffle.[3] One of the strongest statements of its determinative position in narrative plots comes in a passage from Sartre's *La Nausée* which bears quotation at some length. Sartre's protagonist, Roquentin, is reflecting on the meaning of "adventure" and the difference between living and narrating. When you narrate, you appear to start with a beginning. You say, "It was a fine autumn evening in 1922. I was a notary's clerk in Marommes." But, says Roquentin:

In reality you have started at the end. It is there, invisible and present, it is what gives these few words the pomp and value of a beginning. "I was out walking, I had left the town without realizing it, I was thinking about my money troubles." This sentence, taken simply for what it is, means that the guy was absorbed, morose, a hundred miles from an adventure, exactly in a mood to let things happen without noticing them. But the end is there, transforming everything. For us, the guy is already the hero of the story. His moroseness, his money troubles are much more precious than ours, they are all gilded by the light of future passions. And the story goes on in the reverse: instants have stopped piling themselves up in a haphazard way one on another, they are caught up by the end of the story which draws them and each one in its turn draws the instant preceding it: "It was night, the street was deserted." The sentence is thrown out negligently, it seems superfluous; but we don't let ourselves be duped, we put it aside: this is a piece of information whose value we will understand later on. And we feel that the hero has lived all the details of this night as annunciations, as promises, or even that he lived only those that were promises, blind and deaf to all that did not herald adventure. We forget that the future wasn't yet there; the guy was walking in a night without premonitions, which offered him in disorderly fashion its monotonous riches, and he did not choose.[4]

In Roquentin's argument, the beginning presupposes the end, since the concept of an ending is necessary to that of a beginning. The idea of "adventure" has to do with what is to come, the *ad-venire*, so that an adventure is a piece of action in which beginnings are chosen by and for ends. The very possibility of meaning plotted through sequence and through time depends on the anticipated structuring force of the ending: the interminable would be the meaningless, and the lack of ending would jeopardize the beginning. We read the incidents of narration as "promises and annunciations" of final coherence, that metaphor that may be reached through the chain of metonymies: across the bulk of the as yet unread middle pages, the end calls to the beginning, transforms and enhances it. As Roquentin further suggests, we read only those incidents and signs that can be construed as promise and annunciation, enchained toward a construction of significance—those markers that, as in the detective story, appear to be clues to the underlying intentionality of event. The sense of adventure thus plotted from its end, so to speak, has something of the rigor and necessity provided in poetry by meter and rhyme, the pattern of anticipation and completion which overcodes mere succession; or else, to take a banal example, the music of a film, which patterns our understanding of the action. The movie audience, for instance, instinctively recognizes finale music and begins to leave the theater when it tells them to do so.

The sense of a beginning, then, must in some important way be determined by the sense of an ending. We might say that we are able to read present moments—in literature and, by extension, in life—as endowed with narrative meaning only because we read them in anticipation of the structuring power of those endings that will retrospectively give them the order and significance of plot. To say "I have begun . . . " (whatever it may be) acquires meaning only through postulation of a narrative begun, and that beginning depends on its ending. Sartre pursues further his reflection on end-determination in his autobiography, *Les Mots*, describing how in order to escape his sense of himself as unnecessary, utterly contingent, he had recourse to a book discovered in his grandfather's library entitled *L'Enfance des hommes illustres*, which told of children named Johann Sebastian or Jean-Jacques and, without ever mentioning the names Bach and Rousseau, in recounting their childhood constantly inserted casual references to their future greatness, contriving the account so artfully that it was impossible to read of the most trivial incident without relating it to its subsequently revealed significance. These children, Sartre comments, "thought they were acting and talking at random, whereas the real purpose of their slightest remarks was to announce their destiny. . . . I read the lives of those falsely mediocre children as God had conceived them: starting at the end."[5] Sartre in emulation began to see himself as in a book, being read by posterity "from death to birth"; he undertook to live his life retrospectively, in terms of the death that alone would confer meaning and necessity on existence. As he most succinctly puts it, "I became my own obituary" (p. 171).

All narrative may be in essence obituary in that, as our reading of *La Peau de chagrin* suggested, the retrospective knowledge that it seeks, the knowledge that comes after, stands on the far side of the end, in human terms on the far side of death. The further we inquire into the problem of ends, the more it seems to compel a further inquiry into its relation to the human end. As Frank Kermode has put it, man is always "in the middest," without direct knowledge of origin or endpoint, seeking the imaginative equivalents of closure that will confer significance on experience.[6] I have already cited Walter Benjamin's claim that a man's life "first assumes transmissible form at the moment of his death."[7] Benjamin analyzes the implications of the common statement that the meaning of a man's life is revealed only in his death, to reach the conclusion that in narrative, death provides the very "authority" of the tale, since as readers we seek in narrative fictions the knowledge of death which in our own lives is denied to us. Hence Benjamin can state that "Death is the sanction of everything that the storyteller can tell." While this need not be a literal death—it can be some simulacrum, some end to a period, an arrest—very often it is. A popular proto-novelistic form was the Newgate biography, recording the life of a celebrated criminal—especially that life made significant by impending execution. And in the nineteenth-century novel, the deathbed scene repeatedly stands as a key moment of summing-up and transmission. We can at once call to mind Goriot's extended death agony, in *Le Père Goriot*, where he sums up and judges his life and his century; or the dying Miss Havisham's judgment of error and plea for forgiveness in *Great Expectations*; or Aunt Reed's deathbed reparations to Jane in *Jane Eyre*; or the key confession of the publican Luke Marks in *Lady Audley's Secret*; or, in a less sensationalistic vein, the summing-up of Emma's passionate aspirations and their failure in the anointment of her body by the priest during the administration of the last rites in *Madame Bovary*; or the death of the writer Bergotte, obsessed at the last by interpretation—of a detail in a Vermeer painting—in Proust's *Recherche*. Whatever their specific content, and whatever their degree of tragic awareness or melodramatic enunciation, all such scenes offer the promise of a significant retrospect, a summing-up, the coming to completion of a fully predicated, and readable, sentence. It is in this sense that the death of the ending quickens meaning: death in narrative, says Benjamin, is the "flame" at which we as readers, solitary and forlorn because cut off from meaning, warm our "shivering" lives (p. 101).

These arguments from the end are at least apparently paradoxical, since narrative would seem to claim overt authority for its origin, for a "primal scene" from which—as from the scene of the crime in the detective story—"reality" assumes narratability, the signifying chain is established. We need to think further about the deathlike ending, its relation to origin, and to initiatory desire, and about how the interrelation of the two may determine and shape the middle—the "dilatory space" of postponement and error—and the kinds of vacillation between illumination and blindness that we find there. If in the beginning stands desire, and this shows itself ultimately to be desire for the end, between beginning and end stands a middle that we feel to be necessary (plots, Aristotle tells us, must be of "a certain length") but whose processes, of transformation and working-through, remain obscure. Here it is that Freud's most ambitious investigation of ends in relation to beginnings may be of help, and may contribute to a properly dynamic model of plot.

Let us undertake, then, to read *Beyond the Pleasure Principle* (1920) in intertextual relation to narrative fictions and the processes of plotting as we have begun to understand them. We may find a general legitimation for this enterprise in the fact that *Beyond the Pleasure Principle* constitutes Freud's own masterplot, the essay where he lays out most fully a total scheme of how life proceeds from beginning to end, and how each individual life in its own manner repeats the masterplot and confronts the question of whether the closure of an individual life is contingent or necessary. It is indeed so difficult to say what Freud is talking about in this essay—and especially, what he is *not* talking about—that we are almost forced to acknowledge that ultimately he is talking about the very possibility of talking about life—about its very "narratability." His boldest intention may be to provide a theory of comprehension of the dynamic of the life span, and hence of its narrative understanding. It is also notable that *Beyond the Pleasure Principle* is plotted in ways which, Freud suggests, have little to do with its original intention: near the end of the essay he speaks of the need to "throw oneself into a line of thought and to follow it wherever it leads."[8] The plotting of the masterplot is determined by the structural demands of Freud's thought, and it is in this spirit that we must read it as speaking of narrative plots.

Narrative always makes the implicit claim to be in a state of repetition, as a going over again of a ground already covered: a *sjužet* repeating the *fabula*, as the detective retraces the tracks of the criminal.[9] This claim to an act of repetition—"I sing of," "I tell of"—appears to be initiatory of narrative. It is equally initiatory of *Beyond the Pleasure Principle*: it is the first problem and clue that Freud confronts. Evidence of a "beyond" that does not fit neatly into the functioning of the pleasure principle comes first in the dreams of patients suffering from war neuroses or from the traumatic neuroses of peace: dreams that return to the moment of trauma, to relive its pain in apparent contradiction of the wish-fulfillment theory of dreams. This "dark and dismal" example is superseded by an example from "normal" life, and we have the celebrated moment of child's play: the toy thrown away, the reel on the string thrown out of the crib and pulled back, to the alternate exclamation of *fort* and *da*. When he has established the equivalence between making the toy disappear and the child's mother's disappearance, Freud is faced with a set of possible interpretations. Why does the child repeat an unpleasurable experience? It may be answered that by staging his mother's disappearance and return, the child is compensating for his instinctual renunciation. Yet the child has also staged disappearance alone, without reappearance, as a game. This may make one want to argue that the essential experience involved is the movement from a passive to an active role in regard to his mother's disappearance, claiming mastery in a situation to which he has been compelled to submit.

Repetition as the movement from passivity to mastery reminds us of another essay, "The Theme of the Three Caskets" (1913), where Freud, considering Bassanio's choice of the lead casket in *The Merchant of Venice*—the correct choice in the suit of Portia— decides that the choice of the right maiden in man's literary play is also the choice of death; by this choice, he asserts an active mastery of what he must in fact endure. "Choice stands in the place of necessity, of destiny. In this way man overcomes death, which he has recognized intellectually." [10] If repetition is mastery, movement from the passive to the active, and if mastery is an assertion of control over what man must in fact submit to—choice, we might say, of an imposed end—we have already a suggestive comment on the grammar of plot, where repetition, taking us back again over the same ground, could have to do with the choice of ends.

But other possibilities suggest themselves to Freud at this point. The repetition of unpleasant experience—the mother's disappear- ance—might be explained by the motive of revenge, which would yield its own pleasure. The uncertainty that Freud faces here is whether repetition can be considered a primary event, independent of the pleasure principle, or whether there is always some direct yield of pleasure of another sort involved. The pursuit of this doubt takes Freud into the analytic experience, to his discovery of the analysand's need to repeat, rather than simply remember, the past: the analysand "is obliged to *repeat* the repressed material as a con- temporary experience instead of, as the physician would prefer to see, *remembering* it as something belonging to the past" (p. 18). In other words, as Freud argued in two papers that prepare the way for *Beyond the Pleasure Principle*, "The Dynamics of the Transfer- ence" (1912) and "Remembering, Repeating and Working Through" (1914), repetition—including the need to reproduce and to work through—is itself a form of remembering, brought into play when recollection properly speaking is blocked by resistance. Thus the analyst encounters a "compulsion to repeat," which is the work of the unconscious repressed and becomes particularly discernible in the transference, where it can take "ingenious" forms. (I note here, as a subject for later exploration, that the transference is itself a kind of metaphor, a substitutive medium for the analysand's infantile experiences, and thus approximates the status of a text.) The compulsion to repeat gives patients a sense of being fatefully subject to a "perpetual recurrence of the same thing"; it can indeed suggest pursuit by a demonic power. We know from Freud's essay "The Uncanny" (1919) that this feeling of the demonic, arising from involuntary repetition, is a particular attribute of the literature of the uncanny, of texts of compulsive recurrence.[11]

Thus in analytic work (as also in literary texts) there is slim but real evidence of a compulsion to repeat which can override the pleasure principle, and which seems "more primitive, more elementary, more instinctual than the pleasure principle which it overrides" (p. 23). Now, repetition is so basic to our experience of literary texts that one is simultaneously tempted to say all and to say nothing on the subject. To state the matter baldly: rhyme, alliteration, assonance, meter, refrain, all the mnemonic elements of literature and indeed most of its tropes are in some manner repetitions that take us back in the text, that allow the ear, the eye, the mind to make connections, conscious or unconscious, between different textual moments, to see past and present as related and as establishing a future that will be noticeable as some variation in the pattern. Todorov's "same-but-different" depends on repetition. If we think of the trebling characteristic of the folktale, and of all formulaic literature, we may consider that the repetition by three constitutes the minimal repetition to the perception of series, which would make it the minimal intentional structure of action, the minimum plot. Narrative, we have seen, must ever present itself as a repetition of events that have already happened, and within this postulate of a generalized repetition it must make use of specific, perceptible repetitions in order to create plot, that is, to show us a significant interconnection of events. An event gains meaning by its repetition, which is both the recall of an earlier moment and a

variation of it: the concept of repetition hovers ambiguously between the idea of reproduction and that of change, forward and
backward movement (as we shall consider further in the next chapter). Repetition creates a *return* in the text, a doubling back. We
cannot say whether this return is a return *to* or a return *of*: for
instance, a return to origins or a return of the repressed. Repetition
through this ambiguity appears to suspend temporal process, or
rather, to subject it to an indeterminate shuttling or oscillation that
binds different moments together as a middle that might turn
forward or back. This inescapable middle is suggestive of the demonic: repetition and return are perverse and difficult, inter-
rupting simple movement forward. The relation of narrative plot
to story may indeed appear to partake of the demonic, as a kind
of tantalizing instinctual play, a re-enactment that encounters the
magic and the curse of reproduction or "representation." But to
say more about the operations of repetition, we need to read further
in Freud's text.

"What follows is speculation" (p. 24). With this gesture, Freud,
in the manner of Rousseau's dismissal of the facts in the *Discourse
on the Origins of Inequality*, begins the fourth chapter and his sketch
of the economic and energetic model of the mental apparatus: the
system Pcpt-Cs (the perceptual-conscious system) and the unconscious, the role of the outer layer as shield against excitations, and
the definition of trauma as the breaching of the shield, producing
a flood of stimuli which knocks the pleasure principle out of operation. Given this situation, the repetition of traumatic experiences
in the dreams of neurotics can be seen to have the function of
seeking retrospectively to master the flood of stimuli, to perform
a mastery or binding of mobile energy through developing that
anxiety which earlier was lacking—a lack which permitted the breach
and thus caused the traumatic neurosis. Thus the repetition compulsion is carrying out a task that must be accomplished *before* the
dominance of the pleasure principle can begin. Repetition is hence
a primary event, independent of the pleasure principle and more
primitive. Freud now moves into an exploration of the theory of
the instincts, or drives, the most basic forces of psychic life.[12] The

instinctual is the realm of freely mobile, "unbound" energy: the "primary process," where energy seeks immediate discharge, where no postponement of gratification is tolerated. It appears that it must be "the task of the higher strata of the mental apparatus to bind the instinctual excitation reaching the primary process" before the pleasure principle can assert its dominance over the psychic economy (pp. 34–35). We may say that at this point in the essay we have moved from a postulate of repetition as the assertion of mastery (as in the passage from passivity to activity in the child's game) to a conception whereby repetition works as a process of *binding* toward the creation of an energetic constant-state situation which will permit the emergence of mastery and the possibility of postponement.

That Freud at this point evokes once again the demonic and the uncanny nature of repetition, and refers us not only to children's play but to their demand for exact repetition in storytelling as well, points our way back to literature. Repetition in all its literary manifestations may in fact work as a "binding," a binding of textual energies that allows them to be mastered by putting them into serviceable form, usable "bundles," within the energetic economy of the narrative. Serviceable form must, I think, mean perceptible form: repetition, repeat, recall, symmetry, all these journeys back in the text, returns to and returns of, that allow us to bind one textual moment to another in terms of similarity or substitution rather than mere contiguity. Textual energy, all that is aroused into expectancy and possibility in a text, can become usable by plot only when it has been bound or formalized. It cannot otherwise be plotted in a course to significant discharge, which is what the pleasure principle is charged with doing. To speak of "binding" in a literary text is thus to speak of any of the formalizations, blatant or subtle, that force us to recognize sameness within difference, or the very emergence of a *sjužet* from the material of *fabula*. As the word "binding" itself suggests, these formalizations and the recognitions they provoke may in some sense be painful: they create a delay, a postponement in the discharge of energy, a turning back from immediate pleasure, to ensure that the ultimate pleasurable discharge will be more complete. The most effective or, at the least, the most challenging texts may be those that are most delayed, most highly bound, most painful.

Freud now moves toward a closer inquiry concerning the relation between the compulsion to repeat and the instinctual. The answer lies in "a universal attribute of instincts and perhaps of organic life in general" that "*an instinct is an urge inherent in organic life to restore an earlier state of things*" (p. 36). Instincts, which we tend to think of as a drive toward change, may rather be an expression of "the conservative nature of living things." The organism has no wish to change; if its conditions remained the same, it would constantly repeat the very same course of life. Modifications are the effect of external stimuli, and these modifications are in turn stored up for further repetition, so that, while the instincts may give the appearance of tending toward change, they "are merely seeking to reach an ancient goal by paths alike old and new" (p. 38). Hence Freud is able to proffer, with a certain bravado, the formulation: "*the aim of all life is death.*" We are given an evolutionary image of the organism in which the tension created by external influences has forced living substance to "diverge ever more widely from its original course of life and to make ever more complicated *détours* before reaching its aim of death" (pp. 38–49). In this view, the self-preservative instincts function to assure that the organism shall follow its own path to death, to ward off any ways of returning to the inorganic which are not immanent to the organism itself. In other words, "the organism wishes to die only in its own fashion." It must struggle against events (dangers) that would help it to achieve its goal too rapidly—by a kind of short-circuit.

We are here somewhere near the heart of Freud's masterplot for organic life, and it generates a certain analytic force in its superimposition on fictional plots. What operates in the text through repetition is the death instinct, the drive toward the end. Beyond and under the domination of the pleasure principle is this baseline of plot, its basic "pulsation," sensible or audible through the repetitions that take us back in the text. Yet repetition also retards the pleasure principle's search for the gratification of discharge, which is another forward-moving drive of the text. We have a curious situation in which two principles of forward movement operate upon one another so as to create retard, a dilatory space in which pleasure can come from postponement in the knowledge that this— in the manner of forepleasure?—is a necessary approach to the true end. Both principles can indeed become dilatory, a pleasuring in and from delay, though both also in their different ways recall to us the need for end. This apparent paradox may be consubstantial with the fact that repetition can take us both backward and forward because these terms have become reversible: the end is a time before the beginning.

Between these two moments of quiescence, plot itself stands as a kind of divergence or deviance, a postponement in the discharge which leads back to the inanimate. For plot starts (or must give the illusion of starting) from that moment at which story, or "life," is stimulated from quiescence into a state of narratability, into a tension, a kind of irritation, which demands narration. I spoke earlier of narrative desire, the arousal that creates the narratable as a condition of tumescence, appetency, ambition, quest, and gives narrative a forward-looking intention.[13] This is to say as well that beginnings are the arousal of an intention in reading, stimulation into a tension, and we could explore the specifically erotic nature of the tension of writing and its rehearsal in reading in a number of exemplary texts, such as Rousseau's account, in the *Confessions*, of how his novel *La Nouvelle Héloïse* was born of a masturbatory reverie and its necessary fictions, or the similar opening of Jean Genet's *Notre-Dame des fleurs*. The ensuing narrative—the Aristotelian "middle"—is maintained in a state of tension, as a prolonged deviance from the quiescence of the "normal"—which is to say, the unnarratable—until it reaches the terminal quiescence of the end. The development of a narrative shows that the tension is maintained as an ever more complicated postponement or *détour* leading back to the goal of quiescence. As Sartre and Benjamin compellingly argued, the narrative must tend toward its end, seek illumination in its own death. Yet this must be the right death, the correct end. The complication of the detour is related to the danger of short-circuit: the danger of reaching the end too quickly, of achieving the im-proper death. The improper end indeed lurks throughout narrative, frequently as the wrong choice: choice of the wrong casket, misapprehension of the magical agent, false erotic object choice. The development of the subplot in the classical novel usually suggests (as William Empson has intimated) a different solution to the problems worked through by the main plot, and often illustrates the danger of short-circuit.[14] The subplot stands as one means of warding off the danger of short-circuit, assuring that the main plot will continue through to the right end. The desire of the text (the desire of reading) is hence desire for the end, but desire for the end reached only through the at least minimally complicated detour, the intentional deviance, in tension, which is the plot of narrative.

Deviance, detour, an intention that is irritation: these are characteristics of the narratable, of "life" as it is the material of narrative, of *fabula* become *sjužet*. Plot is a kind of arabesque or squiggle toward the end. It is like that arabesque from *Tristram Shandy*, retraced by Balzac, that suggests the arbitrary, transgressive, gratuitous line of narrative, its deviance from the straight line, the shortest distance between beginning and end—which would be the collapse of one into the other, of life into immediate death. The detour of life in fact creates a momentary detour in Freud's essay, in chapter 5, as he considers the sexual instincts, which are in a sense the true life instincts yet also conservative in that they bring back earlier states of living substance; yet again, they stand in dynamic opposition to the death instincts, and hence confer a "vacillating rhythm" on the life of the organism: "One group of instincts rushes forward so as to reach the final aim of life as swiftly as possible; but when a particular stage in the advance has been reached, the other group jerks back to a certain point to make a fresh start and so prolong the journey" (p. 41). Freud's description of the "vacillating rhythm" may in particular remind us of how a highly plotted nineteenth-century novel will often leave one set of characters at a critical juncture to take up another where it left them, moving this set forward, then rushing back to the first, creating an uneven movement of advance, turning back the better to move forward. As with the play of repetition and the pleasure principle, forward and back, advance and return interact to create the vacillating and apparently deviant middle.

Freud's text will in a moment take us closer to understanding the formal organization of this deviance toward the end. But it also at this point offers further suggestions about the beginning. For when he has identified both the death instincts and the life (sexual) instincts as conservative, tending toward the restoration of an earlier state of things, Freud feels obliged to deconstruct the illusion of a human drive toward perfection, an impulsion forward and upward: a force that—this is where he quotes *Faust* as the classic text of man's striving—"presses ever forward unsubdued." As we have already noted, the illusion of a striving toward perfection is to be explained by instinctual repression and the persisting tension of the repressed instinct, and the resulting difference between the pleasure of satisfaction demanded and that achieved, the difference that "provides the driving factor which will permit of no halting at any position attained" (p. 42). This process of subtraction, we saw, is fundamental to Lacan's theory of desire, born of the gap or split between need and demand. Lacan helps us to understand how the aims and imaginings of desire—its enactments in response to imaginary scenarios of fulfillment—move us from the realm of basic drives to highly elaborated fictions. Desire necessarily becomes textual by way of a specifically narrative impulse, since desire is metonymy, a forward drive in the signifying chain, an insistence of meaning toward the occulted objects of desire.

The complexities of the next-to-last chapter of *Beyond the Pleasure Principle* need not be rehearsed in detail. In brief, the chapter leads Freud twice into the findings of biology, first on the track of the origins of death, to find out whether it is a necessary or merely a contingent alternative to interminability, then in pursuit of the origins of sexuality, to see whether it satisfies the description of the instinctual as conservative. Biology can offer no sure answer to either investigation, but it offers at least metaphorical confirmation of the necessary dualism of Freud's thought, and encouragement to reformulate his earlier opposition of ego instincts to sexual instincts as one between life instincts and death instincts, a shift in the grouping of oppositional forces which then allows him to reformulate the libidinal instincts themselves as the Eros "of the poets and philosophers" which holds all living things together and which seeks to combine things in ever greater living wholes. Desire reformulated as Eros thus is a large, embracing force, totalizing in intent, tending toward combination in new unities: metonymy in the search to become metaphor.

But for the symmetry of Freud's opposition to be complete, he needs to be able to ascribe to Eros, as to the death instinct, the characteristic of a need to restore an earlier state of things. Since biology will not answer, Freud, in a remarkable gesture, turns toward myth, the myth of the Androgyne in Plato's *Symposium*, which precisely ascribes Eros to a search to recover a lost primal unity that was split asunder. Freud's apologetic tone in this last twist to his argument is partly disingenuous, for we detect a contentment to have formulated the forces of the human masterplot as "philosopher and poet." As he would write with evident satisfaction late in his career—in the *New Introductory Lectures*—"The theory of the instincts is so to say our mythology. Instincts are mythical entities, magnificent in their indefiniteness." [15] Here in *Beyond the Pleasure Principle*, the apology is coupled with a reflection that much of the obscurity of the processes Freud has been considering "is merely due to our being obliged to operate with the scientific terms, that is to say with the figurative language, peculiar to psychology" (p. 60). *Beyond the Pleasure Principle*, we are to understand, is radically figural, a displaced argument that knows no literal terms. It is not merely metapsychology, but also mythopoesis, necessarily resembling "an equation with two unknown quantities" (p. 57), as Freud concedes, or, we might say, a formal dynamic the terms of which are not substantial but purely relational. We perceive that *Beyond the Pleasure Principle* is itself a plot which has formulated that dynamic necessary to its own detour.

The last chapter of Freud's text recapitulates, but not without difference. He returns to the problem of the relation between the instinctual processes of repetition and the dominance of the pleasure principle. One of the earliest and most important functions of the mental apparatus is to bind the instinctual impulses that impinge upon it, to convert freely mobile energy into a quiescent cathexis. This is a preparatory act on behalf of the pleasure principle, which permits its dominance. Sharpening his distinction between a *function* and a *tendency*, Freud argues that the pleasure principle is a "tendency operating in the service of a function whose business it is to free the mental apparatus entirely from excitation or to keep the amount of excitation in it constant or to keep it as low as possible" (p. 62). This function is concerned "with the most universal endeavour of all living substance—namely to return to the quiescence of the inorganic world." Hence one can consider "binding" to be a preliminary function that prepares the excitation for its final elimination in the pleasure of discharge. In this manner, one could say that the repetition compulsion and the death instinct serve the pleasure principle; in a larger sense, the pleasure principle, keeping watch on the invasion of stimuli from without and especially from within, seeking their discharge, serves the death instinct, making sure that the organism is permitted to return to quiescence. The whole evolution of the mental apparatus appears as a taming of the instincts so that the pleasure principle—itself tamed, displaced—can appear to dominate in the complicated detour called life which leads back to death. In fact, Freud seems here at the very end to imply that the two antagonistic instincts serve one another in a dynamic interaction that is a complete and self-regulatory economy which makes both end and detour perfectly necessary and interdependent. The organism must live in order to die in the proper manner, to die the right death. One must have the arabesque of plot in order to reach the end. One must have metonymy in order to reach metaphor.

We emerge from reading *Beyond the Pleasure Principle* with a dynamic model that structures ends (death, quiescence, nonnarratability) against beginnings (Eros, stimulation into tension, the desire of narrative) in a manner that necessitates the middle as detour, as struggle toward the end under the compulsion of imposed delay, as arabesque in the dilatory space of the text. The model proposes that we live in order to die, hence that the intentionality of plot lies in its orientation toward the end even while the end must be achieved only through detour. This re-establishes the necessary distance between beginning and end, maintained through the play of those drives that connect them yet prevent the one collapsing back into the other: the way in which metonymy and metaphor serve one another, the necessary temporality of the same-but-different which to Todorov constitutes the narrative transformation. Crucial to the space of this play are the repetitions serving to bind the energy of the text so as to make its final discharge more effective. In fictional plots, these bindings are a system of repetitions which are returns to and returns of, confounding the movement forward to the end with a movement back to origins, reversing meaning within forward-moving time, serving to formalize the system of textual energies, offering the pleasurable possibility (or illusion) of "meaning" wrested from "life."

As a dynamic-energetic model of narrative plot, *Beyond the Pleasure Principle* gives an image of how the nonnarratable existence is stimulated into the condition of narratability, to enter a state of deviance and detour (ambition, quest, the pose of a mask) in which it is maintained for a certain time, through an at least minimally complex extravagance, before returning to the quiescence of the nonnarratable. The energy generated by deviance, extravagance, excess—an energy that belongs to the textual hero's career and to the reader's expectation, his desire of and for the text—maintains the plot in its movement through the vacillating play of the middle, where repetition as binding works toward the generation of significance, toward recognition and the retrospective illumination that will allow us to grasp the text as total metaphor, but not therefore to discount the metonymies that have led to it. The desire of the text is ultimately the desire for the end, for that recognition which is the moment of the death of the reader in the text. Yet recognition cannot abolish textuality, does not annul that middle which is the place of repetitions, oscillating between blindness and recognition, between origin and ending. Repetition toward recognition constitutes the truth of the narrative text.

It is characteristic of textual energy in narrative that it should always be on the verge of premature discharge, of short-circuit. The reader experiences the fear—and excitation—of the improper end, which is symmetrical to—but far more immediate and present than—the fear of endlessness. The possibility of short-circuit can, of course, be represented in all manner of threats to the protagonist or to any of the functional logics that demand completion; it most commonly takes the form of temptation to the mistaken erotic object choice, who may be of the "Belle Dame sans merci" variety, or may be the too perfect and hence annihilatory bride. Throughout the Romantic tradition, it is perhaps most notably the image of incest (of the fraternal-sororal variety) that hovers as the sign of a passion interdicted because its fulfillment would be too perfect, a discharge indistinguishable from death, the very cessation of narrative movement. Narrative is in a state of temptation to over-sameness, and where we have no literal threat of incest (as in Chateaubriand, or Faulkner) lovers choose to turn the beloved into a soul sister so that possession will be either impossible or mortal: Goethe's Werther and Lotte, for instance; or Rousseau's *La Nouvelle Héloïse*, where Saint-Preux's letter to Julie following their night of love begins: "Mourons, ô ma douce amie" ("Let us die, my beloved"); or Villiers de l'Isle-Adam's Axël and Sara, who choose death on the threshold of consummation. Incest is only the exemplary version of a temptation of short-circuit from which the protagonist and the text must be led away, into detour, into the cure that prolongs narrative.

It may finally be in the logic of our argument that repetition speaks in the text of a return which ultimately subverts the very notion of beginning and end, suggesting that the idea of beginning presupposes the end, that the end is a time before the beginning, and hence that the interminable never can be finally bound in a plot. Any final authority claimed by narrative plots, whether of origin or end, is illusory. Analysis, Freud would eventually discover, is inherently interminable, since the dynamics of resistance and the transference can always generate new beginnings in relation to any possible end.[16] It is the role of fictional plots to impose an end which yet suggests a return, a new beginning: a rereading. Any narrative, that is, wants at its end to refer us back to its middle, to the web of the text: to recapture us in its doomed energies.

Some demonstration of how the model derived from *Beyond the Pleasure Principle* may be useful in thinking about the plot of a specific text has already been suggested in the discussion of *La Peau de chagrin*, where Raphaël de Valentin's discovery of the talisman and its hyperbolic power to realize desire is simultaneously the discovery of death, and where his subsequent choices to preserve the self can only institute a deathlike existence, devoid of desire and movement, through which desire will once again reassert itself and its drive to the end. Raphaël at the last wishes to will himself into the "conservative law of nature," hoping in his retreat to the mountains of Auvergne to become like a lichen on the rock—nearly quiescent, almost inorganic. The effort is, of course, doomed, and superseded by a last outburst of desire, and then total quiescence. *Le Rouge et le noir* offers a more complex and oblique relation to the model, willing an abrupt and perhaps arbitrary end in such a way as to suggest a permanent deferral and evasion of the problem of the end. I shall in the next chapter discuss Dickens's *Great Expectations* specifically in light of the model, to consider how the energies released in its liminary primal scene (Pip's terrifying encounter with the convict Magwitch in the graveyard) are subsequently bound in a number of wished-for but superficial ways, and in other latent and more effective ways, which have the quality of repetition and return. Each of Pip's choices, consciously life-furthering, apparently forward oriented, in fact seems to lead back to the enigma of origins.

The stories of Raphaël and Pip, perhaps even that of Julien Sorel, and of so many other young protagonists of the nineteenth-century novel, while ostensibly a striving forward and upward, a progress, may also be, perhaps more profoundly, the narrative of an attempted homecoming: of the effort to reach an assertion of origin through ending, to find the same in the different, the time before in the time after. Most of the great nineteenth-century novels tell this same tale. Georg Lukács has called the novel "the literary form of the transcendent homelessness of the idea" and argued that it

is in the discrepancy between the idea and the organic that time,
the process of duration, becomes constitutive of the novel as of no
other genre:

> Only in the novel, whose very matter is seeking and failing to
> find the essence, is time posited together with the form: time
> is the resistance of the organic—which possesses a mere sem-
> blance of life—to the present meaning, the will of life to remain
> within its own completely enclosed immanence. In the epic the
> life-immanence of meaning is so strong that it abolishes time:
> life enters eternity as life, the organic retains nothing of time
> except the phase of blossoming; fading and dying are forgotten
> and left entirely behind. In the novel, meaning is separated
> from life, and hence the essential from the temporal; we might
> almost say that the entire inner action of the novel is nothing
> but a struggle against the power of time.[17]

The understanding of time, says Lukács, the transformation of the
struggle against time into a process full of interest, is the work of
memory—or more precisely, we could say with Freud, of "remembering, repeating, working through." Repetition, remembering, re-
enactment are the ways in which we replay time, so that it may not
be lost. We are thus always trying to work back through time to
that transcendent home, knowing, of course, that we cannot. All
we can do is subvert or, perhaps better, pervert time: which is what
narrative does.[18]

To bring a semblance of conclusion to the discussion of Freud's
masterplot, we may return to the assertion, put forward by Barthes
and Todorov, that narrative is essentially the articulation of a set
of verbs. These verbs articulate the pressure and drive of desire.
Desire is the wish for the end, for fulfillment, but fulfillment must
be delayed so that we can understand it in relation to origin and
to desire itself. The story of Shahrazad again suggests itself as the
story of stories. This implies that the tale as read is inhabited by
the reader's desire, and that further analysis should be directed to
that desire, not his individual desire and its origins in his own

personality, but his transindividual and intertextually determined desire as a reader, including his expectations for, and of, narrative meanings. Because it concerns ends in relation to beginnings and the forces that animate the middle in between, Freud's model is suggestive of what a reader engages when he responds to plot. It images that engagement as essentially dynamic, an interaction with a system of energy which the reader activates. This in turn suggests why we can read *Beyond the Pleasure Principle* as a text concerning textuality and conceive that there can be a psychoanalytic criticism of the text itself that does not become—as has usually been the case—a study of the psychogenesis of the text (the author's unconscious), the dynamics of literary response (the reader's unconscious), or the occult motivations of the characters (postulating an "unconscious" for them). It is rather the superimposition of the model of the functioning of the psychic apparatus on the functioning of the text that offers the possibility of a psychoanalytic criticism. And here the intertextual reading of Freud's masterplot with the plots of fiction seems a valid and useful move. Plot mediates meanings within the contradictory human world of the eternal and the mortal. Freud's masterplot speaks of the temporality of desire, and speaks to our very desire for fictional plots.

5

Repetition, Repression, and Return: The Plotting of *Great Expectations*

We have defined plot, for our purposes, as a structuring operation deployed by narratives, or activated in the reading of narratives: as the logic and syntax of those meanings that develop only through sequence and succession. We noted that the range of meanings assigned to the word plot in the dictionary includes the sense of the scheme or machination to the accomplishment of some end—the sense apparently derived from the "contamination" of the French *complot*—and we suggested that nineteenth-century novels regularly conceive plot as *complot*: they are structured by a plotting for and toward something, a machination of desire. Some narratives clearly give us a sense of plotting and of "plottedness" more than others, and in particular a sense that their central meanings come to us through plotting: that there is no disjuncture between idea and symbol on the one hand, and the requirements of narrative design on the other. Such a disjuncture will, I think, be characteristic of the novel in its "modernist" and "postmodernist" phases, where there is a pervasive suspicion that plot falsifies more subtle kinds of interconnectedness. If the novels of Joyce and Woolf and Proust and Gide, and then Faulkner and Robbe-Grillet, cannot ultimately do without plotting insofar as they remain narrative structures that signify, they plot with irony and bad conscience, intent (in their very different ways) to expose the artifices of formal structure and

113

human design.[1] Whereas it was part of the triumph of the nine-teenth-century novel in its golden age to plot with a good conscience, in confidence that the elaboration of plot corresponded to, and illuminated, human complexities. The intimacy of Balzac, Dickens, Eugène Sue, Wilkie Collins (to name only the most popular) with a large audience inclusive of different social strata was both a result of and a license to the working out of their deepest intentions through plotted action, in a demonstrative mode.

I want in this chapter to discuss in the light of Freud's masterplot a novel that stands firmly within the golden age of plot, one that is centrally, unashamedly, and—at first glance—unsuspiciously concerned with issues of plot and plotting. It is indeed plotting, as an activity, as a dynamic machination, that may provide our best way into the reading of a fully achieved plot. And this activity of plotting may be most readily discernible in a retrospective first-person narrative. When we ask the questions, How do we find significant plots for our lives? How do we make life narratable? we find that the answers are most clearly dramatized in narratives of an autobiographical cast, since these cannot evade an explicit con-cern with problems of closure, authority, and narratability. As Sartre argued, autobiographical narration must necessarily be "obitu-ary"—must in any event explicitly show margins outside the nar-ratable, leftover spaces which allow the narrating *I* to objectify and look back at the narrated *I*, and to see the plotted middle as shaped by and as shaping its margins. Hence rather than such novels as *Bleak House* or *Our Mutual Friend*, highly elaborated lengthy ara-besques of plot, I choose *Great Expectations*, a more compact ex-ample, but one that gives in the highest degree the impression that its central meanings depend on the workings-out of its plot. For in this fictional pseudo-autobiography, Dickens adopts the revealing strategy of taking a "life" and creating the demarcations of a "plot" within it. The novel will indeed be concerned with finding a plot and losing it, with the precipitation of the sense of plottedness around its hero, and his eventual "cure" from plot. The novel images in its structure the kind of structuring operation of reading that plot is.

I

Great Expectations is exemplary for a discourse on plot in many respects, not least of all for its beginning. For what the novel chooses to present at its outset is precisely the search for a beginning. As in so many nineteenth-century novels, the hero is an orphan, thus undetermined by any visible inheritance, apparently unauthored. This clears away Julien Sorel's problems with paternity. There may be sociological and sentimental reasons to account for the high incidence of orphans in the nineteenth-century novel, but clearly the parentless protagonist frees an author from struggle with pre-existing authorities, allowing him to create afresh all the determinants of plot within his text. He thus profits from what Gide called the "lawlessness" of the novel by starting with an undefined, rule-free character and then bringing the law to bear upon him—creating the rules—as the text proceeds. With Pip, Dickens begins as it were with a life that is for the moment precedent to plot, and indeed necessarily in search of plot. Pip when we first see him is himself in search of the "authority"—the word stands in the second paragraph of the novel—that would define and justify—author-ize—the plot of his ensuing life.

The "authority" to which Pip refers here is that of the tombstone which bears the names of his dead parents, the names that have already been displaced, condensed, and superseded in the first paragraph, where Pip describes how his "infant tongue" (literally, a speechless tongue: a catachresis that points to a moment of emergence, of entry into language) could only make of the name, Philip Pirrip, left to him by the dead parents, the monosyllabic Pip. "So, I called myself Pip, and came to be called Pip." [2] This originating moment of Pip's narration and his narrative is a self-naming that already subverts whatever authority could be found in the text of the tombstones. The process of reading that text is described by Pip the narrator as "unreasonable," in that it interprets the appearance of the lost father and mother from the shape of the letters of their names. The tracing of the name—which he has already distorted in its application to self—involves a misguided attempt to remotivate the graphic symbol, to make it directly mimetic, mimetic specifically of origin. Loss of origin, misreading, and the problematic of identity are bound up here in ways we will further explore later on. The question of reading and writing—of learning to compose and to decipher texts—is persistently thematized in the novel.[3]

The decipherment of the tombstone text as confirmation of loss of origin—as unauthorization—is here at the start of the novel the prelude to Pip's *cogito*, the moment in which his consciousness seizes his existence as other, alien, forlorn:

> My first most vivid and broad impression of the identity of things seems to me to have been gained on a memorable raw afternoon towards evening. At such a time I found out for certain, that this bleak place overgrown with nettles was the churchyard; and that Philip Pirrip, late of this parish, and also Georgiana, wife of the above, were dead and buried; and that Alexander, Bartholomew, Abraham, Tobias, and Roger, infant children of the aforesaid, were also dead and buried; and that the dark flat wilderness beyond the churchyard, intersected with dykes and mounds and gates, with scattered cattle feeding on it, was the marshes; and that the low leaden line beyond was the river; and that the distant savage lair from which the wind was rushing, was the sea; and that the small bundle of shivers growing afraid of it all and beginning to cry, was Pip.
>
> "Hold your noise!" cried a terrible voice. . . . (p. 1)

The repeated verbs of existence—"was" and "were"—perform an elementary phenomenology of Pip's world, locating its irreducible objects and leading finally to the individual subject as other, as aware of his existence through the emotion of fear, fear that then appears as the origin of voice, or articulated sound, as Pip begins to cry: a cry that is immediately censored by the command of the convict Magwitch, the father-to-be, the fearful intrusive figure of future authorship who will demand of Pip: "Give us your name."

The scenario is richly suggestive of the problem of identity, self-consciousness, naming, and language that will accompany Pip throughout the novel, and points to the original decentering of the subject in regard to himself. For purposes of my study of plot, it is important to note how this beginning establishes Pip as an existence without a plot, at the very moment of occurrence of that event which will prove to be decisive for the plotting of his existence, as he will discover only two-thirds of the way through the novel. Alien, unauthorized, self-named, at the point of entry into the language code and the social systems it implies, Pip will in the first part of the novel be in search of a plot, and the novel will recount the gradual precipitation of a sense of plot around him, the creation of portents of direction and intention.

Schematically, we can identify four lines of plot that begin to crystallize around the young Pip, the Pip of Part 1, before the arrival of his "Expectations":

1. Communion with the convict/criminal deviance.
2. Naterally wicious/bringing up by hand.
3. The dream of Satis House/the fairy tale.
4. The nightmare of Satis House/the witch tale.

These plots, we will see in a moment, are paired as follows: $2/1 = 3/4$. That is, there is in each case an "official" and censoring plot standing over a "repressed" plot. In terms of Pip's own choices, we could rewrite the formula: $3/4/2/1$, to show (in accordance with one of Freud's favorite models) the archaeological layering of strata of repressed material.[4] When the Expectations are announced by Jaggers at the end of part one, they will apparently coincide with Pip's choices ("My dream was out; my wild fancy was surpassed by sober reality" [Chapter 18, p. 130]), and will thus appear to take care of the question of plot. But this will be so only on the level of official plots; the Expectations will in fact only mask further the problem of the repressed plots.

I choose the term "communion" for the first plot because its characteristic symbolic gesture is Pip's pity for the convict as he swallows the food Pip has brought him, a moment of sympathetic identification which focuses a series of suggestive sympathies and identifications with the outlaw: the bread and butter that Pip puts down his leg, which makes him walk like the chained convict; Mrs. Joe's belief that he is on his way to the Hulks; Pip's flight from the Christmas dinner table into the arms of a soldier holding out handcuffs, to give a few examples. Pip is concerned to assure "his" convict that he is not responsible for his recapture, a point he conveys in a mute exchange of glances which the convict understands and which leads him to make a public statement in exoneration of Pip, taking responsibility for stealing the food. This in turn provokes an overt statement of community with the outlaw, which comes from Joe: "We don't know what you have done, but we wouldn't have you starved to death for it, poor miserable fellow-creatur.— Would us, Pip?" (Chapter 5, p. 36)

The fellowship with the convict here stated by Joe will remain with Pip, but in a state of repression, as what he will later call "that spell of my childhood" (Chapter 16, p. 114)—an unavowable memory. It finds its official, adult, repressive version in the conviction— shared by all the adults in Pip's life, with the exception of the childlike Joe—that children are naturally depraved and need to be corrected, kept in line with the Tickler, brought up by hand lest their natural willfulness assert itself in plots that are deviant, transgressive. Pumblechook and the Hubbles, in their Christmas dinner dialogue, give the theme a choric statement:

"Especially," said Mr. Pumblechook, "be grateful, boy, to them which brought you up by hand."

Mrs. Hubble shook her head, and contemplating me with a mournful presentiment that I should come to no good, asked, "Why is it that the young are never grateful?" This moral mystery seemed too much for the company until Mr. Hubble tersely solved it by saying, "Naterally wicious." Everybody then murmured "True!" and looked at me in a particularly unpleasant and personal manner. (Chapter 4, pp. 22–23)

The "nateral wiciousness" of children legitimates communion with the outlaw, but legitimates it as that which must be repressed, forced into other plots—including, as we shall see, "binding" Pip as an apprentice.

The dream of Satis House is properly a daydream, in which "His Majesty, the Ego" pleasures himself with the phantasy of social ascension and gentility. Miss Havisham is made to play the role of Fairy Godmother, her crutch become a magic wand, explicitly evoked twice near the close of part 1.[5] This plot has adult sanction; its first expression comes from Pumblechook and Mrs. Joe when they surmise that Miss Havisham intends to "do something" for Pip, and Pip comes to believe in it, so that when the "Expectations" arrive he accepts them as the logical fulfillment of the daydream, of his "longings." Yet to identify Satis House with the daydream is to perform a repression of all else that Satis House suggests and represents—all that clusters around the central emblem of the rotting bride cake and its crawling things. The craziness and morbidity of Satis House repose on desire fixated, become fetishistic and sadistic, on a deviated eroticism that has literally shut out the light, stopped the clocks, and made the forward movement of plot impossible. Satis House, as the circular journeys of the wheelchair to the rhythm of the blacksmith's song "Old Clem" may best suggest, constitutes repetition without variation, pure reproduction, a collapsed metonymy where cause and effect have become identical, the same-as-same. It is significant that when Pip returns from his first visit to Satis House, he responds to the interrogations of Pumblechook and Mrs. Joe with an elaborate lie—the story of the coach, the flags, the dogs fighting for "weal cutlets" from a silver basket—a phantasy that we can read as his response to what he calls a "smart without a name, that needed counteraction" (Chapter 8, p. 57). All the attempts to read Satis House as a text speaking of gentility and social ascension may be subverted from the outset, in the passage that describes Pip's first impression of Miss Havisham:

It was not in the first few moments that I saw all these things, though I saw more of them in the first moments than might be supposed. But, I saw that everything within my view which ought to be white, had been white long ago, and had lost its lustre, and was faded and yellow. I saw that the bride within

the bridal dress had withered like the dress, and like the flow-
ers, and had no brightness left but the brightness of her sunken
eyes. I saw that the dress had been put upon the rounded
figure of a young woman, and that the figure upon which it
now hung loose, had shrunk to skin and bone. Once, I had
been taken to see some ghastly waxwork at the Fair, representing I know not what impossible personage lying in state.
Once, I had been taken to one of our old marsh churches to
see a skeleton in the ashes of a rich dress, that had been dug
out of a vault under the church pavement. Now, waxwork and
skeleton seemed to have dark eyes that moved and looked at
me. I should have cried out, if I could. (Chapter 8, p. 53)

The passage records the formation of a memory trace from a moment of unmastered horror, itself formed in repetition of moments
of past visual impression, a trace that forces its way through the
mind without being grasped by consciousness and is refused outlet
in a cry. Much later in the novel, Pip—and also Miss Havisham
herself—will have to deal with the return of this repressed.

We have, then, a quadripartite scheme of plots, organized into
two pairs, each with an "official" plot, or interpretation of plot,
standing over a repressed plot. The scheme may lead us in the first
instance to reflect on the place of repression as one of the large
"orders" of the novel. Repression plays a dominant role in the
theme of education which is so important to the novel, from Mrs.
Joe's bringing up by hand, through Mrs. Wopsle's aunt's school-
room, to Mr. Pocket's career as a "grinder" of dull blades (while
his own children meanwhile are "tumbling up"). Bringing up by
hand in turn suggests Jaggers's hands, representation of accusation
and the law, which in turn suggest all the instances of censorship
in the name of high authorities evoked from the first scene of the
novel onward: censorship is repression in the name of the Law.[6]
Jaggers's sinister hand-washings point to the omnipresent taint of
Newgate, which echoes the earlier presence of the Hulks, to which
Mrs. Joe verbally assigns Pip. Then there is the moment when Pip
is "bound" as apprentice blacksmith before the magistrates, in a

scene of such repressive appearance that a well-meaning philan-
thropist is moved to hand Pip a pamphlet entitled *To Be Read in
My Cell*. There is a constant association of education, repression,
the threat of prison, criminality, the fear of deviance. We might
note in passing Dickens's capacity to literalize the metaphors of
education—"bringing up by hand," "grinding"—in a manner that
subverts the order that ought to assure their figural validity. The
particularly sinister version of the *Bildungsroman* presented by *Great
Expectations* derives in some measure from the literalization of metaphors pertaining to education and upbringing. Societal repression
and censorship are, of course, reinforced by Pip's own, his inter-
nalization of the law and the denial of what he calls the "old taint"
of his association with the criminal. The whole theme of gentility,
as represented by the Finches of the Grove, for instance, or the
punishment of Trabb's boy, consistently suggests an aggressivity
based on denial. One could reflect here on the splendid name of
Pip's superfluous valet: the Avenger.

The way in which the Expectations are instituted, in seeming
realization of the Satis House dream, comprehends "bringing up
by hand" (the other official plot) in that it includes the disciplines
necessary to gentility: grinding with Mr. Pocket, lessons in manners
from Herbert, learning to spend one's time and money in appropriate gentlemanly pursuits. There is in this manner a blurring of
plot lines, useful to the processes of wish fulfillment in that education and indeed repression itself can be interpreted as agencies
necessary to the pursuit of the dream. Realization of the dream
permits acceptance of society's interpretations, and in fact requires
the abandonment of any effort at personal interpretation: Pip is
now enjoined from seeking to know more about the intentions of
his donor, disallowed the role of detective which so much animates
him in part three of the novel—when the Expectations have proved
false—and is already incipiently present in part one.

Taking our terminology from the scene where Pip is bound as
apprentice, we may consider that education and repression operate
in the novel as one form of "binding": official ways of channeling
and tying up the mobile energies of life. It is notable that after he

has become apprenticed to Joe, Pip goes through a stage of purely iterative existence—presented in chapter 14—where the direction and movement of plot appear to be finished, where all life's "interest and romance" appear shut out as by a "thick curtain," time reduced to repetitive duration. Conversely, when the Expectations have arrived, Miss Havisham is apparently identified as the fairy-tale donor, and the Satis House plot appears securely bound, Pip need only wait for the next stage of the plot to become manifest. Yet it is clear that for the reader neither binding as an apprentice (the first accomplishment of an upbringing by hand) nor the tying up of Satis House as a fairy-tale plot constitutes valid and adequate means of dealing with and disposing of the communion with the convict and the nightmare of Satis House. The energy released in the text by its liminary "primal scene"—in the graveyard—and by the early visits to Satis House, creating that "smart without a name," simply is not and cannot be bound by the bindings of the official, repressive plots. As readers we know that there has been created in the text an intensive level of energy that cannot be discharged through these official plots.

In fact, the text has been working simultaneously to bind these disavowed energies in other ways, ways over which Pip's ego, and the societal superego, have no control, and of which they have no knowledge, through repetitions that, for the reader, prepare an inevitable return of the repressed. Most striking are the periodic fragmentary returns of the convict-communion material: the leg iron used to bludgeon Mrs. Joe, guns firing from the Hulks to signal further escapes, and especially the reappearance of Joe's file, the dramatic stage property used by Magwitch's emissary in a "proceeding in dumb show . . . pointedly addressed at me." His stirring and tasting his rum and water "pointedly at" Pip suggests the establishment of an aim (Pip calls his proceeding "a shot"), a direction, an intention in Pip's life: the first covert announcement of another plot which will come to govern Pip's life, but of course misinterpreted as to its true aim. With the nightmare energies of Satis House, binding may be at work in those repetitive journeys around the rotting bridal cake, suggestive of the reproduction or working through of the traumatic neurotic whose affects remain fixed on the past, on the traumatic moment that never can be mastered. For Miss Havisham herself, these energies can never be plotted to effective discharge; and we will have occasion to doubt whether they are ever fully bound for Pip as well. The compulsive reproductive repetition that characterizes every detail of Satis House lets us perceive how the returns of the convict-communion suggest a more significant working through of an unmastered past, a repetition that can alter the form of the repeated. In both instances—but ultimately with different results—the progressive, educative plots, the plots of repression and social advancement, are threatened by a repetitive process obscurely going on underneath and beyond them. We sense that forward progress will have to recover markings from the beginning through a dialectic of return.

II

In my references to the work of repetition as the binding of energies, I have been implicitly assuming that one can make a transfer from the model of psychic functioning proposed in *Beyond the Pleasure Principle* to the literary text, an assumption that no doubt can never be "proved" and must essentially find its justification in the illumination it can bring to texts. We saw in Chapter 2 that texts represent themselves as inhabited by energies, which are ultimately images of desire, and correspond to the arousals, expectations, doubts, suspense, reversals, revaluations, disappointments, embarrassments, fulfillments, and even the incoherences animated by reading. If we can accept the idea of a textual energetics, we can see that in any well-plotted novel the energies released and aroused in the text, especially in its early moments, will not be lost: the text is a kind of thermodynamic plenum, obeying the law of the conservation of energy (as well, no doubt, as the law of entropy). Repetition is clearly a major operative principle of the system, shaping energy, giving it perceptible form, form that the text and the reader can work with in the construction of thematic wholes and narrative orders. Repetition conceived as binding, the creation of cohesion—see the French translation of Freud's *Verbindung: liaison*, a word we would commonly use in the description of discourse and argument—may allow us to see how the text and the reader put energy into forms where it can be mastered, both by the logics set in motion by the plot, and by interpretive effort.

Repetition is, of course, a complex phenomenon, and one that has its history of commentary in philosophical as well as psychoanalytic thought. Is repetition sameness or difference? To repeat evidently implies resemblance, yet can we speak of resemblance unless there is difference? Without difference, repetition would be identity, which would not usually appear to be the case, if only because the chronological context of the repeated occurrence differs from that of the "original" occurrence (the "original" is thus a concept that repetition puts into question). In this sense, repetition always includes the idea of variation in time, and may ever be potentially a progressive act. As Kierkegaard writes near the beginning of *Repetition*, "Repetition and recollection are the same movement, only in opposite directions; for what is recollected has been, is repeated backwards, whereas repetition properly is repeated forwards."[7] Freud, as we noted, considers repetition to be a form of recollection, brought into play when conscious mental rememoration has been blocked by repression. Lacan argues that Freud distinguishes between repeating (*wiederholen*) and reproducing (*reproduzieren*): reproduction would be the full reliving, of the original traumatic scene, for instance, that Freud aimed at early in his career, when he still believed in "catharsis"; whereas repetition always takes place in the realm of the symbolic—in the transference, in language—where the affects and figures of the past are confronted in symbolic form.[8] We can thus perhaps say that for Freud repetition is a symbolic enactment referring back to unconscious determinants, progressive in that it belongs to the forward thrust of desire and is known by way of desire's workings in the signifying chain, but regressive in its points of reference.

We cannot and should not attempt to reduce and resolve the ambiguities of repetition since they are indeed inherent to our experience of repetition, part of what creates its "uncanny" effect and allows us to think about the intractable problem of temporal form, in our lives and in our fictions. In *Great Expectations*, the repetitions associated with Satis House, particularly as played out by Miss Havisham herself, suggest the reproductive in that they aim to restore in all its detail the traumatic moment—recorded by the clocks stopped at twenty minutes to nine—when erotic wishes were abruptly foreclosed by Compeyson's rupture of faith. On the other hand, the repetitions of the convict material experienced by Pip all imply something to come—something to come that, as we shall see, will take him back, painfully, to the primal scene, yet take him back in the context of difference. Repetition in the text is a return, a calling back or a turning back. And as I suggested earlier, repetitions are thus both returns to and returns of: for instance, returns to origins and returns of the repressed, moving us forward in Pip's journey toward elucidation, disillusion, and maturity by taking us back, as if in obsessive reminder that we cannot really move ahead until we have understood that still enigmatic past, yet ever pushing us forward, since revelation, tied to the past, belongs to the future.

The novelistic middle, which is perhaps the most difficult of Aristotle's "parts" of a plot to talk about, is in this case notably characterized by the return. Quite literally: it is Pip's repeated returns from London to his home town that constitute the organizing device of the whole of the London period, the time of the Expectations and their aftermath. Pip's returns are always ostensibly undertaken to make reparation to the neglected Joe, an intention never realized; and always implicitly an attempt to discover the intentions of the putative donor in Satis House, to bring her plot to completion. Yet the returns also always bring his regression, in Satis House, to the status of the "coarse and common boy" (Chapter 29, p. 222) whose social ascension is hallucinatorily denied, his return to the nightmare of unprogressive repetition; and, too, a revival of the repressed convict association, the return of the childhood spell. Each return suggests that Pip's official plots, which seem to speak of progress, ascent, and the satisfaction of desire, are in fact subject to a process of repetition of the yet unmastered past, the true determinant of his life's direction.

The pattern of the return is established in Pip's first journey back from London, in Chapter 28. His decision to visit Joe is quickly thrown into the shade by the presence on the stagecoach of two convicts, one of whom Pip recognizes as the man of the file and the rum and water, Magwitch's emissary. There is a renewed juxta-position of official, genteel judgment on the convicts, voiced by Herbert Pocket—"What a vile and degraded spectacle"—and Pip's inward avowal that he feels sympathy for their alienation. On the roof of the coach, seated in front of the convicts, Pip dozes off while pondering whether he ought to restore the two one-pound notes that the convict of the file had passed him so many years before. Upon regaining consciousness, the first two words he hears, continuing his dream thoughts, are: "Two one-pound notes." There follows the convict's account of his embassy from "Pip's convict" to the boy who had saved him. Although Pip is certain that the convict cannot recognize him, so changed in age, circumstance, and even name (since Herbert Pocket calls him "Handel"), the dreamlike experience forces a kind of recognition of a forgotten self, refound in fear and pain:

> I could not have said what I was afraid of, for my fear was altogether undefined and vague, but there was great fear upon me. As I walked on to the hotel, I felt that a dread, much exceeding the mere apprehension of a painful or disagreeable recognition, made me tremble. I am confident that it took no distinctness of shape, and that it was the revival for a few minutes of the terror of childhood. (Chapter 28, p. 217)

The return to origins has led to the return of the repressed, and vice versa. Repetition as return becomes a reproduction and re-enactment of infantile experience: not simply a recall of the primal moment, but a reliving of its pain and terror, suggesting the im-possibility of escape from the originating scenarios of childhood, the condemnation forever to replay them.

This first example may stand for the other returns of the novel's middle, which all follow the same pattern, which all double return to with return of and show Pip's ostensible progress in the world to be subverted by the irradicable presence of the convict-communion and the Satis House nightmare. It is notable that toward the end of the middle—as the novel's dénouement approaches—there is an acceleration in the rhythm of these returns, as if to affirm that all the clues to Pip's future, the forward movement of his plot, in fact lie in the past. Repetition as return speaks as a textual version of the death instinct, plotting the text, beyond the seeming dominance of the pleasure principle, toward its proper end, imaging this end as necessarily a time before the beginning. In the moment of crisis before the climax of the novel's action, Pip is summoned back to the marshes associated with his infancy to face extinction at the hands of Orlick—who has throughout the novel acted the role of Pip's "bad double," a hateful and sadistic version of the hero—in a threatened short-circuit of the text, as Pip indicates when he thinks how he will be misunderstood by others if he dies prematurely, without explanation: "Misremembered after death . . . despised by unborn generations" (Chapter 53, p. 404).[9] Released from this threat, Pip attempts to escape from England, but even this voyage out to another land and another life leads him back: the climax of Magwitch's discovery and recapture are played out in the Thames estuary, where "it was like my own marsh country, flat and monotonous, and with a dim horizon" (Chapter 54, p. 416). We are back in the horizontal perspectives and muddy tidal flats that are so much a part of our perception of the childhood Pip.

But before speaking further of resolutions, I must say a word about the novel's great "recognition scene," the moment at which the latent becomes manifest, the repressed convict plot is forcibly brought to consciousness, a scene that decisively re-enacts both a return of the repressed and a return to the primal moment of childhood. The recognition scene comes in chapter 39, and it is preceded by two curious paragraphs at the end of chapter 38 in which Pip as narrator suggests that the pages he has just written, concerning his frustrated courtship of Estella, constitute, on the plane of narration itself, a last binding of that plot in its overt version, as a plot of romance, and that now he must move on to a

deeper level of plot—reaching further back—which subsumes as it
subverts all the other plots of the novel: "All the work, near and
afar, that tended to the end had been accomplished." That this
long-range plot is presented as analogous to "the Eastern story" in
which a heavy slab of stone is carved out and fitted into the roof
in order that it may fall on "the bed of state in the flush of conquest"
seems in coded fashion to suggest punishment for erotic transgression, which we may want to read as return of the nightmare plot
of Satis House, forcing its way through the fairy tale, speaking of
the perverse, sadistic eroticism that Pip has covered over with his
erotic object choice—Estella, who in fact represents the wrong choice
of plot and another danger of short-circuit. To anticipate later
revelations, we should note that Estella will turn out to be approx-
imately Pip's sister—natural daughter of Magwitch as he is Magwitch's adoptive son—which lends force to the idea that she, like
so many Romantic maidens, is marked by the interdict, as well as
the seduction, of incest, which, as the perfect androgynous coupling, is precisely the short-circuit of desire.[10]

The scene of Magwitch's return operates for Pip as a painful
forcing through layers of repression, an analogue of analytic
work, compelling Pip to recognize that what he calls "that chance
encounter of long ago" is no chance, and cannot be assigned to the
buried past but must be repeated, reenacted, worked through in
the present. The scene replays numerous details of their earlier
encounter, and the central moment of recognition comes as a re-
enactment and revival of the novel's primal scene, played in dumb
show, a mute text which the more effectively stages recognition as
a process of return to the inescapable past:

Even yet I could not recall a single feature, but I knew him!
If the wind and the rain had driven away the intervening years,
had scattered all the intervening objects, had swept us to the
churchyard where we first stood face to face on such different
levels, I could not have known my convict more distinctly than
I knew him now, as he sat in the chair before the fire. No need
to take a file from his pocket and show it to me; no need to

take the handkerchief from his neck and twist it round his
head; no need to hug himself with both his arms, and take a
shivering turn across the room, looking back at me for recognition. I knew him before he gave me one of those aids,
though, a moment before, I had not been conscious of remotely
suspecting his identity. (Chapter 39, p. 301)

The praeterition on which the passage is constructed—"no need . . .
no need"—marks the gradual retrieval of the past as its involuntary
repetition within the present. The repetition takes place—as Magwitch's effective use of indicative signs may suggest—in the mode
of the symbolic, offering a persuasive instance of Freud's conception of repetition as a form of recollection brought into action by
repression and resistance to its removal. It becomes clear that the
necessity for Pip to repeat and work through everything associated
with his original communion with Magwitch is a factor of his "forgetting" this communion: a forgetting that is merely conscious. The
reader has undergone a similar process through textual repetition
and return, one that in his case has had the function of not per-
mitting him to forget.

The scene of Magwitch's return is an important one for any study
of plot since it demonstrates so well how such a novelist as Dickens
can make plotting the central vehicle and armature of meaning in
the narrative text. All the issues raised in the novel—social, ethical,
interpretive—are here simultaneously brought to climax through
the peripety of the plot. Exposure of the "true" plot of Pip's life
brings with it instantaneous consequences for all the other "codes"
of the novel, as he recognizes with the statement, "All the truth of
my position came *flashing* on me; and its disappointments, dangers,
disgraces, consequences of all kinds" (Chapter 39, p. 303—my ital-
ics). The return of the repressed—the repressed as knowledge of
the self's other story, the true history of its misapprehended desire—forces a total revision of the subject's relation to the orders
within which it constitutes meaning.

Magwitch poses unanswerable questions, about the origins of
Pip's property and the means of his social ascent, which force home

to Pip that he has covered over a radical lack of original authority. Like Oedipus—who cannot answer Tiresias's final challenge: who are your parents?—Pip does not know where he stands. The result has been the intrusion of an aberrant, contingent authorship—Magwitch's—in the story of the self. Education and training in gentility turn out to be merely an agency in the repression of the determinative convict plot. Likewise, the daydream/fairy tale of Satis House stands revealed as a repression, or perhaps a "secondary revision," of the nightmare. That it should be the criminally deviant, transgressive plot that is shown to have priority over all the others stands within the logic of the model derived from *Beyond the Pleasure Principle*, since it is precisely this plot that most markedly constitutes the detour from inorganic quiescence: the arabesque of the narratable. One could almost derive a narratological law here: the true plot will be the most deviant. We might be tempted to see this deviant arabesque as gratuitous, the figure of "pure narration." Yet we are obliged to remotivate it, for the return of the repressed shows that the story Pip would tell about himself has all along been undermined and rewritten by the more complex history of unconscious desire, unavailable to the conscious subject but at work in the text. Pip has in fact misread the plot of his life.

III

The misreading of plots and the question of authority bring us back to the question of reading with which the novel began. Pip's initial attempt to decipher his parents' appearance and character from the letters traced on their tombstones has been characterized as "childish" and "unreasonable." Pip's decipherment in fact appears as an attempt to motivate the arbitrary sign, to interpret signs as if they were mimetic and thus naturally tied to the object for which they stand. Deriving from the shape of the letters on the tombstones that his father "was a square, stout, dark man, with curly hair," and that his mother was "freckled and sickly," for all its literal fidelity to the graphic trace, constitutes a dangerously figural reading, a metaphorical process unaware of itself, the mak-

ing of a fiction unaware of its status as fiction making. Pip is here
claiming natural authority for what is in fact conventional, arbitrary, dependent on interpretation.

The question of texts, reading, and interpretation is, as we earlier
noted, consistently thematized in the novel: in Pip's learning to
read (using that meager text, Mrs. Wopsle's aunt's catalogue of
prices), and his attempts to transmit the art of writing to Joe; the
expressive dumb shows between Pip and Joe; messages written on
the slate, by Pip to Joe, and then (in minimum symbolic form) by
the aphasic Mrs. Joe; the uncanny text of Estella's visage, always
reminding Pip of a repetition of something else which he cannot
identify; Molly's wrists, cross-hatched with scratches, a text for the
judge, and eventually for Pip as detective, to decipher; Mr. Wopsle's
declamations of *George Barnwell* and *Richard III*. The characters
appear to be ever on the watch for ways in which to textualize the
world, so that they can give their readings of it: a situation thematized early in the novel, at the Christmas dinner table, as Pumblechook and Wopsle criticize the sermon of the day and propose
other "subjects":

Mr. Pumblechook added, after a short interval of reflection,
"Look at Pork alone. There's a subject! If you want a subject,
look at Pork!"

"True, sir. Many a moral for the young," returned Mr. Wopsle; and I knew he was going to lug me in, before he said it,
"might be deduced from that text."

("You listen to this," said my sister to me, in a severe
parenthesis.)

Joe gave me some more gravy.

"Swine," pursued Mr. Wopsle, in his deepest voice, and
pointing his fork at my blushes, as if he were mentioning my
christian name, "Swine were the companions of the prodigal.
The gluttony of Swine is put before us, as an example to the
young." (I thought this pretty well in him who had been prais-
ing up the pork for being so plump and juicy.) "What is detestable in a pig, is more detestable in a boy."

"Or girl," suggested Mr. Hubble.

"Of course, or girl, Mr. Hubble," assented Mr. Wopsle, rather irritably, "but there is no girl present."

"Besides," said Mr. Pumblechook, turning sharp on me, "think what you've got to be grateful for. If you'd been born a Squeaker—"

"He *was*, if ever a child was," said my sister, most emphatically.

Joe gave me some more gravy.

"Well, but I mean a four-footed Squeaker," said Mr. Pumblechook. "If you had been born such, would you have been here now? Not you—"

"Unless in that form," said Mr. Wopsle, nodding towards the dish. (Chapter 4, pp. 23–24)

The scene suggests a mad proliferation of textuality, where literal and figural switch places, where any referent can serve as an interpretant, become the sign of another message, in a wild process of semiosis which seems to be anchored only insofar as all texts eventually speak of Pip himself as an unjustified presence, a presence demanding interpretation.

The novel constantly warns us that texts may have no unambiguous referent and no transcendent signified. Of the many examples one might choose in illustration of the status of texts and their interpretation in the novel, perhaps the most telling is the case of Mr. Wopsle. Mr. Wopsle, the church clerk, is a frustrated preacher, ever intimating that if the church were to be "thrown open," he would really "give it out." This hypothetical case never coming to realization, Mr. Wopsle is obliged to content himself with the declamation of a number of secular texts, from Shakespeare to Collins's ode. The church indeed remains resolutely closed (we never in fact hear the word of the preacher in the novel, only Mr. Wopsle's critique of it), and Mr. Wopsle "has a fall": into play-acting. He undertakes the repetition of fictional texts which lack the authority of that divine word he would like to "give out." We next see him playing *Hamlet*, which is of course the text par excellence about usurpation, parricide, lost regal authority, and wrong relations of transmission from generation to generation. Something of the problematic status of textual authority is suggested in Mr. Wopsle's rendition of the classic soliloquy:

> Whenever that undecided Prince had to ask a question or state a doubt, the public helped him out with it. As for example: on the question whether 'twas nobler in the mind to suffer, some roared yes, and some no, and some inclining to both opinions said "toss up for it"; and quite a Debating Society arose. (Chapter 31, p. 240)

From this uncertainty, Mr. Wopsle has a further fall, into playing what was known as "nautical melodrama," an anonymously authored theater played to a vulgar public in the Surreyside houses. When Pip attends this performance, there occurs a curious mirroring and reversal of the spectacle, where Mr. Wopsle himself becomes the spectator, fascinated by the vision, in the audience, of what he calls a "ghost" from the past—the face of the novel's hidden arch-plotter, Compeyson. The vision leads to a reconstruction of the chase and capture of the convicts, from the early chapters of the novel, a kind of analytic dialogue in the excavation of the past, where Mr. Wopsle repeatedly questions: "You remember?" and Pip replies: "I remember it very well . . . I see it all before me." This reconstruction produces an intense visual, hallucinatory reliving of a charged past moment:

> "And you remember that we came up with the two in a ditch, and that there was a scuffle between them, and that one of them had been severely handled and much mauled about the face, by the other?"
> "I see it all before me."
> "And that the soldiers lighted torches, and put the two in the centre, and that we went on to see the last of them, over the black marshes, with the torchlight shining on their faces— I am particular about that; with the torchlight shining on their

faces, when there was an outer ring of dark night all about
us?" (Chapter 47, p. 365)

By an apparently gratuitous free association, from Mr. Wopsle's
play-acting, as from behind a screen memory, emerges a drama on
that "other stage": the stage of dream, replaying a past moment
that the characters have never exorcised, that moment of the buried
yet living past which insists on repeating itself in the present.

Mr. Wopsle's career as a whole may exemplify a general movement in the novel toward recognition of the lack of authorship and
authority in texts: textures of codes without ultimate referent or
hierarchy, signs cut loose from their apparent motivation, capable
of wandering toward multiple associations and of evoking messages
that are entirely other, and that all speak eventually of determinative histories from the past. The original nostalgia for a founding
divine word leads to a generalized scene of writing, as if the plotting
self could never discover a decisive plot, but merely its own arbitrary
role as plotmaker. Yet the arbitrary is itself subject to an unconscious determinant, the reproductive insistence of the past history.

Mr. Wopsle's career may stand as a figure for Pip's. Whereas the
model of the *Bildungsroman* seems to imply progress, a leading
forth, and developmental change, Pip's story—and this may be true
of other nineteenth-century educative plots as well—becomes more
and more as it nears its end the working through of past history,
an attempted return to the origin as the motivation of all the rest,
the clue to what must else appear, as Pip puts it to Miss Havisham,
a "blind and thankless" life (Chapter 49, p. 377). The past needs
to be incorporated *as past* within the present, mastered through the
play of repetition in order for there to be an escape from repetition:
in order for there to be difference, change, progress. In the failure
ever to recover his own origin, Pip comes to concern himself with
the question of Estella's origin, searching for her patronymics where
knowledge of his own is ever foreclosed. Estella's story in fact eventually links all the plots of the novel: Satis House, the aspiration to
gentility, the convict identity, "naterally wicious" (the status from
which Jaggers rescued her), bringing up by hand, the law. Pip's

investigation of her origins as substitute for knowledge of his own has a certain validity in that, we discover, he appeared originally to Magwitch as a substitute for the lost Estella, his great expectations a compensation for the impossibility of hers: a chiasmus of the true situation. Yet when Pip has proved himself to be the successful detective in this quest, when he has uncovered the convergence of lines of plot that previously appeared distinct and indeed proved himself more penetrating even than Jaggers, he discovers the knowledge he has gained to be radically unusable. When he has imparted his knowledge to Jaggers and Wemmick, he reaches a kind of standoff between what he has called his "poor dreams" and the deep plot he has now exposed. As Jaggers puts it to him, there is no gain to be had from knowledge. We are in the heart of darkness, and the articulation of its meaning must simply be repressed. In this novel full of mysteries and hidden connections, detective work turns out to be both necessary and useless. It can offer no comfort and no true illumination to the detective himself. Like deciphering the letters on the tombstone, it produces no authority for the plot of life.

The novel in fact toward its end appears to record a generalized breakdown of plots: none of the schemes machinated by the characters manages to accomplish its aims. The proof *a contrario* may be the "oversuccessful" result of Miss Havisham's plot, which has turned Estella into so heartless a creature that she cannot even experience emotional recognition of her benefactress. Miss Havisham's plotting has been a mechanical success but an intentional failure, as her final words, during her delirium following the fire, may suggest:

> Towards midnight she began to wander in her speech, and after that it gradually set in that she said innumerable times in a low solemn voice, "What have I done?" And then, "When she first came, I meant to save her from misery like mine." And then, "Take the pencil and write under my name, 'I forgive her'!" She never changed the order of these three sentences, but she sometimes left out a word in one or other of them;

never putting in another word, but always leaving a blank and going on to the next word. (Chapter 49, pp. 381–82)

The cycle of three statements suggests a metonymic movement in search of arrest, a plot that can never find satisfactory resolution, that unresolved must play over its insistent repetitions, until silenced by death. Miss Havisham's deathbed scene transmits a "wisdom" that is in the deconstructive mode, a warning against plot.

We confront the paradox that in this most highly plotted of novels, where Dickens performs all his thematic demonstrations through the manipulation of plot, we witness an evident subversion and futilization of the very concept of plot. If the chosen plots turn out to be erroneous, unauthorized, self-delusive, the deep plots when brought to light turn out to be criminally tainted, deviant, and thus unusable. Plot as direction and intention in existence appears ultimately to be as evanescent as Magwitch's money, the product of immense labor, deprivation, and planning, which is in the end forfeit to the Crown. Like money in its role as universal modern (capitalist) signifier as described by Roland Barthes in *S/Z*, tied to no referent (such as land), defined only by its exchange value, capable of unlimited metonymic circulation, the expectations of fortune, as both plot and its aim or intention, as vehicle and object of representation, circulate through inflation to devaluation.

The ultimate situation of plot in the novel may suggest an approach to the vexed question of Dickens's two endings to the novel: the one he originally wrote and the revision (substituted at Bulwer Lytton's suggestion) that was in fact printed. I think it is entirely legitimate to prefer the original ending, with its flat tone and refusal of romantic expectation, and find that the revision, with its tentative promise of reunion between Pip and Estella, "unbinds" energies that we thought had been thoroughly bound and indeed discharged from the text. We may also feel that choice between the two endings is somewhat arbitrary and unimportant in that the decisive moment has already occurred before either of these finales begins. The real ending may take place with Pip's recognition and acceptance of Magwitch after his recapture—this is certainly the ethical dénouement—and his acceptance of a continuing existence without plot, as celibate clerk for Clarrikers. The pages that follow may simply be *obiter dicta*.

If we acknowledge Pip's experience of and with Magwitch to be the central energy of the text, it is significant that the climax of this experience, the moment of crisis and reversal in the attempted escape from England, bears traces of a hallucinatory repetition of the childhood spell—indeed, of that first recapture of Magwitch already repeated in Mr. Wopsle's theatrical vision:

> In the same moment, I saw the steersman of the galley lay his hand on the prisoner's shoulder, and saw that both boats were swinging round with the force of the tide, and saw that all hands on board the steamer were running forward quite frantically. Still in the same moment, I saw the prisoner start up, lean across his captor, and pull the cloak from the neck of the shrinking sitter in the galley. Still in the same moment, I saw that the face disclosed was the face of the other convict of long ago. Still in the same moment, I saw the face tilt backward with a white terror on it that I shall never forget, and heard a great cry on board the steamer and a loud splash in the water, and felt the boat sink from under me. (Chapter 54, pp. 421–22)

If this scene marks the beginning of a resolution—which it does in that it brings the death of the arch-villain Compeyson and the death sentence for Magwitch, hence the disappearance from the novel of its most energetic plotters—it is resolution in the register of repetition and working through, the final effort to master painful material from the insistent past. Pip emerges from this scene with an acceptance of the determinative past as both determinative and as *past*, which prepares us for the final escape *from* plot. It is interesting to note that where the "dream" plot of Estella is concerned, Pip's stated resolution has none of the compulsive energetic force of the passage just quoted, but is rather a conventional romantic fairy-tale ending, a conscious fiction designed, of course, to console the dying Magwitch, but possibly also a last effort at self-delusion: "You had a child once, whom you loved and lost. . . . She lived and found powerful friends. She is living now. She is a lady and very beautiful. And I love her!" (Chapter 56, p. 436). If taken as anything other than a conscious fiction—if taken as part of the "truth" discovered by Pip's detections—this version of Pip's experience leads straight to what is most troubling in Dickens's revised version of the ending: the suggestion of an unbinding of what has already been bound up and disposed of, an unbinding that is indeed perceptible in the rather embarrassed prose with which the revision begins: "Nevertheless, I knew while I said these words, that I secretly intended to revisit the site of the old house that evening alone, for her sake. Yes, even so. For Estella's sake" (Chapter 59, p. 458). Are we to understand that the experience of Satis House has never really been mastered? Is its nightmare energy still present in the text as well? The original end may have an advantage in denying to Pip's text the possibility of any reflux of energy, any new aspirations, the undoing of anything already done, the unbinding of energy that has been bound and led to discharge.

As at the start of the novel we had the impression of a life not yet subject to plot—a life in search of the sense of plot that would only gradually begin to precipitate around it—so at the end we have the impression of a life that has outlived plot, renounced plot, been cured of it: life that is left over. What follows the recognition of Magwitch is left over, and any renewal of expectation and plotting—such as a revived romance with Estella—would have to belong to another story. It is with the image of a life bereft of plot, of movement and desire, that the novel most appropriately leaves us. Indeed, we have at the end what could appropriately be called a "cure" from plot, in Pip's recognition of the general forfeiture of plotting, his renunciation of any attempt to direct his life. Plot comes to resemble a diseased, fevered state of the organism caught in the machinery of a desire which must eventually be renounced. Plot, we come to understand, was a state of abnormality or deviance, suggested thematically by its uneasy position between Newgate and Old Bailey, between criminality and the law. The nineteenth-century novel in general—and especially that highly symptomatic development, the detective story—regularly conceives plot as a condition of deviance and abnormality, the product of cities and social depths, of a world where *récit* is *complot*, where all stories are the result of plotting, and plotting is very much machination. Deviance is the very condition for life to be "narratable": the state of normality is devoid of interest, energy, and the possibility for narration. In between a beginning prior to plot and an end beyond plot, the middle—the plotted text—has been in a state of *error*: wandering and misinterpretation.

IV

That plot should prove to be deviance and error is fully consonant with Freud's model in *Beyond the Pleasure Principle*, where the narratable life of the organism is seen as detour, a deviance from the quiescence of the inorganic which has been maintained through the dynamic interaction of Eros and the death instinct. What Pip at one point has called his "ill-regulated aspirations" (Chapter 29, p. 223) is the figure of plot as desire: Eros as the force that binds integers together in ever-larger wholes, totalizing, metaphoric, the desire for possession of the world and for the integration of meaning—whereas, concomitantly, repetition and return have spoken of the death instinct, the drive to return to the quiescence of the inorganic, of the nontextual. Yet the repetitions, which have served to bind the various plots, both prolonging the detour and more effectively preparing the final discharge, have created that delay necessary to incorporate the past within the present and to let us understand end in relation to beginning. Through the erotics of the text, we have inexorably been led to its end, which is precisely quiescence: a time after which is an image of the time before. We have reached the non-narratable. Adducing the argument of "Remembering, Repeating and Working Through" to that of *Beyond the Pleasure Principle*, we perceive that repetition is a kind of remembering, and thus a way of reorganizing a story whose connective links have been obscured and lost. If repetition speaks of the death instinct, the finding of the right end, then what is being played out in repetition is necessarily the proper vector of the drive toward the end. That is, once you have determined the right plot, plot is over. Plot itself is working-through.

Great Expectations is exemplary in demonstrating both the need for plot and its status as deviance, both the need for narration and the necessity to be cured from it. The deviance and error of plot may necessarily result from the interplay of desire in its history with the narrative insistence on explanatory form: the desire to wrest beginnings and ends from the uninterrupted flow of middles, from temporality itself; the search for that significant closure that would illuminate the sense of an existence, the meaning of life. The desire for meaning is ultimately the reader's, who must mime Pip's acts of reading but do them better. Both using and subverting the systems of meaning discovered or postulated by its hero, *Great Expectations* exposes for its reader the very reading process itself: the way the reader goes about finding meaning in the narrative text, and the limits of that meaning as the limits of narrative.

In terms of the problematic of reading which the novel thematizes from its opening page, we could say that Pip, continuously returning toward origins in order to know the plot whose authority would lead him to the right end but never recovering origins and never finding the authoritative plot, never succeeds in going behind his self-naming to a reading of the missing patronymic. He is ever returned to a rereading of the unauthorized text of his self-given name, Pip. "Pip" sounded like a beginning, a seed. But, of course, when you reach the end of the name "Pip," you can return backward, and it is just the same: a repetitive text without variation or point of fixity, a return that leads to an unarrested shuttling back and forth. The name is in fact a palindrome. In the rereading of the palindrome the novel may offer its final comment on its expectative plot.

What, finally, do we make of the fact that Dickens, master-plotter in the history of the novel, in this most tightly and consistently plotted of his novels seems to expose plot as a kind of necessary error? Dickens's most telling comment on the question may come at the moment of Magwitch's sentencing. The judge gives a legalistic and moralistic version of Magwitch's life story, his violence, his crimes, the passions that made him a "scourge to society" and led him to escape from deportation, thus calling upon his head the death sentence. The passage continues:

> The sun was striking in at the great windows of the court, through the glittering drops of rain upon the glass, and it made a broad shaft of light between the two-and-thirty [prisoners at the bar] and the Judge, linking both together, and perhaps reminding some among the audience, how both were passing on, with absolute equality, to the greater Judgment that knoweth all things and cannot err. Rising for a moment, a distinct speck of face in this way of light, the prisoner [Magwitch] said, "My Lord, I have received my sentence of Death from the Almighty, but I bow to yours," and sat down again. There was some hushing, and the Judge went on with what he had to say to the rest. (Chapter 56, p. 434)

The passage is sentimental but also, I think, effective. It juxtaposes human plots—including those of the law—to eternal orders that render human attempts to plot, and to interpret plot, not only futile but ethically unacceptable. The greater Judgment makes human plots mere shadows. There is another end that recuperates passing human time, and its petty chronologies, to the timeless. Yet despite the narrator's affirmations, this other end is not visible, the other orders are not available. As Mr. Wopsle's case suggested, the divine word is barred in the world of the novel (it is suggestive that Christmas dinner is interrupted by the command to repair handcuffs). If there is a divine masterplot for human existence, it is radically unknowable.

In the absence or silence of divine masterplots, the organization and interpretation of human plots remains as necessary as it is problematic. Reading the signs of intention in life's actions is the central act of existence, which in turn legitimizes the enterprise of reading for the reader of *Great Expectations*—or perhaps, vice versa, since the reading of plot within the text and as the text are perfectly analogous, mirrors of one another. If there is by the end of the narrative an abandonment of the attempt to read plot, this simply mirrors the fact that the process of narration has come to a close—or, again, vice versa. But that there should be a cure from the reading of plot within the text—before its very end—and the creation of a leftover, suggests a critique of reading itself, which is possibly like the judge's sentence: human interpretation in ignorance of the true vectors of the true text. So it may indeed be: the *savoir* proposed by Balzac's antique dealer is not *in* the text. But if the mastertext is not available, we are condemned to the reading of erroneous plots, granted insight only insofar as we can gain disillusion from them. We are condemned to repetition, rereading, in the knowledge that what we discover will always be that there was nothing to be discovered. Yet the process remains necessary if we are not to be caught perpetually in the "blind and thankless" existence, in the illusory middle. Like Oedipus, like Pip, we are condemned to reinterpretation of our names. But it is rare that the name coincide so perfectly with a fullness and a negation of identity as in the case of Oedipus. In a post-tragic universe, our situation is more likely to be that of Pip, compelled to reinterpret the meaning of the name he assigned to himself with his infant tongue, the history of an infinitely repeatable palindrome.

6

The Mark of the Beast: Prostitution, Serialization, and Narrative

My understanding of plot as intention and dynamic in narrative, as that which actively shapes our experience as readers of narrative, has led me to talk of desire as a thematic instrumentality of plot and as a basic motivation of its telling and its reading. If plots seem frequently to be about investments of desire and the effort to bind and master intensive levels of energy, this corresponds on the one hand to narratives thematically oriented toward ambition, possession, mastery of the erotic object and of the world, and on the other hand to a certain experience of reading narrative, itself a process of reaching for possession and mastery. Speaking reductively, without nuance, one might say that on the one hand narrative tends toward a thematics of the desired, potentially possessable body, and on the other toward a readerly experience of consuming, a having that, in an era of triumphant capitalism, is bound to take on commercial forms, giving to the commerce in narrative understandings a specifically commercial tinge. What follows is a reflection largely devoted to the vicissitudes and destinies of the erotic body in a context of commercialized literature, specifically in a prime example of the popular serialized novel characterized by the critic Sainte-Beuve as "industrial literature."

It might be possible to trace a kind of progressive unveiling of the erotic body in the nineteenth-century novel. This, of course, occurs with far more reticence and delay in England than in France, and in more displaced and kinky forms. The eroticism of *Great Expectations*, we saw, is most powerfully felt in the place of its greatest negation and repression, in the story of Miss Havisham. The angelic young women of Dickens—Agnes, Little Dorrit, Rose Maylie, Little Nell—have been voided of sexuality, but this often shows up in displaced and deviant forms: in Tattycoram and the "self-tormentor" Miss Wade of *Little Dorrit*, for instance, or the prostitute (though with a heart of gold) Nancy of *Oliver Twist*. Any adolescent reader of the Brontës, of *Jane Eyre* and *Wuthering Heights*, is obscurely aware of how erotic Jane and Catherine can be, even if the consummation of desire must be accompanied by maiming or blindness, or pushed into the grave. It would be worth making the argument that Henry James's heroines create a far more erotic bodily presence than has usually been allowed, especially those such as Kate Croy in *The Wings of the Dove* and Charlotte Stant in *The Golden Bowl* who use the body as power, and by that power indeed create the deviation of plot. One might also maintain that it is Thomas Hardy who finally unveils the body in the English novel, most particularly in *Tess of the d'Urbervilles*, facing at last, in relative nakedness, the presence and power of Eros, and making the next step—to D. H. Lawrence—merely inevitable. In France, not only is the weight of self-censorship so much lighter (as James plaintively noted on several occasions), there is also the unavowed but nonetheless living inheritance from the eighteenth-century novel, especially its masterpiece, Laclos's *Les Liaisons dangereuses*, which has never been surpassed as an account of the political erotic body and its place in the network of writing and reading. If Stendhal's bodies are subject to a kind of elliptical *pudeur*, suggesting more than it designates, Balzac's are extraordinarily present, even in the more exotic reaches of desire—in *La Fille aux yeux d'or*, for instance, and *La Duchesse de Langeais*—and the substitute formations, including "Platonic" romance, produced by repression are explicitly dismantled, most magisterially in *Le Lys dans la vallée*.[1] Flaubert's *Madame Bovary* continues the unveiling, though in the mode of irony and banality. And Proust brings it to a kind of meditative climax, in

Marcel's reflections on the nude sleeping body of Albertine, at once prisoner and fugitive. In between Flaubert and Proust stands Zola, who made it a point to unveil, but who was also obsessed with the female body as something whose force and emanations were almost too powerful to tolerate. The vast machinery of commerce and industrialism ultimately is set in motion by the body, as in *Au Bonheur des dames*, where Octave Mouret's construction and expansion of the department store is based explicitly on the need to seduce and master women. Zola's most telling expression no doubt comes in *Nana*, where the body of the prostitute is clearly the meeting point of Eros and commerce.

Close to the midpoint of this novel, Nana is completely unveiled— without her shift, without the mesh bodice worn when she represented a nude Venus in the operetta *La Blonde Vénus*—in the scene where she undresses before the mirror as her lover, the Comte Muffat, watches. This self-unveiling is animated by two desires: Nana admires and caresses her own body, while Muffat watches her from behind, taking in both Nana herself and her frontal image in the mirror. Muffat then interrupts his contemplation of the body to read an article in *Le Figaro* by the journalist and critic Fauchery entitled "La Mouche d'or," which in a thinly veiled allegory describes Nana herself as a venomous insect from the gutter who has gradually infected the upper classes, thus avenging the class of the destitute from which she sprang—daughter of workers whose miserable lives have been detailed in *L'Assommoir*—carrying forward social warfare by means of her golden body, "corrupting and disorganizing Paris between her snowy thighs."[2] When Muffat looks up from his reading, he follows Nana's autoerotic looks and touches, leading his, and our, glance finally to her *sexe*, described as both marked and veiled by the pubic hair, revealed but never wholly so. Perhaps in reaction to the frustration of this revelation, and explicitly provoked by Nana's solitary pleasure, Muffat seizes Nana and throws her on the carpet, to possess her in an act he senses is less a demonstration of his own power than a concession of defeat by a power he can neither resist nor control.

The newspaper column, "La Mouche d'or," introduced into this scene of Nana's golden body fully unveiled, may suggest a certain affinity between the body of the prostitute and commercial writing, which the considerable literature on prostitution—sometimes serious, more often exploitative—at this period only confirms. The Second Empire of Napoleon III marked the emergence of the high-class prostitute as a noticeable and much-discussed public figure, whose biography could be highly narratable, whose career could lead to immense wealth and even respectability—the case of Irma d'Anglars, in *Nana,* who becomes country gentry—or else the plunge into the depths of destitution. But the popularity of the literary figure of the prostitute reaches back to Romanticism, to such characters as Victor Hugo's Marion Delorme and Fantine, to Balzac's Coralie and Esther, and a host of other touching and victimized creatures who spoke to the reformist social conscience that became an important factor of French Romantic doctrine. What sealed the alliance of the figure of the prostitute with both social conscience and popular, commercially successful literature was Eugène Sue's *Les Mystères de Paris,* perhaps the most widely read novel of the nineteenth century, which was published serially in the *Journal des Débats* from June 9, 1842, to October 15, 1843.

The *roman-feuilleton*—the serial novel running in regular installments in the daily newspaper—was an early capitalist invention that helped to create modern mass-circulation journalism. In France, the process began when Emile de Girardin founded *La Presse* as the first low-cost newspaper in 1836. His idea was to cut the normal subscription price by half (there were no single-issue sales at the time) and at least to double the number of subscribers, which would then permit an increase in the price and amount of advertising, which would thus take the place of subscription income as the basis of newspaper financing. What permitted the speculation—the oil of this revolutionary new machinery—was the daily dose of fiction of the *feuilleton,* printed on the "ground floor," or bottom quarter of the front page, which aimed to attract a readership which had never before felt the need for a newspaper. The formula launched by *La Presse* was immediately successful: the paper quickly had four times the customary number of subscribers, and the rest of the press hastened to follow suit. Subscriptions began to reach figures unimaginable a decade earlier. A secondary industry sprang into existence with the creation of advertising agencies feeding the press; the financing of newspaper publishing became capitalistic; the economic and political power of the press increased immensely. A shift in the balance of political forces was inaugurated as public opinion, expressed, interpreted, aroused by the mass-circulation newspaper, became a potent fourth estate.

Hence the creation of modern mass journalism, and its power, not only permitted the emergence of the *roman-feuilleton*; it quite directly depended on this first industrial form of literature. The successful *feuilletonistes* not only learned to live exclusively by the products of their pens, they were paid by the line and learned to shape their plots to the exigencies of serialization. Each installment had to fit the space allotted, of course, and to move the story forward to a new moment of suspense and expectation so that the terminal tag, "*la Suite à demain*" (the nineteenth century's "tune in tomorrow"), could take its full toll on the reader. In addition, since newspaper subscriptions were renewable quarterly, it was necessary that a plot be brought to a particularly dire moment of cliff-hanging just before renewal date, so that readers would be sure to sign on for more. *Les Mystères de Paris* gave the genre its classic instance. Readers of all classes—from the king and his ministers on down—awaited eagerly and sometimes even fought over each installment as it appeared; and for those who could not read, there was a public reading in cafés and workshops throughout France. Sue's work in fact rescued the rather staid *Journal des Débats* from financial crisis. More important, it realized a fusion of the "popular" in theme, audience, and mode of production. In particular, Sue opened to popular novelistic treatment a certain urban topography and demography, of crime and social deviance finding and exploiting a new form of the narratable.[5]

We must turn to the novel itself for a closer scrutiny of the body, prostitution, and the commercialization of narrative plot. At its outset, Monsieur Rodolphe—otherwise Son Altesse le Grand-Duc Rodolphe de Gerolstein—is on one of his errands of general and incognito mercy in the social depths of Paris when he meets Fleur-de-Marie, the prostitute known to her low-life companions as "La Goualeuse" (slang for "la chanteuse") from her irrepressible love of song, and hears her story in a typically sordid *tapis-franc*, or cabaret, of the Ile de la Cité—labyrinthine core of Parisian crime—in the company of assorted thieves, murderers, pimps, stool pigeons, and other recruits for the guillotine. The destiny of Fleur-de-Marie, prostitute with a heart of gold, virginal flower anomalously growing in the urban slime, is our principal guiding thread through the labyrinth of multiple plots and realms which constitutes *Les Mystères de Paris*. When she declares herself an orphan of unknown parentage, and when we learn that Rodolphe takes a special interest in her because she is just the age that his daughter would have been had she lived, instead of dying as an infant in mysterious circumstances, we can already, if we are attuned to the necessities of melodramatic plotting, divine the higher pathos of this confrontation which, unbeknownst to its actors, is of father and daughter.

While this information will be furnished to the reader after a few hundred pages (since the reader must have guessed already, Sue cavalierly decides to let the cat officially out of the bag), it will take Rodolphe over three thousand pages to bring it to light, through a series of peripeties, dramatic ironies, *coups-de-théâtre*, and startling coincidences, motivating the convergence of nearly the whole cast of characters and all the lines of plot on the loss and recovery of this unfortunate creature who, after a battered and starving childhood begging on the streets of Paris and a term in prison, was intoxicated with *eau-de-vie* and sold into prostitution. Rodolphe's discovery is the occasion for a full articulation of the antitheses and oxymorons of Fleur-de-Marie's existence: the hereditary princess destined to a life of beggary and blows; the pure, blond child delivered to the hands of a putrid mob of convicts and degenerates; the singing bird in the urban jungle; the "angelic and candid" girl of sixteen smeared with all the filth to be found in the underbelly of Paris. In the body and the history of Fleur-de-Marie, all social and moral extremes meet in a rhetoric of pathos and excruciation.

When all has come to light, Rodolphe undertakes not only to

rehabilitate Fleur-de-Marie—a process begun earlier when, before knowing her to be his daughter, he removed her from the Ile de la Cité and placed her in the model farm of Bouqueval, a place of virtue, industry, and simplicity, from which, alas, she was abducted once again by her former associates and tormentors—but also to restore her to her rightful place in his palace in the Duchy of Gerolstein. But the plan cannot succeed: despite the kindnesses that Rodolphe lavishes on her, Fleur-de-Marie remains a victim of past remembrances. When Rodolphe and his new bride, Clémence, explain to her that she is blameless, a victim of social misery, constrained to degradation, she replies: "But, that infamy . . . I experienced it. . . . Nothing can efface those frightful memories."[4] The past persists, ineffaceable; and when Fleur-de-Marie receives an offer of marriage from Prince Henri of Herkaüsen-Oldenzaal, whom she loves, the promise of final happiness only reveals its final impossibility in the ultimate oxymoron of the prostitute-become-mother, making a *mère* of what was once a *fille*: " 'I a mother,' replied Fleur-de-Marie with a desperate bitterness, 'I respected, blessed by an innocent and candid child! I, once the object of everyone's contempt! To have me thus profane the name of mother. . . . Oh! never' " (Volume 10, p. 151). The inexorable logic continues with her decision to seek refuge in the convent. Yet even this compromise cannot subsist. She no sooner takes the veil than she succumbs to the secret illness that is sapping her from within, and dies.

When she is explaining to Rodolphe and Clémence why she can never marry Prince Henri, Fleur-de-Marie concludes her pathetic confession: "I love Prince Henri too much, I respect him too much, ever to give him a hand that has been touched by the bandits of the Cité" (Volume 10, p. 153). The formula recapitulates the antithesis that governs her existence, and suggests the uncrossable bar separating the terms of the antithesis. Calling upon Freud's concept of the "displacement upwards" that can occur in the symptoms of hysteric neurotics, we can say that "hand" here is a metonymy, a euphemism that displaces the place of uncleanness, of *souillure*.[5] The despoiled can never again be made whole. One can, of course, see in Fleur-de-Marie's refusal to give her soiled body

to a legitimate husband, and in her decorous choice of death as
the only solution to the oxymorons of her existence, a simple sign
of Sue's capitulation to conventional bourgeois morality: there are
limits beyond which even so angelic a creature as Fleur-de-Marie
cannot be revirginized. Yet something more appears to confront
us in the death of Fleur-de-Marie: what I would read as a symbolic
representation of the impossibility of ever effacing the mark of the
Cité, of the lowest of the social depths, once one has descended
into them. There is here at the end of *Les Mystères de Paris* perhaps
simultaneously a dissent from the Romantic cliché of the redeemed
prostitute, a bad faith capitulation to bourgeois morality, and a
representation of how the novel itself—and its author—have undergone marking by the indelible trace of misery, crime, and the sold
body. That these conflicting messages should all be encoded at the
end of *Les Mystères de Paris* is, I think, typical of the book as a whole,
in its presentation of the Parisian underclass from initial motives
that must appear sensationalistic and exploitative, but which changed
considerably as the novel pursued its protracted course of composition and publication in the *Journal des Débats*—in the audacity
of Sue's enterprise which one feels to be tempered not so much by
caution as by unacknowledged ambivalences and blindness, which
may ultimately be inherent to his subject and his interest in it. We
are left saying that if Fleur-de-Marie cannot escape the mark, the
indelible trace of the Cité, this may on the one hand be a sop to
morality and a sign of loss of novelistic nerve, yet on the other
hand it may stand as a sign of a certain realism about the limits of
redemption and also perhaps of Sue's personal confession that the
bodily experience of certain markings is indeed ineffaceable.

   Toward the midpoint of the novel, when the society lady Clémence d'Harville is preparing to visit the prostitutes confined in
Saint-Lazare Prison (it was used for female thieves and prostitutes)
to work toward the rehabilitation of those whose "degraded souls
show the slightest aspiration toward good" (Volume 5, p. 99), Sue
draws an explicit parallel between the mission of the charity ladies.
and his own. The gesture in both cases is one of *descent*, indeed of
condescension, from the heights into the very abysses of society, to

bring the lamp of knowledge and reform to the darkest recesses of the social order. A contemporary reviewer in *La Revue Indépendante* caught the movement and meaning of Sue's novel when he wrote: "Up until now, the novel, almost exclusively lordly, had kept proudly to the social summits, without deigning to look down. . . . This is the first time that it has penetrated so deeply into the miseries of the people; it is the first time that it has stirred up so profoundly the social slime, and that it has descended into these somber abysses where human suffering seems forever cast away from the pity of man and the justice of God."[6]

The original motives of Sue's descent must appear somewhat suspect, possibly less well intentioned than Clémence d'Harville's. Sainte-Beuve saw the situation accurately:

It is doubtful that in beginning his famous work, this man of wit and invention intended to do anything other than persist more than ever in his pessimistic line, and, bringing together all its secrets, create a spicy and salty novel for the consumption of good society. I imagine that he wished to see, in a kind of wager, just how far, this time, he could lead his pretty women readers from the outset, and if great ladies wouldn't recoil from the *tapis-franc*. . . . The result of his success has been to make of someone who was an ironical and skeptical aristocratic writer—or aspired to be one—a popular author henceforth enslaved to his public.[7]

The comment perceptively suggests Sue's point of departure as the fashionable *dandy*, read by a bourgeois audience with aspirations to gentility, who sought a *frisson nouveau* in the novelistic exploitation of the social underbelly. Sue at the inception of *Les Mystères* can validly be accused of slumming, and with less benevolent curiosity than his hero Rodolphe. Yet as he went on, not only did he become the slave of a popular audience which waited eagerly to read—or to hear read—each of the 147 installments of the *Journal des Débats*, he also developed a new concern with documenting, understanding, and dramatizing the miseries of the people. Sue began to imitate his fictive hero Rodolphe, to put on worker's clothes and to visit garrets and workshops and prisons. He began to inquire into the causes of misery, prostitution, and crime; he discovered the precariousness of the artisan's condition, the lack of social resources for those living on the brink of pauperization, the unequal hand of justice, the iniquities of the penal system. He became more than a simple entrepreneur of the new industrial literature: working within its conditions, he grew to be aware of the general conditions of which it was a part, the world of rapid urbanization, nascent industrialism, and exploitative capitalism. A novel that had begun as a descent into the Parisian underbelly in search of exciting and amusing quarry became as it went along a "popular novel" in terms of its subject, as well as its audience and its mode of production. While he began Les Mystères de Paris with the vaguest of ideological orientations—and without knowing at all how the novel's plot and meaning would evolve—Sue emerged from it a declared socialist, a rare case of conversion through one's own work of fiction. He would indeed go on to become a deputy from a working-class district of Paris during the Second Republic, and then figure among the banished after the coup d'état that ushered in the Second Empire.[8]

The sensationally melodramatic, we could say, led to an inquest into the system responsible for the melodramatic contrasts of urban life. Sue's friendships with such socialist writers as Félix Pyat were a factor in his "conversion"; so were the enthusiastic reviews in the reformist and socialist press that greeted the early installments of the novel; and also Sue's vast fan mail which, along with letters pleading that the novelist alleviate Fleur-de-Marie's sufferings or that he dispatch Rodolphe to succor some real-life victim, included urgings from reformers to persist in the exploration of this new terrain and testimonials from the people themselves, recounting anecdotes of their lives. In an increasing number of polemical digressions as the novel advanced, Sue put forth a series of proposals: for model cooperative farms, workingmen's interest-free loan associations, penal reform. The melodramatic imagination working on the world begins to open up its depths; as in the stage melodramas of Félix Pyat and a number of other playwrights, melo-drama becomes a chosen vehicle for the attempt to change the world. In the marriage of melodrama and reformist socialism we find the same ambivalent blend of boldness and blindness that characterizes the death of Fleur-de-Marie and the very choice of prostitution as Sue's way into representation of the social under-world.

The initial descent into the Parisian social inferno is represented by Rodolphe himself, who in expiation of a personal sin has un-dertaken to succor the virtuous poor by exercising a "police of virtue," which, as the novel goes on, itself becomes a blueprint for a new social organism: a bureau of the police charged with dis-covering and rewarding unrecognized virtue, empowering its con-tinued existence in resistance to the demands of vice. The obverse of Rodolphe's vigilantism of virtue is his arrogation to himself of the power to punish those who cause the sufferings of the perse-cuted virtuous, most notably in the horrendous (and immediately famous) scene in which he has his private physician blind the arch-villain, the Maître d'Ecole. The blinded evildoer will be rendered harmless, and will in darkness meditate his sins. As urban Robin Hood, Rodolphe exercises power over the body, and in this case we recognize the equivalence established by Freud between blind-ing and castration, since the Maître d'Ecole represents a powerful sexuality as well as a thoroughly perverse criminality. Rodolphe thus redresses the wrong of Fleur-de-Marie's having been subjected to power over the body. The descent, which ever matches crimi-nality with punishment, as it matches the aspiration to virtue with rehabilitation, constantly juxtaposes fear and power. Policing and surveillance are directed at the body and its deviant sexual power. And here all themes converge on the question of prostitution.

To elucidate the place of prostitution in *Les Mystères de Paris*—and beyond that, its privileged place in the nineteenth-century novel in general—we need to reflect further on the indelible mark that prostitution has left on Fleur-de-Marie. Karl Marx, in some brilliant and scathing pages of *The Holy Family* (1845), demonstrates how Rodolphe "saves" Fleur-de-Marie by first transforming her from prostitute into repentant sinner, then from repentant sinner into nun, then from nun into corpse. Marx argues that Rodolphe teaches Fleur-de-Marie to internalize her "fault," which in large measure means abstracting her fault. That is, to Fleur-de-Marie prostitution is originally a lived situation, a situation external to her humanity, not an abstraction in terms of which she must condemn herself. Rodolphe—when he begins her rehabilitation at the model farm of Bouqueval—turns Fleur-de-Marie over to the Abbé Laporte, who makes her aware of her condition as one of sin inhabiting within. "In making me understand virtue," Fleur-de-Marie tells him, "you have also made me understand the depths of my past abjection" (Volume 3, p. 61). To which the good priest replies: "However generously endowed by the Creator, a nature that has been plunged, if only for a day, into the slime from which we rescued you, keeps from it an ineffaceable stigma." Whereas, comments Marx, Fleur-de-Marie knew herself as human before, now she knows herself as fallen: the filth that previously had only soiled her on the outside now has become her internal essence; God, and then death, are the only answers. Fleur-de-Marie's *sold* body has become the Abbé Laporte's *sinning* body—perhaps because she is to Sue unavoidably the *erotically deviant* body.

Marx's analysis here is characteristically remarkable, but perhaps not wholly faithful to Sue's script. Marx makes too much of the Abbé Laporte. Fleur-de-Marie herself assigns the precipitating cause of her feeling of inner *souillure* and unworthiness to her meeting with Clara Dubreuil, an innocent young girl of her own age, and the sense of distance between the two of them: "For the first time, I felt that there are blots that nothing can efface" (Volume 3, p. 56). In particular, Fleur-de-Marie describes the horror she feels when Clara recounts the story of her "simple, calm, happy life," and then asks Fleur-de-Marie to narrate her own life. The Abbé Laporte really only confirms what Fleur-de-Marie has discovered in juxtaposition and contrast to the normal existence of the unsullied girl of her age: that her own life, her own past, is not narratable. The story of the mark she bears cannot be told, the past cannot be recovered in a full, candid narrative of her life. Hence the mark is ineffaceable, the past irremediable.

The apparent paradox here is that the ostensibly unnarratable life is the very one Sue has chosen to narrate: the novel, after all, is concerned with Fleur-de-Marie's story, not Clara Dubreuil's. What Sue chooses for narration—what comprises the very definition of the "narratable" in *Les Mystères de Paris*—is the deviant, the shameful, the criminal, that which most clearly diverges from the "simple, calm, happy life." The situation is by no means confined to this novel; it is at least characteristic of the nineteenth-century novel, and perhaps in some degree of all narrative, which in general has precious little use for the simple, calm, and happy, since whatever moral obeisance one makes to these, they lack narrative interest. And there is a certain novel, of which Sue, along with Balzac, Dickens, Hugo, Wilkie Collins, Dostoevsky, might be considered a most notable practitioner, which in full contrast seeks the narratable in that which deviates most markedly from the normal, in the criminal, the outside-the-law, the unsocialized, and ungoverned. André Gide referred to the novel as a "lawless" form, using this word in English to suggest the novel's freedom from rules. Yet he might with equal pertinence have used the French term *hors-la-loi*, since it is what lies outside the law, the state of infraction and deviance in its interaction with the controlling pressures of the law, that increasingly in the nineteenth century preoccupies narrative. In this context, Sue's descent into the Parisian depths can be read as a foray into that world which remains potentially storied, where there is to be found the greatest fund of the narratable. If we think of traditional storytelling as allied with travel, with the reports of those coming from afar, and with the marvelous, the realm of the folktale and its story of victory over hostile forces, we may conceive that in the banal nineteenth century, where (as Balzac, for instance, frequently complains) everything is becoming standardized and boring, the world of the social depths—of the professionally deviant, so to speak—comes to appear the last place of stories ready to hand, the last refuge of the narratable. Deviance as a question in social pathology offers an opportunity for tracing its arabesque figure as plot. That "arabesque"—the figure found in *La Peau de chagrin*—represents the opposite of the straight line: it is the longest possible line between two points, or rather, the maintenance of the greatest possible deviance and detour between beginning and end, depending on the play of retardation, repetition, and return in the postponement and progressive unveiling of the end. As in the model of plot we derived from *Beyond the Pleasure Principle*, the drive toward the end is matched by an ever more complex, deviant, transgressive, tension-filled resistance to the end: the space of the plotted existence. If the wretched of the earth are Sue's preferred subject, it may be first of all because, for a bourgeois public at least, they are eminently the stuff of plotted story; though—to preserve the full measure of ambiguity in Sue's descent—their stories may lead to a new understanding of the causes of that deviance which is the object of representation.

When one reflects upon the place of prostitution in this context, one begins to perceive its special and exemplary role in the nineteenth-century narratable. Albert Béguin once noted that a census of *La Comédie humaine* would reveal a percentage of prostitutes far in excess of that in the world outside the novel, no doubt because the prostitute is pre-eminently someone with a novelistic destiny: a special, idiosyncratic form of life.[9] The prostitute's plot is by definition a deviance, and in literary terms she is often seen as herself defining an original trajectory through the world, a plot by which her life achieves a new and exemplary style and meaning. Within the limits set by her social role and function, the prostitute is conceived as an essentially theatric being, capable of making mask into meaning. Balzac's prostitutes—sometimes the lowest class of streetwalker that Fleur-de-Marie represents, more often courtesans, expensive kept women, or else dancers, *rats d'opéra* and the like—have a special capacity to cross social barriers, to exist in all milieux, to make it to the top but through a kind of demonstration that the top is in essence no different from the bottom.

The prostitute in this view would deserve that sobriquet applied in American gangster lore to the automatic pistol: the old equalizer. Balzac's Fanny Beaupré, Jenny Cadine, Tullia, Florine, Suzanne du Val-Noble, and the touching Esther Gobseck play a compensatory social role that Balzac explicitly, if ironically, compares to socialist ideology in a phrase from *Splendeurs et misères des courtisanes*, where he describes the banker Nucingen's passion for Esther and notes that an honest bourgeois wife cannot understand "how a fortune melts between the hands of these creatures whose social function, in the Fourierist system, is perhaps to make up for the sorrows caused by Avarice and Cupidity." [10] For the prostitute speculates on the *libido universalis*, on the capacity to make every man succumb to his erotic needs, each according to his means. The journalist Etienne Lousteau describes Esther's magical powers near the start of *Splendeurs et misères*: "At age eighteen, that girl has already known the highest opulence, the lowest misery, men on each social storey. She has a manner of magic wand with which she unleashes the brutal appetites so violently suppressed in men who, while concerning themselves with politics, science, literature, art, still are passionate at heart. There is no woman in Paris who can say as well as she does to the Animal: 'Come out! . . .' And the Animal leaves its cage, and wallows in excess" (p. 442). The subjacent image here is no doubt Circe, turning men into pigs. In her transformational role, in her capacity to provoke metamorphoses, the prostitute is not only herself narratable, she provokes the stuff of story in others.

If prostitution is as old as human civilization, as an organized and everyday phenomenon it has close ties to industrial capitalism. Prostitution in Paris in fact took on new dimensions with the large increase of population in the first half of the nineteenth century and the creation of an impoverished urban proletariat. As Louis Chevalier writes in his remarkable book *Classes laborieuses et classes dangereuses*, "Prostitution was a basic phenomenon of urban life, more particularly of working-class life, during the first half of the nineteenth century." [11] Investigators began to discover that it had a discernible geographical organization, considerable diversification of function, and a set of police regulations. In 1836, Dr. A.-J.-B. Parent-Duchatelet published *De la prostitution dans la ville de Paris*, an extensive and serious study that details the different categories of prostitute, running from the *fille à carte* (the common streetwalker obliged to carry a registration card issued by the police) to the *fille à numéro* (occupying a brothel) on up to the *femme galante*, *femme à parties, femme de théâtres* (all of which we might now label "call girls").[12] From Parent-Duchatelet's work emerge the contours of an entire subsociety, a subterranean world with its own social organization, its manners, even its language—its special slang—analyzed and documented with great detail and authority. It is not surprising that the study was of the greatest interest to those novelists fascinated by the social underground—the "sub-basement of society," as Balzac sometimes called it—and that such novelists as Balzac, Dumas, Hugo, and Sue put Parent-Duchatelet's research largely to profit. Having read Parent-Duchatelet, one easily recognizes the frequent moments at which the novelists liberally borrow from him, working from suggestive details on the prostitute's manner of life to the creation of such characters as Esther or Fleur-de-Marie.

Parent-Duchatelet's work is one of the most remarkable of an impressive group of contemporary inquiries into the condition of the Parisian underclass, and the work of novelists—most fully, no doubt, Sue and Hugo—went very much in the same direction and belonged to the same movement.[13] The great question of the nineteenth century was to be that of social destitution, or, as Victor Hugo expressed it in the working title to his great novel, *Les Misères*. As translated into the ordinary bourgeois perception of the world, the issue tended to be, as Louis Chevalier has so well demonstrated, most immediately that of criminality: the threat from the dangerous classes. The criminal act and the criminal mind, we have seen, become major novelistic themes, from Balzac to Dostoevsky and beyond. The novel tends to maintain its plots between exploration of the maximal, most daring social deviance on the one hand, and the counter-discipline of the police on the other: it is no surprise that the detective novel and cops-and-robbers fiction are nineteenth-century inventions.[14] While Sue eventually discovers the powerless, what really interests him more are the discontents of power, those in the depths who use it in reverse, perverse ways. Ultimately, as Fleur-de-Marie's profession and the Maître d'Ecole's symbolic castration together imply, the deviant power of the underworld is in essence sexual. This suggests further motivation for the fact that access to the underworld passes most readily through the Circe's den of prostitution.

The subject of prostitution is perhaps necessarily and of itself fraught with the ambiguities we noted in Sue's descent into the realms of social misery: it is never certain whether the novelist's interest is primarily in the sold body or in the deviant body. Social misery, the working class, and criminality, approached through their relation to and manifestation in prostitution, are gilded by the erotic. The descent of the novel here mimes the traditional descent of bourgeois men who, buying the erotic through money, enter a special world that is at least on the threshold of the nether regions. There is also a parallel imagery of psychological descent, into the unavowable erotic, where in darkness and secret the beast is liberated. One can speculate that prostitutes allowed nineteenth-century novelists to deal with the dangerous and fearful subject of female sexuality in a manner not possible when portraying women of the upper and middle classes. Balzac is perhaps the most striking case here, in that such sublime and flaming creatures as Esther, Coralie, or the sequestered Paquita Valdès of *La Fille aux yeux d'or* are vehicles for the exploration of intense female sexuality, extending even to its "perverse" forms. But Balzac's treatment of the subject appears daring in good measure because the courtesan-esque potential is present even in his well-bred women, who, as Proust noted, tend to behave like *filles* when moved by passion. Sexuality circulates across class lines, the low and the high meet, extremes converge.

In Sue, Fleur-de-Marie, promised to attempted redemption, is preserved from too much personal sexuality (as opposed to the male sexuality she has merely endured) by her pairing with another prostitute, La Louve ("the She-Wolf"), whose sexuality is explicit, and explicitly violent and bestial, both frightening and exciting:

La Louve was a large girl, twenty years old, agile, strapping in a virile way, and of quite regular features; her rude black hair shone with reddish tints; the ardor of her blood blotched her complexion; dark down shadowed her full lips; her chestnut eyebrows, thick and coarse, met over her large savage eyes; something violent, fierce, bestial, in the expression of the phys- iognomy of this woman; a kind of habitual mocking grin which, pulling back her upper lip during her fits of anger, revealed her widely-spaced white teeth, explained her given name, the She-Wolf. (Volume 5, p. 133)

Female sexuality is handled in this passage by its assignment to animal sexuality; rhetorically, the whole description is constructed to explain and justify the animal nickname, which in turn explains and justifies the presence of such overt sexuality. La Louve's sexual presence acts as "lightning rod" to draw away any undue worry on the reader's part about Fleur-de-Marie's inner relationship to the sexuality on which her trade is founded, and allows her to speak of the degradation of prostitution solely in moral terms. La Louve is deviant erotic body, while Fleur-de-Marie—who as the novel goes on appears increasingly passive, sweet, almost maidenly—becomes exclusively sold body. Yet, of course, it is she who will eventually succumb to the mark of the beast, die repining for an unrestorable virginity. Whereas La Louve, rehabilitated through Fleur-de-Marie's good offices, is married off to Martial who, originally a poacher and prostitute's consort, becomes a gamekeeper, legitimate hus- band, and father of a numerous progeny. (The poacher become gamekeeper is, of course, a good example of power inverted, turned from deviance and reinvested in policing.) The reason La Louve can survive rehabilitation while Fleur-de-Marie ultimately cannot must be attributed to social class: a prostitute may be reclaimed for the proletariat, become an honest working-class wife, but not for the bourgeoisie. There are limits. The sold body must have been deviant after all. La Louve shows Sue's humanitarian liberalism, whereas Fleur-de-Marie suggests its profoundly bourgeois char- acter and its limitations.

Parent-Duchatelet's *De la prostitution* is itself not exempt from these contradictions. As a piece of social-scientific research, it is remarkably advanced, consciously rejecting prejudice and received ideas in favor of a scrupulous examination of records and statistics.

The sections concerning the physiology and medical histories of prostitutes show considerable freedom from prejudice and folklore concerning female sexuality, and the discussions of the causes of prostitution insist upon poverty, illegitimacy, lack of education, and destitution, rather than moral turpitude. And yet, Parent-Duchatelet can turn around and talk about the moral degradation of these shameful creatures, who suffer all consequences as an inevitable result of "a first lapse from the most important of duties," that is, female chastity. Many chapters begin or end with sententious moral homilies, and the introduction to the study makes its apologia concerning the material to be treated by comparing this investigation to Parent-Duchatelet's earlier inquiry into the condition of the Paris sewer system: "Why should I blush to enter this other kind of cesspool (a cesspool more frightful, I admit, than all the others) in the hope of doing some good . . . ?"[15] Parent-Duchatelet's investigation, we realize, itself marks an exercise of power over the lower depths: it belongs to the larger nineteenth-century project of organizing and policing deviance. Even its exposition of the organization of prostitute society constitutes a surveillance of the criminal body, to use the terms suggested by Michel Foucault's book on nineteenth-century penology, *Surveiller et punir*.[16]

Foucault demonstrates the interdependence of policing and delinquence, criminality as a way of life—what we might call the criminal biography. Like the "carceral institution" itself, the text on criminality responds to the presence of deviance by the power of sight: there is a convergence of intent in the *panopticon* prison invented by Jeremy Bentham, the official investigative report, and the popular social novel. As Alain Corbin argues in his recent and thorough study, *Les Filles de noces*, throughout most of the nineteenth century French thought about prostitution was characterized principally by a *discours réglementariste*, predicated on the idea that one should not attempt to abolish prostitution but rather control it, confine it, keep track of it.[17] The dominant fear, Corbin claims, was prostitution become clandestine, looking like other than what it is. The fear of disguise and clandestinity touched directly on the problem of ex-prostitutes attempting to re-enter mainstream society: police regulations made erasure from the rolls of prostitution extremely difficult, and much reformist doctrine centered on this issue of erasure, *radiation*, arguing that reconversion to virtue should be facilitated. But the dominant view, for much of the century, seemed to be that society needs the deviant body yet needs to maintain that deviance in a marginal space where it can be watched, its trajectories carefully traced.

Sue's novel, in its contradictory attitudes toward the prostitute and in the limits it sets to its reformist verve, displays many of the same ambivalences as Parent-Duchatelet and his successors. Sue describes prostitution as a socially generated evil, insisting on its virtual inevitability in sectors of the proletariat where families are piled together in one room, where incest is common, where a girl's only salable commodity is her body, and he issues diatribes—applauded by the reformists—against a system that, after creating and tolerating prostitution, goes on to regularize and register it through the Bureau des Moeurs and to make rehabilitation nearly impossible. But in the case of Fleur-de-Marie, *radiation* cannot ensure real erasure of the marks of the sold body. What makes Sue's treatment of the prostitute most interesting, and subversive, is his response to the sexual body, which is most fully orchestrated in the episode—which created something of a scandal among his readers—in which Rodolphe uses the lascivious creole Cécily to provoke the downfall of the infamous *notaire* Jacques Ferrand, who quite literally dies of unsatisfied lust. Prostitution in *Les Mystères de Paris* is first and foremost the means of access to a lower world both psychic and social, the place where the manhole cover lifts up to reveal the existence of deviant possibilities. The bourgeoisie comes in contact both with the proletariat and with a "slumming" potential in itself by way of erotic curiosity mediated by money. No doubt this is a curious and ambivalent way to open up the question of the social depths, but it may with a certain historical inevitability have been the first way.

The prostitute, then, stands out as the key figure and term of access to that eminently storied subworld, realm of power, magic, and danger; she exemplifies the modern narratable. One of Balzac's witty courtesans, Suzanne du Val-Noble, exactly makes the point as she shows her guests around her sumptuously furnished apartment: "Voilà les comptes des mille et une nuits," she tells them ("Here are the accounts of a thousand and one nights").[18] The phrase plays on the "*Contes* des mille et une nuits"—the Thousand and One Nights, or Arabian Nights—to suggest that *accounts* in two senses, the narrative and the financial, are interchangeable; that in the life of a prostitute at least, the accounting gives something to recount, money and story flow from the same nights of sexual exchange. The ramifications of Suzanne du Val-Noble's pun are everywhere in *Illusions perdues*, whose very subject, in Georg Lukács's description, is the "capitalization of spirit"—the transformation into commodity of the products of intelligence—and whose intricate plots turn on recountings of accountings, and accountings for recountings.[19] That this aphorism, which might stand as epigraph to the whole of *La Comédie humaine*, should be spoken by a prostitute suggests how the narratable of Balzac's world is found in the conjunction of sexuality and monetary circulation. As Roland Barthes has suggested, money is the universal modern bourgeois signifier, tied to no referent (such as land), defining of value only in terms of its circulation. In the nexus of sexuality, money, and storytelling lie the source and subject of Sue's novel as well, and indeed also its mode of production.

Yet we face the further paradox that this novel so closely tied to new industrial means of production and commercial modes of finance and publicity created a kind of intimacy with its readers that almost evokes the Edenic context of oral storytelling that Benjamin uses as a utopian cultural standard in contrast to the privatized "fallen" world of the novel. Because publication of *Les Mystères de Paris* extended across some sixteen months—generally running four times weekly, but with some long interruptions when Sue ran out of copy—and because Sue had no very precise outline for the yet unwritten pages, not only could readers express their responses to the novel, Sue could respond to their responses in future installments. The result was a dialogue that shaped both the ideology and the form of the novel. Since many of the letters to Sue have been preserved, we can study the readers' responses, for instance, the demands that Le Chourineur, a favorite character whom Sue had sent off to Algeria, return to the novel (Sue complied); that the wicked Martial family be thoroughly punished; that the virtuous seamstress Rigolette be protected from all lurking seducers; and that Fleur-de-Marie variously be granted full rehabilitation, or a life devoted to serving the poor, or orphans, or the church—letters written from a sense of foreboding that Sue was preparing a somber end to his fiction.[20] A number of readers appeared ready to take the fictional for the real: they implored Sue to dispatch Rodolphe to arrest criminal designs, or Clémence d'Harville to succor the unfortunate. Other readers argued rather that the creator of Rodolphe and Clémence d'Harville must himself have a compassionate soul, and thus stand ready to help: the calls for Sue's charity were numerous.

More interesting is the evidence that Sue's fictional situations were mirrored in real life: time and again, his correspondents come forward with descriptions and stories to confirm those in the novel. Thus Sue's readers provided him with the "hard" information he sometimes lacked, as well as material suggestive of future episodes. In addition, social reformers and socialists of various persuasions sent exhortations, tracts, and books, some of which made their mark, for instance Prosper Tarbé's *Travail et salaire* (1841), which Sue will mention in a note to his text. Other readers, often members of the professions, offered schemes for reform: of the law courts (proposing in particular the institution of public defenders for the indigent), of the penal system, of orphanages, and even of the pawnshop. Sometimes the correspondents were able to point to existing projects—workers' benevolent associations, agricultural cooperatives—that seemed to meet Sue's reformist views; and sometimes they told of new institutions—an orphanage, a hospice for the destitute—created in response to the impact of *Les Mystères de Paris*. Others, finally, implored Sue to extend his penetrating vision to further areas of abuse and injustice in order to make of his novel a full new scripture of humanity.

The most interesting and moving of the letters to Sue may be those that contain "counter-stories" elicited by the novel: letters, usually from the poor and sometimes marginally literate, that extend and supplement *Les Mystères de Paris* as they confirm it. For instance, one Louise Crombach, who identifies herself as a "surveillante surnuméraire à Saint-Lazare," writes to thank Sue for making the public appreciate the role of the prison *surveillante*, whom society tends to denigrate since it stigmatizes the warden along with the prisoner. Sue has helped her to understand her job as a mission and an apostolate. As she goes on to describe her work with the female thieves and prostitutes under her care, she more and more espouses their condition, confounding policing and criminality, reversing perspectives through the play of sympathy:

> Poor and obscure like the poorest and most obscure of our prisoners, raised like them by indigent and ignorant parents, like them having been cold and hungry in the streets during the whole of my childhood, I necessarily felt myself attracted to them! Not being able to provide for myself and for two old people, devoting all my time to charity work in the prisons, after two years as a volunteer in this service I had to ask for a job, which provides my daily bread and lets me stay in the midst of my poor captive sisters. . . . If you only knew, Sir, what riches of the heart! how many resources are hidden deep in these souls that are merely *paralyzed*. And then, they are of the people, as am I. I speak the same language and, especially, I understand and I love it, for it is the language of my mother! [21]

It is not only that this has the force of witness, and that it gives voice, for a moment, to a consciousness unrecorded by official history. It is also that we grasp here the power of narrative, even the lurid melodramatic fictional narrative, to generate narrative, and the power of reading to illuminate not merely the text read but other texts of everyday life as well, creating new possibilities of meaning in the world. Eventually, such a reading is transformatory, both of the life led by Louise Crombach and our understanding of *Les Mystères de Paris*. The text of the novel does not change, but its potentialities are transformed by the proliferation of narratives it provokes. Here we may understand something more about our uses of and our need for narrative plots.

The most decisive moment of reader-recognition and reader-participation appears to have come with Sue's introduction, well into the novel, of the jewel-cutter Morel, the poor and honest artisan who lives and labors in a cold garret with his four children, his invalid wife, and her idiot mother, and whose misfortunes, and victimization, accumulate with relentless progression: one child dead of malnutrition and exposure; his daughter Louise seduced, made pregnant, then accused of infanticide upon her child's death; Morel himself accused of theft, cleared through Rodolphe's intervention, then reduced not only to penury but to madness by Louise's misfortunes, confined among the insane at Bicêtre prison, and his family left in total destitution. Morel's story unfolds with all the excruciating excess of melodrama, but for thousands of Sue's readers, the melodrama was *of* reality. In the situation of Morel, Sue touched on a scandal from which there was no escape through moralizing: the lot of the honest artisan victimized by a system that made even hard labor insufficient to assure protection from pauperization, and guaranteed that a single misfortune would quickly plunge a whole family into depths of misery. Here were the powerless, more serious stuff for reformers and socialists than the lurid criminal population of the Ile de la Cité. Yet it remains within the logic of Sue's descent, via the prostitute, into the social depths that pauperization should be discovered through criminality, the laboring classes by way of the dangerous classes, the sold body from the deviant body.

It may be significant that the publication of *Les Mystères de Paris* in the *Journal des Débats* ended, following Fleur-de-Marie's death at Gerolstein, with an open letter from Sue to the paper's editor-in-chief, drawing the attention of readers to a new periodical, *La Ruche Populaire*, written and produced exclusively by workers and addressed to their interests, which in its first issue takes its epigraph, concerning the idea of the "police of virtue," and indeed its inspiration, from *Les Mystères de Paris*. Sue, that is, closes his *novel* with announcement of a *newspaper* that will continue his work; and he ends his letter to the editor by recapitulating a four-point legislative program aimed toward the relief of social misery. The novel passes on into the world of the readers, whom it has defined and who have defined it, becoming part of the movement toward reform and social justice, putting itself at the service of a political world discovered by way of the melodramatic fiction.

There was an assumption on the part of his readers that Sue himself was ready to move from fiction to action when the moment presented itself in 1848. His election as socialist deputy representing working-class *arrondissements* of Paris came as a direct response to his novels, particularly *Les Mystères de Paris.* When the dream of 1848 collapsed into bourgeois reaction after the bloodbath of the June Days, Sue in a final novel, the twelve volumes of *Les Mystères du Peuple* (1849–57), summed up in a fictional history of a French proletarian family from the time of the ancient Gauls to the betrayal of the June Days of 1848, demonstrating (in accord with the theories of the historian Augustin Thierry) that the French ruling classes are descended from the Frankish invader, while the people, oppressed throughout history, are the true children of the Gauls, who will one day reclaim their homeland and overthrow the tyrants. Thus 1848 is made to appear only one more episode in a long struggle toward justice, equality, and freedom, and betrayal by the bourgeoisie a repeated historical pattern. *Les Mystères du Peuple*—sixty thousand copies of which were seized and destroyed in mid-publication by Louis-Napoleon's censors, while Sue was living out his last months as an exile in Savoie—makes it evident that Sue's socialism was sincere, if sentimental, based on humanitarian and fraternal sympathies rather than a cogent analysis of capitalism and the class struggle. As his famous conception of the "police of virtue" (which particularly drew Marx's ire) well implies, Sue's stance is tinged with bourgeois paternalism; it never wholly ceases to resemble Clémence d'Harville's condescension to the wretched of Saint-Lazare who are capable of redemption, but only within limits. And the body of the prostitute, stamped with excitement, fear, pity, and adventure, remains the token of his entry into the underclass.

Nonetheless, *Les Mystères de Paris* constitutes a remarkable descent beneath the "vast smug surface" of society, to use Henry James's words in his preface to *The Princess Casamassima*, his own attempt to plumb the social depths. Before "social realism" could become a watchword—and perhaps with greater effect than was ever achieved by more sober novels—the lurid and melodramatic fiction opens up social concerns, makes them imaginatively available. That the point of entry into the depths should be found in prostitution has the logic of connection, as also of uncanny metaphor. Here, sexuality, money, danger, deviance converge to form a powerful potential for story. "Les Comptes des mille et une nuits" offers the best source of a contemporary Arabian Nights of Paris in the era of capitalist development. In the story of Fleur-de-Marie, the arabesque of the transgressive, hyperbolic plot plays itself out to an end that signals the inevitable victory of social policing power over the sexually aberrant body, yet records also the ineffaceable mark of the sold body. Like its heroine, Sue's novel may be judged to have received the mark of the beast, and with the same ambivalent messages. "Sombre et cruel spectacle!" writes Sue in presenting the tableau of Morel and his family reduced to the final extremities. In this insistent invitation to see—both to be spectator at and to bear witness to—the drama of a misery both real and melodramatically heightened, Sue's narrative suggests both its force and its limitations, the ambiguous power of half-understood discoveries.

Sue's fusion of the popular in terms of subject, audience, and form of publication makes him the logical and necessary example in any exploration of serialization and its relation to narrative meanings. Yet Sue is by no means the popular novel's most accomplished plotter, in our common understanding of plotting as the masterful management of suspense and mystery, artfully leading the reader through an elaborate dilatory space that is always full of signs to be read, but always menaced with misreading until the very end. The novelist who would most claim our attention here is no doubt Wilkie Collins, who at the height of his career was the century's best-selling and highest-paid novelist in English. Collins apparently used to argue with his friend and employer Dickens about the relative merits of "plots of surprise," which Dickens preferred, and "plots of suspense," which Collins so consummately practiced. Through his success, Collins pushed Dickens toward the more suspenseful plots of his maturity, in *A Tale of Two Cities* and *Great Expectations*, for instance, which alternated with Collins's productions in the columns of Dickens's periodical, *All the Year Round*.[22] *The Woman in White*, Collins's masterpiece in the genre of the thriller, appeared in weekly installments in *All the Year Round* over some eight and a half months, and kept the English reading public in thrall as, some twenty years earlier, Sue had held the French. Collins uses the periodization of serial publication to delay, divert, and spin out the narrative. As in the later detective novel *The Moonstone*, he uses multiple narrators to maintain interest and to create a nearly epistemological form of suspense, a deep uncertainty of perspective. It is within the logic of its multiple narrative perspectives and voices that *The Woman in White* should be filled with readers and the exchange of written texts. Each narrator's act of narration is explicitly motivated: the keeping of a record is the necessary way to the eventual unveiling of the obdurate mysteries. At the center of the novel stands Marian Halcombe's diary, which, at the moment she falls ill and ceases to write, is read by the villain it seeks to track, Count Fosco—a remarkable moment of reversal in which our readerly intimacy with Marian is violated, our act of reading adulterated by profane eyes, made secondary to the villain's reading and indeed dependent on his permission. We then continue with a number of narratives that are in the nature of depositions, solicited (we later learn) by Walter Hartright to build his case for the true identity of Laura Fairlie, Lady Glyde: including a deposition labeled "The Narrative of the Tombstone," an ultimate, graven text that will turn out to be false, written by the villains. The most important text of all, predictably, concerns origins: the parish register in which Sir Perceval Glyde has forged the entry testifying to his parents' marriage. It is his attempt to destroy the register before it is read by his enemies that brings Sir Perceval's fiery end. There is much rereading and reinterpreting of these and other evidentiary narratives—and eventually the arch-villain Fosco will be forced into inditing his own narrative, filling in (with high literary gusto) the remaining narrative blanks. Collins's world is a veritable utopia of reading and writing, pursued both for the solution of enigmas and their prolongation in suspense, in the pleasure of the text: the best possible case of plot for plot's sake.

It is perhaps with this image of the slightly perverse, dilatory, almost fetishistic text of narrative pleasure that we may best end this brief exploration of the popular novel. Collins's representation of readers and writers constantly scribbling and constantly reading one another, even when they weren't meant to, suggests an image of the popular serial novel as a prelapsarian age of unlimited storytelling and the unlimited consumption of story: a world in which narrative, whatever the subject, enormously mattered. Yet, of course, the age of the popular serial novel was tied firmly to the new industrial means and modes of production and distribution, to the devouring presses that it had to feed. With the vastly increased circulation of fact goes a similarly multiplied circulation of fictions. The middle decades of the nineteenth century seemed to have an unlimited appetite for narrative.

7

Retrospective Lust,
or Flaubert's Perversities

The novels of Flaubert appear to us today to mark a turning point in the history of the novel. Any discussion of plot and the sense of plottedness needs to confront Flaubert, since his relation to traditional uses of plot can only be described as perverse. His mature work is indeed carefully structured by a systematic perversion of plot as a central system of narrative organization and meaning. The development of perversion as a system becomes evident as one follows its uses from *Madame Bovary* through *L'Education sentimentale* to the unfinished *Bouvard et Pécuchet*, this last a glorious summa of what can be done to parody and explode the ordering discourses elaborated over the ages by mankind to make sense of nature, society, and human history. My choice to focus on *L'Education sentimentale* is motivated by the judgment that it is Flaubert's most fully accomplished and most ambitious novel—the history of his generation, he called it—and also by the generic reference of its title and theme to the "novel of education," which puts it squarely in the main tradition of nineteenth-century plots and allows us to see its intertextual relations to such precursors as Stendhal and Balzac. *L'Education sentimentale* is in fact a novel whose tenuous readability depends directly on its intertextual support, its presupposition of a certain standard novelistic mode which it resolutely refuses to endorse.[1]

Most explicitly and importantly, the intertextual referent of *L'Education sentimentale* is the Balzacian novel, which for Flaubert's generation (and still perhaps for our own) best defines what the dramatic and significant novel is all about. Yet the "Balzacian novel" does not by itself seem an adequate term to describe the entire presuppositional ground of *L'Education sentimentale*: in a novel even more explicitly intimate with the historical evolution of modern French politics and society than most of Balzac's, Flaubert takes on history itself as a signifying system and a sense-making discourse. The novel reaches its climax in the events of the Revolution of 1848, which are supposed to be part of its protagonist's history, elements in the demonstrations worked by his plot of education. Hence my discussion of plotting in *L'Education sentimentale* can be set against a ground defined by the practice of the novel as represented by Balzac and the uses of history as represented by the Revolution of 1848 and its aftermath.

I

Balzac's novels are explicitly present in *L'Education sentimentale*. In the second chapter of the novel, Frédéric Moreau is reunited with his old schoolmate and closest friend, Charles Deslauriers, who advises him to cultivate the acquaintance of the banker Dambreuse, becoming his wife's lover if necessary. When Frédéric protests, Deslauriers replies that he is simply offering classic advice: "Remember Rastignac in the *Comédie humaine*! You'll succeed, I'm sure of it!"[2] This reference, early in the novel, to the best-known of Balzac's ambitious young heroes is the first in a series of allusions to episodes of the *Comédie humaine*, all of them formulated by Deslauriers. He later reminds Frédéric of their early resolve to "imitate *les Treize* of Balzac": that is, to constitute a secret society of strongmen for their mutual aid and success (p. 185). In an unlabeled allusion that is nonetheless perfectly clear to the reader of Balzac, Deslauriers argues his theory of how *le monde*—Parisian high society—functions: "A Parisian dinner party, meeting a well-placed personage, the smile of a beautiful woman, could, by a series of actions logically connected, have gigantic results. Certain Parisian drawing rooms were like those machines which take matter in its

raw form and give it back centupled in value. He believed in courtesans counselling diplomats, in rich marriages obtained by in-
trigues, in the genius of jailbirds, in the docility of fortune in the
hands of the strong" (p. 111).[3] Each phrase here alludes to a specific
Balzacian plot element, and the whole reads as Deslauriers's understanding of the dynamics of Balzacian plot. Moreover, Deslauriers announces the key to the dynamics as well: "The clerk had
his theories. In order to obtain things, it was enough to desire them
strongly" (p. 107). Deslauriers is a good enough reader of Balzac
to have seized the essence: that the concentration of desire pro-
jected onto the world as will constitutes the *primum mobile* of plot,
leverage on circumstance, movement forward and upward. The
ambitious Deslauriers stands as the figure of the Balzacian novel
within Flaubert's novel. And it is part of Flaubert's almost didactic
demonstration that however well Deslauriers understands the system of the Balzacian novel, he is doomed to failure in the Flaubertian novel. Deslauriers will by the end stand as the figure of a
failed will to power, as Frédéric will be that of a failed sentimental
and erotic passion.

To anticipate outcomes, one can find an implicit comment on
the dénouement of the Balzacian plot of ambition when Frédéric
attends M. Dambreuse's funeral, in Père-Lachaise cemetery. The
scene alludes to the famous close of *Le Père Goriot*, where Rastignac,
after burying "the last tear of youth" in Goriot's grave, stands at
the summit of this hill of the dead and looks out over Paris lying
at his feet, possessing with his glance that world of high society
demarcated by the Column of the Place Vendôme on the one hand
and the Dome of the Invalides on the other (Napoleonic markers,
both of them), seeking to "pump the honey" from this beehive of
power, money, and love, and concludes with his celebrated challenge to the City and Society: "A nous deux maintenant!"—the
dueler's announcement that he is ready to begin combat. Paris here
has become a legible topography and text of manners for Rastignac:
his dominating height and panoramic vision presage the extraordinary success that will be chronicled in subsequent volumes of the
Comédie humaine.[4]

The burial of Dambreuse—staged by Frédéric who, like Rastignac for Goriot, has made all the "arrangements"—reads as a res-
olute de-dramatization of its intertext. The record of the six eulogies
pronounced in the name of various societies with which Dambreuse
was connected insists on their verbal and intellectual nullity, their
composition from a tissue of clichés. As the mourners leave to
return to their occupations, we are told: "the ceremony hadn't
lasted too long; they congratulated themselves on this" (p. 413). At
the center of the scene, we have a description of the steeply sloping
terrain of the cemetery, and the descriptive glance continues on to
what one can see from it: "One has under one's feet the green tree
tops; further on, the chimneys of fire pumps, then the whole of
the great city." Then, in a one-sentence paragraph, we are told:
"Frédéric was able to admire the view while the speeches were going
on." And that is all: there is no last tear of youth, no visionary
possession, no challenge: no attempt to dramatize the situation of
death and ambition (Frédéric will soon be engaged to marry the
widowed Mme Dambreuse), no attempt to read the significance of
the place, the position, the moment. This is the essential point: the
failed coherence of the Balzacian "system" of will, desire, and ambition produces a failure of coherence in the novelistic plot itself,
a refusal of the narrative to achieve the kinds of significance that
we expect from narrative arrangements of experience—or simply
from narrative arrangements of discourse.

Of the putative hero, Frédéric, we learn on the second page of
the novel: "He found that the happiness merited by the excellence
of his soul was slow in coming" ("Il trouvait que le bonheur mérité
par l'excellence de son âme tardait à venir") (p. 34). The sentence—
as is so often the case in this novel—appears all the more treacherous the more one looks at it, in part because it offers a typical
instance of how Flaubert's use of *style indirect libre* or "free indirect
discourse" (of which more later) thoroughly confounds the attribution of judgment and tone. The principal verb of the sentence,
Il trouvait, offers the rest as Frédéric's sentiment, yet the use of
trouvait rather than *pensait* ("thought") or *se disait* ("said to himself")
appears at least to pseudo-objectify the sentiment, as if it were an

objective condition there to be found. Then, *le bonheur mérité par l'excellence de son âme* can be read as simply the standard illusion of youth, that a sensitive soul deserves and will attain happiness, or more specifically as the illusion of youth fed on Romantic readings—a number of Frédéric's literary enthusiasms, of the most self-exalting Romantic type, will be enumerated a few pages later—or possibly as a more judgmental irony on the part of the narrator: *l'excellence de son âme* surely teeters on the brink of mockery in the absence of any objective validation. Had the longings of the soul been spoken of, or its feelings or aspirations, there would be less of a problem, since these are subjectively verifiable, whereas "excellence" is one of those words—and we will encounter many other cases—that bewilder as to their source: whose word is it, Frédéric's, the impersonal narrator's, Flaubert's own?[5] Furthermore, that this happiness delays in coming also raises problems of agency: the construction of the sentence gives the distinct impression that Frédéric expects this happiness, the just recompense of his soul's merits, to come by itself, without his doing anything. And this is an impression that the rest of the novel will only confirm, since, as we have already suggested, there seems to be a problem of will and desire, an inability of the hero to invest the world and his career with coherent and sustained desire.

The situation of Frédéric and his plot may be illuminated by an argument advanced by André Malraux in an essay on Choderlos de Laclos's *Les Liaisons dangereuses*, where he suggests that the Vicomte de Valmont marks the end of the traditional hero and the start of something new, what he calls the *personnage significatif*: the significant and signifying character, whose acts are premeditated, based on a conception of the self which structures and gives meaning to his plot, conceived as an intrigue.[6] Such a character, says Malraux, must have a decisive sense of man's goal, the will to reach the goal, and then a methodical system for reaching it. Malraux's representative figures, beyond Valmont, are Julien Sorel, Vautrin, Rastignac, Raskolnikov, Ivan Karamazov; and he notes Flaubert's explicit reversal of this tradition: "Flaubert's characters are often Balzac's characters conceived in the mode of failure rather than success: Madame Bovary become mistress of the Château de la Vaubyessard [where she briefly discovers a glamorous world, at the Vicomte's ball] is a novel by Balzac, and *L'Education sentimentale* is Balzac's *Illusions perdues* whose author no longer believes in ambition."

This both correctly identifies the pertinent intertext and suggests the perverse reversal of perspective on plot that Flaubert has worked. The energies associated with the Romantic hero and his avatars seem to dissipate remarkably quickly in this novel, as if the steam engine had sprung leaks in its valves. When Frédéric imagines his future happiness, it takes forms that suggest passivity, a decadence of desire: "Frédéric furnished a Moorish palace for himself, to live reclining on divans of cashmere, amidst the murmur of a fountain, waited on by negro pages; and these things dreamed of became so well defined that they saddened him, as if he had lost them" (p. 85). Desire here (as so often in Flaubert's novels) creates hallucinatory scenarios of its satisfaction,[7] yet in doing so it reaches at once over and through its objects, exhausting them in the realm of the imaginary, reaching a regret for their fictive loss before their actual possession. The dynamics of ambition are lost.

The problem cannot be confined to the "hero": it is not simply an issue in "character." As Malraux suggests, it is not only Frédéric who no longer believes in ambition, but also the very novel in which he figures. Proust made essentially the same point when, in his remarkable essay on Flaubert, he undertook to show how Flaubert's style, the construction of paragraphs and chapters, the rhythms of sentences, work to de-dramatize the novel, indeed to de-novelize it.[8] The Balzacian novel is constructed precisely on a dramatic, even a theatrical, model, by which will and action are plotted toward major "showdowns," scenes of confrontation in which characters act out, give full expression to the issues in conflict, and where the dramatic moment produces changed relations, a significant outcome to the problems posed. And one can legitimately argue that Balzac defines and illustrates the main tradition of the novel, the tradition as understood by Dickens, Dostoevsky, James, Proust, Hardy, Malraux, Faulkner, for instance.

Proust, Malraux, and other perceptive critics of Flaubert (notably Gérard Genette and Jonathan Culler) have detailed various ways in which Flaubert works to disappoint our expectations of drama and coherence. Culler in particular analyzes Flaubert's role as "demoralizer," his use of the twin tropes of irony and stupidity to "deconstruct" our usual systems for constructing meaning and significance from the elements of the novelistic world. Novels, Culler says, tend to offer us "paradigms of organization" which invite us to "read our own lives as novels," thus opening up opportunities for the demoralizer intent upon denying the validity of life as the novelistic.[9] From my perspective, Flaubert's designifying practice becomes most interesting and significant when considered in the interanimating context of traditional novelistic sense-making. As, for instance, in the work of a "new novelist" such as Alain Robbe-Grillet, the fragmentary structures of the detective story remain present in a text which does not believe in any clear truth of incident or motive to be detected, and these residual structures provide a necessary armature of readability—the signals of a possible narrative construction that are necessary to the reader's exploration of the text's redefinitions of "meaning"—so in Flaubert the model of the Balzacian novel is ever present as an "as-if," a model against which to play. The result of this play is not nothingness but an uncertain vacillation of meaning and its impossibility, a troubled search, through inadequate traditional systems of meaning, for a decision about whether any order of signs and sense could create a significant version of life and history.

We could restate the problem by recalling Barthes's eloquent remark that the reading of narrative, traditionally, is animated by the "passion for (of) meaning." We read no doubt for the satisfaction of all sorts of passions, but surely always aroused by the passion to know, to find and to make sense: to find out, to discover "how it comes out," if not "whodunit"; to discover the semantic ordering conferred on experience by the shape of fiction. But *L'Education sentimentale* continually denies us the satisfactions of full meaning, significance, and even signification. A paragraph near the start of the novel, describing Frédéric's boat trip up the Seine, concludes, as if in warning: "The countryside was completely empty. In the sky were motionless small white clouds—and boredom, vaguely pervasive, seemed to slow the progress of the boat and make the appearance of the voyagers yet more insignificant" (pp. 35–36). The sentence may be taken as emblematic: we as readers expect that voyages will lead somewhere, and that the voyagers who fare forth on them will make not only their goal but their experience along the way the source of significance. To be told that we are scarcely advancing, in the company of the insignificant, makes us wonder why we are to bother at all with a five-hundred-page novel. And this, I think, is a fairly accurate report of a reader's initial reaction to the novel. If the reader goes on to find certain pleasures in reading *L'Education sentimentale*—to find it, perhaps, an indispensable as well as a frustrating book—it is in a radically redefined mode of reading, a redefinition of what it means to "read a novel."

What is at stake, then, is the traditional readability of the novelistic text. The world of *L'Education sentimentale* is not invested with the coherence and significance traditionally conferred on it by the protagonist's desiring. Furthermore, past, present, and future are not held together by the temporal bonding created by scenarios of desire, seeking realization of its objects—themselves often a creation of the past—in a conceived future. Hence the relation of the protagonist to his world and to plotting has been radically altered from the Balzacian model. As a result, the reader's relation to the protagonist, and to the novel itself, has also undergone a profound change. No longer can the reader espouse the protagonist's desire, no longer can he read in the forward-moving expectation created by the force of that desire. The binding, totalizing work of Eros seems to have reached a halt.

I want now to focus more closely on the question of desire, and the novelistic results of Frédéric's relation to the role of novelistic protagonist. Early in his Parisian existence, Frédéric strolls in the Tuileries Gardens—in the hope of seeing Mme Arnoux—and in fine weather he extends his promenades the length of the Champs-Elysées. The passage that follows, describing the world of Parisian luxury, makes reference to a passage from Balzac's *Illusions perdues*, also set in the Champs-Elysées, where Lucien de Rubempré, who has just received a note of dismissal from his protectress, Mme de Bargeton, wanders as the alienated outsider excluded from the world of luxury. In the bedazzling press of carriages and their fashionable occupants, and the gentlemen on horseback paying court to them, Lucien comes upon Mme de Bargeton and her cousin Mme d'Espard (the "summit" of Faubourg Saint-Germain society)—both of whom had announced themselves "indisposed"—and they simply ignore his pedestrian presence; while the dandy Henri de Marsay, who is in attendance on them, eyes Lucien doubtfully through his lorgnon, then lets it fall so singularly that it appears to Lucien "the fall of the blade of the guillotine," signifying his social execution. Lucien's reaction offers no surprise to the habitual reader of Balzac: " 'Great Heavens, gold at any price!' Lucien said to himself. ' . . . I'll triumph. I'll roll down this avenue in a *calèche* complete with footman! I'll have some Marquises d'Espard!' " [10] And he will in fact realize these declarations of desire, with phenomenal rapidity. The experience of exclusion from the desirable world inevitably triggers in the Balzacian protagonist an intense flow of desire and its concentration on the objects invested with desirability, an almost magnetic impulsion toward their possession. To want to have is to be: the self—as in *La Peau de chagrin*—is most typically and fully the self in a state of arousal.

It is worth quoting the whole of the central paragraph in the corresponding passage of *L'Education sentimentale*:

Women, nonchalantly seated in barouches, their veils fluttering in the breeze, passed close by him at the steady pace of their horses with a slight swaying that made the polished leather creak. The carriages became more and more numerous and, slowing down beyond the Rond-Point, they filled the entire avenue. Mane was next to mane, lantern next to lantern; steel stirrups, silver curb-chains, brass buckles threw out points of light here and there among the knee breeches, the white gloves, and the furs hanging over the crests emblazoned on the carriage doors. He felt as if he were lost in a far-off world. His

eyes wandered over the women's faces; and vague resemblances recalled Mme Arnoux. He imagined her amidst the
others, in one of those little broughams, like Mme Dambreuse's
brougham. But now the sun was setting, and the cold wind
stirred up swirling clouds of dust. The coachmen tucked their
chins into their neckcloths, wheels started to turn faster, the
pavement grated; and all the carriages moved down the long
avenue at a brisk trot, pressing against one another, passing,
pulling apart, then, in the Place de la Concorde, scattering.
Behind the Tuileries, the sky took on the color of the slate
roofs. The trees of the garden formed two huge masses, violet
at the top. The gas-lamps lit up; and the Seine, greenish in all
its length, was torn into strips of silky silver against the piles
of the bridges. (pp. 54–55)

[Des femmes, nonchalamment assises dans des calèches, et
dont les voiles flottaient au vent, défilaient près de lui, au pas
ferme de leurs chevaux, avec un balancement insensible qui
faisait craquer les cuirs vernis. Les voitures devenaient plus
nombreuses, et, se ralentissant à partir du Rond-Point, elles
occupaient toute la voie. Les crinières étaient près des crinières,
les lanternes près des lanternes; les étriers d'acier, les gour-
mettes d'argent, les boucles de cuivre, jetaient çà et là des points
lumineux entre les culottes courtes, les gants blancs et les four-
rures qui retombaient sur le blason des portières. Il se sentait
comme perdu dans un monde lointain. Ses yeux erraient sur
les têtes féminines; et de vagues ressemblances amenaient à sa
memoire Mme Arnoux. Il se la figurait, au milieu des autres,
dans un de ces petits coupés, pareils au coupé de Mme Dambreuse.—Mais le soleil se couchait, et le vent froid soulevait
des tourbillons de poussière. Les cochers baissaient le menton
dans leurs cravates, les roues se mettaient à tourner plus vite,
le macadam grinçait; et tous les équipages descendaient au
grand trot la longue avenue, en se frôlant, se dépassant, s'é-
cartant les uns des autres, puis, sur la place de la Concorde,
se dispersaient. Derrière les Tuileries, le ciel prenait la teinte

des ardoises. Les arbres du jardin formaient deux masses én-
ormes, violacées par le sommet. Les becs de gaz s'allumaient;
et la Seine, verdâtre dans toute son étendue, se déchirait en
moires d'argent contre les piles des ponts.]

Here is the same world of Parisian luxury evoked in *Illusions perdues*,
detailed, even more than in Balzac—who is nonetheless the master
of what we might call the Parisian "accessory"—through its smallest
elements: the polished leather, the furs and the gloves, and the
stirrups, silver curb-chains, brass buckles which become, along with
the lanterns, so many luminous points, catching and reflecting the
late afternoon sun. What more and more seems to preside at the
composition (the painterly analogy is forced on us) of the first part
of the paragraph is the play of sunlight, which provides visual
highlights, selects the details. When we reach Frédéric, he is lost,
like Lucien, but without in his case encountering the objects of
either desire or resentment. His eyes "wander" without coming to
focus. The lack of an object for Frédéric's dispossessed glance points
to a more general devaluation of human agency in the passage,
which may be consubstantial with a lack of human desire investing
the world. Frédéric is characterized by a vague imagining of Mme
Arnoux in this world, but never by a decision to put her or himself
there. There is no passage to arousal, no gesture of future possession. As a result, the described world, though it is clearly by
conventional standards eminently desirable, does not appear to be
animated by human desire: it remains other, a world of surfaces
contemplated for themselves. And just at the point where we expect
a reaction and a decision from the human agent, we pass from
Frédéric through a *mais* that marks a change in the hour and the
weather—what we might call an atmospheric change—which leads
back to the objects themselves, now jolted into faster motion as they
head down the Champs-Elysées.

The descriptive glance now apparently has nothing to do with
Frédéric's angle of vision; it seems rather to follow some other
compositional principle, clearly painterly in intent, sweeping down
the avenue after the retreating carriages, then noticing the evening

sky over the Tuileries (that is, behind the Place de la Concorde), then the effect of the trees in the setting sun, the lighting of the lamps, and, finally, the Seine, dark but streaked with light where it meets the bridges. It might be possible to attribute all that is observed to the perspective of Frédéric (assuming far fewer buildings along the avenue in the 1840s than there are today, when one cannot see the Seine from the Champs-Elysées) but there is no compelling reason for doing so, since we are given no indication of his personal investment in the seen. The human agency within the text seems to have been set aside in favor of a recording and composing vision of a more impersonal sort which finally insists, not on the human, but on the aesthetic: on a superior beauty that can be found in the play of light and mass in a world voided of human actors. If there is significance here, it is not that of the human subject as vehicle of desire and focus of the plot of ambition, but rather that of a world viewed, an aesthetic vision shared, over the head of the protagonist, by the reader and whoever it is—a narrator so uncharacterized we might as well call him the author?— who sees, arranges, writes this beautiful and inhuman text. As is so very often the case in this novel, the significant—possibly even redemptive—picture of the world is offered as an aesthetic vision in which the actors of the novel do not appear to participate.

Balzac's *La Peau de chagrin* suggested in an allegorical mode that a world disinvested of desire—the world as Raphaël de Valentin attempts to live it in part three of the novel, "The Agony"—is ugly, inert, alien: a world seen through those special opera glasses that distort lines and destroy form. The world seen in *L'Education sentimentale* is often beautiful—many critics have noted how often Flaubert makes us think of the paintings of Degas and Manet—but it does not appear to be the hero's desiring eyes that make it so. Rather, there is another glance at work, a superior aesthetic desire exercised by the hidden yet present artist. This aesthetic desire, deployed at a distance from the traditional novelistic registers of character and plot, brings no coherence to *L'Education sentimentale* *qua* novel, whatever else it may offer, if anything, in the place of the novelistic—a question to which I shall return. In talking about the novel, the coherence of its plot and its imagined human world, one is forced to the conclusion that it reveals a problem in desire: its lack of durable potency, an inability to maintain that aroused state of the self that characterizes the typical nineteenth-century narrative.

Frédéric will in fact enter the world of Parisian luxury, but unlike Lucien de Rubempré and his peers he will accede to it without doing much of anything, remaining largely a passive agent. As we move through the last chapter of part one of the novel, we have a series of peripeties that might have furnished the plot of an entire novel by Balzac: Frédéric, who has finally passed his law exams and sees before him "an interminable series of years full of love" (p. 120), goes home to visit his mother in Nogent, to discover that the family fortune has been heavily compromised, that he is "Ruined, destitute, lost!" (p. 122). Sinking into provincial lassitude, Frédéric allows his mother to arrange a clerkship for him with the local *avoué* and drifts toward a sentimental attachment with the neighbor's daughter, Louise Roque. Then one day a letter arrives informing him that he has inherited the wealth of a rich uncle. At once, the possibility of a Parisian existence captures him as a "hallucination," a life with Mme Arnoux at its center, furnished with all the accessories of the Champs-Elysées passage: "bringing her a present wrapped in tissue paper while outside would be standing his tilbury, no, a brougham rather! a black brougham, with a footman in brown livery; he heard his horse snorting and the noise of the curb-chain mingling with the murmur of their kisses" (p. 129). The hallucination quickly extends to furnishings for the imagined apartment: "the dining room would be in red leather, the boudoir in yellow silk, divans everywhere! And what cabinets, what china vases, what carpets!" This hallucinatory scenario of desire fulfilled is of course focused by the desired woman, Mme Arnoux, but it characteristically fragments into what may appear to be synecdoches, parts that represent a totality that may be labeled (in Balzacian fashion) luxury and love. Yet we may wonder whether they are true synecdoches, whether they ever really evoke the harmonious whole they allude to. They seem rather a string of random metonymies, moving from one *article de luxe* to another, from one accessory to another without ever naming—even in visionary form—the essential act of possession of the desired woman. We never accede to a full image, we are left with fragments. Our sense that desire is somehow enfeebled is confirmed when Frédéric's mother—who would prefer him to put the inheritance to productive use in the provinces—asks him what he intends to do if he returns to Paris, and Frédéric answers: "Nothing!"

What would have been the matter for several chapters of breathtaking twists and reversals in Balzac's writing here occupies under ten pages of undramatized presentation, ending with the protagonist, passive recipient of great wealth, returning to Paris to do nothing. The return leads him to the episode of the masked ball presided over by the courtesan Rosanette Bron, herself *en travestie* as "la Maréchale," where the costumes of the collected women represent different forms of erotic possibility. This chapter—the first installment of Frédéric as rich inheritor in Paris—ends in a dream, beginning in "the hallucination of first sleep," in which he sees pass before him different bodily parts of the different costumed women of the ball, "the shoulders of the Fishwife, the back of the Stevedore, the ankles of the Polish beauty, the hair of the Savagess" (p. 159). The erotic object—the female body—is fragmented, a *corps morcelé* that offers no focus and no hold for desire. As we move to the chapter's end, Frédéric slips deeper into sleep, to dream that he is "harnessed next to Arnoux, in the shafts of a cab," while Rosanette, "La Maréchale," is astride him, "ripping open his flanks with her golden spurs." The final image of desire is passive and masochistic, offering no promise of Frédéric's dominion over the objects of desire, indeed no hope of his ever reuniting the fragmented parts of the body. The action of desire remains radically discontinuous; it does not work as an ordering principle; it offers no anticipation of arrest and cohesion.

When Frédéric eventually becomes the lover of Mme Dambreuse, who represents the apex of high bourgeois society, he demonstrates that he has very much found a place within the desirable world. Well before that, he enters the realm of luxury and erotic gratification represented by Rosanette, a star of that special *monde* which here (as in Zola's *Nana*) so often appears a more amusing imitation of the real one. When Frédéric accompanies Rosanette to the races at the Hippodrome of the Champ de Mars, there is an explicit re-evocation of the earlier Champs-Elysées passage, as the luxurious carriages on their way home from the races crowd together at the top of the avenue: "Then Frédéric remembered those already distant days when he coveted the ineffable happiness of being in one of these carriages, next to one of these women. Now he possessed that happiness, and it didn't make him any more joyful" (p. 240). That this passage follows another aesthetic evocation of the beauty of the scene composed by carriages, accessories, sun and sky, offers confirmation that it is not Frédéric who finds joy in the world viewed. His desires are banal rather than transcendent, and their realization as flawed as their conception. But this episode goes further still in suggesting the nature of desire. When he sees that he has been seen in Rosanette's company by Mme Arnoux, whose carriage chances to pass close to his, he senses that the possibility of desire fulfilled—the "joyous and easy love" at hand—has created an irreparable check to romantic passion. So that "worn out, full of contradictory desires and no longer even knowing what he wanted, he felt an overwhelming sadness, a wish to die" (p. 238). With this *tristesse démesurée* and this *envie de mourir*, Frédéric seems to run through the trajectory of desire, to discover its eventual cooperation with the death instinct. It appears indeed to be in the logic of the critique of desire offered in *L'Education sentimentale* that it should discover and lay bare, with a rare explicitness, the cohabitation of the death instinct with desire: that immediately and visibly beyond the pleasure principle, as it were, the death instinct should be present.

The novel in fact rarely presents a moment of Eros without introducing a *memento mori*, as for instance at Rosanette's ball, when Frédéric's dinner companion, the "Sphinx," suddenly coughs up blood into her napkin and provokes in Frédéric a hallucinatory representation of Parisian misery and death: "He shivered then, taken by a glacial sadness, as if he had glimpsed whole worlds of misery and despair, a charcoal brazier next to a trestle bed, and the corpses of the Morgue in leather aprons, with the tap of cold water that runs on their hair" (p. 155).[11] The mental representation of death here has a force and presence that we rarely find in Frédéric's erotic hallucinations, in part because the present tense of the last clause—"le robinet d'eau froide qui *coule* sur leurs cheveux"—violates the grammatical rules of indirect discourse, making present this terrible image in a manner that exceeds Frédéric's perceptions, giving it an absolute and eternal status. The very enfeeblement and contradictoriness of desire in the novel appear ever to strip away erotic embellishments to reveal the drive toward extinction that underlies them.

But what is the place in this scheme of desire of the true focus of Frédéric's sentimental life, Mme Arnoux, the woman met in the first pages of the novel and loved, but never possessed, throughout? Her introduction into his life virtually takes the form of the supernatural, the moment of divine intervention; it is "like an apparition," and presented in a one-line paragraph:

Ce fut comme une apparition. (p. 46)

And she will by the end of the first chapter have become a "luminous point" in Frédéric's existence. The moment of Mme Arnoux's Dantesque apparition to Frédéric is clearly an instant of great power and privilege, a truly "primal scene" in that it will determine the destinies of Frédéric's future sentimental life. And yet, for all its force, the moment is somewhat compromised by Frédéric's inability to see Mme Arnoux without the rather tawdry trappings of Romantic passion: "He supposed her to be of Andalusian origin, creole perhaps: she had brought the negress servant back from the islands with her" (p. 37)—Mme Arnoux in fact comes from near Chartres—"She resembled the women in Romantic books" (p. 41). The reader in fact is never vouchsafed any "objective" view of Mme Arnoux, any perspective that would allow us to step outside Frédéric's mystified vision of her. Late in the novel, Rosanette provides a distinctly unflattering portrait of Mme

Arnoux—"a middle-aged woman with a complexion the shade of licorice, a thick waist, eyes as big as manholes, and just as empty" (p. 441)—but Rosanette can hardly be considered an objective observer in the case.

Henry James argued that the exclusive presentation of Mme Arnoux through the eyes of Frédéric, an "abject" human specimen and a "limited" register and reflector, marked a serious failure on Flaubert's part, a failure not simply artistic but "moral" as well:

> What *was* compromising—and the great point is that it remained so, that nothing has an equal weight against it—is the unconsciousness of error in respect to the opportunity that would have counted as his finest. We feel not so much that Flaubert misses it, for that we could bear; but that he doesn't *know* he misses it is what stamps the blunder. We do not pretend to say how he might have shown us Madame Arnoux better—that was his own affair. What is ours is that he really thought he was showing her as well as he could, or as she might be shown; at which we veil our face. For once that he had a conception quite apart, apart I mean from the array of his other conceptions and more delicate than any, he "went," as we say, and spoiled it.[12]

James's strictures are of course "right" in terms of the premises of the Jamesian novel—which is also the Balzacian novel—by which every major character must be freely and fully developed enough to enact his or her moral being. But his strictures reveal a considerable failure or unwillingness to understand the anti-Balzacian, or antinovelistic, premises of Flaubert's novel, which preclude turning fascination into knowledge.

One could juxtapose comments from Flaubertian criticism to illustrate that there is a debate—a debate that in some sense touches on the heart of the matter—as to whether or not *L'Education sentimentale* is "a great love story."[13] I would suggest that the novel gives us no sure basis for deciding this question. *L'Education sentimentale* could be considered a great love story in the courtly tradition, where the failure to possess the desired object works in concert with the lover's absolute and continuous fidelity to the object. Mme Arnoux's status as "luminous point" in Frédéric's existence never undergoes the possible tarnishment of possession, nor simply the changes that would be wrought by an altered relation to desire. Yet *L'Education sentimentale* might equally well be described as "the story of a delusion," where Frédéric's failure ever to possess stands as a sign of his failure—and the reader's—ever to know Mme Arnoux, an uncertainty as to whether she is correctly cast as the great beloved, and more generally, uncertainty as to whether one can extract much in the way of meaning from so tenuous, interrupted, and undeveloped a love story. To prove the validity of the label "great love story," one would expect to be able to point to some narrative transformations, even in—perhaps especially in—the lack of possession, some change or recognition in the protagonists. Our resistance to the label "great love story" may be motivated less by uncertainty about the status of "love" in the novel than by doubt about the status of "story." The "luminous point" that is Mme Arnoux resolutely refuses to be narrativized; it does not move, change, provoke recognition. In terms of narrative progression, it is less a luminous point than a black hole. When, in his final meeting with Mme Arnoux (a scene I shall come back to), Frédéric turns aside from what appears to be the possession finally offered to him, too late, because he feels "a repulsion, and something like the fear of incest," we must recognize that this love remains in the sphere of infantile investments of desire, incapable of inventing scenarios of change.

Another way of stating the case would be to say that *L'Education sentimentale* tends to invalidate the "great love story" as genre, both through the refusal of story, and through an implicit demonstration that the sociohistorical conditions of "love" have changed since the era of the great Romantic novelists. The most exemplary representation of this change comes when Frédéric pursues Mme Arnoux to her husband's chinaware factory at Creil, knowing Arnoux is absent, and determined to bring things to a resolution. What follows is a tragicomic grotesque of an episode, with Frédéric pursuing Mme Arnoux through the different workshops of the factory, which she insists that he visit, placing sentimental declarations at each step, only to have them interrupted and canceled by the clash of machinery and the vocabulary of industrial manufacture. "Ce sont les patouillards," she tells him at one point—"These are the drabblers"—and he finds the word "unseemly" in her mouth, as if the language of passion and that of manufacture created a standoff that he cannot resolve (p. 227). He then risks a romantic phrase, prelude to a declaration, only to have his words covered by the clanging of a fire-pump. When Sénécal, the socialist become fore-man, joins the tour, he takes over the role of guide, and launches into a paragraph of technical terms in which Flaubert clearly takes pleasure in defying common understanding, as well as creating a maximum verbal cacophony: "ovens, pyroscopes, hovel hearths, types of slip, glazes, and metals, with a wealth of chemical terms such as chloride, borax, and carbonate" (p. 228). Back in the Ar-noux' lodgings, Frédéric picks up a volume of Alfred de Musset, lying "by chance" on a table, and uses it as a prop to talk "of love, its despair and its transports." But the spirit of the quintessential Romantic poet is invoked in vain: Mme Arnoux replies that "all that"—"tout cela"—is "either criminal or false" (p. 230). Frédéric is reduced to complaining that her rules of conduct are "bourgeois," to which she replies that she has never claimed to be a "grande dame." Frédéric's thought of throwing himself at her feet is aborted when he hears a creaking, as of steps, in the corridor. The scene ends without resolution, even without real declaration, and Fréd-éric stumbles outside, and loses his way in the bleak landscape of the industrial suburbs. The episode constitutes one of a number of understated demonstrations that the very march of history, the coming of the age of high capitalism and industrial manufacture, has made the Romantic passion represented by Musset somehow superfluous, in excess of objective conditions. As Arnoux's dream of "L'Art industriel" slips progressively, in the course of the novel, from its first term to its second, so "love" as believed in by the generation prior to Flaubert's appears to be attenuated and com-promised by the progress of history. Another story is at work.

The impression that another story is working to infirm the one at hand is everywhere present in *L'Education sentimentale*, and the creaking floor—real or imagined sign of someone coming to interrupt—returns repeatedly as its sign. There is a kind of anti-principle of form at work in the novel: the principle of interference. Its theory is first explicitly offered when Frédéric finds himself dividing his life between sacred and profane love, as it were, paying court to both Mme Arnoux and Rosanette:

> The frequentation of these two women created as it were two melodies in his life: one playful, wanton, diverting, the other serious and almost religious; and, vibrating at the same time, they continued to swell, and little by little mingled;—for, if Mme Arnoux happened to brush him merely with her finger, the image of the other at once presented itself to his desire, because in that quarter his chance of success was less distant; —and when in the company of Rosanette it happened that his heart was touched, he at once remembered his great love. (pp. 175–76)

By couching the passage in terms of music, pre-eminently the artistic medium of passion and the apex of the Romantic hierarchy of the arts, Flaubert appears to promise some superior harmonic resolution of Frédéric's passional conundrum. But the start of the next paragraph characterizes the blending of the two melodies as "this confusion," and such clearly is the result. No harmony can be achieved from these two musical strains. Rather, we have a systematic playing-out of the interference of systems, a narrative dissonance.

Systematic interference takes the forms of missed rendezvous, interrupted meetings, wrong addresses, mistaken objects. To note briefly a few examples: When the long-awaited Deslauriers finally arrives in Paris to join Frédéric, Frédéric spoils their reunion because he cannot miss dining out at the Arnoux'. When Frédéric has an appointment with M. Dambreuse which should result in his becoming Dambreuse's executive secretary, he suddenly departs for Creil, having learned that Mme Arnoux is alone there. When Deslauriers has made him promise a subsidy of 15,000 francs for a new journal, Arnoux arrives needing 18,000 francs to pay his debts—and Frédéric gives the money to him instead. When Frédéric is away at Nogent, Deslauriers attempts to seduce Mme Arnoux. The failure of this attempt leads Deslauriers to tell Mme Arnoux that Frédéric is going to marry Louise Roque. This in turn leads to Mme Arnoux's recognition that she is in fact in love with Frédéric—who, at that very moment, the text tells us, is strolling with Louise in Nogent. When, later on, Frédéric finally does hold Mme Arnoux in his arms, "a creaking was heard on the floor," and Rosanette (now Frédéric's mistress) is there, looking for Jacques Arnoux. One could continue to accumulate examples, which all seem to obey some perverse logic of not being there where and when one ought to be.

On the level of relations among persons, interference characteristically takes the form of betrayal: the betrayal of loves and friendships, which the novel presents in a crushing accumulation, and which extends to the ideological-political sphere, where Sénécal's evolution from revolutionary socialist to murderous police agent is the key example. The omnipresent go-between and procuress, La Vatnaz, represents betrayal as a profession. In narratological terms, betrayal is interference, the dissonance of the two melodies, the clash of two sets of signals that results in a jamming of voices, a near semiotic incoherence. The system of plot seems to be an anti-system of randomized coincidence, as if one had taken a cast of characters—Sénécal, Dussardier, Hussonnet, Pellerin, Regimbart, Cisy, Martinon, and so forth—and so programmed them that they will return at unpredictable intervals, usually at the wrong time and in the wrong place. Proust noted this aspect of the novel when he described it as a *trottoir roulant*, a mechanical moving sidewalk that brings the characters back again and again without any apparent motivation.[14] Georg Lukács has convincingly argued that coincidence in Balzac's novels—the apparently fortuitous meeting of characters and the conjuncture of circumstances—is really motivated by the deep structures and the basic contradictions of the society Balzac represents. The truth of Lukács's comment is demonstrated by what Balzac does with the coincidental meeting: he makes it into an essential confrontation, where the actors play out everything that they represent, bringing a crisis and a change of position. Whereas Flaubert's coincidences are carefully nonessentialized, as they are de-dramatized: they are not confrontations, but simple encounters, unfolding the narrative as something close to pure metonymy without metaphoric arrest.[15]

Late in the novel, when Frédéric has made himself simultaneously the lover of Rosanette and of Mme Dambreuse, and is obliged to play more actively within two melodies—using the image of Rosanette to work up some passion when he's with the rather dry Mme Dambreuse, for instance—he lives the systematics of a double life, "diverting" himself with his lies. After he has made his first conquest of Mme Dambreuse, he pays a visit to Rosanette, and, finding her irresistible, draws her onto his knees: "And he said to himself, 'What a bastard I am!' congratulating himself on his perversity" (p. 401). "Perversity"—the condition of being turned around—well characterizes the curious motors and motions of this narrative plot. Desire and its objects are ever in a relation of chiasmus: you are never there where desire is to be realized; and when desire is realized, it is never in the right place or with the right person. The best illustration of this—one that the novel highlights by making it the conclusion of part 2—comes when Frédéric has finally won a rendezvous with Mme Arnoux, at the corner of the rue Tronchet and the rue de la Ferme, which he intends to make into an erotic conquest, renting a room nearby and furnishing it elaborately. When Mme Arnoux misses the rendezvous—"saved" by the illness of her child—Frédéric picks up Rosanette instead. And, "by a refinement of hatred, the better to outrage Mme Arnoux in his soul, he led her to the building in the rue Tronchet, to the room prepared for the other." In the other's room, then, he finally becomes the lover of the wrong woman, Rosanette, completing the profanation of his ideal passion. Rosanette wakes in the middle of the night to find Frédéric sobbing into his pillow. When she asks him what's wrong, he replies: "It's too much happiness.... I've been wanting you too long!" (p. 315). It is in the logic of chiasmatic desire realized that it should lead both to tears and to mendacity about their source.

II

The missed rendezvous with Mme Arnoux is the occasion of another failure to connect, for this very day Frédéric also misses his rendezvous with history. We are now at the start of the Revolution of 1848: the government's banning of the Reform Banquet, which led to street demonstrations, the arrest of the demonstrators, and that evening, February 23, 1848—as Frédéric is on his way to bed with Rosanette—the fusillade of the boulevard des Capucines, which provoked the first barricades and the uprising that, by the next day, would be a full-scale insurrection. Frédéric had moreover been convoked to the demonstrations by Deslauriers, in a note beginning: "La Poire est mûre"—"The Pear is ripe," "pear" being the caricaturists' way of portraying the king, Louis-Philippe. Deslauriers's message completes a series of statements that "the moment is approaching," promising a political crisis and culmination, a dramatic event that will install new meaning in history and in the characters' lives. Frédéric's amorous rendezvous makes him turn his back on the political dreams that have been the most generous aspiration of his group of friends and of his whole generation. He refuses to protest even as his friends are arrested by the police, since he might himself be compromised and miss his rendezvous. Thus the chiasmus of erotic desire is doubled by the crossing and interference of two systems, the amorous and the political.

But before considering more fully what the order of historical event, as represented by the Revolution of 1848, means in the novel, it may be well to complete the discussion of interference and chiasmus by a word on *style indirect libre*, whereby interference and chiasmus come to inhabit the text in its very verbal texture. As the best recent critics of Flaubert have shown, traditional discussions of *style indirect libre* as a technique for reporting speech and its characteristic

patterns, rhythms, and key words without recourse to direct quotation and without overt intervention of an authorial-narratorial
voice—discussions that see the technique as part of an increasingly
sophisticated mimesis whereby the novel appears to "write itself"
in the absence of the author—fail to appreciate the most radical
consequences of Flaubert's practice, which are indeed consonant
with the interference of systems and orders as I have sketched it.[16]
To understand how this is so, we ought to take the time to demonstrate how Flaubert uses *style indirect libre* to avoid and prevent direct attribution of what is spoken and reported, as a technique of irresponsibility, in that it refuses to designate who is
responsible for any given statement. Brief illustration will have
to suffice. To take first a relatively simple example, an evening in Mme Dambreuse's drawing room following the marriage
of her "niece" (in fact her husband's illegitimate daughter)
Cécile:

> That evening, a few friends came by to congratulate her and
> to condole with her: she must be missing her niece so much?
> It was a very good idea, though, for the newlyweds to have
> gone on a trip; later, difficulties, children come along! But
> Italy didn't live up to the idea one had of it. Granted, they
> were at the age of illusions! and then, the honeymoon embel-
> lished everything! (p. 401)

The lack of attribution here—we don't even know who the "few
friends" are, though we could no doubt reconstruct the cast of
characters from other Dambreuse gatherings—signals the commonplace nature of what is said, its status as cliché, belonging to
everyone and to no one. The commonplace statements are presented in the imperfect tense, the usual tense of indirect discourse,
but with a use of punctuation, question marks and especially exclamation points, which in Flaubert's usage seem to be almost musical notations of "voicing": they suggest the intonation of those
phrases which are being only indirectly quoted. And the sentence
on the newlyweds' trip violates—in a manner once again typical of

Flaubert—the normal structure of verb tenses in indirect discourse by moving into the present with *surviennent* ("come along"), as if voice broke through the reportorial convention to assert its presence.

Flaubert creates here the voice of a collectivity, and the lack of an answer to the question, who is speaking? does not much concern us, since what is being said is so banal. Nor are we much concerned here to say why we find the sentiments uttered banal—why we automatically read them with the distance of irony—so obvious does the point seem. Yet we should note that the passage gives no overt indications of ironization: our judgment that it is to be "taken ironically" must derive from our recognition of the perfect banality of the reported speech—a recognition of Flaubert's artistry in creating the perfectly stupid. This was indeed a basic Flaubertian ambition, mentioned many times in his correspondence, perhaps best expressed in his goal for the *Dictionnaire des idées reçues*, in which he wished to construct a book where "there would not be a single word invented by me"—where both the entries and their definitions would be made of the *sottises*, the stupidities, of others—and the reader would stand in the uneasy position of being uncertain whether to read it ironically or not.[17] Thus would the dream of the perfectly disguised author be realized.

Other situations of *L'Education sentimentale* can, however, be more treacherous, especially if more happens to be at stake. We could take, as a kind of intermediate instance, the speeches proffered at M. Dambreuse's funeral, at the graveside. There are six such speeches, each presented in the name of a collectivity, running from the Chambre des Députés (where Dambreuse was a representative) to the Society of Antiquaries of Amiens:

And they all profited by the occasion to thunder against Socialism, from which M. Dambreuse had died a victim. It was the spectacle of anarchy and his devotion to order that had cut short his days. They exalted his enlightenment, his probity, his generosity, and even his mutism as representative of the people, for if he was not an orator, he possessed on the other

hand those solid qualities, a thousand times preferable, etc.,
with all the consecrated terms one uses on such occasions:
"Untimely end,—eternal regrets,—that other homeland,—
farewell, or rather, till we meet again!" (p. 413)

This is a fine example of the *sottisier*, the lexicon of stupidity, complete with an apology for mutism as the ultimate sign of good
character. Yet the editorial hand intrudes in a strange manner,
inserting an "etc." just as we are coming to the list of preferable
qualities. Where does "etc." come from? Surely not from the orators
who, on the contrary, must be imagined as filling in each detail *in
extenso*. There is interference at work here—an interference confirmed by the break in the syntactic progression of the sentence,
followed by "with all the consecrated terms" ("avec tous les mots
qu'il faut dire"), which implies the judgment of an external critic
or editor. Critic/editor is, of course, never identified. We might be
tempted to make him coincide with Frédéric—a move typical of
critics who try to see a coherent point of view in the novel—but
nothing in the syntax suggests this identification, and we have in
fact been told that Frédéric is admiring the view while the speeches
are going on. It appears rather to be that impersonal person—so
often, in fact, hidden under the impersonal pronoun *on* ("one")—
whom we would like to pin down as the author. Our desire to pin
him down here is not caused by any hesitation in our judgment of
M. Dambreuse, whom we know to be a perfectly corrupt financial
dealer and politico. But we would be interested in knowing something more about the authorial view of that specter which common
stupidity holds to be the cause of Dambreuse's death: Socialism.

It is in fact issues of ideology that make the studied irresponsibility of *style indirect libre* most frustrating to the reader, its use of
interfering voices without apparent privilege of one or another
most distressing. A final example—more extended this time—should
make the point. This passage starts from a direct quotation from
"the Citizen," Regimbart, sometime in March, 1848, that is, between
the initial (February) Revolution and the turning point, the workers'
uprising known as the June Days.

"Take the Rhine, I tell you, take the Rhine, dammit."

Then he denounced the reaction.

It was beginning to show its hand. The sack of the châteaux of Neuilly and Suresnes, the fire at Les Batignolles, the riots in Lyon, all the excesses and all the grievances, they exaggerated them now, adding in Ledru-Rollin's circular, the fixed rate of banknotes, the fall in government notes to sixty francs, finally, as a supreme iniquity, as the last straw, as the horror of horrors, the forty-five-centime tax! And on top of all this there was Socialism as well! Although these theories, as new as tic-tac-toe, had been sufficiently debated for forty years to fill libraries full, they terrified the bourgeois, like a hail of meteorites; and they were indignant, in virtue of that hatred provoked by the advent of any idea because it's an idea, an execration which will later make its glory, and which ensures that its enemies are always inferior to it, however mediocre it may be.

Now Property rose in consideration to the level of Religion and was confused with God. The attacks made on it appeared a sacrilege, almost cannibalism. Despite the most humane legislation ever, the specter of '93 reappeared, and the blade of the guillotine resonated in each syllable of the word Republic; —which didn't prevent people from despising it for its weakness. France, feeling herself without a master, began to cry out in terror, like a blind man without his stick, like a kid who has lost his nurse. (pp. 326–27)

[—Prendre le Rhin, je vous dis, prendre le Rhin! fichtre!

Puis il accusa la réaction.

Elle se démasquait. Le sac des châteaux de Neuilly et de Suresnes, l'incendie des Batignolles, les troubles de Lyon, tous les excès, tous les griefs, on les exagérait à présent, en y ajoutant la circulaire de Ledru-Rollin, le cours forcé des billets de Banque, la rente tombée à soixante francs, enfin, comme iniquité suprême, comme dernier coup, comme surcroît d'horreur, l'impôt des quarante-cinq centimes!—Et, par-dessus tout cela, il y avait encore le Socialisme! Bien que ces théories, aussi neuves que le jeu d'oie, eussent été depuis quarante ans suffisamment débattues pour emplir des bibliothèques, elles épouvantèrent les bourgeois, comme une grêle d'aérolithes; et on fut indigné, en vertu de cette haine que provoque l'avenèment de toute idée parce que c'est une idée, exécration dont elle tire plus tard sa gloire, et qui fait que ses ennemis sont toujours au-dessous d'elle, si médiocre qu'elle puisse être.

Alors, la Propriété monta dans les respects au niveau de la Religion et se confondit avec Dieu. Les attaques qu'on lui portait parurent du sacrilège, presque de l'anthropophagie. Malgré la législation la plus humaine qui fut jamais, le spectre de 93 reparut, et le couperet de la guillotine vibra dans toutes les syllabes du mot République;—ce qui n'empêchait pas qu'on la méprisait pour sa faiblesse. La France, ne sentant plus de maître, se mit à crier d'effarement, comme un aveugle sans bâton, comme un marmot qui a perdu sa bonne.]

We have no trouble in ascribing these sentiments and phrases to Regimbart until we reach the verb "terrified"—*épouvantèrent*—which gives us pause because its tense, the preterite, violates the system of indirect discourse and seems to imply a narrator, since it is the tense of literary narrative discourse. That is, *épouvantèrent* appears to present the action of terrifying as a narrative fact, not simply as part of Regimbart's reported discourse. When it is followed by another preterite in *on fut*, we are put directly before the question, who is speaking? A narrative change of gears has taken place: we are in the tense, and the perspective, of retrospective (and judgmental) narration.

Upon inspection, the following paragraph has abandoned the claim to reported speech entirely: it is no longer in realm of *mimesis*, but rather in the mode of *diegesis*: telling, narrative "summary."[18] If this is the case, it would tend to make us want to attribute the judgments of the paragraph—and they are among the most overt and unambiguous of the entire novel—to a narrator. And since this narrator has been given no independent characterization in the text, we are tempted to equate his opinions directly with those of the author. And no doubt we can: at least as a judgment on the bourgeois reaction to the Second Republic, the sentiments coincide pretty clearly with Flaubert's—though it would be unwarranted to go further and present Flaubert as a partisan of the Second Republic, since other passages will pronounce a plague on that house as well.[19] But it is surely characteristic that the arrangement of the passage quoted is such as to disguise agency: the passage from Regimbart, an incessant commentator on public affairs and a mouthpiece of conventional wisdom, to "Flaubert"—if one may so state the case—is dissimulated, and intentionally so. The reader is led into believing that he is at a mimetic moment—learning "what the characters think"—and is not likely to be fully aware of the moment at which the text changes to another mode of discourse. In Barthes's terms, we pass from "the voice of the person" to the "voice of Science," without quite knowing it. The result, surely, is to make both notions, person and science, somewhat uncertain, and to make ideological evaluations impossible. The novel refuses to allow itself to be pinned down, to be made to declare its opinions. Like its hero's desires, it exists in a mode of uncertainty and inconsistency.

The uncertainty and inconsistency that arise from interfering voices and ideological systems characterize the whole presentation of 1848. Frédéric, who leaves Rosanette's arms to view the events, first comes on a group of insurgents who are attacking the guardhouse at the Château-d'Eau, "in order to free fifty prisoners, who weren't there" (p. 317). There is thus an immediate ironic disjuncture between heroic action and its results—the very irony of History. Frédéric, joined by Hussonnet, is then witness to the sack of the Tuileries Palace, where his insistence on the "sublimity" of the people is counterpointed by Hussonnet's sardonic comments on the bad odors of the sovereign mob. The terminal image of the scene—witnessed as the two leave the palace from fear of suffocation—is telling: "In the antechamber, raised on a pile of clothing, stood a prostitute, in the pose of a statue of liberty,—immobile, her eyes wide open, terrifying" (p. 321). Revolution here appears to present itself not only as the farcical repetition of history (see Marx) but as degradation and mute immobility, which terrifies with the terror of the nonsignificant.[20] Ideology parodies language and gesture to the point that rational discourse is silenced. We could set in counterpoint the moment when Frédéric decides to run for election to the Assemblée Nationale, which the reader tends to take as a favorable sign of resolution and activity on the part of the hitherto passive hero, only to be told: "Frédéric, man of all weaknesses, was won over by the universal madness. He wrote a speech . . ." (p. 330). We begin to suspect that all action, activity itself, belongs to the world of mindless madness, of *démence*. And Frédéric's attempt to speak to the Club de l'Intelligence becomes a perfect carnival of clichés and contradictory commonplaces, ending in the absurdity of the speech, in Spanish, of the "patriot from Barcelona." When Frédéric, still vainly attempting to begin his discourse, objects: "This is too absurd: no one can understand a word!" the crowd becomes exasperated, and demands his expulsion from the meeting. "Understanding," we must understand, has also lost its currency.

A further reduction in understanding is assured when Flaubert has Frédéric, along with Rosanette, leave Paris on the eve of the June Days, to pass a quiet idyll in Fontainebleau. Thus Frédéric, who was absent from the first call to rendezvous with the major historical event of his lifetime, will also miss its climactic moment, the bloody confrontation of class warfare in the June Days. But history is not abandoned during the Fontainebleau episode. Rather, it is shifted into another temporal register, set in the context of a *longue durée* which gives a curious new perspective on the Parisian struggle. Essentially, the Fontainebleau episode works through three widening spirals of history, in its presentation of the château, the forest, and the rocks.

The château is placed under the sign of Diane de Poitiers, figured in a series of mythological metamorphoses. Faced with the "symbols" of her glory, creating as her residue "an indistinct voice, a continuing splendor," Frédéric "was taken with an inexpressible retrospective lust" (p. 352). This "concupiscence rétrospective et inexprimable," desire oriented toward an irretrievable past and therefore silenced, blocked, figures well the incapacity of Frédéric's desiring to serve as the motor of action oriented toward the future. The phrase also, I think, reveals the kind of hyper-retrospectivity characteristic of Flaubert's narrative and specifically prepares the ending of the novel. In the immediate context of the château, Frédéric's retrospectivity leads him to evoke all the famous names of the past associated with it, from Charles Quint and the Valois kings up to Louis-Philippe, but the meditation leads to a kind of cancellation of the historical memorial—or of memorializing history—in its final paragraph, which evokes the "peculiar melancholy" of royal palaces, which has to do with their vast dimensions and "their immobile luxury, proving by its age the fugacity of dynasties, the eternal misery of everything" (p. 353). The passage ends with Rosanette's ear-to-ear yawn.

From the château, we move to the forest, which Frédéric and Rosanette visit as tourists. First comes a carefully constructed description of the stands of trees, which come to appear "a group of Titans immobilized in their anger," as if we were on the traces of a legendary world of forest spirits, a nature once animated and now alienated from man. Then we move on to the rock quarry, and a proto-cubist landscape strewn with boulders:

> They were multiplied in all directions, and ended by filling the entire landscape, cubic like houses, flat like paving stones, angled up against one another, hanging over one another, confused together, like the unrecognizable and monstrous ruins of some lost city. But the very fury of their chaos makes one rather imagine volcanoes, floods, vast unknown cataclysms. Frédéric said that they had been there since the beginning of the world and would remain until its end; Rosanette turned aside, claiming that "that would drive her crazy," and went to pick heather. (p. 357)

We seem to have moved from the immediate history of political event—what is going on in Paris—to the larger history of the dynasties of French rulers, to a mythicizing natural history, finally to reach a kind of geo-history. Those rocks evocative of unknown and unknowable cataclysms from prehistory, rocks that were there at the unimaginable beginning and will be there still at the unimaginable end, create a scope for history that is beyond the reach of mind, and Rosanette's remark that such an idea is enough to drive one crazy no doubt signals the healthy simple human response. This geo-history does not work to establish a more significant context for the Revolution of 1848 in general—nor for the human and social cataclysm of the June Days which are bloodying Paris at the very moment Frédéric and Rosanette view forest and rocks. On the contrary, geo-history rather feeds a certain attitude of quietism: the historical act is disinvested of significance in a world that begins and ends with boulders. The June Days, whichever side might win, can have no incidence on the geo-historical.[21]

When Frédéric suddenly decides to return to Paris—having found Dussardier's name among the wounded listed in the newspaper—we live the end of the sociopolitical cataclysm in two modes. The first is again the sense that Frédéric has missed history, a sense furnished by his nighttime passage across Paris as in a fantasmagoria of event, as troops move through the city in preparation for the final assault on the Faubourg Saint-Antoine. Frédéric is here the anguished and alien witness to something grandiose that passes his own understanding and dimension. The second mode asserts itself when he finally finds Dussardier, to discover that this man of the people who has fought heroically for the National Guard is in an anguish of doubt about whether he chose the right side: perhaps he should have been on the other side of the barricades, with the workers, who after all were witnessing the liquidation of the social republic. The account of the June Days then ends with a description of the prisoners in the cellars of the Tuileries, under the pitiless hand of the National Guard, and an evocation of the vengeful reaction of all sectors of the middle class on all that had caused it fear. Once again, we have a paragraph where we seem to detect Flaubert speaking in his own voice. It concludes: "Public reason was troubled as after the great upheavals of nature. Men of intelligence were made idiots by it for the rest of their lives"

(p. 368). If there is a final overt judgment by Flaubert, on the June Days and their aftermath, and indeed on the whole of the Revolution of 1848, it may be here: political event ends in idiocy, the cretinization of the otherwise and the formerly intelligent.

It is not, I think, that Flaubert condemns the ideals of the insurgents—though these are in fact seen mainly in their more ludicrous forms—and surely not that he is a defender of the established order, which is simply the *sottisier* in power. That the revolution ends in idiocy has to do rather with revolutionary action, and indeed with action itself, of which revolutionary action is perhaps simply the paroxystic condition. To act as if the world could be changed is the error. To act in the belief that it must change as the result of your action risks the result of idiocy. If *L'Education sentimentale* claims to be the history of Flaubert's generation, it appears to pass its severest judgment on that generation's belief that change is within the grasp of human agency. Like another summing-up on the first half of the nineteenth century, Baudelaire's "Le Voyage"— the terminal poem of *Les Fleurs du mal*—*L'Education sentimentale* presents a negative balance sheet, the end of action in *ennui* and the failure of intelligence. Hence the promise that the novel seemed to tender its readers, that Frédéric's hitherto aimless career might take on meaning when "the moment" finally came, and that the novel itself might become structured by the superior orderings of history, comes to naught. Like the model of the Balzacian novel, history is finally a deceptive ordering, a fiction, and what's more, a corrosive fiction in that it leads men to kill one another in the streets. Following the heightened replay of the June Days in the uprising and suppression of the Paris Commune in 1871, Flaubert said of his contemporaries, "If only they had understood *L'Education sentimentale*, none of this would have happened." [22] The remark may reveal a strange infidelity to Flaubert's avowed beliefs about the separation of the realms of life and art, and it may suggest a very high ideal of readership. But it does confirm our sense that the lesson of history in *L'Education sentimentale*—from human history to geo-history—appears to counsel passivity, the knowledge that action is futile.

What follows June, 1848, in the novel works toward something like a resolution of the system of interferences it has established. But the form taken by resolution seems to be insistently, repeatedly, that of liquidation, in all the senses we commonly attribute to the term: selling off, killing off, closing up shop, giving up hope, losing form and substance. Arnoux, the most entrepreneurial and energetic figure in the novel, falls into decadence and premature senility as a merchant of religious icons, then, having declared one bankruptcy too many, flees to the depths of Brittany, taking Mme Arnoux with him. Frédéric, who has never managed to attach himself to a father figure, despite M. Dambreuse's paternal overtures—a situation that may offer another comment on the ineffectuality of Frédéric's desire—himself becomes a father in the parodistic mode: it is Rosanette who bears him a child, while he daydreams that it might instead have been Mme Arnoux. The parody ends in a grim grotesque, as the baby dies—not only dies, but is made to undergo the indignity of having its deathbed portrait painted by Pellerin, a work that turns out to be "something hideous, almost derisory" (p. 437). Dambreuse dies, willing his fortune to his illegitimate daughter, Cécile, and Mme Dambreuse sitting before the empty safe—where she has in vain sought a contradictory testamentary document—offers an explicit link to Frédéric's unsuccessful parenthood: "A mother mourning next to an empty cradle is not more lamentable than was Mme Dambreuse in front of the gaping safe" (p. 414). Frédéric is about to realize his most Balzacian success in the novel through marriage to the widowed Mme Dambreuse—rich enough still, if no longer a millionaire—but this will also come to nothing, in the scene that best represents the liquidation of the sentimental side of Frédéric's youth: the auction of the Arnoux family belongings, caused by Mme Dambreuse, who has used some old unpaid notes found in her husband's desk to pursue Arnoux for debt, in order to avenge herself for Frédéric's continuing attachment to Mme Arnoux; while Frédéric suspects it is Rosanette who has caused the legal action, and thus has declared a definitive rupture with her just before the auction scene.

Frédéric attends the auction, under duress, at Mme Dambreuse's side. It is for him a "distribution of [Mme Arnoux's] relics, by which he recalled confusedly the form of her limbs . . . an atrocity, as if he had seen crows pecking at her dead body" (p. 432). When the auctioneer comes to the furnishings of her bedroom, we have a passage that proceeds in the same manner as the scene of the last rites administered to Emma in *Madame Bovary*, where each part of the body touched by the holy oil is remembered for its erotic and intense existence.[23] Here, it is not the parts of the body that are touched (and not a priest officiating, but an auctioneer) but rather furnishings and accessories, resulting in a metonymic liquidation, the liquidation of an absent presence:

> Thus there disappeared, one after another, the large blue car-pet strewn with camelias that her delicate feet brushed across in coming toward him, the little needlepoint *bergère* where he always sat facing her when they were alone; the two fireplace screens, whose ivory was made softer by the contact of her hands; a velvet pincushion, still stuck full of pins. It was as if parts of his heart were carried off with these things; and the monotony of the same voices and the same gestures overcame him with fatigue, brought him a deathlike torpor, a dissolution. (pp. 443–44)

In liquidation and dissolution, the hero begins to melt away, to lose the last vestiges of outline and shape. When Mme Dambreuse treacherously decides that she will buy a little casket of Mme Arnoux's—one tied to Frédéric's "dearest memories"—Frédéric finally has a moment of moral revolt, breaking with Mme Dambreuse as the auctioneer's hammer comes down.[24] It is a break with the corruption of the living in fidelity to an ideal woman who now belongs to the past—whose obituary has, so to speak, been performed.

The selling-off of the Arnoux belongings and the break with the future promised by Mme Dambreuse prepare the two final liquidations of this antepenultimate chapter of the novel. First, having decided that he needs the restorative virtues of the countryside, Frédéric takes the train to Nogent and starts to dream again of

Louise Roque, the provincial girl who loved him passionately and to whom he was once engaged—only to arrive in Nogent at the moment when Louise is coming out of the church, in her wedding dress, on the arm of her new husband, Deslauriers. "Shamed, beaten, crushed," Frédéric takes the next train back to Paris, to encounter the aftermath of the coup d'état of December 2, 1851, when Louis-Napoléon Bonaparte dissolved the Assembly, interned the leaders of the Opposition, and declared martial law—the coup d'état that would lead, within a year, to his becoming Napoleon III, ruler of the Second Empire. Frédéric is witness to the last vestiges of resistance by the republicans, in a scene made the more terrifying for its muteness, its inarticulate playing-out of a historical tragedy:

> It was five o'clock, a fine rain was falling. Some bourgeois were on the sidewalk by the Opera. The buildings opposite were shuttered. No one at the windows. Across the whole width of the Boulevard, dragoons were galloping, at full speed, leaning forward on their horses' necks, their sabres drawn; and the plumes of their helmets, and their large white cloaks lifted behind them passed across the light of the gaslamps, which writhed in the wind in the twilight. The crowd watched them, mute, terrified.
>
> Between the cavalry charges, squads of police appeared, to push the crowds back into the sidestreets.
>
> But on the steps of Tortoni, a man, Dussardier, recognizable from far off because of his height, remained motionless, like a caryatid.
>
> One of the policemen at the head of the file, his three-cornered hat down on his eyes, menaced him with his sword.
>
> The other, then, moving forward a step, cried out:—"Long live the Republic!"
>
> He fell on his back, his arms in a cross.
>
> A howl of horror arose from the crowd. The policeman looked all around him; and Frédéric, open-mouthed, recognized Sénécal. (p. 448)

The scene completes the betrayals of the novel, as one member of Frédéric's original circle of companions executes another; and Sénécal's evolution from revolutionary socialist to murderous police agent marks a historical betrayal only too familiar in modern history. The scene also completes the liquidation of all the generous political dreams of Frédéric's generation which, however misguided Flaubert may judge them to have been, were on the side of humanity. Not only a life but life itself seems to go under in this brutal act, which can be recorded only in a howl of horror, resisting articulate commentary. Flaubert has brought his most important lines of plot—personal and ideological—to climax at a moment of world-historical importance, in what is pre-eminently a *scène-à-faire* of the Balzacian variety. The scene is dramatic enough, yet it achieves its effect through the inarticulate, the very opposite of the achievement of stated meaning. Rather than reminding us of the hyper-articulateness of the Balzacian melodramatic showdown, the scene may evoke Lear at his "promised end": "Howl, howl, howl, howl!"

Moreover, the scene stops here and is followed by a blank—a silence that Proust identified as the most admirable thing in the novel—and when the next chapter begins, it is as if the temporal gearbox of the narrative had made a radical change in its ratios, leaping over years: "He traveled. . . . He returned. . . . Years passed; and he endured the idleness of his intellect and the inertia of his heart" (p. 448). Following this great gap of time scarcely recorded, this narrative void, we are in 1867—sixteen years after the preceding scene, twenty-seven years after the start of the novel—when Mme Arnoux comes back from Brittany to pay Frédéric a visit.

III

The claim that *L'Education sentimentale* is "a great love story" must rest much of its case on this scene, where Mme Arnoux and Frédéric for the first time give full expression to their love for one another. And it is undeniable that the scene represents a remarkable fidelity in a novelistic world characterized by flux, dissolution, liquefaction, and liquidation: Mme Arnoux has remained that fixed "luminous point" in Frédéric's existence; and now we discover that he has played much the same role for her—if not the requited lover, nonetheless the ever-faithful courtly lover, the incomparable and unique man in a world of infidelities and betrayals. As Jonathan Culler has argued, one can in effect read these pages both as "a great love scene" and as a deconstruction thereof: Frédéric and Mme Arnoux play out and quote the roles of romantic lovers.[25] Indeed, bookish models are very much present: Mme Arnoux tells Frédéric, "It seems to me that you are there when I read passages about love in books." And Frédéric replies, "You have made me feel everything they fault as exaggerated in books. . . . I understand Werther, who isn't disgusted by Charlotte's bread and butter" (pp. 450–51). What ultimately may most deconstruct the sublimity of the moment, however, is its temporal place: it comes too late. It cannot be a moment of romantic plenitude and presence because its verb tenses are wrong. The whole scene is played out in the retrospective mode, as the articulation of a sublime love that belongs to the past, and indeed derives its sublimity from its pastness.

Mme Arnoux says to Frédéric: "Never mind, we will have loved each other well." And Frédéric answers, "Without belonging to one another, however." Then she replies: "Perhaps it's better that way." And Frédéric: "No, no! What happiness we would have had!" To Mme Arnoux's future perfect—we will have loved well—which already sees their (unconsummated) love as capped and made definitive by an impending end, the final separation that will conclude this last meeting, Frédéric replies by a past conditional, evoking the missed possibilities of the past. Both tenses—that which already foresees their love as fixed by their future separation, that which regrets the unfulfilled promise of happiness in the past—render the impossibility of the present moment. It is the wrong moment, coming too late.

When Mme Arnoux takes off her hat, Frédéric receives a "blow in the heart": her hair has turned white. To "hide his disappointment from her," he sits at her knees and begins a rapture of praise for what she was in the past—the whole passage is spoken in the imperfect tense—while she accepts "with ravishment these adorations addressed to the woman she no longer was." But retrospectivity then is compromised by the feedback effect of his own words on Frédéric: "Frédéric, intoxicating himself on his own words, began to believe in what he was saying." The moment begins to take on the possibility of presence. Frédéric takes her in his arms. She speaks, now using his past conditional:

> "I would have liked to make you happy."
> Frédéric suspected that Mme Arnoux had come to offer herself to him; and he was repossessed by desire stronger than ever, furious, raging. However, he sensed something inexpressible, a repulsion, as if the fear of incest. Another fear stopped him, that of feeling disgust afterward. Moreover, what a nuisance it would be! and at once from prudence, and in order not to degrade his ideal, he turned on his heel and began to roll a cigarette.
> She looked at him, in wonder.
> "How fine you are! There's no one like you, no one!" (p. 452)

The possibility of presence, of fulfillment, provokes simultaneously desire and fear, the sense of taboo and the anticipation of disgust, and Frédéric's turning away from the possession offered is motivated both by prudence and by homage to the ideal. Mme Arnoux's praise of his delicacy thus is partly justified, partly delusion. To the extent that he is sublime, and the whole moment one of sublimity, this depends on its being maintained in the retrospective mode, as another example of *concupiscence rétrospective*. After the tacit recognition that they will not become lovers—that the present will not recapture the past—Frédéric and Mme Arnoux have nothing left to say to one another: "There comes a moment in partings when the beloved already is no longer with us." The end has been written before the end arrives. Mme Arnoux leaves, and the text is brutally reticent, monosyllabic: "And that was all"—"Et ce fut tout."

Earlier in the scene, we are told: "Ils se racontèrent leurs anciens jours . . . " ("They recounted old times to one another"). Not only is the tense of the scene retrospective, oriented toward the irrecoverable past, thematically it is concerned with the recall and the recounting of the past. Mme Arnoux professes herself astonished by Frédéric's memory, and she herself still hears his words from the past, "like a far-off echo, like the sound of a bell carried on the wind." It is as if in the past and present failure of fulfillment, the memory of the past began to take on a privilege of its own. It is as if desire, failing to capture its objects, comes to be reinvested in the recapitulative act of narration. Such a transfer of desire is even more strongly felt in the next, brief chapter (the last), which brings together Frédéric and Deslauriers "near the beginning of last winter"—in an unspecified but recent past—who sum up their experience of life, which they both have botched. Together, they blame "chance, circumstances, the times in which they lived." Frédéric notes the gap between what they are and what they had planned to become as schoolboys. This return to the beginnings of their friendship provokes an orgy of memory. "And, exhuming their youth, with each sentence they said to one another, 'Do you remember?' " (p. 455). In the debacle of their dreams and plans and ambitions, memory and the telling of the remembered assume dominating importance and become the source of pleasure.

Their telling takes them back to the summer vacation of 1837, and their visit to the bordello of La Turque in Nogent, their first attempt to realize erotic desire, thoroughly frustrated since Frédéric, unstrung by fear, remorse, and the pleasure of seeing so many women offered to him, was immobilized and, when the ladies laughed at his embarrassment, ran away. And since Frédéric had the money, Deslauriers was obliged to follow. They are seen leaving the place of perdition, thus furnishing Nogent a story "that wasn't forgotten three years later."

Now, "three years later" brings us up to 1840, when the novel begins—"On September 14, 1840, around six o'clock in the morning," the first sentence starts—thus connecting end to beginning, buckling the chronological loop. Frédéric and Deslauriers in fact allude to this adventure and the calumny it provoked during their reunion in chapter 2 of the novel, though the reader has no way of understanding their allusion until he has read the last page of the novel. A moment's reflection makes us appreciate Flaubert's architectural skill, the perfection of the form he has created. Yet further reflection suggests how curious the implications of this form are. Frédéric will say of the visit to La Turque—and it is his last statement in the novel—"That was the best we ever had!"; and Deslauriers responds, to close the novel, "Yes, you may be right! That's the best we ever had!" Critics since the novel's publication have noted the cynicism of the remark, and also its pathos, and have underlined the fairly vicious irony of ending a sentimental education with the evocation of the whorehouse, which of course caps the important theme of prostitution in the novel: prostitution which is profanation, to be sure, but also for Flaubert, unlike Balzac and Sue, somehow the inevitable response to the lies of Romantic passion, the most characteristic and even the most lucid form of "love" in a world where everything is subject to the marketplace.[26]

But a more "narratological" point must be made. The novel ends with Frédéric and Deslauriers conferring special privilege on a moment that does not fall within the normal chronology of the novel, a moment presented at the very end that in fact predates the beginning.[27] This striking analepsis, prefigurative of such a later novelist as Faulkner, seems to say that everything we have read in this very long novel is somehow secondary to the unrecorded moment of three years before it began. It is as if the novel suddenly discovers that it began too late, that the *sjužet* started out without knowing or accounting for an essential moment of the *fabula*—as if we had all along been reading a detective story that only at the end leads us to its essential clue, and an unfair detective story, in that it gave us no way of knowing that the essential clue really lay outside the time frame it originally established; or as if we were in one of Freud's case histories, where it transpires that all that has been remembered must be conceived as a screen memory, masking the real scene of trauma, which comes out only at the end. Closure here also uncloses, suggesting that novels, like analyses, may in essence be interminable.

One should not overprivilege this threshold moment in Frédéric's sentimental education, but it is important to note the curious and perverse effect of the privilege Frédéric, and Flaubert, accord to it, last and first, exhuming it from a literally prehistoric time to make it close the novel. It is perhaps most important to emphasize that the novel thus closes with the telling of an incident which was already in the state of a memory when the novel opens. The ultimate privilege involved may be that of memory itself, and its telling. Recalling their visit to La Turque, Frédéric and Deslauriers, we are told, "told it to one another prolixly, each completing the memories of the other": "Ils se la contèrent prolixement, chacun complétant les souvenirs de l'autre." The word *prolixement* suggests an excess of the *sjužet* in regard to the *fabula*: the story not only is told, it is told excessively, overtold. And it is told by each to himself and to the other—or so the reflexive verb permits us to say—in a dialogic act of exhumation, the two of them creating between them a kind of text of narrative pleasure, where the act of narrating clearly produces a sort of pleasure that the incident in itself did not comport. The pleasure of narration, exercised on a piece of story that did not even make it into the novel in its "original" chronology, seems at the last to confer a special status on telling itself, on the retrospective recapitulation of that which it is too late to change.

I noted earlier that moments of *L'Education sentimentale* tend to compose themselves into an aesthetic vision that does not belong to any character within the novel, but rather to an impersonal person, the composer of tableaux, the author. And what seems to arise from the ruins at the end of this education in failure is again the figure of the novelist, or, to put it less in terms of person, the figure of novelizing, of the narrative act, as that which continues even when the ostensible objects of narrative have revealed their insignificance. While we may find this a fitting final emphasis of the novel, and one that perhaps sets an ideal—narrative art—in resistance to betrayal, liquidation, and failure, we should not fall into the illusion of believing that the pleasure of retrospective narration in any way redeems the unsuccess and insignificance of the lives that are its object. The *concupiscence rétrospective* of narrative here never binds or transforms the past. If there is a knowledge provided by narrative—a *savoir* wrested from the doomed dialectic of *vouloir* and *pouvoir*, to use again the terms of Balzac's antique dealer in *La Peau de chagrin*—it is of a particularly ironic sort: not only knowledge that comes too late, but recognition of the perpetual belatedness of cognition in relation to action. The traditional Aristotelian recognition—*anagnorisis*—also came too late in terms of the life of the hero, who in tragedy most often died of the knowledge gained. But in tragedy, we the spectators share in the knowledge won by the hero's sacrifice: tragedy, as Northrop Frye pointed out, is like the Mass, a "mimesis of sacrifice" in which we the audience are communicants.[28] As the Chorus puts it at the end of Milton's *Samson Agonistes*, speaking of the dispositions of "Highest Wisdom":

> His servants he, with new acquist
> Of true experience from this great event
> With peace and consolation hath dismissed
> And calm of mind, all passion spent. (lines 1755–58)

Milton's restatement of the Aristotelian catharsis emphasizes the shared enlightenment it brings. But the negativity of Flaubert's education—a kind of "leading out" to nowhere—makes our sharing in the final moment of memorializing narration appear bitter and barren. Frédéric and Deslauriers appear to speak from beyond any possible pertinence of narrative to life, as if they had already lapsed into Freud's "preorganic quiescence." They speak—as the novel in which they figure so often has—against the normal terminal dynamics of narrative: the moment of plot's consummation as the moment of meaning. It is as if repetition had failed to achieve the binding that would permit a final discharge.

A far more optimistic reading of this ending is implicit in the whole of Georg Lukács's discussion of *L'Education sentimentale* in his *Theory of the Novel*, where he claims exemplary status for this novel because of its representation of "time as duration," the medium of man's search for meaning, which, no longer "transcendental," must lie within time. In Lukács's description, time is antagonist but also virtually protagonist since it gives the characters "the essential quality of their existence." What works on time is memory: "Memory transforms the continual struggle [with time] into a process which is full of mystery and interest and yet is tied with indestructible threads to the present, the unexplained instant." [29] This captures the apparent privilege Flaubert would seem to give to memory and its exercise in the present of narration. The power of rememoration working on time is of course a creative force in all narrative, perhaps particularly evident in retrospective first-person novels—*Great Expectations*, for instance, or, in more complex dialogic form, *Absalom, Absalom!*—which tend to dramatize what is at stake in the act of remembering, what the temporal gap between narrated and narrating means. The creative role of memory is implicit in the very postulate of any classic novel, that it is essential to understand what has happened because meaning lies only in a process of temporal struggle and unfolding, not, as in epic or drama, in the revelation of the transcendent within the human. In this sense, one might say that *L'Education sentimentale* at the last calls attention to narrating not as the act of a single person but as the very gesture of narrative itself, as what the novel as genre is about.

Yet our reading of the novel cannot sustain so optimistic a tone. Lukács surely misstates the effect of the novel when he goes on to conclude: "And so, by a strange and melancholy paradox, the moment of failure is the moment of value: the comprehending and experiencing of life's refusals is the source from which the fullness of life seems to flow." The terminal moment of retrospection in the novel offers no fullness, and little comprehension. While the recapitulative repetition of the past may in itself be pleasurable, a moment of dialogue and participation, its impotence to bind and master the past may also render it futile and gratuitous. Frédéric and Deslauriers at the end already resemble Bouvard and Pécuchet, the two copyists who recapitulate encyclopedias of human experience without a gain in understanding.

We may feel that Flaubert has come rather too close to his ideal of writing "a book about nothing." Yet something, some energy, keeps the novel and its reading going. If we feel we need to pay attention to the long chronicle of Frédéric's failure, it is because of the intertexts we have discussed—subsumed for our purposes under the broad categories of "the Balzacian novel" and "History"— and the energy that is generated by reading *against* them. The achievement of *L'Education sentimentale* does not reach us as a direct commentary on life, but rather as a commentary on the narrative forms in which life has traditionally been rendered. This commentary eventually, and no doubt logically, works toward bringing into the foreground the place from which all commentary proceeds, the act of narration. And when the nature of narration as a repetitive recapitulative mechanism—almost independent of what it recapitulates—has been laid bare, the threat of return to "preorganic quiescence" becomes clear and present: what is to keep the narrative going? Only—we have almost reached the situation of Samuel Beckett's narrators—the act of narration itself.

L'Education sentimentale in its very perversity does assume an exemplary position in the history of the novel. By way of its studious, even laborious, deconstructions of the contents of education and the sentiments, its critical examination of systems of meaning applied to life—or claimed to be immanent to life—it reaches a truly "melancholy paradox" in the claim that the memory and narration of failed meanings is somehow in itself a matter of compelling interest. Retrospective desire satisfies itself in the recall and recounting of unobtainable objects. Such a claim may not only be perverse; it may be wholly demoralizing. Yet it may also lay bare some essential factor of our need for, and our desire for, the novel as genre and narrative itself as a form of human discourse.

8

Narrative Transaction
and Transference

I

We have by now frequently evoked questions having to do with narrative situation: with how stories are told and how they are listened to. The motivation of plotting, I have argued, is intimately connected to the desire of narrating, the desire to tell, which in turn has much to do with the need for an interlocutor, a listener who enters into the narrative exchange. The shapes taken by stories and the reasons for their telling suggest the need to explore more fully the narrative situation—narrative *in situation* between teller and listener—and the kinds of reaction and understanding that narratives appear to want to elicit. All storytelling, Roland Barthes maintains, is contractual: it asks for something in return for what it supplies.[1] The contract can take many forms, from the seductive example of Balzac's *Sarrasine* discussed by Barthes—a story for a night of love—to the "metaseductive" of the *Thousand and One Nights*: a story instead of a simple night of love (ended by a beheading), a story to keep desire alive, to prolong and renew the intersubjective and interlocutionary relation. In fact, we shall see that "contract" is too simple a term, and too static; something more active, dynamic, shifting, and transformatory is involved in the exchange.

One of the most prolific of the nineteenth century's producers of story—the commercial term seems appropriate to the case—was

Guy de Maupassant, and several of his short stories provide interesting examples of the narrative situation. One in particular is
worth a moment's attention. "Une Ruse" presents the situation of
a newlywed young woman in conversation with her old doctor. The
woman is not ill, really, only a bit unwell, tired, slightly anemic,
such as is often the case with newlyweds "at the end of the first
month of their union, when they have married for love."[2] The
slightly prurient and cynical implication of too much lovemaking
sets the tone for what will follow. We enter the midst of a conversation where the young woman is protesting that she does not
understand how a wife can deceive her husband and give herself
to another man. To which the doctor replies that a woman is "ripe"
for "real love" only after she has been prepared by marriage. And
he suggests a comparison to a house, which is inhabitable "only
after a husband has cured the plaster." Finding the young woman
still incredulous about a wife's capacity to deceive, the doctor begins
a story (a tale-within-the-tale) that tells how he was once roused in
the middle of the night by a young woman who told him her lover
had just died in her bedroom—and her husband would soon be
home from his club. Most of the story recounts the doctor's visit
to her bedroom, his decision to pass the corpse off as a live man
who has suffered an attack while calling on the woman along with
the doctor, and the woman's energy, courage, and sang-froid in
helping him dress the corpse, get it out to the carriage, and then
meeting the returning husband with this fabricated story. When
the doctor has finished the tale of his successful ruse, we return to
the frame, and the newlywed woman—who now is "tense" (*crispée*)—
says to him: "Why have you told me this frightful story?" To which
he replies, "To offer you my services, should they be needed."

In a sense, the doctor's tale—and Maupassant's—is a dirty joke,
designed to ensure the listener's complicity in what could not otherwise be said or acknowledged. Whether or not the young wife will
ever be in a situation where she will need such "services" from the
doctor, she has already undergone some kind of a loss of innocence
simply in hearing them offered. The listening to his tale itself
implicates the listener. In this sense, the young woman's question,

"Why have you told me this?" comes too late: she has already heard, and that is irreparable. She is contaminated by the doctor's story. And we may impute such contamination to be his motive in the telling: his act of narration is aggressive, a kind of violation. Indeed, when we reflect on the title, "A Ruse," we understand that it applies not only to the ruse recounted by the doctor, but also to the ruse of the recounting itself: he has made her listen to something she did not want to acknowledge. And if the relation of framed to frame is one of ruse, so is the relation of both to the other listener, the reader—who not only has been lured into hearing the passably sordid little story, but who also must at the end consider his relation to the young woman and to the doctor. As a reader, can he maintain the innocence originally displayed by the young woman? Does not reading—having read—put him, like it or not, on the side of fallen knowledge?

In "Une Ruse," then, the contract of narrative leads to a contamination, the acquisition of an unwanted, sullying wisdom. In Balzac's *Sarrasine*, the story told by the narrator to the Marquise de Rochefide in order to satisfy her curiosity concerning the old specter seen at the Lantys' ball, and his connection with the Lanty fortune—a curiosity whose satisfaction should lead to her reciprocal satisfaction of the narrator's desire for her—leads to abrogation of the contract because of the content of the framed story. For the "specter" is the once-famous *castrato* Zambinella, mistakenly loved as a woman by the sculptor Sarrasine, whose love and desire are themselves unmanned and killed by the revelation of what he has desired. And the narrator's telling of this tale equally brings castration into his relation with the Marquise, who turns away when she has heard him out, telling him that he has created a disgust for love. "Ah, you know how to punish," replies the narrator, acknowledging that castration has moved out of the framed tale to strike at the desire that the telling of that tale was supposed to bring to satisfaction.[3]

Balzac offers a particularly rich array of framed narratives, from full-length novels such as *Le Lys dans la vallée* to novellas and short stories such as *Honorine, Gobseck, Adieu*, "Z. Marcas," "Facino Cane," all of which in various ways stage the relation of tellers to listeners and the problematic questions of narrative understanding and transmission.[4] "Facino Cane" in particular deserves mention, since its introductory frame has traditionally been read as a Balzacian *ars poetica*, presenting the narrator's penetrating powers of observation, his capacity to delve beneath the surfaces of other people's lives, to discover the stuff of their hidden stories. This power of observation "gave me the faculty to live with the life of the individual on whom it was exercised, allowing me to substitute myself for him as the dervish of the *Thousand and One Nights* took the body and the soul of those persons over whom he pronounced certain words."[5] The power of observation thus becomes the faculty of substitution and exchange by which the narrator (explicitly identified as scholar and author) espouses the story of another, makes it his own, speaks it. "To give up one's habits, to become another than oneself by the intoxication of the moral faculties, and to play this game at will, such was my distraction," says the narrator. Then he adds the question: "Is this a second sight? Is it one of those gifts whose abuse would lead to madness?" (p. 1020). The assumption of another's story, the entry into narratives not one's own, runs the risk of an alienation from self that in Balzac's work repeatedly evokes the threat of madness and aphasia, the possibility that, as in *Sarrasine*, *Le Lys dans la vallée*, *Adieu*, the communicative network may be violently ruptured.

The narrator goes on to tell of his meeting with the old blind musician who gives the impression of being "an old Homer who kept within himself an Odyssey condemned to oblivion." In fact, the ragged musician will identify himself as Marco Facino Cane, Principe de Varese, a Venetian nobleman who tells the narrator that he must listen to the tale Facino will tell, for it will make him immensely rich. "I thought that this man was mad; but there was in his voice a power that I obeyed," the narrator comments: like Coleridge's Wedding Guest (and he is in fact guest at a working-class wedding, where Facino is part of the wretched three-piece band) held in thrall by the Ancient Mariner, he must perforce listen to Facino's tale. This is a remarkable story of intrigue, adventure, and the erotic that turns on Facino's visionary power to detect the presence of gold, which guides his escape from the state prison into the state treasury, piled with gold, yet leads also to blindness, which he interprets as retribution for "an abuse of the visual power," echoing the narrator's fears about his own faculty of vision. The treasury still stands in Venice, and Facino's powers could again lead him to his secret tunnel if only the narrator will guide his steps to Venice: his tale thus holds out the possibility of fortune if only the original narrator, now become Facino's narratee, will act on it, realize it, make it his own. "We will go to Venice," the narrator finally exclaims; and when he escorts Facino back to the Quinze-Vingts (hospice for the blind), he promises to act on the narrative "contract" thus established. They will leave for Venice as soon as they have saved a bit of money. Whereupon the tale ends brusquely: "Facino Cane died during the winter, after having lingered on for two months. The poor man had a catarrh" (p. 1032).

Since Facino dies before the narrator-narratee can act on his promise to guide Facino to Venice, we do not know for certain whether the narrator really believes the story he has been told. Has he just been humoring the blind musician? Or has he in fact been convinced by Facino's magnetic presence and the haunting power of his story? Balzac's narrative gives us no principle for deciding this question. The status of Facino's tale within its frame remains indeterminate. All that we know is that Facino's tale has been retold by this narrator expert in transference and substitution, that from narratee he has again become narrator, assuming Facino's story and passing it on to us. The reader's situation in regard to the narrator mirrors the narrator's situation in regard to Facino: he senses the seductive possibility of fiction realized in life, the framed tale brought to realization, and riches, in the frame. That is, in the framed-tale structure, the outer frame comes to represent "the real," and movement from inner to outer tales suggests the movement of reference, making real. But of course such movement is frustrated here. The reader is finally left with a story on his hands, a story he doesn't know what to do with, except perhaps eventually to retell it. In this sense, the movement of reference is one of "contamination": the passing-on of the virus of narrative, the creation of the fevered need to retell. Such may be the "madness" that the narrator fears.

"The Story in It," Henry James entitled one of his short stories, and narratives repeatedly speak of the problem of what there is to know and to tell, of the problematic boundaries of telling and listening, and of the process of transmission. Balzac's framed tales appear often to confront the situation of tales that have been lost from sight, buried, and that must be unearthed, brought alive again, re-established in a circuit of communication. There is an allegory of the problem in *Le Chef d'oeuvre inconnu*, where the painter Frenhofer's visionary masterpiece never manages to get represented on the canvas in visible form, as there is also in *Adieu*, where Stéphanie de Vandières's love story is condemned to an amnesia and aphasia lifted only by a cure that at once proves mortal. Here, as in "Facino Cane," we have narratives that contain within their frames stories that never quite manage to be fully told, in the sense that their transmission or realization is blocked. Perhaps the most haunting case of all is presented by the short novel *Le Colonel Chabert*, whose hero has suffered the ultimate horror of burial alive.

I I

Burial alive has a rich literary career, running at least from M. G. Lewis's *The Monk* through the tales of Edgar Allan Poe. As a nightmare responding to our most primitive fears, beyond its specifically Gothic literary manifestations burial alive may evoke ancient punishments for the transgression of impurity (as with sinning vestal virgins, sealed alive in the tomb), or the entire mechanism and burden of repression, burying and encrypting a past that insists on continuing to live: the "archaeological" image of repression which Freud found so well represented in the Pompeii of Jensen's *Gradiva*. The fascination exercised by burial alive on the literary imagination may point to a specifically literary obsession with the buried utterance: the word, the tale, entombed without listener. In *Le Colonel Chabert*, the hero has managed to escape his bodily entombment, digging his way out of the mass battlefield grave with a dead comrade's detached arm. The true horror of his situation may lie in an even more painful analogue and product of his living entombment: the possibility that his *story* may remain buried, the nightmare of a certain narrative situation and the vicissitudes of the narrative desire. In *Le Colonel Chabert*, a text originally entitled *La Transaction*, the insistence on telling a story is matched by a resistance to hearing it, thus generating an attempt to transact a place for the story.

Chabert was a colonel in Napoleon's armies. Victim of a deep head wound at the battle of Eylau, he is judged dead and buried in a mass grave on the battlefield. Regaining consciousness in the silence of the tomb, he manages to dig his way out and to emerge, naked, in a second birth, to be cared for by Prussian peasants, until one day he remembers who he is, or was. Returning destitute to Paris, he finds that, since his death was recorded in the official bulletin of the battle, his wife not only has inherited his property and received his death benefit but also has remarried, to a Faubourg Saint-Germain aristocrat, member of the class which now is in the ascendancy with the Bourbon Restoration following the fall of Napoleon. Chabert must therefore struggle not only to assert his living identity against a historical record that says he is dead, and against a wife who has repudiated him, but also to make good the rights of a Napoleonic hero in a regime that wishes to suppress the Napoleonic episode, indeed to claim, by a massive act of historical repression, that it never occurred. As Balzac's text opens, the clerks in Derville's law office are in fact copying a decree by Louis XVIII restituting to the nobility those lands confiscated during the revolutionary period—an act of restoration and denegation which augurs ill for Chabert's claims. Chabert then enters these "caverns of chicanery" in search of legal counsel toward the recovery of his status, his fortune, his name, his very existence; and the story of his death and rebirth will be told by him to Derville as a tale within Balzac's tale.

We may begin to approach Chabert's narrative problem through the comment made by one of the clerks during Chabert's first visit to the law office. The clerk remarks of Chabert that "Il a l'air d'un déterré," which of course "means" that he looks dreadful, pale as death: like a corpse dug up.[6] But what does it mean to look *like* a man dug up from the grave—to have that "air"—when literally you *are* thus dug up? There is here an example of Balzac's insistent "strange but true," claiming the presence of the Gothic in the real, but also some problem of collapsed metaphor, a metaphor unaware that its tenor and its vehicle have become identical, that it has lost the tension of displacement inherent to metaphor, ceased to function as that active "transaction between contexts," to use I. A. Richards's definition of metaphor.[7] In the clerk's remark, there is an unwitting tautology. To introduce difference, to reinstate transaction within this tautology becomes a central problematic of Chabert's telling of his tale within the framework of Balzac's tale. "Transaction" is, of course, another word for "metaphor," as is "transference," which we shall use in a moment; all three terms image a process of substitution, cross-over, exchange. *Le Colonel Chabert* first of all, in the manner of *Sarrasine* and "Facino Cane," represents the contract that calls the narrative into existence, and the work of exchange that confers its value. Inserting the framed tale of Chabert's supreme adventure at the frontiers of life and death within the chicanery of the law office, it makes the active negotiation of the contract of Chabert's tale the very subject of the framing narrative, thus demonstrating with particular force what may be at stake in telling and listening and their transactive relation.

We need to dwell for a moment on Chabert's act of narration and its situation. When Chabert announces to Derville that he is Colonel Chabert, "dead at Eylau," he engages a first willingness on Derville's part to listen. The "signs" of his face confirm the potential of story implicit in this oxymoronic announcement that Chabert is the living bearer of his own obituary. As the narrator has told us, "A doctor, an author, a magistrate would have sensed an entire drama at the sight of this sublime horror whose least merit was to resemble those fantasies which painters sketch at the bottom of their lithographic stones to amuse themselves while chatting with their friends" (p. 322). Those who spend their lives listening to, or creating, stories must recognize that here narrative makes a

special claim to attention. "Parlez," says Derville, making a preliminary commitment to the narrative contract, as narratee to Chabert
as narrator. When Chabert proceeds to tell his story with "perfect
lucidity," to "recount facts so true seeming, although strange"
(p. 324), Derville affirms and reinforces the contract by his request
for continuation: "Monsieur, veuillez poursuivre" (p. 328). To which
Chabert reacts with "metalinguistic" rapture, commenting on the
veuillez, the first engaging form of address he has heard since his
official death. Upon conclusion of the colonel's tale, the contract
is fully validated as Derville strikes his hand in sign of agreement.
More important still, Derville announces his intention to stake
twenty-five louis—money he has won at the gambling table— on
the authenticity of Chabert's story, as support for the colonel while
the process of establishing his identity goes forward. We have a
first and unusually clear answer to the question posed by Barthes
in his discussion of narrative contracts: "Que vaut le récit?"—What
is narrative worth? What is it proposed that it be exchanged
for? A life's story here is worth the gamble of twenty-five louis.

Yet Derville also says to Chabert at this point, "Il faudra peut-
être transiger" (p. 333)—that is, it may be necessary to make a
settlement out of court, arrange a "transaction," as Derville later
names it in the substantive form (p. 342), negotiate a compromise.
To this proposal, Chabert replies with absolutist logic that he must
be either dead or alive, that compromise is not at issue: " 'Transiger,' répéta le colonel Chabert. 'Suis-je mort ou suis-je vivant?' "
The question is to the point—it is the point—but it is not susceptible
of a simple answer, any more than the question of what it means
to have the air of the disinterred when one is in fact disinterred.
What Derville understands is that the simple telling of Chabert's
story—which reduced to its elements reads: "Dead Colonel Chabert
lives"—lacks adequate communicative value. The tale needs the
proper listener—needs, beyond Derville himself, a narratee representative of society and its conditions of meaning and understanding. Without such a narratee, Chabert's affirmation of existence
risks resembling Frenhofer's incommunicable vision or Facino
Cane's imprisoned Odyssey. The telling of the tale is not enough;

there must be listening too. The narrator alone is insufficient to narrative; there must be a narratee as well. There must be a validated narrative contract for narrative to take place. And it is this contract that Derville, in his gamble on the authenticity and force of Chabert's narrative, undertakes to enact, by making signatory to it Chabert's quondam wife, the Comtesse Ferraud, who must serve as the first and representative narratee through whom the whole of society, and indeed the historical epoch of the Restoration, will accept Chabert's story.

The main action of *Le Colonel Chabert* is hence Derville's proposed negotiation, *La Transaction*, as the novel's earlier title explicitly emphasized; and this transaction concerns not only Chabert's claim to fortune, but the very status of his narrative as well. The structure of the framed tale in this instance overtly dramatizes not only the contractuality of narrative, and the place of the act of narration between narrator and narratee, but also the activity required to disinter the buried story. The bulk of the novel will concern the attempted working out of the framed narrative within the narrative frame, its attempted entry into a situation of exchange. In contrast to *Sarrasine* or "Facino Cane," here the size and importance of the frame exceeds that of the framed, suggesting the shift in emphasis from teller to listener. If in *La Peau de chagrin* listening eventually broke down, lapsed into unconsciousness, to give us telling alone, here telling comes from nowhere—from beyond life, from the silence of the tomb—whereas listening is seen to be pre-eminently a social act, conferring currency on stories that the society accepts as negotiable instruments. As we follow the work of negotiation undertaken by Derville the narratee in his effort to make Chabert's narrative come alive, his mediations between impossible telling and productive listening, we perceive that something yet more active and dynamic than contract is being played out. To restore the force of the "collapsed metaphor," to regain its difference, Chabert's story must undergo a metonymic process, the movement of exchange and reception. Derville's transaction might better be conceived as in the nature of the transference, in the psychoanalytic sense, since it intends to make an obsessive story from the past present and to assure its negotiability within the framework of "real life"—the outer narrative frame—and thus to work the patient's "cure."

Chabert returned from the grave is a curiously infantile figure, despite his cadaverous appearance, often referred to as "naive" and "candid." He has lost his father, Napoleon—who called him "mon Chabert"—and has been left unprotected, shivering: "Our sun has set, we are all cold now" (p. 331). He delivers himself to Derville as a dependent, financially as in all other respects, making of Derville the mediator of his affective existence and the representative of all the figures of authority from his past life. Their relationship is propitious to the full development of the transference, where the analyst in dialogue with the analysand becomes the fictive object of all past investments of desire, and where the interlocutionary situation becomes the place of repetition and working through of a past not yet mastered and brought into correct, therapeutic relation with the present.

Whatever the "lucidity" of Chabert's narrative of his death and rebirth, it is a story of the subject's alienation from himself—am *I* that Chabert whose obituary is written in the history books, or something other?—put together from fragments—personal memories, others' reports, hypotheses filling in the blanks of memory and evidence—and obsessively caught in the unanswerable question: Am I, as what I think I am, alive or dead?[8] It is a story whose paradoxes and oxymorons, whose obsessive desire to recover a *status quo ante mortem*, assure its blockage in the past, its inability to accede to integration with a possible present and future existence for Chabert. The repetitive insistence of desire that we hear in Chabert's discourse suggests something even more imperious and inherently unsatisfiable than what his demand explicitly formulates: his desire is in essence oriented toward total resuscitation of a past that can come no more, toward scenarios of satisfaction that are infantile in their refusal of present reality. Freud's characterization of the "dynamics of the transference" (in the 1912 essay of that name) seems pertinent here:

> The unconscious impulses do not want to be remembered in the way the treatment desires them to be, but endeavour to

reproduce themselves in accordance with the timelessness of the unconscious and its capacity for hallucination. Just as happens in dreams, the patient regards the products of the awakening of his unconscious impulses as contemporaneous and real: he seeks to put his passions into action without taking any account of the real situation. The doctor tries to compel him to fit these emotional impulses into the nexus of the treatment and of his life-history, to submit them to intellectual consideration and to understand them in the light of their psychical value.[9]

Freud's terms here echo those of Derville, and of Barthes: "Que vaut le récit?" What is its value, and how can it be put right?

The analysand always has a story to tell to the analyst, but it is always a story that is not good enough: links are missing, chronologies are twisted, the objects of desire are misnamed. In his act of narration, the analysand, as Freud puts it in his paper of 1914 "Remembering, Repeating and Working Through," "does not listen to the precise wording of his obsessional ideas" (Volume 12, p. 152). The analyst must help the analysand listen to the discourse of desire in order to grasp its intention. Analysis works toward the more precise and orderly recollection of the past, no longer compulsively repeated, insistently reproduced in the present, but ordered as a retrospective narrative. The analyst, like Derville, must deal with the actuality of a force—the force of past desire unconsciously enacting itself in the present—while ever attempting to translate it back into the terms of the past, in which it can recover its meaning. In other words, the goal which the analyst sets himself in dealing with the actings-out of the transference is "remembering in the old manner," that is, recall in the mind (p. 153); though this can work only through the kinds of memory—repetition and reproduction—that come into play when memory properly speaking is blocked. While the transference manifestations are troublesome to the analyst, they are, of course, also useful, for "it is precisely they that do us the inestimable service of making the patient's hidden and forgotten erotic impulses immediate and manifest" (p. 108). So that there is in the dynamics of the transference at once the drive to make the story of the past present—to actualize past desire—and the countervailing pressure to make the history of this past definitively past: to make an end to its reproductive insistence in the present, to lead the analysand to understanding that the past is indeed past, and then to incorporate this past, as past, within his present, so that the life's story can once again progress.

"The transference," Freud writes further, "creates an intermediate region between illness and real life, through which the transition from the one to the other is made" (p. 154). The transference as transition through an intermediate region closely resembles the "transaction" of Chabert's narrative proposed by Derville. Chabert's incredulity at the idea of transaction—his grand antithesis, "Am I dead or am I alive?"—represents the core resistance with which the transference must deal, the analysand's insistence on the continuing force of his identity as established in the past, at a time before his death and the Emperor's fall, whereas Derville understands that he must be led from this claim of identity to a revised one. The analysand-narrator must gain the conviction that he is indeed Chabert, the colonel whose deeds are recorded (in the mode of obituary) in the *Victoires et conquêtes*; yet this must be known as retrospective knowledge, as a past come to its end, which must be incorporated into a different present. When Derville tells Chabert (in their second meeting) that his case is "excessively complicated," he receives the reply that it is "excessively simple": Chabert continues, "Give me back my wife and my fortune . . ." (p. 340). Here we have the continuing reproductive thrust of desire in the transference, its hallucinatory insistence on the denial of time and sequence, its inability to replace repetition by recollection. What Derville must lead Chabert to through the transitional negotiation of his story is not so much a renunciation of this past desire as a transaction between its pastness and the possibilities of the present, a transference of past desire into terms that can be realized and made to render real rewards.

In taking on the negotiation of Chabert's case, then, Derville undertakes his cure—a cure that necessarily takes the form of correcting the narrative rhetoric of his story. The subject of that story must be brought to full predication, and the narrative tense must be made the past definite, so that Chabert's tale, like any successful narrative, may be a full retrospective statement of identity, a book both closed and legible, like that which Rousseau, at the start of the *Confessions*, announces he has brought to his Sovereign Judge. Only the fully framed tale within the tale offers the possibility of life outside the frame, within what the text presents as "reality." Rehabilitation of Chabert depends on a reordering of his narrative according to the rules of narrative syntax, so that the paradoxical figure—the "air d'un déterré"—can be unpacked in the story of a literal *déterré*, so that the antithesis of "dead or alive?" can be superseded by the more sophisticated "once believed dead, now returned to life"—an example of what Todorov calls a "narrative transformation." Thus would the collapsed metaphor gain new transferential properties. The guarantee of this new—transformed, transacted—version of the story must be its acceptance by the narratee, without whom stories are, as it were, entombed.

Derville's transaction must take the form of generalizing the transference established between Chabert and himself, implicating other narratees, eventually society at large, and initially the Comtesse Ferraud, Chabert's wife—once? or still?—now remarried to the Comte Ferraud and possessor of Chabert's fortune. In practical terms, Derville seeks a compromise whereby the Comtesse Ferraud will publicly identify and recognize Chabert, and grant him a regular annuity, in return for annulment of her first marriage and uncontested rights to her inheritance. In order to gain a hold on the Comtesse Ferraud, Derville undertakes to analyze her position as a plebeian who with her inheritance from Chabert was able, during the final years of the Empire, to marry a young aristocrat and make her way in the Faubourg Saint-Germain, but with the coming of the Restoration finds her position threatened by her husband's regret that he has not allied himself with a noble family, one that might bring the transfer of a peerage onto his name. An excuse for annulment of his marriage could only be to the Comte Ferraud's advantage, as the comtesse has divined; thus she lives devoured by "a moral cancer" (p. 349). What Derville has discovered through his analysis is another "tale within the tale," the secret story that the Comtesse Ferraud has buried—*enseveli*—deep in her heart, which forms the "knot of this story" and which, inversely from the colonel's story, she wishes to keep from entering the narrative situation, to block from any action of the narratee, to prevent from reaching its dénouement, its unknotting. Derville's detection of this second story finds its proof when he presents its possible outcome—in the Comte Ferraud's marriage to the daughter of a peer of the realm whose peerage would be transmitted to him by order of the king (in the manner of the order of restitution read aloud by the law clerks at the outset)—and the comtesse displays a mortal pallor. Derville now has what he needs: a counterstory to Chabert's, one that seeks the silence of the tomb. From this silence, this need to *taire l'histoire*—silence the story and even history—should come the basis for transaction, that which will make Chabert's story accede to listening.

The attempted transaction takes place in Derville's office, with the two principals, Chabert and the comtesse, separated in different rooms, and Derville serving as intermediary, shuttling from one to another in literal realization of the desired transference. But his role as intermediary is violated when Chabert, disgusted by the comtesse's unwillingness to sign the contract, leaves his room and confronts her directly. Now the comtesse simultaneously recognizes him and recognizes that he is *méconnaissable*, unrecognizable to the public at large without contractual validation. As Derville right away surmises, Chabert has lost his suit. And with the confrontation of the two principals in the case, there ensues a disappearance of the mediator, loss of the analyst on whose person the transference was played out. In a curious passage describing Chabert's and the comtesse's first moments alone together, the narrator states that in such crucial instants, "Life no longer seems to be in us; it comes out of us, spurts forth, it communicates itself like a contagion . . ." (p. 359). It is one of those virtually illegible Balzacian passages where we never quite grasp the coherence of the figural order employed. But it appears to mark a sudden release of tension and a lowering of the level of energy, resulting precisely from the removal of the agent of mediation, the person on whom the construct of the transference has been built.

The rest of the story unfolds ineluctably from the removal of the mediator, and marks the failure of Derville's proposed transaction, the failure of transmission of Chabert's story into the public domain. The comtesse whisks Chabert off to her country house and works to persuade him to renounce his story "d'une manière authentique" (p. 363)—that is, to use his identity to deny his identity, to be the author of his nonexistence. By the time Chabert comes to understand that the comtesse's sentimental appeals conceal a plot, he has lost the will to begin again a process of transaction, which this time would have to pass through the courts. What he calls "an odious war" (p. 366) stands in such marked contrast to the war in which he gained glory that he decides to give up his claim to the name by which his deeds were recorded in the *Bulletins de la Grande-Armée*, to call himself simply "Hyacinthe"—the name given him as a child in the orphanage—and to "rentrer sous terre," accepting entombment a second time. One consequence of his renunciation is that Derville goes unreimbursed for the sums he advanced Chabert. When this comes to Chabert's attention, he writes a letter (of unrecorded content) to the comtesse which produces immediate payment. For Derville, then, the result of his wager is zero: reimbursement, without either gain or loss from his investment in Chabert's story. When he expresses his astonishment that Chabert in renouncing his claims has not even stipulated an annuity for himself, Chabert replies that he now has only contempt for "that exterior life to which most men cling." And he adds, "When I think that Napoleon is on Saint-Helena, everything else here below is indifferent to me" (p. 370). In his contempt for "exterior life," Chabert articulates a final renunciation of a public narratee for his story, and in juxtaposing his renunciation to Napoleon's exile, he signals his abandonment of any attempt to live within the realities of the Restoration. He pulls all his investments back into the past, within which he died, gloriously.

Transaction of Chabert's narration fails utterly, then. The transference is unsuccessful in producing the cure that would deliver

Chabert back to society. What, then, is the ultimate status and value of Chabert's story? "Que vaut le récit?" Derville and his colleague Godeschal come upon Chabert years later—in 1840, under still another regime—sitting on a stone before the Hospice de la Vieillesse at Bicêtre. Recognizing Chabert, Derville says to Godeschal, "That old man, my friend, is a whole poem, or as the Romantics say, a drama" (p. 371). But Chabert refuses his name: "Pas Chabert! pas Chabert! je me nomme Hyacinthe . . . ." His story is reduced to a minimum syntax of denegation. It has in fact become mute gesture: his last comment in the text is to cry "Vive Napoléon!" and then: "He described in the air with his cane an imaginary arabesque." This tracing of an arabesque sets up resonances: it is like the arabesque that Balzac inscribed as epigraph to *La Peau de chagrin* which, we have seen, in its intertextual reference to *Tristram Shandy* signals a comment on narrative itself, on its gratuitous deviation from the rule-governed line. Are we to understand by the mute, nonsemantic arabesque that "le récit ne vaut rien": that in the absence of a successfully transacted contract of narrative, Chabert's story is worth nothing?

When Godeschal's curiosity is awakened by Derville's preliminary remarks on Chabert, we learn that "Derville told him the preceding story" (p. 372). "L'histoire qui précède" is confusing: are we to understand that Derville has become the narrator of the whole of the narrative, including that part of it which precedes his coming on stage? Has he usurped the place of the unnamed first narrator, moving from picture to frame? Or has he somehow placed the first narrator's tale within another narrative, so that Chabert's narration is now doubly framed? The hierarchy and status of embedded utterances appear to be in doubt with the failure of transaction for the tale within a tale. Derville, after giving a rather conventional summary of Chabert's "destiny"—his career set in retrospect—calls our attention to the listeners to tales, the professional narratees of society. He proposes to Godeschal that there are in society three men who cannot respect others, and who wear black, perhaps in mourning for all virtues and all illusions: the priest, the doctor, and the lawyer. Of the three, it is the lawyer who learns the worst of humanity—and Derville gives a little list of crimes committed in other volumes of *La Comédie humaine* to which he has been privy. "Finally," he says, "all the horrors that novelists think they are inventing are always short of the truth." And he announces his intention to retire from Paris to the country.

The lawyer is the arch-narratee, and also the figure of the novelist: he who listens to, and enters into, all the secret, buried stories of a society. Yet like the priest and the doctor, the lawyer is sworn to professional secrecy: he is precisely the man who does not transmit stories but rather lets them die in his office, encrypted in his vaults. Or rather: the lawyer—unlike the priest on the one hand, whose silence should be absolute, or the doctor on the other, who may give a full report if it is in the anonymous form of the case history—retells stories selectively, rearranged, in the litigation of his client's case. The lawyer as figure of the novelist is ultimately an ambiguous and oblique trope, leaving us uncertain about transmission and transaction. The original power of Chabert's tale from beyond the grave dissipates in the communicative circuit: we are left with a sense of the difficulty of narrative transactions.

It is the mutual implication of narrator and narratee, telling and listening, in the creation and validation of the narrative exchange that *Le Colonel Chabert* most tellingly dramatizes. Like other framed tales of *La Comédie humaine*, *Le Colonel Chabert* reflects on the relation of inner and outer narratives, on the desire, power, and danger of storytelling. The act of narration is compelling, as in "Facino Cane," seductive, as in *Sarrasine*, eliciting contractual relations of promise, conversion, erotic consent, yet both it and the act of listening can be mortal, bringing the annulment of contract, as in *Sarrasine* where castration transgresses the frame to strike at the relationship of narrator and narratee, or as in "Facino Cane" where Facino dies before his vision can be tested by the trip to Venice. Yet *Le Colonel Chabert* presents the power and danger of storytelling in a somewhat different register, recording the consequences of a failed telling in the failure of listening, with the consequent failure of cure, and the reburial of the disinterred hero whose erased name titles the text. More than the other tales mentioned, *Le Colonel Chabert* calls attention to the problem of listening (and the relative length of frame to framed suggests this emphasis), of what it takes to have narrative become operative. In this tale of ultimate Gothic horror articulated in the law office, we have the story not only of narrative's contractual conditions, but also of the necessary activity of narrative transaction that this entails.

The process by which Chabert's buried tale, originally presented as a collapsed metaphor, fails to gain the active, transactive force that it needs to become operative may suggest the broader pertinence of a psychoanalytic model of transference in the study of narrative texts. Freud, as I have noted, calls the transference "a kind of intermediate region between illness and real life, through which the transition from the one to the other is made." He continues, "The new condition has taken over all the features of the illness; but it represents an artificial illness which is at every point accessible to our intervention" (p. 154). This "intermediate region" (*Zwischenreich*), an "artificial illness" reproductive of the past yet accessible to the interventions of the present, surely resembles the narrative text, indeed any text. That is, we may conceive of the text as an as-if medium, fictional (as any set of signs must be) yet speaking of the investments of desire on the part of both addresser and addressee, author and reader, a place of rhetorical exchange or transaction. We as readers "intervene" by the very act of reading, interpreting the text, handling it, shaping it to our ends, making it accessible to our therapies.

In the transference, desire passes through what Lacan calls the "defile of the signifier": it enters the symbolic order, where it can be reordered, reread, rewritten. While other "transactional" models of reading could be proposed, the model of the psychoanalytic transference has the advantage of imaging the productive encounter of teller and listener, text and reader, and of suggesting how their interaction takes place in a special "artificial" medium, obeying its own rules—those of the symbolic order—yet vitally engaged with the histories and intentions of desire. [10] In other words, the transference, like the text as read, becomes the peculiar space of a deadly serious play, in which affect, repeated from the past, is acted out as if it were present, yet eventually in the knowledge that the persons and relations involved are surrogates and mummers. The transference actualizes the past in symbolic form, so that it can be replayed to a more successful outcome. The results of the replay return us to the real: as Freud writes, in the last sentence of "The Dynamics of the Transference," "When all is said and done, it is impossible to destroy anyone *in absentia* or *in effigie*" (p. 108). The statement may appear paradoxical, in that it is precisely in the symbolic mode—in effigy—that the past is laid to rest. But the symbolic making-present of the past in the transference confers on the past the psychic reality needed to rework it. Disciplined and "subjugated," the transference delivers one back to a changed reality. And so does any text fully engaged by the reader.

Those texts that dramatize narrative situation, contract, and transaction may most patently demonstrate the value of a transferential model. This is particularly the case when "framing" is an issue, for the frame of the framed tale comes to represent Freud's "real life," that outer margin that makes the life within narratable, figures it as the "artificial illness" treated for what it has to say about the story written by unconscious desire. In *Le Colonel Chabert*, Derville the narratee is brought into the position of analyst—becomes the present surrogate for past desire—who tries to cure his patient by working through the dynamics of the transference to the point where the story told can be reabsorbed and transcended in the outer frame of reality. In the "playground" of repetition, as Freud at one point characterizes the transference, the narratee listens to narration for the implied plot of past desire as it shapes and disfigures the present discourse, looking for the design of the story it would tell, working toward the recovery of the past as past, syntactically complete and reconciled within the present. The failed transference of *Le Colonel Chabert* may make particularly clear what is at stake in narrative transmission, transaction, transformation: the dynamics released when we try to unbury stories. *Que vaut le récit?* Only the rate of exchange will tell you.

Our exploration of narrative in the situation of its telling and its listening has led to the sketch of a transferential model of the text that seems to me pertinent and even crucial to the description of narrative as a process of dynamic exchange. For it is important to consider not only what a narrative is, but what it is for, and what its stakes are: why it is told, what aims it may manifest and conceal, what it seeks not only to say but to do. There can be a range of reasons for telling a story, from the self-interested to the altruistic. Seduction appears as a predominant motive, be it specifically erotic and oriented toward the capture of the other, or more nearly narcissistic, even exhibitionistic, asking for admiration and attention. Yet perhaps aggression is nearly as common, and, of course, often inextricably linked to the erotic: a forcing of attention, a violation of the listener. The nature of the transference established between speaker and listener can be positive and productive of satisfaction, but it can also involve dependency and abjection, the incapacity to free oneself from the interlocutor—or from the shadowy figures for whom the interlocutor is surrogate—as in the Dostoevskyan monologue which always (as Mikhaïl Bakhtin has shown) is dialogically inhabited by the voice of the other, a type of discourse well illustrated by Jean-Baptiste Clamence, the poor prophet for shabby times who speaks in Albert Camus's *La Chute*.[11] Framed narratives and those, such as *La Chute*, that incorporate the listener in the discourse of the speaker illustrate most explicitly a condition of all narrative: shape and meaning are the product of the listening as of the telling. Further confirmation for such a view could be found in William Labov and Joshua Waletsky's study of oral narratives: these appear always to contain a moment of "evaluation," a moment where the speaker calls attention to and reflects on the "point" of his story, and explicitly or implicitly calls the listener to attention, asking him to judge the story as important.[12]

As we continue to talk of plots and plotting, we shall be paying ever greater attention to dramatizations of telling and their relation to implications of listening. This progression of emphasis is partly in the logic of our argument and partly determined by a historical shift, an increasingly acute self-consciousness about the status of narrative within art that is itself self-consciously "modern." Curiously, this intense awareness of the epistemological and linguistic problems posed by storytelling is less a discovery of "Modernism" than a rediscovery of a concern central to earlier fiction, particularly in the eighteenth century: Sterne's *Tristram Shandy* and Diderot's *Jacques le fataliste* come at once to mind. These issues are not absent, of course, from the nineteenth-century novel. Yet during this golden age of narrative, there was an apparent need for and confidence in the shaping order of plot, whatever its ultimate inconsistencies and limitations as an explanatory system. With what we call, all too loosely, "Modernism," things become more suspicious.

9

An Unreadable Report: Conrad's *Heart of Darkness*

We need now to consider a number of the issues we have raised, concerning endings, authority, repetition, and the transaction of narratives, in the context of the "crisis" in the understanding of plots and plotting brought by the advent of Modernism. Joseph Conrad's *Heart of Darkness*—published in the last year of the nineteenth century—poses in an exemplary way central questions about the shape and epistemology of narrative. It displays an acute self-consciousness about the organizing features of traditional narrative, working with them still, but suspiciously, with constant reference to the inadequacy of the inherited orders of meaning. It suggests affinities to that pre-eminently nineteenth-century genre, the detective story, but a detective story gone modernist: a tale of inconclusive solutions to crimes of problematic status. In its representation of an effort to reach endings that would retrospectively illuminate beginnings and middles, it pursues a reflection on the formal limits of narrative, but within a frame of discourse that appears to subvert finalities of form. Most of all, it engages the very motive of narrative in its tale of a complexly motivated attempt to recover the story of another within one's own, and to retell both in a context that further complicates relations of actors, tellers, and listeners. Ultimately, all these questions, and everything one says about the tale, must be reconceived within the context of Marlow's act of narration aboard the *Nellie* at the moment of the turning of the tide on the Thames, in the relation of this narrator to his narratees and the relation of the narrative situation to the stories enacted within it.

Heart of Darkness is again a framed tale, in which a first narrator introduces Marlow and has the last word after Marlow has fallen silent; and embedded within Marlow's tale is apparently another, Kurtz's, which never quite gets told—as perhaps Marlow's does not quite either, for the frame structure here is characterized by notable uncertainties. Referring again to Gérard Genette's tripartite distinction of narrative levels, it is evident that in *Heart of Darkness* everything must eventually be recovered on the plane of narrating, in the act of telling which itself attempts to recover the problematic relations of Marlow's narrative plot to his story, and of his plot and story to Kurtz's story, which in turn entertains doubtful relations with Kurtz's narrative plot and its narrating. Marlow's narrative plot will more and more as it proceeds take as its story what Marlow understands to be Kurtz's story. Yet Kurtz's story has other plots, ways in which he would like to have it told: for instance, in his *Report to the Society for the Suppression of Savage Customs* (a plot subverted by the scribbled and forgotten footnote "Exterminate all the brutes"); or else the manner in which posthumously he commands Marlow's "loyalty" in retelling it—as lie—to his Intended. Ultimately, we must ask what motivates Marlow's retellings—of his own and Kurtz's mortal adventures—in the gathering dusk on the Thames estuary.[1]

One way to begin to unpack the dense narrative layerings of *Heart of Darkness* may be through the various orders of signification and belief—ready-made life plots—that the text casts up along the way: orders that marshal reality and might explain it if only one could believe them, if only there did not always seem to be something subverting them. One such order, for instance, is the Company, its door flanked by the two knitters of black wool, one of whom—or is it by now a third, to complete the suggestion of the Parcae?—obtrudes herself upon Marlow's memory at the moment of maximum blackness "as a most improper person to be sitting at the other end of such an affair."[2] In the knitted web—shroud, pall, or is it rather Ariadne's thread into a dark labyrinth?—the Company's design reaches to the depths of the dark continent. The Company as ordering is related to the "idea": "The conquest of the earth . . . is not a pretty thing when you look into it too much. What redeems it is the idea only" (pp. 50–51). The "idea" is the fiction of the mission, which upon inspection is seen to cover up the most rapacious and vicious of imperialisms. Here surely is one relation of order as ready-made plot to story in *Heart of Darkness*: a relation of cover-up, concealment, lie. Yet one should note a certain admiration in Marlow for the idea in itself: a recognition of the necessity for plot, for signifying system, even in the absence of its correspondence to reality (which may, for instance, suggest a reason for his effacing Kurtz's scribbled footnote before passing on the *Report to the Society for the Suppression of Savage Customs* to the press). The juxtaposition of ready-made order to reality, and Marlow's capacity to see both the admirable and the absurd in such attempted applications of order, is well suggested by the Company's chief accountant in the lower station, in high starched collar and cuffs, "bent over his books . . . making perfectly correct entries of perfectly correct transactions; and fifty feet below I could see the still tree-tops of the grove of death" (p. 70). The building of the railroad, with its objectless blasting of a path to nowhere, would be another example; even more compelling is perhaps the picture of the French warship shelling an incomprehensible coast:

Once, I remember, we came upon a man-of-war anchored off the coast. There wasn't even a shed there, and she was shelling the bush. It appears the French had one of their wars going on thereabouts. Her ensign dropped limp like a rag; the muzzles of the long six-inch guns stuck out all over the low hull; the greasy, slimy swell swung her up lazily and let her down, swaying her thin masts. In the empty immensity of earth, sky, and water, there she was, incomprehensible, firing into a continent. Pop, would go one of the six-inch guns; a small flame would dart and vanish, a little white smoke would disappear, a tiny projectile would give a feeble screech—and nothing happened. Nothing could happen. There was a touch of insanity in the proceeding, a sense of lugubrious drollery in the sight; and it was not dissipated by somebody on board assuring me earnestly there was a camp of natives—he called them enemies!—hidden out of sight somewhere. (pp. 61–62)

The traditional ordering systems—war, camp, enemies—lead to the logical consequences—men-of-war, cannonades—which are wholly incongruous to the situation requiring mastery. There is an absurd disproportion between the ordering systems deployed and the triviality of their effect, as if someone had designed a machine to produce work far smaller than the energy put into it. And there are many other examples that conform to such laws of incongruous effect.

The question of orderings comes to be articulated within the very heart of darkness in an exchange between Marlow and the manager on the question of Kurtz's "method" in the acquisition of ivory, which, we have already learned from the Russian—Kurtz's admirer, and the chief teller of his tale—Kurtz mainly obtained by raiding the country. The manager's rhetoric is punctuated by Marlow's dissents:

"I don't deny there is a remarkable quantity of ivory—mostly fossil. We must save it, at all events—but look how precarious the position is—and why? Because the method is unsound." "Do you," said I, looking at the shore, "call it 'unsound method'?" "Without doubt," he exclaimed hotly. "Don't you?" ... "No method at all," I murmured after a while. "Exactly," he exulted. "I anticipated this. Shows a complete want of judgment. It is my duty to point it out in the proper quarter." "Oh," said I, "that fellow—what's his name?—the brickmaker, will make a readable report for you." He appeared confounded for a moment. It seemed to me I had never breathed an atmosphere so vile, and I turned mentally to Kurtz for relief—positively for relief. (pp. 137–38)

The result of this exchange is that Marlow finds himself classified with those of "unsound method," which, of course, is a way of moralizing as lapse from order any recognition of the absence of order, using the concept of disorder to conceal the radical condition of orderlessness. The manager's language—"unsound method," "want of judgment," "duty to point it out in the proper quarter"— refers to ordering systems and in so doing finds a way to mask perception of what Kurtz's experience really signifies. The "readable report," which Marlow notes to be the usual order for dealing with such deviations as Kurtz's, would represent the ultimate system of false ordering, ready-made discourse. What we really need, Marlow seems to suggest, is an *unreadable* report—something like Kurtz's *Report*, perhaps, with its utterly contradictory messages, or perhaps Marlow's eventual retelling of the whole affair.

The text, then, appears to speak of a repeated "trying out" of orders, all of which distort what they claim to organize, all of which may indeed cover up a very lack of possibility of order. This may suggest one relationship between story and narrative plot in the text: a relationship of disquieting uncertainty, where story never appears to be quite matched to the narrative plot that is responsible for it. Yet the orders tried out in *Heart of Darkness* may in their very tenuousness be necessary to the process of striving toward meaning: as if to say that the plotting of stories remains necessary even where we have ceased to believe in the plots we use. Certain minimum canons of readability remain necessary if we are to be able to discern the locus of the necessarily unreadable.

Marlow's own initial relationship to the matter of orderings is curious, and recognized by himself as such. Marlow is eminently the man of work, proud of his seamanship, concerned with what he calls the "surface-truth" (p. 97) of steering, mechanics, repairs, devoted to the values of the master mariner codified in Towson's (or Towser's) *Inquiry into Some Points of Seamanship*: "Not a very enthralling book; but at the first glance you could see there a singleness of intention, an honest concern for the right way of going to work, which made these pages . . . luminous with another than a professional light" (p. 99). Yet as he presents his decision to undertake his African journey, it appears capricious, irrational, unmotivated. The decision reaches back to his boyhood passion for maps—which are another external ordering of reality—yet particularly his attraction to the unmapped within them, to their blank spaces. The space to which he will journey in the story recounted in *Heart of Darkness*—for convenience, we may call it the Congo, though it is never so named, never named at all, in the text—appeared "the biggest, the most blank, so to speak" (p. 52). By the time of his journey, the blank has been filled in, "with rivers and lakes and names"; indeed, possibly it has been filled overfull with "ideas," for "It had become a place of blackness" (p. 52). But blackness appears to motivate as strongly as blankness. Marlow in fact appears to recognize that his explanation lacks coherence, when he goes on to describe the "mighty big river ... resembling an immense snake uncoiled," and himself as the "silly little bird" that is "fascinated" by the snake—so fascinated that he began to have recourse, as he never had before, to women relatives on the Continent, in order to have a captaincy in the Company trading on the river. The desire for the journey is childish, absolute, persistent through contradictions; the journey itself appears compulsive, gratuitous, unmotivated. In the manner of Marlow himself, the reader must, in the absence of clear purpose or goal to the journey, be content with a general "fascination." The point bears some insistence, for Marlow's description of his trip up the river will in fact be also a description of how the journey came to be motivated: of the precipitation of a motivating plot within the originally unmotivated journey, and narrative.

"Going up that river was like travelling back to the earliest beginnings of the world ..." (p. 92). The way up is the way back: Marlow's individual journey repeats, ontogenetically, a kind of reverse phylogeny, an unraveling of the threads of civilization. His quest, we might say, is also an inquest, an investigation leading toward beginnings and origins; and the traditional story line of the journey comes to be doubled by the more specifically goal-oriented plot line of the inquest. What makes it so is his discovery that he has been preceded in his journey by the "remarkable" Mr. Kurtz, who becomes the object of inquest, providing a motive for the previously gratuitous voyage. Kurtz in fact provides a magnetizing goal of quest and inquest since he not only has led the way up the river, he has also returned upriver instead of coming back to the central station as he was supposed to do: Marlow indeed is able to "see Kurtz for the first time," in his imagination, in this return upriver, "setting his face towards the depths of the wilderness" (p. 90). It can in fact be pieced together from various remarks of the Company officials that the very reason for Marlow's being sent on his journey upriver is to detect the meaning and the consequences of Kurtz's return upriver—a presiding intention to his voyage of which Marlow becomes aware only in its midst, at the central station. It is thus gradually impressed upon Marlow, and the reader, that Marlow is in a state of belatedness or secondariness in relation to the forerunner; his journey is a repetition, which gains its meaning from its attachment to the prior journey. Marlow's plot (*sjužet*) repeats Kurtz's story (*fabula*), takes this as its motivating force— and then will seek also to know and to incorporate Kurtz's own plot for his story.

So it is that Marlow's inquest, in the manner of the detective's, becomes the retracing of the track of a precursor. We noted earlier, in the discussion of Conan Doyle's "The Musgrave Ritual," that the detective story in its classic form is built on the overlay or super-imposition of two temporal orders, the time of the crime (events and motives leading up to the crime) and the time of the inquest (events and motives leading away from the crime, but aimed at reconstructing it), the former sequence *in absentia*, lost to repre-sentation except insofar as it can be reconstructed in the time of the inquest, the latter *in praesentia* but existing merely to actualize the absent sequence of the crime. Tzvetan Todorov, we saw, iden-tified the relation of these two orders as the relation of *fabula* to *sjužet* that one finds in any narrative: a story postulated as prior gone over by a narrative plot that claims thereby to realize it.[3] The detective story may in this manner lay bare the structure of any narrative, particularly its claim to be a retracing of events that have already occurred. The detective retracing the trace of his prede-cessor and thus uncovering and constructing the meaning and the authority of the narrative represents the very process of narrative representation. This couple, the criminal precursor and the late-comer detective, has special relevance to the situation of Marlow and Kurtz. No more than the detective's, Marlow's narrative is not primary: it attaches itself to another's story, seeking there its authority; it retraces another's path, repeats a journey already undertaken.

In Marlow's narrative, then, we witness the formation of motivation in the middle of the journey, though in his act of narration this motivation may stand at its very inception, as part of the very motive of telling, since his own story has become narratable only in relation to Kurtz's. In a phrase that marks his first explicit recognition of a goal to his journey, and hence of a plot to his story, Marlow states: "Where the pilgrims imagined it [the steamboat] crawled to I don't know. To some place they expected to get something. I bet! For me it crawled toward Kurtz—exclusively" (p. 95). The reason for Marlow's choice of this "exclusive" and seemingly arbitrary motivation is made more specific following the attack on the steamboat, in a manner that helps us to understand the uses of plot. Thinking that the attack may betoken the death of Kurtz (later we learn that Kurtz himself ordered the attack), Marlow feels an "extreme disappointment," as if "I had travelled all this way for the sole purpose of talking with Mr. Kurtz. Talking with . . ." (p. 113). His choice of terms to image his anticipated meeting with Kurtz now leads him to recognition that it was indeed Kurtz as talker that he sought:

I . . . became aware that this was exactly what I had been looking forward to—a talk with Kurtz. I made the strange discovery that I had never imagined him as doing, you know, but as discoursing. . . . The man presented himself as a voice. . . . The point was in his being a gifted creature, and that of all his gifts the one that stood out preëminently, that carried with it a sense of real presence, was his ability to talk, his words—the gift of expression, the bewildering, the illuminating, the most exalted and the most contemptible, the pulsating stream of light, or the deceitful flow from the heart of an impenetrable darkness. (pp. 113–14)

The definition of Kurtz through his "gift of expression" and as "a voice," and Marlow's postulation of this definition of Kurtz as the motivating goal of his own journey, serve to conceptualize the narrative end as expression, voice, articulation, or what Walter Benjamin termed simply "wisdom": the goal of all storytelling which, with the decline of traditional oral transmission, has in the "privatized" genre of the novel come to be defined exclusively as the meaning of an individual life. And we have seen that in Benjamin's argument, the meaning of a life cannot be known until the moment of death: it is at death that a life first assumes transmissible form—becomes a completed and significant statement—so that it is death that provides the authority or "sanction" of narrative. The deathbed scene of the nineteenth-century novel eminently represents the moment of summing-up of a life's meaning and a transmission of accumulated wisdom to succeeding generations. Paternal figures within novels write their own obituaries, transmitting to the younger protagonists something of the authority necessary to view the meaning of their own lives retrospectively, in terms of the significance that will be brought by the as yet unwritten end.

To Marlow, Kurtz is doubly such a deathbed figure and writer of obituary. In the first place, he has reached his journey's end, he is lodged in the heart of darkness and it is from that "farthest point of navigation" that he offers his discourse, that "pulsating stream of light" or "deceitful flow." Kurtz has reached further, deeper than anyone else, and his gift for expression means that he should be able to give articulate shape to his terminus. "Kurtz discoursed. A voice! a voice!" (p. 147) Marlow will later report. But by that point Kurtz's report on the meaning of his navigation into the heart of the jungle will be compounded with his journey to his life's end, and his terminal report on his inner descent into darkness. So that Kurtz's discourse stands to make sense of Marlow's voyage and his life, his journey and his inquest: to offer that final articulation that will give a meaning to journey and experience here at what Marlow has doubly identified as "the farthest point of navigation and the culminating point of my experience" (p. 51). Kurtz is he who has already turned experience into Benjamin's "wisdom," turned story into well-formed narrative plot, matter into pure voice, and who stands ready to narrate life's story in significant form. Marlow's own narrative can make sense only when his inquest has reached a "solution" that is not a simple detection but the finding of a message written at and by the death of another. The meaning of his narrative plot has indeed come to depend on Kurtz's articulation of the meaning of *his* plot: Marlow's structuring of his own *fabula* as *sjužet* has attached itself to Kurtz's *fabula*, and can find its significant outcome only in finding Kurtz's *sjužet*.

For Kurtz, in the heart of darkness and at life's end, has "stepped over the edge" and has "summed up." Since it is a "summing up" that Marlow has discovered to be what most he has been seeking— that summary illumination that retrospectively makes sense of all that has gone before—his insistence that Kurtz has summed up is vitally important. At the end of the journey lies, not ivory, gold, or a fountain of youth, but the capacity to turn experience into language: a voice. But here we are forced to give closer scrutiny to Marlow's affirmations and their curious self-cancellations. Noting that after Kurtz's death he almost died himself, Marlow continues in reflection on ultimate articulations:

> I was within a hair's breadth of the last opportunity for pronouncement, and I found with humiliation that probably I would have nothing to say. This is the reason why I affirm that Kurtz was a remarkable man. He had something to say. He said it. Since I had peeped over the edge myself, I understand better the meaning of his stare, that could not see the flame of the candle, but was wide enough to embrace the whole universe, piercing enough to penetrate all the hearts that beat in the darkness. He had summed up—he had judged. "The horror!" He was a remarkable man. After all, this was the expression of some sort of belief; it had candour, it had conviction, it had a vibrating note of revolt in its whisper, it had the appalling face of a glimpsed truth—the strange commingling of desire and hate. And it is not my own extremity I remember best—a vision of grayness without form filled with

physical pain, and a careless contempt for the evanescence of all things—even of this pain itself. No! It is his extremity that I seem to have lived through. True, he had made that last stride, he had stepped over the edge, while I had been permitted to draw back my hesitating foot. And perhaps in this is the whole difference; perhaps all the wisdom, and all truth, and all sincerity, are just compressed into that inappreciable moment of time in which we step over the threshold of the invisible. Perhaps! I like to think my summing-up would not have been a word of careless contempt. Better his cry—much better. It was an affirmation, a moral victory paid for by innumerable defeats, by abominable terrors, by abominable satisfactions. But it was a victory! That is why I have remained loyal to Kurtz to the last, and even beyond, when a long time after I heard once more, not his own voice, but the echo of his magnificent eloquence thrown to me from a soul as translucently pure as a cliff of crystal. (pp. 151–52)

The passage is one that epitomizes all our difficulties with Marlow as narrator, for the resonance of its ethical pronouncements seems somehow to get in the way of the designation of a starker and possibly contradictory truth: the moral rhetoric appears in some measure a cover-up. Marlow explicitly confirms Benjamin's argument concerning storytelling and wisdom, and confirms his need for Kurtz as the paternal figure whose final articulation transmits wisdom. Kurtz "had summed up." And this summary articulation, which concerns not only Kurtz's individual experience but also penetrates "all the hearts that beat in the darkness," comes from "over the edge," on the other side, *beyond* life, or more accurately, on the threshold of the beyond, with one foot on either side; whereas Marlow has only "peeped" over the edge. In his hypothesis that "all the wisdom, and all truth" are compressed into this moment of termination and threshold, Marlow evokes the tradition of the "panoramic vision of the dying": as he says just before the passage I quoted at length, "Did he [Kurtz] live his life again in every detail of desire, temptation, and surrender during that supreme moment of complete knowledge?" (p. 149) The supremacy of the moment should inform Kurtz's *ultima verba*, his summing-up: in his discourse is wrought his "victory."

And yet, when after considering that "all the wisdom, and all truth" may lie compacted in that last moment, that "last opportunity for pronouncement," Marlow states: "I like to think my summing-up would not have been a word of careless contempt," he may subvert the rhetorical system of the passage quoted by inculcating a major doubt concerning the proper characterization of Kurtz's "word." The uncertainties of Marlow's argument here are suggested by other curiosities of diction and rhetoric. "Better his cry" is a curious comparative to use in regard to a word that Marlow claims was *not* spoken (the word of careless contempt). "But it was a victory" appears somewhat strange in that one doesn't ordinarily introduce a clause by a concessive when the previous clause is ostensibly making the same affirmation. Marlow's discourse seems to shape itself in opposition to the anticipated objections of an imagined interlocutor. By protesting too much, he builds those putative objections dialogically into his own discourse, making it (in Mikhaïl Bakhtin's terms) "double voiced."[4] Double voicing indeed is suggested by the evocation of the "echo" of Kurtz's voice. This "echo of his magnificent eloquence" becomes the most highly problematic element of the passage when, later, we understand that the "soul as translucently pure as a cliff of crystal" is Kurtz's Intended, and that the "echo" which she hears is a pure fiction in blatant contradiction to that which Marlow hears in the same room with her: a lie which Marlow is obliged to confirm as conscious cover-up of the continuing reverberation of Kurtz's last words: "The horror! The horror!"

This is no doubt the point at issue: that Kurtz's final words answer so poorly to all of Marlow's insistence on summing-up as a moment of final articulation of wisdom, truth, and sincerity, as affirmation and as moral victory. Marlow affirms that it is Kurtz's ultimate capacity to judge, to use human language in its communicative and its normative dimensions to transmit an evaluation of his soul's adventures on this earth, that constitutes his victory: the victory of articulation itself. And yet, "The horror! The horror!" is more accurately characterized when Marlow calls it a "cry." It comes about as close as articulated speech can come to the primal cry, to a blurted emotional reaction of uncertain reference and context. To present "the horror!" as articulation of that wisdom lying in wait at the end of the tale, at journey's end and life's end, is to make a mockery of storytelling and ethics, or to gull one's listeners—as Marlow himself seems to realize when he finds that he cannot repeat Kurtz's last words to the Intended, but must rather cover them up by a conventional ending: "The last word he pronounced was—your name" (p. 161). The contrast of this fictive act of naming—"proper" naming—with Kurtz's actual cry may suggest how poorly Kurtz's summing-up fits Marlow's description of it. Indeed, his cry so resembles the "word of careless contempt" that when we find this phrase in Marlow's account, we tend to take it as applying to Kurtz's last utterance, only to find that it is given as the very contrary thereof. Something is amiss.

We can concede to Marlow his reading of the ethical signified of Kurtz's last words, his "judgment upon the adventures of his soul on this earth" (p. 150)—though we may find the reference of this signified somewhat ambiguous: is the horror within Kurtz or without? Is it experience or reaction to experience? But we have a problem conceiving the signifier as fulfilling the conditions of the wisdom-and-truth-articulating function of the end. More than a masterful, summary, victorious articulation, "The horror!" appears as minimal language, language on the verge of reversion to savagery, on the verge of a fall from language. That Kurtz's experience in the heart of darkness should represent and be represented by a fall from language does not surprise us: this belongs to the very logic of the heart of darkness, which is consistently characterized as "unspeakable." There are the "unspeakable rites" at which Kurtz presides (p. 118), the "unspeakable secrets" of his "method" (p. 138), and, at the very heart of the darkness—at the moment when Marlow pursues Kurtz into the jungle at night, to struggle with his soul and carry him back to the steamer—we have only this characterization of the dark ceremony unfolding by the campfire: "It was

very awful" (p. 143). Critics have most often been content to point
to the moral signified of such phrases—or to criticize them, and
Conrad, for a lack of referential and ethical specificity—but we
should feel obliged to read them in their literal statement.[5] What
stands at the heart of darkness—at the journey's end and at the
core of this tale—is unsayable, extralinguistic.

It cannot be otherwise, for the heart of darkness—and Kurtz
himself in the heart—is beyond the system of human social structures which makes language possible and is itself made possible by
language: which is unthinkable except through and as language,
as that which demarcates culture from nature. The issue is most
directly addressed by Marlow when he contrasts Kurtz's position
within the unspeakable and unimaginable darkness to that of his
solidly "moored" listeners aboard the *Nellie*:

> It was impossible—it was not good for one either—trying to
> imagine. He had taken a high seat amongst the devils of the
> land—I mean literally. You can't understand. How could you?—
> with solid pavement under your feet, surrounded by kind
> neighbours ready to cheer you or to fall on you, stepping
> delicately between the butcher and the policeman, in the holy
> terror of scandal and gallows and lunatic asylums—how can
> you imagine what particular region of the first ages a man's
> untrammelled feet may take him into by the way of solitude—
> utter solitude without a policeman—by the way of silence—
> utter silence, where no warning voice of a kind neighbour can
> be heard whispering of public opinion? These little things make
> all the great difference. (p. 116)

Language is here presented, accurately enough, as a system of
police. Incorporate with the *polis*, language forms the basis of social
organization (which itself functions as a language) as a system of
difference, hence of distinction and restraint, which polices indi-
viduality by making it part of a transindividual, intersubjective system: precisely what we call society. To policing is contrasted the
utter silence of utter solitude: the realm beyond interlocution, be-

yond dialogue, hence beyond language. As Marlow puts it when he struggles to return Kurtz from the jungle to the steamboat, "I had to deal with a being to whom I could not appeal in the name of anything high or low.... He had kicked himself loose of the earth" (p. 144).

If Kurtz's summing-up may represent ethically a return to the earth and its names (though the ethical reference of his last pronouncement is at least ambiguous), as an act of language "The horror! The horror!" stands on the verge of non-language, of nonsense. This is not to characterize "The horror!" as the Romantic ineffable: if Marlow appears to affirm an ineffable behind Kurtz's words, his whole narrative rather demonstrates the nothingness of that behind. Marlow continually seems to promise a penetration into the heart of darkness, along with a concurrent recognition that he is confined to the "surface truth." There is no reconciliation of this standoff, but there may be the suggestion that language, as interlocutionary and thus as social system, simply can have no dealings with an ineffable. For language, nothing will come of nothing.[6]

Certainly the summing-up provided by Kurtz cannot represent the kind of terminal wisdom that Marlow seeks, to make sense of both Kurtz's story and his own story and hence to bring his narrative to a coherent and significant end. Kurtz's final articulation should perhaps be typed as more than anything else anaphoric, pointing to the unsayable dumbness of the heart of darkness and to the impossible end of the perfect narrative plot. In this sense, Kurtz's narrative never fully exists, never fully gets itself told. And for the same reason, Marlow's narrative can never speak the end that it has sought so hard to find, and that it has postulated as the very premise and guarantee of its meaning. Marlow's search for meaning appears ever to be suspended, rather in the manner of his description of his encounter with death: "My destiny! Droll thing life is— that mysterious arrangement of merciless logic for a futile purpose. The most you can hope from it is some knowledge of yourself— that comes too late—a crop of unextinguishable regrets" (p. 150). The logic of life's plot is never vouchsafed knowledge of that end which might make its purpose significant. Such knowledge as there is always is caught in a process of suspension and deferral, so that it comes too late. Marlow as the belated follower of Kurtz the predecessor is too late, as, the tale implies, he who seeks to know the end, rather than simply live it, must always be. Ends are not—are no longer?—available.

The necessary syntactic incompletion of the life story is referred to by the Marlow who is one of the narrators of *Lord Jim*, a novel contemporaneous with *Heart of Darkness*:

> And besides, the last word is not said,—probably shall never be said. Are not our lives too short for that full utterance which through all our stammerings is of course our only and abiding intention? I have given up expecting those last words, whose ring, if they could only be pronounced, would shake both heaven and earth. There is never time to say our last word—the last word of our love, of our desire, faith, remorse, submission, revolt.[7]

Marlow here defines the "intention" of life as "utterance," as the articulation of Benjamin's "wisdom," and as the completion of that fully predicated sentence which to Barthes constitutes the classical narrative. Does this Marlow give up the other Marlow's search for the "summing up," or does he rather reaffirm that since it is unknowable in one's own life it must be sought in the voice of another, as in Kurtz's? The word "stammerings" may imply that the search for utterance will always encounter a crossing of voices, creating a dialogic discourse of more complex reference and truth than the heaven-and-earth-shaking last word.

Returning to *Heart of Darkness*, we must ask what we are to make of Marlow's puzzling continued affirmation of Kurtz's "victory," and his proclamation of continued "loyalty" to Kurtz because of this victory. Is it that Marlow recognizes his own continuing need for the terminal articulation by which everything else makes sense, and thus in the face of all evidence to the contrary continues to affirm the articulate significance of Kurtz's final cry? In order to make sense of his own story, Marlow needs an ending "borrowed" from another's story. In the lack of finality of the promised end, Marlow must continue to attach his story to Kurtz's, since to detach it would be to admit that his narrative on board the *Nellie* is radically unmotivated, arbitrary, perhaps meaningless. As he has conceded at the start of his narrative, the story was "sombre" and "not very clear. And yet it seemed to throw a kind of light" (p. 51). His loyalty to Kurtz is perhaps ultimately the loyalty of *sjužet* to *fabula*: the loyalty of telling to told, of detective to criminal, follower to forerunner, repetition to recollection. It is only through the postulation of a repetition that narrative plot gains motivation and the implication of meaning, as if, in the absence of any definable meaning in either *fabula* or *sjužet*, it were in the fact of repetition of one by the other that meaning could be made to inhere.

Marlow's "loyalty" to Kurtz is overtly tested in the last episode recounted in his narrative, the meeting with Kurtz's Intended. She insists that there must be a traditional pattern of transmission from person to person, from one story to another, from precursor to those left behind: " 'Something must remain. His words, at least, have not died.' 'His words will remain,' I said" (p. 156). Since she believes that the meaning of Kurtz's life story lies in the words he has left behind, the Intended naturally demands to know Kurtz's last words, those which, capping the utterance expressing his life, should fix him semantically for posterity, endow his story with authority. If up to now Marlow has insisted that Kurtz's last words constitute a victory, here he discovers that as an official conclusion to Kurtz's story they will not do. The Intended asks that he repeat Kurtz's last words:

I was on the point of crying at her, "Don't you hear them?" The dusk was repeating them in a persistent whisper all around us, in a whisper that seemed to swell menacingly like the first whisper of a rising wind. "The horror! The horror!"

"His last word—to live with," she insisted. "Don't you understand I loved him—I loved him—I loved him!"

I pulled myself together and spoke slowly.

"The last word he pronounced was—your name." (p. 161)

Marlow's retreat here into a conventional ending to Kurtz's story, his telling of a lie—and Marlow hates lies because they have "a flavour of mortality" (p. 82)—marks a decision that Kurtz's last words belong to the category of the unspeakable. Language as a system of social communication and transmission, as the medium of official biographies and readable reports, has no place for the unspeakable; it is used rather to cover up the unnamable, to reweave the seamless web of signification. The cover-up is accomplished by Marlow's substituting "your name"—the name of the Intended, which we are never in fact given—for the nameless, as if to say that any proper name can be used, according to the circumstance, to ward off the threat of a fall from language. This substitutability of names, of course, marks a notable alterability of stories: the narrative of Kurtz composed by Marlow for the Intended is different from that told to the other narratees, those on board the *Nellie.* The way stories are told, and what they mean, seems to depend as much on narratee and narrative situation as on narrator.

That Marlow's narration on board the *Nellie* concludes—or more accurately, breaks off—just after he has told of his lie to the Intended suggests the link between his lie and his narrative. Having once presented a lying version of Kurtz's story, he apparently needs to retell it, restituting its darkness this time, and in particular showing its place in Marlow's own story. Marlow's lie on behalf of Kurtz's official story, alluded to early in his narrative, prior to the account of his meeting with Kurtz, has been from the start implicitly the most powerful motive to Marlow's act of narration, which comes to break the silence of dusk on the Thames without explicit raison d'être. By its end, Marlow's narrative has revealed the central motive that compelled his act of narration. He is not simply a teller of tales, but a reteller. He must retell a story, that of Kurtz, mistold the first time. And in doing so, he must complicate it by telling how he came to know it, thus adding another layer of plot and eventually transforming the relation of telling to told, so that it is finally less Kurtz's story that he tells than his own story inhabited, as it were, by Kurtz's story. The question may then be whether

Marlow can tell the story "right" the second time around: whether the story that needs telling can properly be told at all, since proper telling may imply a conventional semantics and syntax that are unfaithful to Marlow's experience of Kurtz's experience of the heart of darkness.

This brings us back to the final issue we need to address, that of Marlow as storyteller, retelling his story on the deck of the *Nellie* to a certain group of listeners. Marlow's tale is proffered at a moment of suspension: the moment of the turning of the tide, as the mariners wait for the outbound tide in the Thames estuary in order to begin a new voyage. By the time Marlow falls silent, they will have missed the "first of the ebb." Marlow's tale inserts itself, then, in a moment of indefinable suspension between the flood and the ebb of the tide, at a decisive turning point that passes undiscerned to those who depend on it. This suspended temporality finds a counterpart in the first narrator's description of Marlow's tales as reversals or negative images of those usually spoken by seamen, in that they do not frame their wisdom in the conventional manner:

> The yarns of seamen have a direct simplicity, the whole mean-
> ing of which lies within the shell of a cracked nut. But Marlow
> was not typical (if his propensity to spin yarns be excepted),
> and to him the meaning of an episode was not inside like a
> kernel but outside, enveloping the tale which brought it out
> only as a glow brings out a haze, in the likeness of one of these
> misty halos that sometimes are made visible by the spectral
> illumination of moonshine. (p. 48)

This way of characterizing Marlow's narratives first of all puts us on warning that the structure of "framed narration" used in *Heart of Darkness* will not in this instance give a neat pattern of nested boxes, bracketed core structures, nuts within shells. If we consider how each of the inner frames opens and closes, we realize that in a traditional patterning we should have a structure in which the first narrator presents Marlow as the second narrator, who presents Kurtz as the third narrator; then Kurtz would tell his tale to its end and fall silent; Marlow would then finish his own tale, framing Kurtz's; and the first narrator would reappear to close the outer frame.[8] In fact, Kurtz never fulfills the promise of a coherent inner frame, a core structure, for although we are told repeatedly that "he discoursed," we get very little report of what he said. Kurtz never assumes the narration of his own story, which comes to us in a curiously lateral and indeed nonnarrated form, from the Russian: "this amazing tale that was not so much told as suggested to me in desolate exclamations, completed by shrugs, in interrupted phrases, in hints ending in deep sighs" (p. 129). And since Kurtz's story in its telling becomes bound up with Marlow's, it never is clearly demarcated from its frames. Then, at the close of Marlow's narration, where we might expect the first narrator to step in with a closing comment—a final "summing up"—we have an apparent avoidance of explicit reaction to Marlow's narrative. There is simply citation of the Director's remark that they have missed the first of the ebb (ambiguous indication of either inattentiveness or else absorption, pensivity) and the first narrator's final descriptive sentence: "I raised my head. The offing was barred by a black bank of clouds, and the tranquil waterway leading to the uttermost ends of the earth flowed sombre under an overcast sky—seemed to lead into the heart of an immense darkness" (p. 162). Thus there is a generalization of the darkness at the heart of Marlow's (and Kurtz's) stories, rather than any defining illumination. The Thames, which initially was presented as leading up to a place of darkness—a place of gloom, and once itself a heart of darkness—now leads out to darkness as well. Darkness is everywhere visible. The encompassing darkness offers one realization of the image the first narrator has used to describe Marlow's tales, where meaning is not within but "enveloping." The tale, that image tells us, does not contain meaning, but rather brings it out as a surrounding medium, acting itself as a virtual source of illumination which must be perceived in that which, outside itself, it illuminates: "as a glow brings out a haze," in the manner of a misty halo made visible "by the spectral illumination of moonshine." Marlow's tale makes the darkness visible.

If we ask what a meaning that is outside rather than within the narrative might be, what status it might have, we are forced to the conclusion that such meaning must reside in the relation between the tale's telling and its listening, in its reception, its transaction, in the interlocutionary relation. The truth value of Marlow's narrative must be in what his listeners can do with it. Perhaps the most important dramatization of interlocution comes at the moment when Marlow appeals to his listeners to "see":

> "He [Kurtz] was just a word to me. I did not see the man in the name any more than you do. Do you see him? Do you see the story? Do you see anything? It seems to me I am trying to tell you a dream—making a vain attempt, because no relation of a dream can convey the dream-sensation, that commingling of absurdity, surprise, and bewilderment in a tremor of struggling revolt, that notion of being captured by the incredible which is of the very essence of dreams. . . ."
>
> He was silent for a while.
>
> " . . . No, it is impossible; it is impossible to convey the life-sensation of any given epoch of one's existence—that which makes its truth, its meaning—its subtle and penetrating essence. It is impossible. We live, as we dream—alone. . . ."
>
> He paused again as if reflecting, then added—
>
> "Of course in this you fellows see more than I could then. You see me, whom you know. . . ."
>
> It had become so pitch dark that we listeners could hardly see one another. For a long time already he, sitting apart, had been no more to us than a voice. There was not a word from anybody. The others might have been asleep, but I was awake. I listened, I listened on the watch for the sentence, for the word, that would give me the clue to the faint uneasiness inspired by this narrative that seemed to shape itself without human lips in the heavy night-air of the river. (pp. 82–83)[9]

Marlow's appeal to vision, and his attempt to make his own visual presence into his listeners' surrogate assurance of truth in Kurtz's story—the substitute for eyewitness experience—are, of course, subverted by the first narrator's comment that he and the other listeners could in fact no longer see Marlow (or even one another). Like Kurtz himself, Marlow has become a disembodied voice. If Marlow is simply voice, then the authority of his narrative depends wholly on his verbal act, on rhetoric. And as a listener to Marlow's rhetoric, the first narrator—Marlow's principal narratee—tells us that he is on the watch "for the sentence, for the word" that would solve the enigma and the mystery of Marlow's narrative. The first narrator thus characterizes himself as an obtuse narratee, for pinning down "the sentence" and "the word" is precisely what Marlow's narrative will not and cannot do—indeed, what Marlow's narratives never do, according to the first narrator's own characterization of them as "inconclusive" (p. 51). The nearest Marlow will come to speaking "the sentence," "the word," is his report of Kurtz's summing-up, a nonsentence and words that fail as definition, which necessitate the continuing effort to tell, where telling never coincides with designation but is rather a perpetual slippage of meaning, a movement forward in a metonymic chain which can never fix meaning—for meaning is not, whatever the Intended may think, a matter of nomenclature—but simply point to its place, contextualize the desire for it and the movement toward it.

The impossibility of summing-up, the impossibility of designating meaning as within the narrative frame, explains why Marlow must retell his tale on board the *Nellie*, seeking meaning in the "spectral illumination" of narrative transaction. If framed narration in general offers a way to make explicit and to dramatize the motive for storytelling, *Heart of Darkness* shows the motive for retelling. Repetition appears to be a product of failure in the original telling— Kurtz's failure to narrate his own story satisfactorily, Marlow's lying version of Kurtz's story to the Intended—just as, in Freud's terms, repetition and working through come into play when orderly memory of the past—recollection of it *as* past—is blocked. We are fully within the dynamics of the transference. But it does not seem possible to conclude that Marlow's retelling on the *Nellie* is wholly a success: it does not meet the standards of intelligibility sought by the first narrator, and the most that can be said of the other narratees is that they are possibly (though not certainly) absorbed by the tale. We have a feeling at the end of Marlow's act of narration that retelling of his tale will have to continue: that the ambiguous wisdom he has transmitted to his listeners will have to be retransmitted by them as narrative to future listeners. The process is potentially infinite, any closure or termination merely provisional. *Heart of Darkness* does not "end"; it is a potentially interminable analysis that simply breaks off.

Any future retelling of Marlow's tale of Kurtz's story will have to be narrative in nature because there is no way to state its kernel, its wisdom, directly: this can only be approached metonymically, through a trying-out of orders, through plottings. And these will never take you there, they will only indicate where "there" might be located. Meaning will never lie in the summing-up but only in transmission: in the passing-on of the "horror," the taint of knowledge gained. Meaning is hence dialogic in nature, located in the interstices of story and frame, born of the relationship between tellers and listeners. Meaning is indeed the implicit dialogue itself, the "set" of the teller's message toward his listener as much as toward the matter of his tale. Marlow is as fully concerned with the hearing as with the telling of his tale and its truth, equally concerned with the "phatic" as with the "emotive" and "referential" functions of language.[10] If meaning must be conceived as dialogic, dialogue represents a centerless and reversible structure, engendering an interminable process of analysis and interpretation, a dynamics of the transference in which the reader is solicited not only to understand the story, but to complete it: to make it fuller, richer, more powerfully ordered, and therefore more hermeneutic. Summing-up and dialogue are offered as two different modes of understanding, each incompatible with the other, yet neither exclusive. Marlow needs the postulation of Kurtz's summing-up in order to make basic sense of his own narrative. Failing himself to sum up, he must pass on his implication as narratee of Kurtz's story to his listeners, implicating them in turn as narratees, trapping them in the dialogic relationship. Figured here as well is the reader's relationship to the text. The reader's own incapacity to sum up—the frustration promoted by the text—is consubstantial with his dialogic implication in the text. The reader is necessarily part of the process of transmission in this tale that is ultimately most of all about transmission.

I have argued that one finally needs to read *Heart of Darkness* as act of narration even more than as narrative or as story. It shows this act to be far from innocent, indeed as based perhaps most of all on the need and the desire to implicate one's listeners in a taint one can't live with alone. It is not simply, and not so much, that confessing excuses but that properly managed it taints. If the listener has listened, he has assumed the position of "thou" to an "I." Reassuming the first-person pronoun for himself, he makes the former "I" into a "thou." [11] The intersubjective and reversible pattern of dialogue has been created. Why are you telling me this? the interlocutor may want to ask—but by the time he comes to make such a response, it is already too late: like the Ancient Mariner's Wedding Guest, he has been made to hear. If a number of nineteenth- and twentieth-century narrative texts present sophisticated versions of traditional oral storytelling, it is because this gives them a way to force the reader into transferential relationship with what he may not want to see or hear.

Yet another characteristic peculiar to late nineteenth- and early twentieth-century narrative—that which we characterize as modernist—appears to emerge from our study of *Heart of Darkness*. This is the implication that all stories are in a state of being retold, that there are no more primary narratives. Marlow must repeat Kurtz's story, and presumably his listeners will have to repeat Marlow's story of Kurtz's story. Indeed, the very start of Marlow's narrative suggests an infinite possibility of repetition when he reaches back nineteen hundred years to imagine the Roman commander navigating up the Thames, into a land of savagery: a further level of *fabula*, an ancient historical story that all the modern stories must rehearse. One could demonstrate in a number of texts—James's *The Aspern Papers*, for instance, or Gide's *Les Faux-Monnayeurs*, or Faulkner's *Absalom, Absalom!*, even Proust's *Recherche* insofar as Marcel repeats the story of Swann in love—that there seems to be a need for protagonists and storytellers, and particularly protagonists *as* storytellers, to attach their narratives to someone else's, to be ever the belated followers of the track of another. Do we find here once again the influence of the detective story, that genre invented by the nineteenth century and so highly characteristic of it? Partly, perhaps, but also it may be the implicit conviction that there are no new plots, no primary stories left, only the possibility of repeating others. The sons are not free of the fathers but bound to the retracing of their traces. But yet again, the impossibility of original story, the need to retell, places the primary emphasis of the tale on the plane of narration itself, calls attention to the attempt to repeat, reconstruct, retell. In the act of narration, the narrators often end up telling a different story from that they imagined they were telling: the narrator of *The Aspern Papers*, for instance, tells the story of his own crime while intending to tell that of a detection. Marlow, thinking to tell us of Kurtz's victory wrested from innumerable defeats, himself wrests a kind of defeat from the postulated victory.

But to state the outcome of *Heart of Darkness* as either victory or defeat is to posit for it a finality which its very form subverts. In an essay on Henry James, Conrad talks about conventional novelistic ends, what he calls "the usual methods of solution by rewards and punishments, by crowned love, by fortune, by a broken leg or a sudden death." [12] He goes on to note: "These solutions are legitimate inasmuch as they satisfy the desire for finality, for which our hearts yearn, with a longing greater than the longing for the loaves and the fishes of this earth. Perhaps the only true desire of mankind, coming thus to light in its hours of leisure, is to be set at rest." Thus does Conrad offer his version of *Beyond the Pleasure Principle*. That the challenging storyteller should refuse this "rest," postpone and defer the quiescence of the end, becomes clear as Conrad goes on to characterize James's nonfinal, rest-less endings: "You remain with the sense of the life still going on; and even the subtle presence of the dead is felt in that silence that comes upon the artist-creation when the last word has been read." The presence of the dead: certain ghosts, such as Kurtz's, are never laid to rest.

The effort to narrate one's life story as it relates to their numinous and baleful presence is never done. One must tell and tell again, hoping that one's repetition will in turn be repeated, that one's voice will re-echo.

10

Fictions of the Wolf Man: Freud and Narrative Understanding

Sergei P——, otherwise known as the Wolf Man, died in the Vienna Psychiatric Hospital at the age of ninety-two on May 7, 1979. The event passed without much public notice. No doubt most present-day readers of Freud's classic case history of the Wolf Man, *From the History of an Infantile Neurosis*, published in 1918, have assumed that its subject long since passed away, or at least vanished from the context of the narratable into the vague and uninteresting realm of "real life." He had become fixed as a literary figure, a textual creation, evoked to represent a certain psychological configuration, an exemplary biography. The Wolf Man, however, in 1971 published his own memoirs, including his reminiscence of the remarkable Dr. Freud, thus offering a curious moment of reversal, as if the object of investigation in the detective story had suddenly taken over the narrative from the detective himself. Yet he called his memoirs *The Wolf-Man by the Wolf-Man*, signing his own version of his life's story with the name he had been assigned by Freud in the case history, the name derived from his most famous traumatic dream, itself using as its representational material derivatives from fairy tales: a symbolic fictional construct at several removes from "reality" which he yet assumed as his public identity. His identity remained to the end of his life inextricably bound up with his role as the most famous "case" of psychoanalysis, with a biography written by Freud that was essential to a certain conceptual moment and theoretical construction in Freud's thought.[1]

However much for us as readers the Wolf Man belongs to the pages of Freud's case history, he had, of course, his "own" histories. He lived through the individual and collective disasters of two world wars, the Bolshevik Revolution in his native Russia, the Nazi *Anschluss* in Austria, economic inflation, devaluation, and destitution, his wife's suicide, the demise of his two principal psychoanalysts, Freud and Ruth Mack Brunswick, and the persistence to the end of evident obsessional traits. The outer history of the Wolf Man was all too closely intertwined with the cataclysmic political history of twentieth-century Europe; while his inner history, as we know from Freud's case history, remained resolutely fixed on the past, caught in the labyrinth of personal disasters that Freud traces back to his patient's second year. The place of this inner story, this "history of an infantile neurosis," within the context of the experience of modern political and social history already suggests an elusive and particularly "modernist" issue of meaning and understanding. In particular, the case history within history, and personal history within the case history, pose forcefully major questions about the nature of historical and narrative understanding, suggesting both the necessity and the limits of narrative meanings, and the complexity of our uses of narrative plot.

Let me lay out briefly the salient points of personal and general history. The Wolf Man was born on Christmas Day, 1886, according to the Julian calendar used in Russia (January 6, 1887, by the Gregorian calendar), the son of a wealthy Russian landowner and liberal political leader. He arrived in Vienna in January, 1910, a severely debilitated young man accompanied by his valet and his personal physician; he carried a letter of introduction to Freud, who immediately won his confidence, and began analysis. He had spent the previous two years in and out of various sanatoria, undergoing hydrotherapy and every other cure within the arsenal of German alienists, but without remission in his obsessive and hysterical symptoms. It was in a Munich sanatorium that he had fallen violently in love with his nurse, Therese, whom he pursued to her room and besieged with requests for a rendezvous, to become her lover in a brief, stormy, interrupted affair. By 1911, Freud considered the analysis well enough begun to permit the Wolf Man to see Therese again; and in 1914, she came to Vienna, and the couple received Freud's permission to marry at the completion of analysis. This appeared to be at hand: the Wolf Man, preparing to return to Odessa, called upon Freud to bid him goodbye on June 29, 1914. The day before, the Archduke Franz Ferdinand had been shot at Sarajevo. Neither the Wolf Man nor Freud foresaw the consequence: that for the next five years there could be no communication between them. By spring 1918, Odessa was occupied by German troops. Then came the collapse of the Central Powers, the October Revolution, and the arrival of the Red Army. In 1919, the Wolf Man managed to escape from Odessa and make his way along the Black Sea to Rumania, thence to Austria. On very bad advice, he equipped himself for exile by buying an equal number of German marks and Austrian crowns, which by the time of his arrival were close to worthless. His immense fortune had indeed vanished to nothing, and when he returned to Freud in the fall of 1919 to resume analysis of some previously unanalyzed material, he was unable to pay him. Freud undertook this new analysis gratis because the Wolf Man—whose case history he had in the meantime written (in 1914–15), then published with two important bracketed additions (in 1918)—had proved to be so valuable to the progress of psychoanalysis. The Wolf Man indeed became a kind of ward of the Vienna psychoanalytic community, living off its annual dole, a collection undertaken by Freud from among his wealthy patients and disciples that would itself play an important role in the later analyses carried out by Ruth Mack Brunswick, which would be concerned with elements of the transference unresolved in the original analysis. Eventually, the Wolf Man found employment as an insurance agent and lived a petit-bourgeois existence, complete with Sunday painting, in a state of relative peace which was, however, shattered for some time by Therese's suicide shortly following the *Anschluss*. While at times ostensibly skeptical about the lasting therapeutic benefits of psychoanalysis—and himself never wholly free from neurotic obsessions, particularly in his erotic life—he remained a devout admirer of Freud, one who had evidently absorbed the lessons of psychoanalysis so well that they informed his entire world view. He wrote papers on the psychoanalytic study of art and continued to talk of his own biography, his relation to figures past and present, in a nuanced and well-mastered psychoanalytic vocabulary. He was frequently visited by Freud's disciples, and apparently to the last received a small stipend from the Freud Archives, of which indeed he could be said to have constituted a living part.[2]

When he first came to Freud in 1910, the Wolf Man was emblematic of one aspect of European high bourgeois culture in its finest flowering: the morbid narcissism of its most sensitive and artistic souls, those debris of capitalist and imperialist grandeur who perhaps in some measure legitimized empire building and public affairs through the implicit equation of their incapacity to participate with sickness. Dependent on his valet and his personal physician in all the routines of daily life (including dressing in the morning and receiving his regular enema for his hysterical constipation), the Wolf Man reminds us of the decadent des Esseintes, hero of Huysmans's *A Rebours*, indeed of a whole line of valetudinarian heroes reaching back to Villiers de l'Isle-Adam's *Axël*, who some years earlier had spoken the celebrated slogan: "Live? Our servants will do that for us." The cast of characters that moves through his years in the German sanatoria—French princesses, Russian counts, merchants from Hamburg, an occasional spinster from Boston—evokes nothing so much as Thomas Mann's *The Magic Mountain*, with its microcosm of European civilization on the brink of its destruction in the Great War. The Wolf Man's pursuit of Therese has much of the grotesque pathos of Hans Castorp's courtship of Clavdia Chauchat. In his memoirs, the Wolf Man compares his love for Therese, who reminds him of a Leonardo painting, to Swann's passion for Odette, who reminded *him* of a Botticelli painting, in Proust's *Recherche*. Like the novels of Mann and Proust, the Wolf Man's story seems to draw up the balance sheet of European high bourgeois culture at the moment of its apparent triumph as it blindly prepares its self-immolation. By the time of his return to Freud, the social order that produced the Wolf Man, and his story, had been shattered, the "proud tower" of European civilization lay in fragments, its advanced culture stunned by reversal.

Like the two great representative novels of European Modernism that I have evoked, the story of the Wolf Man contains within it the outline of a "standard" nineteenth-century narrative—the story of a coherent individual in society and within history—yet, again like these novels, so complicated and undermined by the process of its telling that the apparent premises of the nineteenth-century narrative mode are put into question. In a manner yet more radical than Mann's or even Proust's—perhaps more nearly approaching Faulkner's—Freud's case history involves a new questioning of how life stories go together, how narrative units combine in significant sequence, where cause and effect are to be sought, and how meaning is related to narration. The case history of the Wolf Man's story, itself embedded in modern history, suggests a paradigm of the status of modern explanation, which must on the one hand see itself as narrative, concerned with a set of histories and the mediations among them, and on the other hand recognizes that the traditional tenets and the very authority of narrative have been subverted, that the bases of explanation have been radically problematized.

I earlier suggested that the life histories of societies, institutions, and individuals assumed a new importance as the idea of a sacred masterplot lost its persuasive and cohesive force. From sometime in the eighteenth century onward, the interpretation of human plots took on new urgency in response to a new centering of perspectives on the individual personality and a search for patterns in the individual existence and understanding of self that might recover some of the explanatory force lost with the decline of the collective myth. Rousseau's effort to get his life into a book that he might present to the Sovereign Judge—if not God, then at least the reader—stands as the emblematic emergence of the biography of the individual personality, announcing the typical focus and concern of modern narrative. The case history brings this form of narrative explanation into the social and medical sciences, presenting the individual's story as exemplary of human stories in general, and the plotted form it assumes, or that one can detect in it, as a generalizable structure of narrative explanation and understanding. Rousseau in such episodes as that of the stolen ribbon indeed stands at the inception of the case history, the use of narrative to grasp patterns of behavior through time and to trace their etiology. And the Freudian case history, privileging the "prehistoric" period of the individual's life, his early childhood, stands as a direct legacy from Rousseau's discovery of the indelible traces of childhood experience in the mature but never quite grown-up adult.

The urgency of narrative explanation in modern times is, we saw, well represented in that nineteenth-century invention, the detective story, which claims that all action is motivated, causally enchained, and eventually comprehensible as such to the perceptive observer. The urgency of the task of interpreting plot in order to analyze social pathology is nicely suggested by a remark of Sherlock Holmes's at the conclusion of a case called "The Cardboard Box": "What is the meaning of it, Watson? . . . What object is served by this circle of misery and violence and fear? It must tend to some end, or else our universe is ruled by chance, which is unthinkable. But what end? There is the great standing perennial problem to which human reason is as far from an answer as ever." [3] In Holmes's question there sounds both the anguish of the investigator who cannot quite put the evidence of individual cases together in an overarching explanatory theory and the apparent Edwardian confidence that there must be an intelligible and motivated pattern, one that should eventually be accessible to human detection. It is the Wolf Man himself, in his memoirs, who provides the explicit link between Holmes's search for explanation and Freud's:

Once we happened to speak of Conan Doyle and his creation, Sherlock Holmes. I had thought that Freud would have no use for this type of light reading matter, and was surprised to find that this was not at all the case and that Freud had read this author attentively. The fact that circumstantial evidence is useful in psychoanalysis when reconstructing a childhood history may explain Freud's interest in this type of literature.[4]

Freud apparently was fully aware of the analogies between psychoanalytic investigation and detective work. Faced with fragmentary evidence, clues scattered within present reality, he who would explain must reach back to a story in the past which accounts for how the present took on its configuration. The detective story exhibits a reality structured as a set of ambiguous signs which gain their meaning from a past history that must be uncovered so as to order the production of these signs as a chain of events, eventually with a clear origin, intention, and solution, and with strong causal connections between each link. The figure of the detective may be seen as an inevitable product not only of the nineteenth century's concern with criminal deviance, but also, more simply, of its pervasive historicism, its privileging of narrative explanation, accounting for what we are through the reconstruction of how we got that way.

Working to trace the etiology of neurosis, Freud occupies this same ground. In his earliest case histories—those in the *Studies on Hysteria* (1895)—he almost explicitly assumes a Holmesian posture, pressing his patients for the symptomatic clues, reaching back to uncover a moment of trauma, a scene of crime that makes sense of all subsequent events. As he finishes his preliminary exposition of the Wolf Man's symptoms, he again sounds like the detective making out his *aide-mémoire* of the facts in the case: "Here, then, in the briefest outline, are the riddles for which the analysis had to find a solution. What was the origin of the sudden change in the boy's character? What was the significance of his phobia and of his perversities? How did he arrive at his obsessive piety? And how are all these phenomena interrelated?"[5] Yet with the case of the Wolf Man, Freud will discover "detection" and its narrative to be extraordinarily more complex and problematic, like the plots of modernist fiction, and indeed inextricably bound up with the fictional. I want to consider how the narrativity of the structure of explanation deployed in this nonfictional genre, the case history, necessarily implicates the question of fictions through the very plotting of that narrativity and what this implies about the nature of modernist narrative understanding.

The problem for this riddle-solver is similar to that posed to his classic precursor, Oedipus, who responds initially to the message of the Delphic oracle—that he can purge Thebes of its pollution only by driving out the murderer of Laius—with the words: "The track of this ancient guilt is hard to detect." [6] Freud at the threshold of his case history warns us that he is dealing with an infantile neurosis analyzed fifteen years after its termination, a "childhood disorder" analyzed "through the medium of recollection in an intellectually mature adult" (p. 9). The "crime" to be detected is again an ancient one, covered over by subsequent events, overlaid by adult disorders, accessible only to rememoration: Freud with the Wolf Man is in a position analogous to that of the Proustian narrator in relation to his own buried past or, better, to those Faulknerian narrators who must unearth, order, make sense of the past stories of others in order to make sense of history and their own understandings of life. Freud writes further:

> I will once more recall the fact that our therapeutic work was concerned with a subsequent and recent neurotic illness, and that light could only be thrown upon these earlier problems when the course of the analysis led away for a time from the present, and forced us to make a *détour* through the prehistoric period of childhood. (pp. 17–18)

The detective here is doubled, in what we know was one of Freud's avocations as well as a source of recurrent imagery, by the archaeologist, digging through the mental strata in order to reconstruct the plan of a primitive organization and its various modifications through time. He will indeed refer us to the archaeological analogy toward the end of the case history as he seeks to image the survival of contradictory impulses in the Wolf Man's psychic history:

> So it was that his mental life impressed one in much the same way as the religion of ancient Egypt, which is so unintelligible to us because it preserves the earlier stages of its development

side by side with the end-products, retains the most ancient gods and their attributes along with the most modern ones, and thus, as it were, spreads out upon a two-dimensional surface what other instances of evolution show us in the solid. (p. 119)

This sentence suggests the problem of an understanding which must both trace narrative evolutions and preserve a sense of structures which resist the passage of time, which maintain their covert force into the present. Explanation must be both narrative and structural, tracing the etiology of neurosis and mapping the interrelationship of elements that define the "set" toward neurosis. There is a tension between spatial and temporal form, neither of which can ever wholly "saturate" the other, which exposition must recover in a relation of complementarity through its own successive ordering of evidence, story, and solution.

But the plot of exposition cannot itself be simple or linear. If Freud's goal can only be reached through a return to beginnings— the "*détour* through the prehistoric period of childhood"—this temporal analepsis provides neither the entire place of explanation nor the whole of what requires narration. Freud encounters not only a problem in investigation but also a problem of exposition, of writing, which he alludes to at the start of his second chapter, where he confesses that he is "unable to give either a purely historical or a purely thematic account" of his patient's story; that he can write a consecutive "history neither of the treatment nor of the illness," but must combine different stories and methods of presentation (p. 13). Attempting to "unpack" Freud's two either/ors here, we find four separable elements in his material and his account: (1) the structure of the infantile neurosis (the history of the neurosis); (2) the order of event in the past providing the cause of the neurosis (the etiology of the neurosis); (3) the order of emergence of past event during the analysis (the history of the treatment); (4) the order of report in the case history.

It may be helpful here to refer once again to the Russian formalist distinction between *fabula*, or story, and *sjužet*, or plot—a distinction that itself belongs to a modernist awareness and, in its application to Freud's case history, suggests how we read even this kind of biographical account with certain narrative expectations. In Freud's text, the *sjužet* must ultimately be the fourth in the series of elements I identified: the order of report of the material that constitutes the "case" of the Wolf Man.[7] But this *sjužet* will alternately choose its *fabula* from among the three other elements, sometimes presenting the history and structure of the infantile neurosis, sometimes tracing the events that caused it, sometimes following the course of the analysis and the way event emerged during it. The "ultimate" *fabula*, one might say, is element number 2, the etiology of the infantile neurosis; but in the presentation, element number 1, the way the neurosis manifested itself and evolved, can serve as its *sjužet*, and so can element number 3, the way the events of childhood emerged during the analytic sessions. The history of the neurosis, element number 1, can in turn be *fabula* to element number 3 as *sjužet*. The elements occupy shifting positions in relation to one another, as the "story" and its "plotting," and it must be the task of the fourth element, the writing of the case history itself, to recover the other elements in their complex interrelationship. Freud evokes frequently the problems of exposition and explanation which this situation poses: he notes, for instance, the limitations encountered in "forcing a structure which is itself in many dimensions" onto a two-dimensional plane (p. 72). He must manage to tell, both "at once" and "in order," the story of a person, the story of an illness, the story of an investigation, the story of an explanation; and "meaning" must ultimately lie in the effective interrelationship of all of these.

One can trace this issue of exposition and explanation in the detail of the analysis itself. To take briefly just one example, consider the dream, the terrifying dream of the six or seven white wolves sitting in a tree which came to name the case, and the patient, and which Freud from its first introduction into the analysis held to be the most important piece of evidence in discovering the causes of the infantile neurosis. This dream from childhood, restaged near the beginning of the analysis but fully elucidated only toward its end, subtends the whole course of the analysis as the ur-text which all the other verbal structures exist to elucidate. For the manifest text of a dream, of course, both conceals and reveals. It demands a decipherment, an understanding of the latent dream thoughts staged and distorted by the dream work, which is comparable to finding the original *fabula* which a displaced and condensed *sjužet* "covers" with clues, at once suggestive and misleading, that must be read by the detective interpreter. My use of terms belonging to the analysis of narrative finds justification here in that the analysis of a dream involves, among other things, unpacking a dense, over-laid, concentrated text and reordering its components as narrative, finding the implications of *story* behind the dream. As in detective narratives—in "The Musgrave Ritual," for instance—the dream's metaphors, and the dream as metaphor, must be plotted out as metonymies. The thematic material suggested by the dream, and the associations that the dreamer is able to articulate in reviewing the dream, can only begin to make sense when narrativized, or-dered as a sequence of events. Yet, of course, in the etiology of the Wolf Man's infantile neurosis, the dream itself is an *event*, indeed the decisive traumatic event, in that by deferred action it produces the neurotic reaction to the "primal scene," witnessed two and a half years earlier, and to the "seduction," which occurred several months earlier. The dream is both, as rememoration, the record of past event, and, in the past, a decisive present event in the Wolf Man's story; a *sjužet* that is itself in turn *fabula*, a text that both explains and alters the reality to which it refers.[8]

The question of narrative ordering—the constitution of a co-herent and explanatory sequence of event, of recognizable units in Barthes's proairetic and hermeneutic codes—is both of overwhelm-ing importance to the analysis and of increasingly problema-tized status. A typical instance concerns the scene with the servant Grusha, which emerges timidly, incompletely, but in strong outline, from unpacking the "screen memory" of the swallowtail butterfly and the child's phobic reaction to it. This is in fact the earliest real remembrance that the Wolf Man will produce—it is prior to the wolf dream—and it pictures Grusha scrubbing the floor on her hands and knees, her buttocks projecting, and includes her scolding the child. Her chastisement Freud reconstructs as the threat of castration in response to the child's urination, an action that can itself be supplied from the association between Grusha's broom, made of a bundle of twigs, and the bundles of firewood used to burn John Huss at the stake (in a story that had impressed the child), where burning is a compensatory image for uncontrolled urination. Grusha's posture on the floor suggests the mother's posture during the earlier scene of *coitus a tergo*, which would make of the urination a childish attempt at seduction; while the association of the two postures explains, by displacement, the Wolf Man's later violent passion for servant girls as a class. Postures appear to indicate the joints and interconnections of event, the way one event "plugs into" another. Yet, Freud asks in one of his bracketed additions to his text, are we justified in regarding the child's urination during this scene as evidence of an earlier impression of sexual excitement, thereby "proving" the infant's observation of parental intercourse? Or is the scene with Grusha itself "innocent," and sexualized only retrospectively, on the basis of later encounters with the postures of intercourse? Is it a case of deferred action or retroaction? Having posed the alternatives, Freud readily concedes that he cannot offer a decision between them; they constitute an either/ or, a moment of sequential and causal undecidability which may revise our very conception of the narrative interrelationship of event. We are faced with a recombinant potential of postures and possibly reversible chains of association. The relation between *fabula* and *sjužet*, between event and its significant reworking, is one of suspicion and conjecture, a structure of indeterminacy which can offer only a framework of narrative possibilities rather than a clearly specifiable plot.

Undecidability becomes a particularly acute issue in the question of origins. The specification of origins should be of the utmost importance in any etiological explanation: to understand causes, one must get back to the beginning. Indeed, a great part of the nineteenth-century confidence in narrative explanation, and the need for it, reposes on the postulate that a history can be and should

be a tracing of origins. We know what we are because we can say
where we are, and we know this because we can say where we came
from. The authority of narrative derives from its capacity to speak
of origins in relation to endpoints. Freud is no exception in his
original postulate. He traces the beginning of the childhood neurosis back to the occurrence of the dream, then traces the origin
of the dream back to the occurrence of the "primal scene"—the
scene of parental intercourse—to which the child, then one and a
half years old, was witness. The primal scene thus appears as the
origin of all origins, the bedrock of the Wolf Man's case, the inception of his story. Like what is often called the *drame du coucher*
in Proust's novel—the drama of the mother's withheld kiss—it is
that moment of the buried yet living past on which the Wolf Man's
subsequent existence is founded.

And yet: when Freud has uncovered—or more accurately, reconstructed—this primal scene, which would appear to be crucial
to his narrative of the Wolf Man's case, he proceeds to erase it. In
the two long bracketed passages added to chapters five and eight
(added in 1918, whereas the bulk of the case history had been
written in 1914–15) he questions whether the primal scene, the
observation of parental coitus, ever had any reality as *event*. It might
rather be a phantasy concocted from the observation of animals
copulating, then referred back to the parents. Thus in the place
of a primal scene we would have a primal phantasy, operating *as*
event by deferred action. And Freud refers us at this point to his
discussion of the problem in the *Introductory Lectures*, where he
considers that such primal phantasies may be a phylogenetic inheritance through which the individual reaches back to the history
of mankind, to a racial "masterplot."

We have at this crucial moment of the case history an apparent
evacuation of the problem of origins, substituting for a founding
event a phantasy or fiction on which is conferred all the authority
and force of prime mover, and the evocation of a possible infinite
regress in the unconscious of the race. This "solution" might appear
irresponsible, an abandonment of all distinction between the fictional and the nonfictional, might indeed appear to build into Freud's

explanatory account a kind of self-destruct mechanism. Worse still, Freud closes his discussion of primal scenes versus primal phantasies with a *non liquet*, arguing that the case is properly undecidable. And then, returning to the question, he argues further that undecidability is not of importance, since the subsequent history, whether it derives from primal scene or primal phantasy, remains unchanged.

We have here one of the most daring moments of Freud's thought, and one of his most heroic gestures as a writer. He could have achieved a more coherent, finished, enclosed, and authoritative narrative by sticking by his arguments of 1914–15, never adding the bracketed passages. Or, given his second thoughts of 1918, he could have struck out parts of the earlier argument and substituted for them his later reflections. What is remarkable is that, having discovered his point of origin, that which made sense of the dream, the neurosis, and his own account of them, Freud then felt obliged to retrace the story, offering another and much less evidential (and "eventimential") kind of origin, to tell another version of the plot, and then finally leave one juxtaposed to the other, indeed one superimposed on the other as a kind of palimpsest, a layered text that offers differing versions of the same story. A narrative explanation that surely foresaw that much of its celebrity would come from its recovery of so spectacular a moment of origin doubles back on itself to question that origin and indeed to displace the whole question of origins, to suggest another kind of referentiality, in that all tales may lead back not so much to events as to other tales, to man as a structure of the fictions he tells about himself.[9]

A narrative account that allows the inception of its story to be either event or fiction—that in turn opens up the potential for another story, anonymous and prehistoric—perilously destabilizes belief in explanatory histories as exhaustive accounts whose authority derives from the force of closure, from the capacity to say: here is where it began, here is what it became. Like Holmes with the text of the Musgrave ritual, Freud has unpacked dreams, screen memories, obsessional and hysterical symptoms—those bodily metaphors through which unconscious desire inscribes its messages—

but here the result is not the neat Holmesian solution but rather a proliferation of narratives with no ultimate points of fixity. Consequently, the shape of the individual and his biography becomes uncontrollable: their etiology and evolution are assigned to an unspecifiable network of event, fiction, and interpretation. It is as if we were condemned always to an understanding of stories and persons as uncertain and troubling as Marlow's version of Kurtz. We should note here not only the possible fictionality of the primal scene (which curiously borrows the structure of the fairy tale, since the coitus is three times repeated) but also that those wolves that were the object of the child's phobia themselves turn out to be a product of fictions, of the fairy tales heard in childhood. The very name of this nonfictional character—born 1887, died 1979—is a derivative of age-old anonymous fictions. The person who signed his autobiographical writings "Wolf Man" should perhaps be considered less a character from Mann or Proust than a Virginia Woolfman.

The Wolf Man's "real" name indeed is inscribed in the text only through his initials, S.P., which make their appearance through the associations of another dream, as a pun on the insect he calls an *Espe*, which is really a mutilated *Wespe*, a wasp with its wings torn off. The psychological subject is present to himself in the text as a linguistic deformation, suggesting the interconnections of anxiety, desire, and language in the problematic identity of the self. This vestigial proper name coded in the condensed and displaced memory, which here covers a wish for revenge against the threat of castration, implies a gap between identity and desire, the uneasy relation of the forward-moving narrative of life to the other story told by indestructible unconscious desire. That is, unconscious desire has its own history, its version of an unsatisfactory past and what would give it satisfaction, a history unavailable to the conscious subject but persistently repeating its thrust and drive in present symbolic formations. As Jacques Lacan puts it, "It is the truth of what desire has been in its history that the subject cries out in his symptom."[10] We know that in Lacan's terms this desire is unappeasable because it is directed toward fictional scenarios of fulfillment from deep in the past. It is the historicity of this fictionally originated desire—buried yet continuing as a filigree of design in the present, inhabiting a language that intends more than it says—that emerges as the plot of analysis and its exposition in the case history. One result is that language itself, as the agency of desire's insistence *toward* meaning, is in a state of displacement and fictionality, ever a mutilated naming or misnaming from which we must try to reconstruct what the name of the lost object might have signified. Biography, even in the form of the case history, appears to be intimate with fiction: it is a hypothetical construction.

That the Wolf Man's narrative and his very identity are bound up with the fictions he was told and read and dreamed as a child suggests a classic trope of the novelistic genre, from Cervantes on, where the hero must be disillusioned of a bookish, mystified conception of reality. What is radically modernist in Freud's narrative is that there is not and cannot be any disillusion: the self is bound in illusory relations, and the most one can hope for is some understanding of the order of relation itself, its uses as symbolic code. Freud's suggestion that the individual life history may open backward onto a phylogenetic masterplot is a further modernist gesture, an example of how we try to account for the insertion of the individual subject within political, biological, and cosmic history. One thinks here of the manner in which Thomas Mann uses the Faust legend or the story of Joseph and his brothers, or Faulkner the widening historical patterns of a man's life, a family's genealogy, the South's history, or Joyce the patterns of Homeric epic as the backdrop to a day in modern Dublin: these examples may in different ways suggest the problematic relation of the seemingly undirected individual existence to large transindividual orders—orders that might explain, organize, justify, if only one were certain of their status, if only one could reinvest them with the explanatory power of sacred myth. The modernist thirst for myth, for explanatory and justificatory masterplots, which we find not only in Joyce, Mann, Faulkner, but also in Yeats, Eliot, Gide, Kafka, Giraudoux, and so many others, is suggested in Freud's comment that a person "catches hold of this phylogenetic experience where his own experience fails him. He fills in the gaps in individual truth with prehistoric truth" (p. 97). The individual, we might say, makes raids on a putative masterplot in order to remedy the insufficiencies of his own unsatisfactory plot—unsatisfactory because unclosed and thus not fully coherent, unilluminated. It is as if the individual, in order to be able to narrate his life story to himself in such a way as to make it coherent and significant, had to reach back toward the idea of a providential plot which, for better or for worse, would subsume his experience to that of mankind, to show the individual as a significant repetition of a story already endowed with meaning, were it to be only the painful and inevitable story of Oedipus of Thebes. Filling in the gaps of individual truth with prehistoric truth may be one possible maneuver to elude Sherlock Holmes's question about the meaning of secular plots.

In Freud's early case histories, those of *Studies on Hysteria*, finding the chain of events leading from the initial trauma, usually infantile, to its sexualized repetition, usually during adolescence, on to the present symptoms provided a seamless narrative that was thought to be cathartic and therefore in itself curative. The detective story in the case of the Wolf Man is evidently far more complex than anything in the Holmes canon; it resembles more the tenuous solutions to uncertain problems presented by *Heart of Darkness* or a number of tales by Jorge Luis Borges. Not only does Freud question whether one can, or need, claim that "in the beginning was the deed"—since the imagined can have the full originary force of the deed—he also proposes a radical revision of conventional notions of narrative causality. The logic of his interpretive work moves Freud to an understanding that causation can work backward as well as forward since the effect of event, or of phantasy, often comes only when it takes on meaning, usually when it takes on sexual significance, which may occur with considerable delay. Chronological sequence may not settle the issue of cause: events may gain traumatic significance by deferred action (*Nachträglichkeit*) or retroaction, action working in reverse sequence to create a meaning that did not previously exist. Thus the way a story is ordered does not necessarily correspond to the way it *works*. Indeed, narrative order, sequence as a logical enchainment of actions and outcomes, must be considered less a solution than part of the problem of narrative explanation. How we narrate a life—even our own life to ourselves—is at least a double process, the attempt to incorporate within an orderly narrative the more devious, persistent, and powerful plot whose logic is dictated by desire.

Freud also recognizes that there are elements of cause and signification that can never really be narrativized at all, but must rather be understood through a structural analysis, in a "mapping" of a certain psychic "set" toward neurosis, a network analyzed with extraordinary complexity in the chapter of this case history entitled "Anal Eroticism and the Castration Complex," which demonstrates explicitly what is implicit throughout the case history, that causality must be thought of in a context of probability, complementarity, and uncertainty. And if we return to Freud's preliminary remarks concerning the analysis, we find an acknowledgment that narrative itself, as a mode of discourse and understanding, has only a provisional status. Its understandings work on and in time, while the unconscious remains timeless. The analyst must patiently submit to this timelessness; yet he must also know when and how to impose a time limit on analysis, in order to speed up the overcoming of resistances—an artificial *finis* which creates temporal form. As the analysis of the Wolf Man proceeds, it reveals (as most narratives do) both a drive toward the end and a resistance to ending. Freud would argue, in one of his last essays, that analysis is inherently interminable, since the dynamics of resistance and the transference can always generate new beginnings in relation to any conceivable end. The narrative of the Wolf Man must be given closure and shape, but these are provisional, and could always reopen to take in further circles of meaning and theory. As Henry James wrote in a famous line from the preface to *Roderick Hudson*, "Really, universally, relations stop nowhere, and the exquisite problem of the artist is eternally but to draw, by a geometry of his own, the circle within which they shall happily *appear* to do so."[11] The closure demanded by narrative understanding—the closure without which it can have no coherent plot—is always provisional, as-if, a necessary fiction.

There is in Freud's case histories an underlying assumption that psychic health corresponds to a coherent narrative account of one's life. As Steven Marcus notes in his discussion of the case history of Dora, "Human life is, ideally, a connected and coherent story, with all the details in explanatory place, and with everything (or as close to everything as is practically possible) accounted for, in its proper causal or other sequence. And inversely illness amounts at least in part to suffering from an incoherent story or an inadequate narrative account of oneself." [12] In *Dora*, Freud claims that "the patients' inability to give an ordered history of their life insofar as it coincides with the history of their illness is not merely characteristic of the neurosis. It also possesses great theoretical significance." Marcus rightly stresses the "tribute" Freud pays here to the culture of narrative, the authority conferred on the great novels of the nineteenth century and after in the illumination of human significances. Marcus also goes on to demonstrate that *Dora* is a more complex and novelistic construction than it might at first appear, and that Freud can be accused of being an "unreliable narrator"— which Freud indeed partly admits, since he confesses that he did not at the time sufficiently understand the role of the transference. *Dora*, it seems to me, reads like a flawed Victorian novel, one with a ramifying cast of characters and relations that never can be brought into satisfactory form. With the case history of the Wolf Man, Freud has advanced to a more sophisticated presentation of complex narrative plots and a more subtle understanding of what the "healthy" narrative of life may be.

It is notable that Freud more than once during the course of this analysis proposes to the Wolf Man a more straightforward, logical, "reasonable" narrative of events, only to have his patient refuse recognition and credence to these standardized plots. Freud and his patient together demonstrate that it is not so much simple coherence and mere plausibility that make our narratives persuasive. Narrative sequences and scenarios must accord with the complex, twisting, subversive patternings of desire. The insistent past must be allowed to write its design at the same time one attempts to unravel it. As well as having form, plots must generate force: the force that makes the connection of incidents powerful, that shapes

the confused material of a life into an intentional str
turn generates new insights about how life can be to
erful fiction is that which is able to restage the comp
past history of desire as it covertly reconstitutes itself in the present
language.

This present language, it should be clear, lacks the firm authority
of the scientific monologue, the unchallenged voice of truth. It is
in fact the meeting place of two voices, that of the patient and that
of the analyst, in the "transitional realm" of the transference, linked
in the dialogue of analysis. As Lacan writes of the transference:
"In psychoanalysis, in fact, the subject, properly speaking, constitutes himself by a discourse where the mere presence of the analyst
brings, prior to any intervention [by the analyst], the dimension of
dialogue."[14] The presence of the analyst as narratee and potential
narrator "dialogizes" the discourse of the analysand. The analytic
transference thus realizes Mikhaïl Bakhtin's conception of the "dialogic," whereby discourse internalizes the presence of otherness,
becomes marked by the alterity inherent in any social use of language.[15] In this medium of the in-between—Freud, we remember,
called the transference a *Zwischenreich*—the "true" narrative lies in-
between, in the process of exchange; it is the product of two discourses playing against one another, often warring with one another, working toward recognitions mutually acknowledged but
internalized in different ways. Analysis hence constitutes itself as
inherently dialogic, a perpetually reversing counterpoint of self and
other, closure and opening, origin and process. Centerless and
never finally terminable, analytic discourse is consubstantial with
the complementarity and uncertainty, either/ors, deferred actions
and retroactions, to which Freud has narrative recourse when he
finds there is no centered and authoritative explanatory history.

As we have said before, the patient comes to the analyst with a
story to tell, a story that is not so much false—since it does in some
manner signify the truth—as it is incomplete and untherapeutic.
Its plot lacks the dynamic necessary to creating sequence and design
that integrate and explain. The fuller plot constructed by the analytic work must be more dynamic, thus more useful as a shaping

and connective force; above all it must be hermeneutically more forceful. It must carry the power of conviction, for its tellers and its listeners, that is the ultimate goal of storytelling. Truth, then, arises from a dialogue among a number of *fabula* and a number of *sjužet*, stories and their possible organizations, as also between two narrators, analysand and analyst. A centerless and reversible structure, dialogue is an agency of narration that creates as it questions the narrative, and designates the field of force of the necessary fiction.

A case history is the story of an individual presented to the public for didactic purposes: it is a form of exemplary biography. In the course of his use of the genre, Freud encounters all the problems of narrative design and exposition faced by biographers, historians, and novelists, and the issues of fictionality that have haunted literature since Plato. A nonfictional genre concerning a real person, the case history of the Wolf Man is radically allied to the fictional since its causes and connections depend on probabilistic constructions rather than authoritative facts, and on imaginary scenarios of lack and desire, and since the very language that it must work with, as both object and medium of its explanations, takes its form from histories of desire consubstantial with what cannot be. In his narratives—as in all his writings—Freud shares with such other modernists as Conrad or Joyce or Proust a basic pessimism about life stories and their putative plots. His vision of man insists on the limits to man's self-knowledge and mastery of his own biography. What man can be depends on the uncertain relation of the conscious subject to the unconscious. "Wo Es war soll Ich werden": the famous dictum is traditionally, and optimistically, translated, "Where Id was shall Ego come to be," but it may rather signify a never-ending struggle of the ego to coincide with and master that otherness within that drives the subject in obscure ways.[16] And the telling of the history of this struggle is always a hypothetical construction.

Like the modernist novel, the case history of the Wolf Man shows up the limits of storytelling while nonetheless insisting that the story must get told. The plots of narrative have become extraordinarily complex, self-subversive, apparently implausible. They have been forced to abandon clear origins and terminations in favor of provisional closures and fictional inceptions; their causes may work by deferred action and retroaction; their connections are probable rather than logical; their individual dramas stand in uncertain tension with transindividual imaginings. But if plot has become an object of suspicion, it remains no less necessary: telling the self's story remains our indispensable thread in the labyrinth of temporality. It is of overwhelming importance to us that life still be narratable, which may mean finding those provisional, tenuous plots that appear to capture the force of desire that cannot speak its name but compels us in a movement—recursive, complex, unclosed—toward meaning. Hence the importance of the issues in narrative that Freud so forcefully poses. Freud's restless thought and his dynamic model of psychic life summon us to think beyond formalist paradigms, to engage the dynamic of memory and desire that can reconnect, however provisionally and tenuously, time lost and time continuing.

11

Incredulous Narration:
Absalom, Absalom!

To a reader concerned with the design and project of narrative, William Faulkner's *Absalom, Absalom!* is full of interest. More than Faulkner's other novels, *Absalom, Absalom!* seems to pose with acute force problems in the epistemology of narrative and the cognitive uses of plotting in a context of radical doubt about the validity of plot. Perhaps even more than such cerebral probes into these issues as Joyce's *Ulysses*, Gide's *Les Faux-Monnayeurs*, Italo Svevo's *La Coscienza di Zeno*, or Michel Butor's *La Modification*, *Absalom, Absalom!* offers an exemplary challenge to the critic since it both sums up the nineteenth-century tradition of the novel—particularly its concern with genealogy, authority, and patterns of transmission—while subverting it, working this subversion in a manner that reaffirms a traditional set of problems for the novel while disallowing its traditional solutions. Here is a novel that in its appendix provides us with a chronology (as in Freud's final footnote to the Wolf Man), a genealogy (as in such familial chronicles as Zola's *Les Rougon-Macquart* and Galsworthy's *The Forsyte Saga*), and a map (furnished implicitly if not literally throughout Balzac, Tolstoy, Hardy, and other novelists who stake out and order terrain). These are traditional schemata for the ordering of time and experience from which *Absalom, Absalom!* markedly departs, yet by which it is also haunted, as by the force of an absence. *Absalom, Absalom!* may indeed be very much the story of the haunting force of absences, including formal absences, in the wake of whose passage the novel constructs itself.

As a first approach to the place of plot in *Absalom, Absalom!*, we can refer again to the concept of narrative as a coded activity, implicit in all narratology and urged most persuasively by Roland Barthes in *S/Z*. That is, a given narrative weaves its individual pattern from pre-existent codes, which derive, most immediately at least, from the "already written." The reading of a narrative then tends to decipher, to organize, to rationalize, to *name* in terms of codes derived from the "already read." We noted that two of Barthes's five codes seem particularly pertinent to the study of plot: the proairetic, or "code of actions," and the hermeneutic, or code of enigmas and answers, ultimately the code or voice of "Truth." The proairetic, it will be recalled, concerns the logic of actions, how the completion of an action can be logically derived from its initiation, and the whole of an action seen as a complete and namable unit, which then enters into combination with other actions, to form sequences. Like its label, this code is essentially Aristotelian, concerned with the wholeness of actions and the logic of their interrelationship. The hermeneutic code rather concerns the questions and answers that structure a story, their suspense, partial unveiling, temporary blockage, eventual resolution, with the resultant creation of a "retarding structure" or "dilatory space" which we work through toward what is felt, in classical narrative, to be meaning revealed. Plot, we suggested, might best be conceived as a combination of the proairetic and the hermeneutic, or better, an over-coding of the proairetic by the hermeneutic. The actions and sequences of action of the narrative are structured into larger wholes by the play of enigma and solution: the hermeneutic acts as a large, shaping force, allowing us to sort out, to group, to see the significance of actions, to rename their sequences in terms of their significance for the narrative as a whole. We read in the suspense created by the hermeneutic code, structuring actions according to its indications, restructuring as we move through partial revelations and misleading clues, moving toward the fullness of meaning provided by the "saturation" of the matrix of the sentence now fully predicated.

A major source of our difficulty in reading *Absalom, Absalom!* may derive from its peculiar use of these two codes, the way they refuse to mesh or synchronize in the traditional mode. As readers, we encounter in the novel certain sequences of action and event that seem to lack any recognizable framework of question and answer, and hence any clear intention of meaning. Worse still, we encounter sequences where the orderly progression of the "proairetisms," the movement of chains of event to their conclusion, is interrupted and interfered with by the formulation of enigmas concerning the actions themselves. It is as if the characters in the novel often turned to the interrogation of a proairetic sequence for its revelatory meaning before we, as readers, have been allowed to see how the sequence runs. The very logic of action is violated by the inquiry into its hermeneutic force, an inquiry that can only derive its sense from an end to the sequence which we have not been privileged to see. Thus it is that we so often find ourselves suddenly faced with hermeneutic shifts of gears, forced to reconsider the very integrity of narrative event in terms of its hermeneutic possibilities and determinations; so that we often find ourselves in the position of Quentin Compson's Canadian roommate at Harvard, Shreve McCannon (relatively, of course, the outsider in the narrative), wanting to shout, as he does, "Wait! For God's sake wait." One quite straightforward instance of the situation I have in mind occurs in the narrative of the killing of Thomas Sutpen by Wash Jones after the birth of the child fathered by Sutpen on Wash's daughter, Milly Jones, where we have this exchange between Shreve and Quentin:

> "Wait," Shreve said. "You mean that he got the son he wanted, after all that trouble, and then turned right around and—"
> "Yes. Sitting in Grandfather's office that afternoon, with his head kind of flung back a little, explaining to Grandfather like he might have been explaining arithmetic to Henry back in the fourth grade: 'You see, all I wanted was just a son. Which seems to me, when I look about at my contemporary scene, no exorbitant gift from nature or circumstance to demand—' "

"*Will you wait?*" Shreve said. "—that with the son he went to all that trouble to get lying right there behind him in the cabin, he would have to taunt the grandfather into killing first him and then the child too?"

"—What?" Quentin said. "It wasn't a son. It was a girl."

"Oh," Shreve said. "—Come on. Let's get out of this damn icebox and go to bed."[1]

We find here a suspension of the revelation that is necessary to make the actions previously recounted (Sutpen's refusal to marry or even to provide for Milly since she has produced a daughter, not a son) into some version of Barthes's fully predicated narrative sentence. This suspension heightens—at the expense of "meaning"—the dramatic rendering of what is the final destruction of Sutpen's life-plot, his "design," itself a major shaping force in the overall hermeneutic code of the narrative.

The reader just as often finds himself witness to a proairetic sequence that appears perfectly logical but lacks the coherence of meaning, as if he had not been given the hermeneutic clues requisite to grasping the intention of event and the motive of its narration. The reader in these cases stands in much the same position as Quentin at the outset of the novel, listening to Rosa Coldfield's narration. I cite a fragment of her narrative from the early pages:

"I saw what had happened to Ellen, my sister. I saw her almost a recluse, watching those two doomed children growing up whom she was helpless to save. I saw the price which she had paid for that house and that pride; I saw the notes of hand on pride and contentment and peace and all to which she had put her signature when she walked into the church that night, begin to fall due in succession. I saw Judith's marriage forbidden without rhyme or reason or shadow of excuse; I saw Ellen die with only me, a child, to turn to and ask to protect her remaining child; I saw Henry repudiate his home and birthright and then return and practically fling the bloody corpse of his sister's sweetheart at the hem of her wedding gown; I

saw that man return—the evil's source and head which had
outlasted all its victims—who had created two children not only
to destroy one another and his own line, but my line as well,
yet I agreed to marry him." (p. 18)

This passage in fact gives virtually the whole of the story to be told,
from Rosa's point of view, and gives it with the insistent veracity
of the eyewitness account: "I saw . . . I saw." What is missing from
her account? In some important sense, everything, for it is a largely
nonhermeneutic narrative, offering no apparent structure of
meaning for this sequence of events, indeed no clue as to how and
even why one should look for meaning in it. There is narrative
aplenty here, as throughout the novel, but inadequate *grounds* for
narrative.

One might generalize from this quotation, to suggest that it characterizes not only a problem *in* the narrative, but the very problem
of narrative in *Absalom, Absalom!*, where ultimately narrative itself
is the problem. Mr. Compson typically generalizes the problem for
us, in one of his noble but slightly futile epic evocations:

"It's just incredible. It just does not explain. Or perhaps that's
it: they don't explain and we are not supposed to know. We
have a few old mouth-to-mouth tales; we exhume from old
trunks and boxes and drawers letters without salutation or
signature, in which men and women who once lived and breathed
are now merely initials or nicknames out of some now incomprehensible affection which sound to us like Sanskrit or Chock-
taw; we see dimly people, the people in whose living blood and
seed we ourselves lay dormant and waiting, in this shadowy
attenuation of time possessing now heroic proportions, per-
forming their acts of simple passion and simple violence, impervious to time and inexplicable— Yes, Judith, Bon, Henry,
Sutpen: all of them. They are there, yet something is missing;
they are like a chemical formula exhumed along with the letters
from that forgotten chest, carefully, the paper old and faded
and falling to pieces, the writing faded, almost indecipherable,
yet meaningful, familiar in shape and sense, the name and

presence of volatile and sentient forces; you bring them together in the proportions called for, but nothing happens; you
re-read, tedious and intent, poring, making sure that you have
forgotten nothing, made no miscalculation; you bring them
together again and again nothing happens: just the words, the
symbols, the shapes themselves, shadowy inscrutable and se-
rene, against that turgid background of a horrible and bloody
mischancing of human affairs." (pp. 100–01)

This passage alludes to all the enigmatic issues of the narrative:
Why did Henry Sutpen kill Charles Bon? What did this killing have
to do with Thomas Sutpen, and with the eventual ruin of the house
of Sutpen? What does this tale of the ancestors have to do with the
present generations? And, especially, how can narrative know what
happened and make sense of the motives of events? And if it cannot,
what happens to lines of descent, to the transmission of knowledge
and wisdom, and to history itself? Is history finally simply a "bloody
mischancing of human affairs"? If for Barthes the resolution of all
enigmas coincides with the full and final predication of the narrative sentence, Mr. Compson here appears to question the possibility of ever finding a predicate: the subjects—the proper names—
are there, but they refuse to accede to meaning.

The quotations from Rosa Coldfield and Mr. Compson both tend
to suggest that on the one hand there is a story to be told—perhaps
even history itself to be told—and on the other hand there is telling
and writing—people writing and reading letters and documents, and
especially, talking—but that somehow what should lie in-between,
the story-as-told, the narrative as coherently plotted, the hermeneutic sentence, is lacking. Referring once again to Gérard Genette's categories, *histoire*, *récit*, and *narration*—"story," "plot," and
"narrating"—it is evident that in *Absalom, Absalom!* we have on the
one hand plenty of narrating, and on the other at least the postulation of a story that may equal history itself. What appears to
be missing is the level of plot, the result of Mr. Compson's chemical
operation, that comprehensible order of event that was the very
substance and raison d'être of the classical narrative.

Another way of stating the problem might be to say that in this

novel which pre-eminently concerns fathers, sons, generation, and
lines of descent, there seems to be no clear authority, not even of
a provisional sort, for the telling of the story, and as a result no
suggestion of how to achieve mastery of its interpretation. The
nineteenth-century novel, we saw, repeatedly concerns issues of
authority and transmission, and regularly plays them out in relations of fathers to sons. From Rousseau to Freud, the discourse of
the self and its origins—so much a matter of patronymics—ultimately concerns the authority of identity, that knowledge of self
which, through all its complex workings-out, aims at the demonstrative statement, "this is what I am." *Absalom, Absalom!* problema-
tizes further this classic issue in that not only does the identity of
all the important characters seem to be in question, but the very
discourse about identity seems to lack authority. As we have argued
in discussion of the narrative situation, stories are told in the name
of something or someone; they are told *for* something. The incessant narrating of *Absalom, Absalom!*, however, seems to bring us
perilously close to narrative without motive: a collection of "letters
without salutation or signature," unable to name their sender or
receiver, and unable to define the subject of their narrative discourse. If we ever are to be able to define the status of plot in this
novel, we will first have to discover the motives of storytelling.
Narrative meaning very much depends on the *uses* of narrative.

These formulations may begin to take on more precise and more
useful meaning if I now return to the beginning of the novel, and
attempt for the moment to be more explicative. We have at the
outset a teller and a listener, or narrator and narratee. Rosa is
doing the telling, "in that grim haggard amazed voice until at last
listening would renege and hearing-sense self-confound and the
long-dead object of her impotent yet indomitable frustration would
appear, as though by outraged recapitulation evoked . . ." (pp. 7–
8). This description could stand as emblem for all of Rosa's narrating, and indeed for much of the storytelling in the novel: an
evocation through outraged recapitulation, where there is evidently
a need not only to remember but also—in Freud's terms—to repeat
and to "work through" an as yet unmastered past, from motives
that are highly charged emotionally but not specified or yet speci-

fiable. Nor does the listener, Quentin, know why he has been chosen as Rosa's narratee, so that we have from the outset an interrogation of the motive and intention of telling. "*It's because she wants it told,* he thought, *so that people whom she will never see and whose names she will never hear and who will never have heard her name nor seen her face will read it and know at last why God let us lose the War . . .*" (p. 11). Quentin's explanation here leaps over what we might have expected to be a formulation of the storyteller's intention in terms of the coherent design given to her story by its shaping plot, leaps to the level of history, to the *fabula* as something truly fabulous: the epic of the Civil War, the tragedy of Southern history. The war and the history of the South may in some ultimate sense be both the final principle of explanation for everyone in the novel, and the final problem needing explanation. But to make a direct leap to that level is to elide the intervening level of plot, of coherently motivated and shaped narrative: between story as history on the one hand, and the recapitulative narrating on the other, plot seems to have been lost, to have failed in its role as the cohesive bond of the narrative construction.

It is worth noting that this initial situation of telling in *Absalom, Absalom!,* which places face to face the one surviving eyewitness to the past (or so we, and Quentin, believe at this point) and the representative of the future, he who is supposed to escape the South, is hermeneutically most significant at the point—the very end of chapter 1—where we are given the fragment of a narrative of what Rosa did *not* see: "But I was not there. I was not there to see the two Sutpen faces this time—once on Judith and once on the negro girl beside her—looking down through the square entrance to the loft" (p. 30). This is far more consequential for a construction of the plot than Rosa's recapitulation of her moral outrage at Sutpen's wrestling bouts with his slaves, which Judith and Clytie are watching from the loft: it is not the seen but the seers, unseen by the eyewitness, which constitute our hermeneutic clue here. For in the doubling of Judith in Clytie, in the Negro version of Sutpen, lies the very trace of difference which is the ironic determinant of Sutpen's plot.

But this is a clue that can only be interpreted later. By the close

of the first chapter, I have suggested, there is a split and a polar-
ization: narrating on the one hand, an epic historical story on the
other, and no narrative plot or design to join them. In this structure
of the absent middle, the failed mediation, the problem of the rest
of the novel is formulated: How can we construct the plot? Who
can say it? To whom? On what authority? The narrative of *Absalom,
Absalom!* not only raises these issues, it actively pursues them. The
novel becomes a kind of detective story where the object of investigation—the mystery—is the narrative design, or plot, itself.

We might note briefly the forms in which this problem develops
over the succeeding chapters. In chapters 2, 3, and 4, Mr. Compson
is telling. (One hesitates to label him, or any other of the tellers, a
"narrator" in the traditional sense, since narration here as elsewhere
in Faulkner seems to call upon both the individual's voice and that
transindividual voice that speaks through all of Faulkner's characters. Certainly the narrative is "focalized" by an individual—to
use Genette's terminology again—but the question of voice is more
difficult to resolve.)[2] Mr. Compson is eminently the figure of transmission, standing between his father, General Compson, the nearest thing to a friend that Sutpen had in Jefferson, and his son
Quentin. Mr. Compson fills in some of the background of Sutpen's
story, his arrival in Jefferson, his marriage to Ellen Coldfield, the
birth of the two children, Judith and Henry, the appearance of
Charles Bon. Chapter 3 ends with the evocation of Wash Jones
appearing before Rosa's house to tell of Henry's shooting of Bon;
then, curiously, chapter 4 ends with the same moment, but with
Wash Jones's message fully articulated this time: "Henry has done
shot that durn French feller. Kilt him dead as a beef" (p. 133). The
two chapter endings force us to ask what has happened in the
intervening pages to advance our understanding of this killing,
which from Rosa's initial presentation of the elements of the story
has stood as a shocking challenge to understanding.

What we have had, essentially, is the elaboration of Mr. Compson's plot, involving Henry and Bon and Judith. It turns on Bon's
earlier morganatic marriage to the octoroon woman in New Orleans, making of him an "intending bigamist" in the betrothal to

Judith. Mr. Compson is a rich scenarist, imaging the meeting of Henry and Bon at the University of Mississippi, Henry's "seduction" by Bon, the scenes at Sutpen's Hundred during vacations, Henry's trip to New Orleans, and so on. It is a narrative in which we are ever passing from the postulation of how it must have been to the conviction that it really was that way: for instance, Mr. Compson imagines the introduction of Henry to Bon in a series of clauses headed "perhaps," ending: "or perhaps (I like to think this) presented formally to the man reclining in a flowered, almost feminized gown, in a sunny window in his chambers" (p. 95), and then a page later has turned the hypothesis into solid narrative event: "And the very fact that, lounging before them in the outlandish and almost feminine garments of his sybaritic privacy . . . " (p. 96). And yet, for all his evident will to construct a hermeneutically powerful plot, Mr. Compson encounters moments of radical doubt, most notably in the passage beginning, "It just does not explain," which I quoted earlier. We have a complex, intricate, seemingly highly motivated plot that ultimately appears to get the story of Bon and Henry all wrong. Like Rosa's narrative, however, Mr. Compson's does include some important hermeneutic clues hidden in its mistaken design: the issue of incest, for instance, is suggested in the relation of Henry and Judith—in the vicarious incest Henry would enjoy in Bon's marriage to Judith, whom Mr. Compson does not suspect to be related by blood—and the issue of miscegenation is posed by the very existence of the octoroon woman. These are latent figures of narrative design which will later provide some of the hermeneutic "chemistry" that Mr. Compson's plotting is unable to activate.

With chapter 5, we return to Rosa's telling, and a nearer approach to the moment of murder. "I heard an echo, but not the shot," she says (p. 150), in a phrase emblematic of her whole relation to narrative event, which is one of secondariness and bafflement. Her narrating takes us precisely to what she did not see and cannot tell: the confrontation of Henry and Judith over Bon's corpse. Imagining the dialogue of brother and sister falls to her listener, Quentin; and we can infer that this need to tell will provide his entry into the narrative structure of the novel more directly than will Rosa's revelation that there is someone other than Clytie currently living at Sutpen's Hundred:

> ... the two of them, brother and sister ... speaking to one another in short brief staccato sentences like slaps. ...
>
> *Now you cant marry him.*
> *Why cant I marry him?*
> *Because he's dead.*
> *Dead?*
> *Yes. I killed him.*
>
> He (Quentin) couldn't pass that. He was not even listening to her; he said, "Ma'am? What's that? What did you say?"
> "There's something in that house."
> "In that house? It's Clytie. Dont she—"
> "No. Something living in it. Hidden in it. It has been out there for four years, living hidden in that house." (p. 172)

What is living in the house is, of course, Henry Sutpen, and Quentin's meeting with him, a few hours following this exchange with Rosa, will possibly constitute the most important event of the story that needs telling in *Absalom, Absalom!* and the key motive of its plot, as well as the original impetus to Quentin's narrating. But representation of this event is deferred until the very last pages of the novel. Here, at the close of Rosa's narrative, the narratee—Quentin—appears to fix on one moment of the narrator's account (why is a question we may defer for now) which he cannot "pass." Since, he seems to imply, the narrator has not done justice to this moment, it is up to the narratee to pursue its true narrative implications and consequences. If we may later want to say that Quentin enters the Sutpen *story* through the meeting with Henry at Sutpen's Hundred, he enters the *narrative* on the plane of *narrating*, as the better artist of the narrative plot. Yet, by what right and in what interest does Quentin claim the role of narrator? And if the listener/narratee has moved into the position of narrator, who has come to occupy the position he has vacated?

From chapter 6 through to the end of the novel, the narrating will essentially be Quentin's. His ostensible narratee will be Shreve, yet Shreve will come to participate in the narrating to such an extent that he too must eventually be considered a narrator. The agency of narration will hence be fully dialogic, which both solves and evades the question of the vacancy created by Quentin's movement into the place of the narrator. We need at this point to ask what kind of a narrative principle and authority is provided, can be provided, by these two young men who have usurped narrating, de-authorized the eyewitness account (Rosa's) and the account at one remove (Mr. Compson's) in favor of something at greater distance (both temporally and spatially) but which claims greater hermeneutic force. We need to ask three straightforward, quite naive questions: What do they recount? How do they know it? What is their motive, their investment in what they recount?

Let me start with the second question, that of the epistemology of their narrative. As source for their narrative, there is first of all something in the nature of "documentary evidence." Chapters 6 through 9 in fact are framed by Mr. Compson's letter recounting Rosa's death and burial, and earlier Mr. Compson had shown Quentin the letter Judith had given Quentin's grandmother, the letter written to Judith by Charles Bon in captured Yankee stovepolish in 1865. Then there are the tombstones, as so often in the nineteenth-century novel—in *Great Expectations*, for instance, and in Wilkie Collins's *The Woman in White*—authoritative texts that nonetheless require decipherment. Quentin and his father, out shooting quail at Sutpen's Hundred, come upon five tombstones. These are: (1) Ellen's (ordered from Italy, brought home by Sutpen in 1864); (2) Sutpen's own (of the same provenance); (3) Charles Bon's (bought by Judith when she sold the store); (4) Charles Etienne Saint-Valery Bon's (paid for partly by Judith, partly by General Compson, and erected by the latter); (5) Judith's (provided by Rosa). The aberrant and enigmatic text here—hence the clue—is the fourth tombstone, that of Charles Etienne Saint-Valery Bon (Charles Bon's child by the octoroon woman), who looks white but chooses blackness: who takes a black wife (their child will be the idiot Jim Bond), and in has black ancestry in both his mother *and* his father, though we do not yet know this. This Bon, who is hauled into court after a fight and admonished by the justice, Jim Hamblett, for "going with blacks," in fact presents a problem in categorization: Hamblett, following the vocative "you, a white man," turns back on his words to find the sign he has used subverted in its referent: "he looking at the prisoner now but saying 'white' again even while his voice died away as if the order to stop the voice had been shocked into short circuit, *'What are you? Who and where did you come from?'* " (p. 203). In this slippage of signified from under its signifier, we encounter a transgression of categories and accepted patternings which provides an essential trace of hermeneutic design.

More important than the documentary evidence is oral transmission. Quentin's main source of knowledge comes from what Sutpen told his grandfather, General Compson, during the hunt for the French architect, and then on another occasion thirty years later when he came to General Compson's office, a narrative which General Compson passed on to Mr. Compson who passed it on to Quentin. But this narrative lacks meaning until it is retroactively completed by what Quentin himself learns from his visit to Sutpen's Hundred with Rosa in 1909:

> "Your father," Shreve said. "He seems to have got an awful lot of delayed information awful quick, after having waited forty-five years. If he knew all this, what was his reason for telling you that the trouble between Henry and Bon was the octoroon woman?"
>
> "He didn't know it then. Grandfather didn't tell him all of it either, like Sutpen never told Grandfather quite all of it."
>
> "Then who did tell him?"
>
> "I did." Quentin did not move, did not look up while Shreve watched him. "The day after we—after that night when we—"
>
> "Oh," Shreve said. "After you and the old aunt. I see." (p. 266)

This dialogue marks the supersession of Mr. Compson's, General Compson's, even Sutpen's own narratives in favor of Quentin's, since Quentin has been able to supply essential "delayed information" previously missing, thus creating a narrative that has retroactive explanatory force. The nature of this information is further specified a few pages later:

> "Your old man," Shreve said. "When your grandfather was telling this to him, he didn't know any more what your grandfather was talking about than your grandfather knew what the demon was talking about when the demon told it to him, did he? And when your old man told it to you, you wouldn't have known what anybody was talking about if you hadn't been out there and seen Clytie. Is that right?"
>
> "Yes," Quentin said. (p. 274)

This information, then, does not come from anything Quentin has read or been told, but simply from seeing Clytie. Here, a decisive clue finally is witnessed and interpreted by an adequate narrator. Clytie, who in Rosa's words *"in the very pigmentation of her flesh represented that debacle which had brought Judith and me to what we were"* (p. 156), is a Negro Sutpen.[3] Clytie's identity opens the possibility of other part-Negro Sutpen children and alerts the narrators (and readers) to the significant strain of miscegenation; it also sets a model of narrative repetition which will allow Quentin and Shreve to see how Henry and Bon will be acting out Sutpen's script, but in the mode of irony. It is Quentin—the narratee become narrator—who will eventually be able to postulate the essential discovery: that Charles Bon was also Sutpen's child, and that he, too, was part Negro. The source of that postulation, we should emphasize, is the discovery of a certain formal pattern of the crossing of categories: Clytie's Sutpen face with its Negro pigmentation, the very design of debacle. The "truth" of narrative may have come to depend, more than on any fact, on powerful formal patternings, designs, eventually, of the narrative itself; a question to which we shall return.

I have by no means said all that needs to be said about the epistemological issues of Quentin's and Shreve's narrative, but I want for a moment to return to the first of the three questions I

identified, the question of what they recount. The story they tell
is in the first instance, and essentially, that of Sutpen, which has
come to appear the necessary myth of origins of all the problems
under consideration, and which in itself very much concerns origins.
It has become apparent that nothing can be solved or explained
without getting Sutpen's story straight. We could say that it has
become apparent that horizontal relationships, those of siblingship
and courtship—Judith, Bon, Henry—which were at the center of
Mr. Compson's narrative have come to show their hermeneutic
inadequacy and their insolubility in isolation. As Quentin reflects,
in one of several meditations on the inescapable issue of paternity:
"*Yes, we are both Father. Or maybe Father and I are both Shreve, maybe
it took Father and me both to make Shreve or Shreve and me both to make
Father or maybe Thomas Sutpen to make all of us*" (pp. 261–62).[4] Consideration must now be directed to a vertical problem, an issue in
genealogy and the transmission of paternal authority through historical time.

Sutpen's story, filled in mainly in chapter 7, has its thematic summary in the statement, "Sutpen's trouble was innocence" (p. 220).
It is the story of a hillbilly boy from the mountains who comes
down to the Tidewater with his family and is sent by his father to
a plantation house with a message, only to be turned away from
the front door and told to come round to the back. In this moment
of barred passage, Sutpen discovers the existence of difference:
difference as an abstract and formal property which takes precedence over all else—since, for instance, it is more important than
the content of the message he was supposed to deliver. Good and
evil, morality, social position, worth are not substantial, but belong
rather to the order of the signifier. The scenario reads like a version
of Rousseau's *Discourse on the Origins of Inequality*: the creation of
possession and differentiation where previously there had been
none. The difference is symbolized by that between black and white,
though this is but the most immediate and visible realization of a
larger problem, one indeed so basic that even the boy Sutpen can
begin to understand its primordial role in the organization and
assignment of meaning. Sutpen's compensatory plot, what he re-

peatedly calls his "design," will be conceived to assure his place on the proper side of the bar of difference. He goes off to Haiti to make his fortune on a sugar plantation, and there takes a wife who he believes to be part French and part Spanish, but who— after she has borne his son—is revealed to be part Negro, a fact that, as he puts it, makes an "ironic delusion" of his entire design (p. 263), which depends upon genealogical clarity and purity, on the ability to chart a clear authoritative relationship between origin and endpoint. So Sutpen repudiates his wife and starts over again at Sutpen's Hundred, in a new originating creation: "creating the Sutpen's Hundred, the *Be Sutpen's Hundred* like the olden-time *Be Light*" (p. 9). But then, his son by the first wife, Charles Bon, appears from the past to threaten "a mockery and a betrayal" of his design (p. 274): asking through the vessel of Judith that the new pure Sutpen line be intermixed with the dark blood of the past. So it is that Sutpen must turn Charles Bon, his first-born son, from the front door of his own plantation house. In the wake of all disasters, Sutpen goes on trying: after the war, and the disappearance of Henry, he proposes to Rosa that they breed together, then marry if she produces a son. After she has fled back to Jefferson in out-rage, he makes a last attempt with Milly Jones—poor white, but white—which results in a daughter, and Sutpen's death at the hand of Wash Jones.

I have dwelt on Sutpen's "design" because it is a key not only to the overriding thematic issues of the novel but, more important, to the symbolic field in which it inscribes its reflection on narrative meaning. Sutpen himself is a master-plotter, endowed with an ab-stract, formalist sense of what the future shape of his life must be. Yet his repeated attempts to found a genealogy do not work, no doubt because one cannot postulate the authority and outcome of a genealogy from its origin. The authority of genealogy is known only in its outcome, in its *issue*, using that word in all its possible senses. Sutpen attempts to write the history of the House of Sutpen prospectively, whereas history is evidently always retrospective. I have indeed argued that all narrative must, as a system of meaning, conceive itself as essentially retrospective. Only the sons can tell the

story of the fathers. Narrative, like genealogy, is a matter of patronymics. And here we may find both a source of Quentin's relative
success as narrator of the past and a source of his anguish at being
condemned to narrate the past, the world of ghosts which has fallen
to his inheritance and which one can attempt to placate only through
acts of genealogical narration.

When Quentin and Shreve have given shape to Sutpen's story,
they turn to Sutpen's immediate issue, to the sons, Bon and Henry.
Bon, too, we learn, has a design. Its parodic form—a parody of all
the plots in the novel—is represented by the figure of Bon's mother's lawyer, scheming to blackmail Sutpen through the threat of
incest, maintaining his secret notations:

> *Today Sutpen finished robbing a drunken Indian of a hundred miles
> of virgin land, val. $25,000. At 2:31 today came up out of swamp
> with final plank for house, val. in conj. with land 40,000. 7:52 p.m.
> today married. Bigamy threat val. minus nil. unless quick buyer. Not
> probable. Doubtless conjoined with wife same day. Say 1 year* and
> then with maybe the date and the hour too: *Son. Intrinsic val.
> possible though not probable forced sale of house & land plus val.
> crop minus child's one quarter. Emotional val. plus 100% times nil.
> plus val. crop. Say 10 years, one or more children. Intrinsic val. forced
> sale house & improved land plus liquid assets minus children's share.
> Emotional val. 100% times increase yearly for each child plus intrinsic
> val. plus liquid assets plus working acquired credit* and maybe here
> with the date too: *Daughter* and you could maybe even have
> seen the question mark after it and the other words even:
> *daughter? daughter? daughter?* trailing off. . . . (p. 301)

The lawyer's calculations here devastatingly lay bare the plot of the
nineteenth-century social and familial novel, with its equations of
consanguinity, property, ambition, and eros, that is ever the backdrop for the plottings of *Absalom, Absalom!* Yet Bon appears as the
hero of romance, with a simpler and more absolute design. He
simply wants a sign—any sign—of recognition from his father. "*He
would just have to write 'I am your father. Burn this' and I would do it*"

(p. 326). Bon's insistence on marriage to Judith becomes the choice of scandal in order to force the admission of paternity. What appears to be erotic desire reveals itself to be founded on the absolute demand for recognition by the father.

The working-out of Bon's design leads to the key scene, in 1865, as the Confederate army falls back toward Richmond and final defeat, when Colonel Sutpen summons Henry to his tent and speaks the essential words: "*Henry, . . . my son*"—the words Bon will never hear—and delivers the final answer to the enigma, completes the hermeneutic sentence that should allow us to explain the mischancings of the affairs of the House of Sutpen: "*He must not marry her, Henry. His mother's father told me that her mother had been a Spanish woman. I believed him; it was not until after he was born that I found out that his mother was part negro*" (pp. 354–55). And Bon draws the conclusion: "*So it's the miscegenation, not the incest, which you cant bear*" (p. 356). Thus it is that at this belated point in the novel, knowledge catches up with event, and Henry, along with the reader, learns what those narrators who originally were narratees have learned.

But wait. On what basis and by what authority do Quentin and Shreve narrate this scene, the scene that articulates the revelations necessary to constructing a coherent plot? Whereas for many earlier parts of their narrative we glimpsed sources and documents, here there are none. Indeed, the narrators have clearly passed beyond any possible evidence for their narrative. As Shreve has stated some pages earlier, "Let me play a while now" (p. 280). And before that, "All right. Dont bother to say he stopped talking now; just go on" (p. 258). These and a number of other indications signal clearly that we have passed beyond any narrative reporting, to narrative invention; that narrating, having failed to construct from the evidence a plot that would make sense of the story, turns to inventing it. Even what we normally call "reported speech"—direct quotation—is the product of an act of ventriloquism, in a duet for four voices in which Quentin and Shreve become compounded with Henry and Bon, "compounded each of both yet either neither" (p. 351). To the question, Who is speaking here? the text replies, Everyone and no one:

... it might have been either of them and was in a sense both: both thinking as one, the voice which happened to be speaking the thought only the thinking become audible, vocal; the two of them creating between them, out of the rag-tag and bob-ends of old tales and talking, people who perhaps had never existed at all anywhere, who, shadows, were shadows not of flesh and blood which had lived and died but shadows in turn of what were (to one of them at least, to Shreve) shades too, quiet as the visible murmur of their vaporizing breath. (p. 303)

What can this mean, if not that the narratees/listeners/readers have taken over complete responsibility for the narrative, and that the "voice of the reader" has evicted all other voices from the text, eliminated all the syntactic subordinations of reportage ("He said that she said that . . . ") in favor of a direct re-creation, and has set itself up, by a supreme act of usurpation, as the sole authority of narrative? Commenting on a particularly ambiguous case of voicing in Balzac's *Sarrasine*, Barthes reaches the conclusion that ultimately the voice that speaks in the text is that of the reader, in that it is in the reader's interest, in his name, that the story must be told. Here, as narrators, narratees, and characters become compounded and interchangeable—and the narrated and the narrating occupy shifting positions—we have very nearly a literal realization of Barthes's point: the distance between telling and listening, between writing and reading, has collapsed; the reader has been freed to speak in the text, toward the creation of the text.[5]

The passage quoted shows us how narration can become fully dialogic, centerless, a transaction across what may be a referential void—filled perhaps only with phantasies from the past—yet a transaction that creates, calls into being, a necessary hermeneutic fiction. The narrative transaction thus appears fully consonant with the psychoanalytic transference, a *Zwischenreich* in which narration works through and works out a narrative solution. Furthermore, here the transferential dialogue is carried out by those who were originally narratees and readers, as if the analysts had also become analysands, assuming the burden of all stories, as also the power to reorder them correctly. To the literary analyst, this may imply that the reader, like Quentin and Shreve, will always take over the text, both reading and (re)writing it to his own design, finding in it "what will suffice" to his own hermeneutic need and desire. As Bon's desire once postulated develops by the dynamics of its own internal tension toward the scene in Sutpen's tent in 1865, so the reader's desire inhabits the text and strives toward the fulfillment of interpretation. A further, more radical implication might be that the implied occurrences or events of the story (in the sense of *fabula*) are merely a by-product of the needs of plot, indeed of plotting, of the rhetoric of the *sjužet*: that one need no longer worry about the "double logic" of narrative since event is merely a necessary illusion that enables the interpretive narrative discourse to go further, as in the mind of some Borgesian demiurge. This in turn might imply that the ultimate subject of any narrative is its narrating, that narrative inevitably reveals itself to be a Moebius strip where we unwittingly end up on the plane from which we began. Origin and endpoint—and, perforce, genealogy and history—are merely as-if postulations ultimately subject to the arbitrary whims of the agency of narration, and of its model in readership. Narrative plots may be no more—but of course also no less—than a variety of syntax which allows the verbal game—the dialogue, really—to go on.

To extend these implications further may be simply to encounter the commonplaces of artistic modernism, and these need to be tempered by a sense of the urgency of the narrative act, which may restitute reference and the "double logic" of narrative in other forms. But before turning to that consideration, I want to return to the specific issue of plot, to ask whether the story *Absalom, Absalom!* claims to tell ever gets told: whether the novel ever records the invention of a plot that is hermeneutically satisfying, and where our interpretive desire ought to rest its case. Here we must refer to a scene that ought to be a revelatory moment in both the story and its plot: a scene held in suspense nearly the length of the novel, and one that ought to offer key insight into Quentin's relationship to the narrative since it marks the moment at which the time of the narrators intersects with the time of the narrated—the moment at which it is revealed that one of the protagonists of the past drama lives on into the present of narration, offering the promise that the past can be recuperated within the present. This is of course Quentin's meeting with Henry Sutpen at Sutpen's Hundred in the fall of 1909, just before his departure for Harvard. What happens in this meeting?

> *And you are—?*
> *Henry Sutpen.*
> *And you have been here—?*
> *Four years.*
> *And you came home—?*
> *To die. Yes.*
> *To die?*
> *Yes. To die.*
> *And you have been here—?*
> *Four years.*
> *And you are—?*
> *Henry Sutpen.* (p. 373)

Does anything happen here? The passage reads as nearly a palindrome, virtually identical backward and forward, an unprogressive, reversible plot. It seems to constitute a kind of hollow structure, a concave mirror or black hole at the center of the narrative. It generates no light, no revelation. If we have been led to feel that we understand the events that precipitated the fall of the House of Sutpen, we may sense that we are still at a loss to understand the larger plot that should link the sons to the fathers, motivate not only the story from the past, but the present's relation to it.

We do know, however, that Quentin's narrating seems to impel him toward recollection and replay of the scene with Henry Sutpen, deferred to climactic position, disappointing in that it offers no revelation, yet evidently constitutive of compulsive narrative desire since the result of this scene for Quentin is "Nevermore of peace" (p. 373): an anxiety never to be mastered, a past come alive that never can be laid to rest. If we can understand in a general way how this "afterlife" of the Sutpen story creates an influx of energy which Quentin's narrative can never quite bind and discharge, can we say specifically why it is Henry Sutpen who emerges as the traumatic figure of Quentin's narrative desire?

We must face the question left hanging earlier: what is the motive of the narrating? One could address this question (and some critics have done so) by way of the intertextual relation between *Absalom, Absalom!* and *The Sound and the Fury*, calling upon Quentin's incestuous desire for his sister Candace to explain his fixation on the story of Henry, Judith, and Bon, equating Judith with Candace and Bon the seducer with Dalton Ames, thus assigning Henry and Quentin to the same tortured place in the triangle of desire. Yet *Absalom, Absalom!* doesn't even mention Quentin's having a sister, and in any case using the intertext to explain, rather than enrich and extend the novel, seems reductive and impoverishing.[6] *Absalom, Absalom!* in fact offers no certain answer to the question of motivation. Yet I think it would also be a mistake simply to note the "arbitrariness" of the narrative and its undecidable relations of event and interpretation: so simplistic and sweeping a deconstructive gesture eludes the challenges the text poses to us. We should rather, I think, consider further how the text may suggest a remotivation of narrative through narration and the need for it.

As its title, and its biblical intertext, so clearly signal, *Absalom, Absalom!* addresses centrally the question of fathers and sons, perhaps the dominant thematic and structural concern and shaping force in the nineteenth-century novel, ultimately perhaps constituting a theme and a structure incorporate with the very nature of the novel as we know it. Circling about the problem of what Shreve calls "that one ambiguous eluded dark fatherhood" (p. 299), *Absalom, Absalom!* raises the related issues of fraternity (Henry and Bon, Quentin and Shreve), paternity (including genealogy), and filiality (if I can know who my father is, will he consent to know me?). Eventually these issues may point to the problematic status of narrative meaning itself: meaning as a coherent patterning of relation and transmission, as the possibility of rule-governed selection and combination, as the sense-creating design of writing. Is coherent understanding, the explanatory narrative plotted from origin to endpoint, possible and transmissible? Do the sons inherit from the fathers, do they stand in structured and significant relation to an inheritance which informs the present? Can the past speak in a syntactically correct and comprehensible sentence?

Two threads of patterning, two elements of design, seem to be woven throughout the book. On the one hand there is incest, which according to Shreve (and Quentin does not contradict him) might be the perfect androgynous coupling, from which one would not have to uncouple: "maybe if there were sin too maybe you would not be permitted to escape, uncouple, return" (p. 324). Incest is that which overassimilates, denies difference, creates too much sameness. If, as Lévi-Strauss has claimed, it is the taboo on incest that creates the differentiated society, the attraction to incest raises the threat of the collapse of difference, loss of tension, and the stasis of desire extinguished in absolute satisfaction. On the other hand there is miscegenation, mixture of blood, the very trace of difference: that which overdifferentiates, creates too much difference, sets up a perpetual slippage of meaning where (as in the case of Charles Etienne Saint-Valery Bon brought before Justice Hamblett) one cannot find any points of fixity in the signifying chain. Incest thus would belong to the pole of metaphor, but as static, inactive metaphor, the same-as-same; whereas miscegenation would be a "wild," uncontrollable metonymy. The story of the House of Sutpen as told by the younger generation seems to be caught between these two figures, never able to interweave them in a coherent design.[7] To give just one brief example, from the scene in Colonel Sutpen's camp in 1865, Quentin and Shreve narrate this exchange between Henry and Bon:

—*You are my brother.*
—*No I'm not. I'm the nigger that's going to sleep with your sister. Unless you stop me, Henry.* (pp. 357–58)

Incest and miscegenation, sameness and difference, here as elsewhere in the narrative—including, notably, the working-out of Sutpen's design—fail to achieve a pattern of significant interweaving, and give instead a situation of paradox and impossibility: for instance, the nigger/brother conundrum that can be solved only by a pistol shot. Shreve at the end offers a parodic summing-up of this problem in design as it concerns the Sutpen "ledger" when he notes that it takes two Negroes to get rid of one Sutpen. "Which is all right, it's fine; it clears the whole ledger, you can tear all the pages out and burn them, except for one thing. . . . You've got one nigger left. One nigger Sutpen left. . . . You still hear him at night sometimes. Don't you?" (p. 378). The one left is, of course, Jim Bond, the idiot, the leftover who can be heard howling at night. The tale he would tell would be full of sound and fury, signifying nothing. He stands as a parodic version of Barthes's contention that the classical narrative offers at its end the implication of a residue of unexhausted meaning, a "pensivity" that remains to work in the reader.

The narrative ledger cannot be cleared by a neat calculation; the tale can never be plotted to the final, thorough, Dickensian accounting; and the *envoi* to the reader—the residual meaning embodied in Jim Bond—seems the very principle of nonsignificance. But of course this is not all that the text has to say about design and the making of patterns. Of the many metaphors of its own status and production presented by the text, all of which would bear consideration, I shall quote only Judith's extraordinary evocation of the loom, which she articulates when she comes to Quentin's grandmother, to ask her to keep the letter she received from Charles Bon during the war, a letter "without date or salutation or signature" which nonetheless constitutes a precious act of communication. It is an extended image, which moves from the letter to the entanglement of marionettes, which then modulates to the loom and the weaving of the rug, then moves on to another kind of text, the legend scratched on the tombstone, then back to the letter and the act of transmission of the letter:

"... and your grandmother saying, 'Me? You want me to keep it?'

" 'Yes,' Judith said. 'Or destroy it. As you like. Read it if you like or dont read it if you like. Because you make so little impression, you see. You get born and you try this and you dont know why only you keep on trying it and you are born at the same time with a lot of other people, all mixed up with them, like trying to, having to, move your arms and legs with strings only the same strings are hitched to all the other arms and legs and the others all trying and they dont know why either except that the strings are all in one another's way like five or six people all trying to make a rug on the same loom only each one wants to weave his own pattern into the rug; and it cant matter, you know that, or the Ones that set up the loom would have arranged things a little better, and yet it must matter because you keep on trying or having to keep on trying and then all of a sudden it's all over and all you have left is a block of stone with scratches on it provided there was someone to remember to have the marble scratched and set up or had time to, and it rains on it and the sun shines on it and after a while they dont even remember the name and what the scratches were trying to tell, and it doesn't matter. And so maybe if you could go to someone, the stranger the better, and give them something—a scrap of paper—something, anything, it not to mean anything in itself and them not even to read it or keep it, not even bother to throw it away or destroy it, at least it would be something just because it would have happened, be remembered even if only from passing from one hand to an-other, one mind to another, and it would be at least a scratch, something, something that might make a mark on something that *was* once for the reason that it can die someday, while the block of stone cant be *is* because it never can become *was* be-cause it cant ever die or perish. . . .' " (pp. 127–28)

If Judith's images suggest an ultimate pessimism about the status of texts—woven or graven or written—her insistence on passing on the fragile letter as an instance of something that possesses ontological gravity because it was written by a living hand, ad-dressed from someone to someone, suggests that the process of sense-making retains a tenuous privilege of which its products are drained. Judith's statement concedes the evanescence or even the impossibility of the "referential" and "metalinguistic" functions of language (in Roman Jakobson's sense) while arguing the continuing pertinence of and need for the "phatic": the way we use language to test the communicative circuit, to confirm the conductive properties of the medium of words.[8] She makes a claim neither for story nor for plot, but rather for narrating as, in Genette's terms, the narrative act productive of plot and story. This is not simply to state—in a modernist commonplace—that *Absalom, Absalom!* is a "poem about itself," but rather to contend that narrating is an urgent function in itself, that in the absence of pattern and structure, patterning and structuration remain necessary projects, dynamic intentions. Judith's struggle with the tenses of the verb "to be" suggests the whole problem of narrative as recovery of the past and makes us note how in the passing-on of Bon's letter of 1865 (whose very inscription—on the finest watermarked French notepaper taken from a gutted Southern mansion, in stovepolish manufactured by the victorious Union and captured by the doomed Confederate raiders in the place of the food or ammunition they had hoped to find—is marked by the cosmic ironic laughter of History) the reader is linked not only to the reading but to the writing of "historical" documents, and how, as a belated reader of the document—following Judith herself, Quentin's grandmother, grandfather, father, and then Quentin himself—he is summoned to take his place in the activity of transmission, to join the ventriloquized medium of history as fiction and fiction as history, perhaps finally to become, in a modification of Proust's phrase, the writer of himself.

The recovery of the past—which I take to be the aim of all narrative—may not succeed in *Absalom, Absalom!*, if by the recovery of the past we mean its integration within the present through a coherent plot fully predicated and understood as past. Yet the attempted recovery of the past makes known the continuing history of past desire as it persists in the present, shaping the project of telling. As the psychoanalyst Stanley Leavy has written, perhaps in too optimistic a tone, "All desire aims at the future, and this especially, because it is a desire for a revelatory knowledge to come, often first and naively experienced as the desire for the recovery of a buried memory, a lost trauma. To speak at all is to express the desire to be recognized and heard, whether the speech is in the form of a demand or not."[9] The seemingly universal compulsion to narrate the past in *Absalom, Absalom!*, and to transmit its words, may speak both of an unmasterable past and of a dynamic narrative present dedicated to an interminable analysis of the past. Faulkner's present is a kind of tortured utopia of unending narrative dialogue informed by desire for a "revelatory knowledge." That knowledge never will come, yet that desire never will cease to activate the telling voices.

Quentin alludes to the tentative and dialogic quality of narrating in a parenthetic reference to General Compson's view of language: "language (that meager and fragile thread, Grandfather said, by which the little surface corners and edges of men's secret and solitary lives may be joined for an instant now and then before sinking back into the darkness where the spirit cried for the first time and was not heard and will cry for the last time and will not be heard then either)" (p. 251). This is certainly no triumphant apology for narrative; it makes the patternings of plot tentative indeed, ready to come unwoven as soon as they are stitched together. It is, perhaps, tentatively an apology for narrating, an enterprise apparently nostalgic, oriented toward the recovery of the past, yet really phatic in its vector, asking for hearing. I will here raise the question, to leave it unanswered, whether at the end of the novel Shreve has heard Quentin, whether his last question, "Why do you hate the South?" marks a failure of comprehension of all that has been told, or on the contrary too full an understanding of the desire animating the narrative act. And I will close by returning to the first agent of narration in the novel, Rosa Coldfield, to give her the last word, for it is she who speaks of *"the raging and incredulous recounting (which enables man to bear with living)"* (p. 161).

In Conclusion:
Endgames and the Study
of Plot

Any closure to our subject would be artificially imposed: the story of plot may be interminable, the examples calling for attention are legion, and any terminus reached suggests the need for a revisionary epilogue, another perspective, a different narrative. But perhaps it is fair to say at this point that we have accumulated a sufficient number of instances, and that two tasks remain, to be briefly touched on rather than truly accomplished. The first is to suggest some elements of an epilogue on plot: what has happened to plot in our time, in the space of years following *Absalom, Absalom!*—roughly in the period that carries the questionable label of "postmodernist." The second is to return to our models of narrative and its analysis, especially those derived from Freud, to meditate further, briefly, on the uses of psychoanalysis in criticism and on the understanding of narrative.

I

Toward the end of Samuel Beckett's *Endgame*, Clov speaks ("imploringly") to Hamm: "Let's stop playing." Hamm replies: "Never!" Then, after a pause: "Put me in my coffin." And Clov answers: "There are no more coffins." Ends, it seems, have become difficult to achieve. In their absence, or their permanent deferral, one is condemned to playing: to concocting endgames, playing in anticipation of a terminal structuring moment of revelation that never comes, creating the space of an as-if, a fiction of finality. There is

313

a wait for the end that never achieves satisfaction. When ending comes, it is more in the nature of stalemate than victory. The story could be continued, it could belong to another story, one might invent a sequel. Our most sophisticated literature understands endings to be artificial, arbitrary, minor rather than major chords, casual and textual rather than cosmic and definitive. Yet they take place: if there is no spectacular dénouement, no distribution of awards and punishments, no tie-up, through marriages and deaths, of all the characters' lives, there is a textual finis—we have no more pages to read.

This tenuous, fictive, arbitrary status of ends clearly speaks to and speaks of an altered situation of plot, which no longer wishes to be seen as end-determined, moving toward full predication of the narrative sentence, claiming a final plenitude of meaning. We have, in a sense, become too sophisticated as readers of plot quite to believe in its orderings. Part of our sophistication no doubt has to do with the cinema, a form that is consubstantial with temporal successiveness and has made the syntax of plot so available it seems to offer no further challenges. Whereas plot continues in our time to be a dominant element in popular narrative fictions of many sorts and to proceed on principles little changed from the nineteenth century, in those works that claim to challenge their readers, that are in various ways experimental, plot is often something of an embarrassment. Other users of narrative—historians and anthropologists, for instance—have also rebelled against the plotted sequence of events in favor of presentation by way of structural homologies or transverse cuts through moments of history, to present patterns and complexes of attitudes and ways of being. Yet there has recently been a discernible return to narrative on the part of many professional historians, since there appear to be kinds of understanding and explanation that demand narrative form, demand that the mind move over events in their temporal interrelation, setting up patterns of sequence and consequence. And the experimental narrative fictions that have most claimed our attention have not, I think, so much illustrated the far too uncritically accepted notion of "spatial form" as they have shown a fragmentation of plot, using it in residual and parodistic ways, working to disappoint the reader's normal expectations concerning the plotted narrative, yet nonetheless carrying reading forward by way of plotted narrative elements.[1]

From the many examples that might be adduced here, surely some representative of the French "new novel" may claim our momentary attention, since when this work first began to be published—in the 1950s—it seemed marginally readable, radically taxing of the reader's skills, yet it was subsequently assimilated with remarkable rapidity. Readers learned to read the new novel, partly by abandoning certain expectations of coherence and meaning that these texts refused to fulfill and partly by learning to use the plot elements offered, in playful and fragmentary form, to construct fictions that, in the absence of any more immediate referent—any more definite *fabula*—became fictions of fiction making. Alain Robbe-Grillet (to take the new novelist who to my mind offered the most radical and interesting challenge to the traditional novel) in a work such as *Le Voyeur* uses elements of the detective story to create readerly expectations which the text will disappoint, since there is no certain crime to be detected, yet which lead the reader to the central gap or split—the *faille* or fault—of the text: the time and place that the protagonist, and the text, never can account for, a black hole that is also animating of plotting and meaning since it provokes the reader's search. The protagonist here is a traveling salesman of watches, and the detective story modeling of experience is like the modeling of time by timepieces: both ineffectual and necessary. The reader is invited to play with and against traditional novelistic devices, constructing a model that denies narrative's privilege while it confirms narrative's necessity.

For there is in Robbe-Grillet's work a radically "constructivist" sense of narrative: the reader is asked to build a novel, not as the traditional plenum of meaning but as a possible model of narrative itself, a kind of laboratory experiment. Since I have discussed repetition as a major plot element, it is worth quoting a passage of *La Jalousie* referring to the song, apparently sung by a native workman, that is one of the repeated motifs of the novel:

No doubt it is always the same song that goes on. If sometimes the themes blur, it is only to come back a little later, more
marked, very close to identical. Nonetheless, these repetitions,
these minute variants, these elisions, these turnings back, can
produce modifications—moving eventually quite far from the
point of departure.[2]

The passage not only serves as one possible *mise-en-abyme* for *La
Jalousie*—and for later novels such as *Projet pour une révolution à
New-York*, which the reader must construct from the banalized and
sensationalistic elements of a New York landscape given in novelistic kit form—it suggests as well the constructive role of repetition
in all of Robbe-Grillet's fiction. Repetition is one of the few factors
of the text that allow a reader to see patterns of coherence, and
thus at least the incipience of meaning, and to perceive how modification works, how the idea of repetition is linked to the idea of
variation, indeed how an entire narrative might be constructed on
the minute variations within repetition.

Robbe-Grillet remains in my view one of the most impressive
examples of what can be done with the leftovers of the traditional
novel, as with the "ready-mades" of consumer society: the man-
nequins and glossy photos, the clichés of desire and the claptrap
of eroticism that pervade his novels and films. The ready-made
and the leftover (the "surplus") can be treated as camp or, more
simply, as an object of bemused interest, to be tried in different
contexts and combinations. Narrative becomes a *combinatoire*: a game
of putting together, a kind of generalized metonymy in which the
given elements—as the given products and paradigms of culture
and society—provide, as it were, the metaphoric glue. Thus our
sense of plot in Robbe-Grillet's novels is most often serial (borrow-
ing the term from serial music): the trying-out of one possible
ordering of materials which is then superseded by another "reel,"
which will play itself out in turn. The reader never is vouchsafed
anything we would want to call a plot, in the traditional sense, but
he is himself forced to engage in plotting, if not toward the creation
of meaning, at least in exploration of the conditions of narrative
meaning.

Other experimental novelists of our time, perhaps especially in North and South America, have worked more specifically with the parody of traditional plot, developing in part the model furnished by Joyce's use of Homeric plot. John Barth, for instance, constructs *The Sot-Weed Factor* on an elaborate parodic resurrection of eighteenth-century plotting (in the manner of Fielding), very much including plot as machination and conspiracy, which in its modern context is made to seem both an obsolete system of meaning and a paradigm of our desire for epic adventure and its coherent fulfillment. The remarkable energy of Barth's fiction comes in part from the exuberance of his pastiches of past forms: repeating with ludic variation the outmoded forms gives the narrative its motor force. And one could say similar things about Thomas Pynchon or Julio Cortázar or Manuel Puig or Carlos Fuentes: Fuentes indeed in the novella *Aura* pulls off the tour-de-force of a narrative that proceeds chronologically backward, from death to birth, both parodying traditional forms and showing us something about how we always decoded such forms, from the end.

Such texts have been called metafictions or, more soberly, critical fictions, in that they reflect upon traditional novelistic devices in a highly self-conscious way and use them only in quotation marks, so to speak. This is, of course, not new in the history of the novel. One could argue with some plausibility that the novel as genre incorporates the antinovel—its critical reflection—from the earliest stages of its history: certainly in *Don Quixote*, perhaps even in the earlier picaresque; and surely from Flaubert onward into Modernism, the self-reflexive ironies of the novelistic enterprise have been a major preoccupation. The difference of the postmodern is, I think, one of degree: a greater explicitness in the abandonment of mimetic claims, a more overt staging of narrative's arbitrariness and lack of authority, a more open playfulness about fictionality. The most exemplary of all the instances one could cite here might well be Jorge Luis Borges, who notes in his preface to *Ficciones* that rather than write books, or commentaries on existing books, he has preferred to write glosses on imaginary books, presenting in each case a problem in the nature of fictions reduced to essential outline.

One Borges story speaks directly to some of the issues of plot that have concerned us. "The Garden of Forking Paths" is in some manner a framed tale. Its outer and ostensible action concerns the need of one Yu Tsun, German-employed spy in Britain, to communicate to his chief in Germany the name of the town (in Belgium) where there is a new British air base, so the Germans can bomb it—before Yu Tsun's voice is silenced by Captain Richard Madden, who is hot in pursuit. How can Yu Tsun make the "report" of his revolver heard in Germany in the minutes left to him? The answer lies in the telephone book, a text that—rather like the Musgrave ritual—will prove capable of a metonymic unpacking that will provide a plot: shooting the one person with the surname "Albert" listed in the telephone book will, by the instant publicity of the murder, its perpetrator, and its victim, transmit the name of the town—Albert—to Germany. Catching the train to Ashgrove just before Richard Madden arrives at the station—and thus gaining forty minutes in which to perform his crime and send its message—Yu Tsun has defined a problem in space and time, in metaphor (one thing substituted for another), and metonymy (the slippage from one name, or its referent, to another).

At the core of Borges's tale stands the *mise-en-abyme* of this problem, the labyrinth-novel known as *The Garden of Forking Paths*, written by Yu Tsun's ancestor Ts'ui Pên, reconstructed and translated by the sinologist Stephen Albert. This maze of a novel undertakes to represent, not a single plot—following a protagonist through that career defined and delimited by the choices he makes, leading to an outcome—but all possible plots: in "The Garden of Forking Paths," there are no roads not taken, since all can be taken, with wholly different outcomes. The novel—which Yu Tsun has always considered "an indeterminate heap of contradictory drafts"[3]—is in fact a utopia of plotting, creating all possible futures and holding them all in the present, allowing all possible, even contradictory, outcomes to occur. As such, it is "an enormous riddle, or parable, whose theme is time"—the one problem that is never mentioned in its text. As Stephen Albert continues his exposition: "*The Garden of Forking Paths* is an incomplete, but not false, image of the universe as Ts'ui Pên conceived it. In contrast to Newton and Schopenhauer, your ancestor did not believe in a uniform, absolute time. He believed in an infinite series of times, in a growing, dizzying net of divergent, convergent and parallel times." Thus the future always exists as one potential present, even as an accomplished past, and when Yu Tsun shoots Stephen Albert, he realizes his earlier maxim: "*The author of an atrocious undertaking ought to imagine that he has already accomplished it, ought to impose upon himself a future as irrevocable as the past.*" Yet this dastardly future of treachery and murder (which will entail Yu Tsun's execution as well) is "merely" an escape from the labyrinth, which remains unaffected, which indeed deconstructs this outcome as simply one contingency, a possible *fabula* produced by a truly infinite *sjužet*. Forking paths and crossroads— such as the one where Oedipus unwittingly, yet predictably, killed his father, Laius—are both random and determined. The labyrinth is ultimately that of narrative literature, which is ever replaying time, subverting and perverting it, in order to claim that it is not simply "time lost," always in the knowledge that this loss is the very condition of the meanings that narrative claims to relate.

II

We can let Borges and "The Garden of Forking Paths" stand as a final paradigm of plot, understood in its utopian promise and impossibility, and turn to a few last words on our own discourse on plot, especially the emphasis we have given to psychoanalytic models of understanding. Working with the tools provided by "narratology," I have argued that such a formalist approach, while indispensable, does not provide—and generally does not seek to provide—an understanding of the dynamics of narrative, of what impels its movements of transformation, and thus its engagement with human memory and desire and its status as a form of thinking. Hence such useful formalist terms of analysis as the distinction of *fabula* and *sjužet*, the operation of function and sequence, or of the proairetic and hermeneutic codes, and the interplay of metaphor and metonymy, need to be rethought through concepts of recollection, repetition, desire, and transference, where our best guide may be Freud since his analyses of these questions touch directly on the "narratability" of life and the uses of the stories we tell. We have essentially used two different models derived from Freud to talk about two different aspects of narrative: the energetic-dynamic model, which speaks to the question of the human life-span, its movement and arrest, and hence to the organization of biography and the energetics of the life story; and the model of the psychoanalytic transference as consonant with the narrative situation and text.

In an overarching theory of narrative, the energetic-dynamic model of *Beyond the Pleasure Principle*, in which repetition as binding prolongs and formalizes the middle, and also prepares the end, should be integrated with the transactive and transferential model we found in a number of Freud's papers on technique and in the "Wolf Man" case history. One could begin to look for such an integration in the role of repetition in the transference, repetition that takes the place of intellectual recall and, in a symbolic enactment of the past as if it were present, puts the story of the past in such a form—within the as-if medium of the transference—that it can become the subject of dialogic reorderings and understandings on the part of analysand and analyst, teller and listener or reader. Thus the shaping force of the life story that we found referred to in *Beyond the Pleasure Principle* enters the situation of telling, listening, and understanding provided by the transference. What is made present in the transference is in some measure an individual version of the energetic masterplot. The narrative text conceived as transference then becomes the place of interpretation and construction of the plotted story.

In an essay from his very last years, "Constructions in Analysis" (1937), Freud reminds us that psychoanalysis involves two people, analysand and analyst, and says of the latter: "His task is to make out what has been forgotten from the traces which it has left behind or, more correctly, to *construct* it." [4] Freud then notes that the "time and manner in which he conveys these constructions to the person being analyzed, as well as the explanations with which he accompanies them, constitute the link between the two portions of the work of analysis," the analyst's and his patient's. Such constructive work figures the link between *fabula* and *sjužet* as we have conceived it: the working-out of a coherent and interpretive relation between "events" (real or imagined) and their significant ordering. Thus the analysand/analyst relation in the reconstruction of the past images the relation of story to the plotted narrative discourse, and it also, of course, images the relation of text to reader, especially in those problematic narratives where the reader is called upon to participate in the telling and the completion of the narrative in order to make it fully hermeneutic. The analyst, Freud writes further, like the archaeologist has "an undisputed right to reconstruct by means of supplementing and combining the surviving remains" (p. 259). Yet the analyst has this advantage over the archaeologist, that the buried material he is dealing with is "still alive," repeating and working through in the dynamics of the transference, thus still covertly expressing its design and intention. If narrative indeed has to do with the recovery of the past, and more generally with the attempted rescue of meaning from passing time, the psycho-analytic model of remembering is invaluable since it reaches out to include repeating, working-through, and reconstructing—all of which seem to me to characterize the literary text and our reading of it, to define the text-as-read.

The construction practiced by the analyst takes a more dynamic and dialogic form than the archaeologist's. "The analyst finishes a piece of construction and communicates it to the subject of the analysis so that it may work upon him; he then constructs a further piece out of the fresh material pouring in upon him, deals with it in the same way and proceeds in this alternating fashion until the end" (pp. 260–61). This alternation between interpretation and the production of fresh material once again suggests the relation of discourse and story, and the way in which interpretations elicit and create story, extend and complete the narrative construction, both within the narrative—as, for instance, Sherlock Holmes and Marlow, with varying degrees of success, construct a plot that will fill in the gaps of the stories they seek to understand—and in its reading, which constantly calls on the same process of building interpretive models and testing them against their narrative productivity.

When he comes to the problem of the analysand's assent to the constructions made by the analyst, Freud notes that a simple "yes" may have no value "unless it is followed by indirect confirmations, unless the patient, immediately after his 'yes,' produces new memories which complete and extend the construction" (p. 262). Something similar, I think, happens when the reader's hypotheses of interpretation are strong and valuable: they produce new confirmation from the text, setting up previously unperceived networks of relation and significance. Freud writes further that the path starting from the analyst's construction ought to lead to the patient's recollection but does not always succeed in doing so. Instead of recollection of the repressed, the analysis may produce in the analysand something else: "an assured conviction of the truth of the construction which achieves the same therapeutic result as a recaptured memory" (p. 266). This conviction is not so far from the conviction—mental and juridical—sought by Sherlock Holmes: it is the conclusion that a *sjužet* has been so well formed, so tightly enchained, that the *fabula* derived from it must be right. Plots are valuable for the use-value they give to stories, the way they make them exchangeable, transactable.

The Freud I have evoked is not only a man of great literary culture and a highly perceptive reader, he is also—in a sense that may legitimate the somewhat pretentious word—a semiotician, intent to read all the signs produced by humans, as individuals and as a culture, and attentive to all behavior as semiotic, as coded text that can be deciphered, as ultimately charged with meaning. The "conquistador"—as he was pleased to call himself—Freud extends the empire of signs and meaning. Thus he (and the follower who best has understood his semiotic message, Lacan) points us toward a convergence of semiotics and psychoanalysis which can open up important perspectives to the literary critic who is concerned to connect literary texts to human experience.

Narrative, I suggested, may work according to a model that begins with a blinded and collapsed, inactive metaphor, unpacks the givens of this initial figure through the enactments of metonymy, then reaches a terminal enlightened, transactive metaphor. I have been interested by how often the initial blinded metaphor seems to concern transmission blocked—not only in the brief narratives "All-Kinds-of-Fur" and "The Musgrave Ritual," but also in *Heart of Darkness*, where Marlow seeks illumination of his life in another's death; in *Great Expectations*, where deciphering his parents' tombstones is Pip's impossible but necessary task; in *Le Rouge et le noir*, which entitles its fourth chapter "Un Père et un fils"; and in *Absalom, Absalom!*, where Rosa Coldfield in the first pages calls attention to the relation of telling and transmission. The successfully transacted and transactive metaphor of the end ought to permit a passing-on. This may not be so clear an articulation as what Walter Benjamin called "wisdom." Since ends have ceased to be simple—indeed, on inspection we realize they never were simple—the end that narrative seeks, in its anticipation of retrospection, may disappoint and baffle. Yet this may only make it the more necessary to construct meaning *from* that end, moving back to recover markings from the past, reconstructing the outposts of meaning along the way. If nothing certain is transmitted by a narrative, it may be that the reader's role in attempting the construction of what needs transmission carries the assurance of conviction.

Henry James, in his well-known discussion of "the romantic" versus "the real" in the preface to *The American*, allows romance to stand for "the things that can reach us only through the beautiful circuit and subterfuge of our thought and our desire." [5] James by sleight-of-hand seems to have embraced under the term romance all narrative fiction, if we are ready to see narrative as a form of understanding motivated by our desire and narrative fictions as what trace the circuit and subterfuge of that desire working out its patterns of meaning. Narrative is one of the ways in which we speak, one of the large categories in which we think. Plot is its thread of design and its active shaping force, the product of our refusal to allow temporality to be meaningless, our stubborn insistence on making meaning in the world and in our lives.

NOTES

1. Reading for the Plot

1. E. M. Forster, *Aspects of the Novel* (New York: Harcourt, Brace, 1927), p. 126.

2. One of the ambitions of Northrop Frye in *Anatomy of Criticism* (Princeton, N.J.: Princeton Univ. Press, 1957) is to provide such a typology in his *mythoi*. Yet there is in Frye a certain confusion between *mythoi* as plot structures and as myths or archetypes which to my mind makes his work less valuable than it might be.

3. On historical narrative as a form of understanding, see the fine essay by Louis O. Mink, "Narrative Form as Cognitive Instrument," in *The Writing of History*, ed. Robert H. Canary and Henry Kozicki (Madison: Univ. of Wisconsin Press, 1978), pp. 129–49. Mink calls narrative "a primary and irreducible form of human comprehension" (p. 132). Of interest also is Dale H. Porter, *The Emergence of the Past* (Chicago: Univ. of Chicago Press, 1981).

4. See "All-Kinds-of-Fur" [*Allerleirauh*], in *The Grimms' German Folk Tales*, trans. Francis P. Magoun and Alexander H. Krappe (Carbondale: Southern Illinois Univ. Press, 1960), pp. 257–61.

5. See Walter Benjamin, "The Storyteller" [*Der Erzähler*], in *Illuminations*, trans. Harry Zohn (New York: Schocken Books, 1969), p. 91. On the place of incest and the incest taboo in the Grimms' tales, see Marthe Robert, "The Grimm Brothers," in *The Child's Part*, ed. Peter Brooks (rpt. Boston: Beacon Press, 1972), pp. 44–56.
One might offer the following diagram of the movement of the plot in "All-Kinds-of-Fur," from the initial overeroticization of the daughter (as the object of prohibited desires), through the undervaluation of the feminine (becoming the simulated beast), to the state of equilibrium achieved

at the end: $++/--/+-$. Without attaching too much importance to such a formula, one can see that it describes a process of working-out or working-through common to many tales.

6. On the Oedipus myth, see Claude Lévi-Strauss, "The Structural Study of Myth," in *Structural Anthropology* (Garden City, N.Y.: Anchor-Doubleday, 1967), pp. 202–28. On the "atemporal matrix structure," see Lévi-Strauss, "La Structure et la forme," *Cahiers de l'Institut de Science Economique Appliquée* 99, série M, no. 7 (1960), p. 29.

7. Aristotle, *Poetics*, trans. Ingram Bywater, in *Introduction to Aristotle*, ed. Richard McKeon (2nd ed.; Chicago: Univ. of Chicago Press, 1973), p. 678.

8. See Seymour Chatman, *Story and Discourse* (Ithaca, N.Y.: Cornell Univ. Press, 1979). Chatman's book offers a useful summary, and attempt at synthesis, of narrative analysis in the structuralist tradition; he also gives extended bibliographical references. One can find an exposition of many of the issues that concern us here in Robert Scholes, *Structuralism in Literature* (New Haven: Yale Univ. Press, 1974).

Fabula and *sjužet* are rendered as "story" and "plot" by Lee T. Lemon and Marion Reis in their anthology, *Russian Formalist Criticism* (Lincoln: Univ. of Nebraska Press, 1965). Equating the *fabula/sjužet* distinction with "story"/"plot" is much criticized by Meir Sternberg in *Expositional Modes and Temporal Ordering in Fiction* (Baltimore: Johns Hopkins Univ. Press, 1978), chap. 1. But Sternberg's understanding of the concept of plot is based exclusively on E. M. Forster's definition in *Aspects of the Novel*, where plot is distinguished from story by its emphasis on causality. To offer causality as the key characteristic of plot may be to fall into the error of the *post hoc ergo propter hoc*, as Roland Barthes suggests in "Introduction à l'analyse structurale des récits" (*Communications* 8 [1966], English trans. Stephen Heath, in *A Barthes Reader*, ed. Susan Sontag [New York: Hill and Wang, 1982]), and as Vladimir Propp implicitly demonstrates in *The Morphology of the Folktale* (trans. Laurence Scott [2nd ed.; Austin: Univ. of Texas Press, 1970]): if plot appears to turn sequence into consequence, this may often be illusory; causality can be produced by new material, by changes in mood or atmosphere, by coincidence, by reinterpretation of the past, and so forth. Some of these issues will be taken up in chapter 10.

Sternberg argues further that the *sjužet* is properly the whole of the text, whereas plot is an abstraction and reconstruction of it. But I think that *sjužet* as used by such Russian Formalists as Boris Tomachevsky and Victor

Shklovsky is similarly an abstraction and reconstruction of the logic of the narrative text, and in this sense quite close to Aristotle.

For a useful discussion of the concept of plot, especially as related to the notion of mimesis, see Elizabeth Dipple, *Plot* (London: Methuen, 1970).

9. Paul Ricoeur, "Narrative Time," in *On Narrative*, ed. W. J. T. Mitchell (Chicago: Univ. of Chicago Press, 1981), p. 167. Compare Louis O. Mink on historical narrative, when he argues that the past "is not an untold story but can be made intelligible only as the subject of stories we tell" ("Narrative Form as Cognitive Instrument," p. 148). Ricoeur offers a more extended presentation of his ideas in the recent *Temps et récit* (Paris: Editions du Seuil, 1983), which primarily concerns historical narrative and will be followed by a second volume devoted to fictional narrative.

10. The work I refer to here is available in English translation primarily in two anthologies: Lee T. Lemon and Marion Reis, eds., *Russian Formalist Criticism*, which contains Tomachevsky's essay in synthesis, "Thematics"; and Ladislav Matejka and Krystyna Pomorska, *Readings in Russian Poetics* (Cambridge: MIT Press, 1971). The major study of the Russian Formalists remains Victor Erlich, *Russian Formalism* (The Hague: Mouton, 1955). See also the anthology in French translation edited by Tzvetan Todorov, *Théorie de la littérature* (Paris: Editions du Seuil, 1965).

11. Propp, *The Morphology of the Folktale*, p. 21.

12. The paradigmatic axis is the "axis of selection" in Roman Jakobson's terms, the set of rules and virtual terms that are activated along the syntagmatic axis, or "axis of combination." For a good discussion of the uses of the two axes, see Jakobson, "Closing Statement: Linguistics and Poetics," in *Style in Language*, ed. Thomas Sebeok (Cambridge: MIT Press, 1960), pp. 350–77.

13. See A. J. Greimas, *Sémantique structurale* (Paris: Larousse, 1966). One of Greimas's more amusing illustrations is Karl Marx's *Capital*, which according to the model gives the following "actants": Subject: Man; Object: Classless Society; Sender: History; Receiver: Humanity; Helper: Proletariat; Opposer: Bourgeoisie.

14. See in particular Tzvetan Todorov, *Grammaire du Décameron* (The Hague: Mouton, 1969), and the essays of *Poétique de la prose* (Paris: Editions du Seuil, 1971), English trans. Richard Howard, *The Poetics of Prose* (Ithaca, N.Y.: Cornell Univ. Press, 1977). On Todorov's contribution to the poetics of narrative, see Peter Brooks, "Introduction" to Todorov, *Poetics*, trans. Richard Howard (Minneapolis: Univ. of Minnesota Press, 1981). See also Gerald Prince, *A Grammar of Stories* (The Hague: Mouton, 1973).

15. See Roland Barthes, *S/Z* (Paris: Editions du Seuil, 1970), English trans. Richard Miller (New York: Hill and Wang, 1974).

16. The notion of "literary competence," implicit in Barthes's view of reading, is very well discussed by Jonathan Culler in *Structuralist Poetics* (Ithaca, N.Y.: Cornell Univ. Press, 1975), pp. 113–30. Culler's book as a whole offers a lucid and useful discussion of structuralist approaches to the study of literature.

17. Barthes, "Introduction à l'analyse structurale des récits," p. 27.

18. See Gérard Genette, "Discours du récit," in *Figures III* (Paris: Editions du Seuil, 1972), English trans. Jane Lewin, *Narrative Discourse* (Ithaca, N.Y.: Cornell Univ. Press, 1980). To the *histoire/récit* (*fabula/sjužet*) distinction, Genette adds a third category, which he calls *narration*—"narrating"—that is, the level at which narratives sometimes dramatize the means and agency (real or fictive) of their telling. This category will prove of use to us later on. On the "perversion" of time in Proust, see "Discours du récit," p. 182.

19. Genette, "Discours du récit," pp. 77–78.

20. See Jean-Jacques Rousseau, "Seconde Préface," *La Nouvelle Héloïse* (Paris: Bibliothèque de la Pléiade, 1964), p. 18.

21. Marcel Proust, *A la recherche du temps perdu* (Paris: Bibliothèque de la Pléiade, 1954), vol. 3, p. 1045.

22. Genette, "Discours du récit," p. 228.

23. Benjamin, "The Storyteller," p. 94.

24. See Frank Kermode, *The Sense of an Ending* (New York: Oxford Univ. Press, 1967); Jean-Paul Sartre, *La Nausée* (Paris: Gallimard, 1947), pp. 59–60; Sartre, *Les Mots* (Paris: Gallimard, 1968), p. 171.

25. Jean Pouillon, *Temps et roman* (Paris: Gallimard, 1946). See also Claude Bremond, *Logique du récit* (Paris: Editions du Seuil, 1973).

26. On the resistance to the end, see D. A. Miller, *Narrative and Its Discontents* (Princeton, N.J.: Princeton Univ. Press, 1981). It is to Miller that I owe the term and concept "the narratable," which will be used frequently.

The relation of past and future to present is the subject of a famous meditation by Saint Augustine, in book 11 of the *Confessions*, where he finds a "solution" to the problem by the argument that there is a present of the past, in the form of memory, and a present of the future, in the form of anticipation or awaiting—a situation that he illustrates by the example of reciting a psalm. If Augustine does not solve the problem of temporality here, he surely offers a suggestive comment on the particular temporality of recitation or reading, its play of memory and anticipation. See the very rich analysis of Augustine's meditation in Ricoeur, *Temps et récit*, pp. 19–53.

27. Sir Arthur Conan Doyle, "The Musgrave Ritual," in *The Complete Sherlock Holmes* (New York: Doubleday, 1953), vol. 1, p. 445.

28. This use of metaphor and metonymy, as representing the selective or substitutive and the combinatory poles of language respectively (or the paradigmatic and syntagmatic), comes from Roman Jakobson's influential essay, "Two Types of Language and Two Types of Aphasic Disturbances," in Roman Jakobson and Morris Halle, *Fundamentals of Language* (The Hague: Mouton, 1956).

29. Todorov, "Typologie du roman policier," in *Poétique de la prose*, pp. 57–59.

30. Todorov, "Les Transformations narratives," in *Poétique de la prose*, pp. 225–40.

31. Jonathan Culler, "Story and Discourse in the Analysis of Narrative," in *The Pursuit of Signs* (London: Routledge and Kegan Paul, 1981), p. 178. Culler's discussion here is partly in reference to my essay, "Fictions of the Wolfman," *Diacritics* 9, no. 1 (1979), pp. 72–83, which forms the core of chapter 10 of the present study.

32. Cynthia Chase, "The Decomposition of the Elephants: Double Reading *Daniel Deronda*," *PMLA* 93, no. 2 (1978), p. 218.

33. Sir Arthur Conan Doyle, "The Naval Treaty," in *The Complete Sherlock Holmes*, vol. 1, p. 540.

34. Jean-Jacques Rousseau, *Confessions* (Paris: Bibliothèque de la Pléïade, 1959), p. 85.

35. On the "text as machine" in Rousseau, and on the episode of the stolen ribbon as a whole, see the notable essay by Paul de Man, "The Purloined Ribbon," in *Allegories of Reading* (New Haven: Yale Univ. Press, 1979), pp. 278–301. While my use of the episode of the stolen ribbon is substantially different from de Man's, I am indebted to his remarkable analysis.

36. For the most succinct statement of this research, see William Labov and Joshua Waletsky, "Narrative Analysis: Oral Versions of Personal Experience," in *Essays on the Verbal and Visual Arts* (Proceedings of the 1966 Annual Spring Meeting of the American Ethnological Society), ed. June Helm (Seattle: Univ. of Washington Press, 1967), pp. 12–44. In general, Labov and Waletsky's analysis of the form of oral narratives tends to confirm the work of the structural narratologists. Their identification of the

self-reflective moment of "evaluation" offers an extremely useful addition.

37. Susan Sontag, *Against Interpretation* (New York: Farrar, Straus and Giroux, 1966), p. 14.

2. *Narrative Desire*

1. Sigmund Freud, *Beyond the Pleasure Principle* [*Jenseits des Lustprinzips*] (1920), in *The Standard Edition of the Complete Psychological Works of Sigmund Freud*, ed. James Strachey (London: Hogarth Press, 1953–74), vol. 18, p. 50. Subsequent references to Freud are to this edition, and simple page citations will be given in the text.

2. On this plot structure, traditionally considered to be the structure of Greek "new comedy," see Northrop Frye, *Anatomy of Criticism* (Princeton, N.J.: Princeton Univ. Press, 1957), pp. 163–85; and Erich Segal, "The φύσις of Comedy," *Harvard Studies in Classical Philology* 77 (1973), pp. 129–36. On *Lazarillo de Tormes* and its place in the history of the novel, see Walter L. Reed, *An Exemplary History of the Novel* (Chicago: Univ. of Chicago Press, 1981), pp. 43–70.

3. On the bourgeoisie and the novel, see Harry Levin, *The Gates of Horn* (New York: Oxford Univ. Press, 1963), especially chap. 2; and Ian Watt, *The Rise of the Novel* (3rd ed.; Berkeley and Los Angeles: Univ. of California Press, 1962), which also discusses the protestant and dissenting role represented by the female consciousness, as in *Clarissa*. On women's plots, see Nancy K. Miller, *The Heroine's Text* (New York: Columbia Univ. Press, 1980). One might recall here that the folktale "All-Kinds-of-Fur" in some measure represents the female plot, a resistance and what we might call an "endurance": a waiting (and suffering) until the woman's desire can be a permitted response to the expression of male desire.

4. Honoré de Balzac, *Le Père Goriot*, in *La Comédie humaine* (Paris: Bibliothèque de la Pléïade, 1976–81), vol. 3, pp. 77–78. Subsequent references to Balzac are to this edition, and simple page citations will be given in the text.

5. See Michel Serres, *Feux et signaux de brume: Zola* (Paris: Grasset, 1975), pp. 209–10. Serres's book has in general been an inspiration to my consideration here of motors and engines.

6. Ernest Jones, *The Life and Work of Sigmund Freud* (New York: Basic Books, 1953), vol. 1, p. 41. On Freud's scientific background, see also Frank J. Sulloway, *Freud: Biologist of the Mind* (New York: Basic Books, 1979).

7. "Instincts and Their Vicissitudes" [*Triebe und Triebschicksale*], in *Standard Edition*, vol. 14, p. 122.

8. Harry Levin aptly notes: "This criterion [*énergie*] combined the old rhetorical term for emphasis with the new concept of power, *puissance motrice*, which Nicolas Carnot and other physicists were developing. It might be glossed as the thermodynamics of genius." *The Gates of Horn*, p. 115.

9. For one possible treatment of this notion, see J.-F. Lyotard, *Economie libidinale* (Paris: Editions de Minuit, 1974).

10. Balzac was, of course, a self-proclaimed monarchist and Catholic, who regarded modern capitalist society, society without organic hierarchy or spiritual form, as headed toward chaos; and this position of dissent made him a particularly lucid critic of the contradictions of his time, as Marx and Engels recognized. Balzac was particularly acerbic in criticism of the Restoration for having bungled the chance to rehabilitate true monarchy; he claims that the mostly aged leadership of the Restoration failed to gain the energy it needed to re-establish dynastic power through a pact with the active, intellectual youth of France—young men like Balzac himself, and like Lucien, who with the other *viveurs* of his generation is condemned to "moral Helotism." His most cogent sociopolitical indictment of the Restoration may be that in *La Duchesse de Langeais*, in *La Comédie humaine*, vol. 5, pp. 927–32.

11. Charles Dickens, *Hard Times* (London: J. M. Dent, 1957), p. 19.

12. Gustave Flaubert, *L'Education sentimentale*, in *Oeuvres* (Paris: Bibliothèque de la Pléïade, 1952), vol. 2, p. 352.

13. Emile Zola, *Nana*, in *Oeuvres complètes* (Paris: Cercle du Livre Précieux, 1967), vol. 4, pp. 321–22.

14. Jacques Derrida, "Force et signification," in *L'Ecriture et la différence* (Paris: Editions du Seuil, 1967), pp. 29, 11.

15. Balzac, *La Peau de chagrin*, in *La Comédie humaine*, vol. 10, p. 202.

16. See Freud, *Beyond the Pleasure Principle, Standard Edition*, vol. 18, pp. 53–54. These questions, and the interpretation of *Beyond the Pleasure Principle*, will be more fully discussed in chapter 4.

17. On some of these questions, see Françoise Gaillard, "L'Effet Peau de chagrin," in *Le Roman de Balzac*, ed. R. Le Huenen and P. Perron (Montreal: Marcel Didier, 1980), pp. 213–20.

18. This is one version of the "panoramic vision of the dying," a question that interested Henri Bergson and is discussed by Georges Poulet in "Bergson: le Thème de la vision panoramique des mourants et la juxtaposition,"

L'Espace proustien (Paris: Gallimard, 1963). Whether the scenes of the panoramic vision are simultaneous or rather successive, we recognize in the theme further evidence of the importance accorded to the moment of death in the nineteenth-century novel as a privileged moment of understanding, a question that will receive further discussion in chapter 4.

19. Gérard Genette defines "narration" as "l'acte narratif producteur du récit et, par extension, l'ensemble de la situation réelle ou fictive dans laquelle il prend place" ("Discours du récit," in *Figures III* [Paris: Editions du Seuil, 1972], p. 72; English trans. Jane Lewin, *Narrative Discourse* [Ithaca, N.Y.: Cornell Univ. Press, 1980]). Mieke Bal has argued that *narration* does not properly constitute a third narrative level distinct from *récit* (*sjužet*): see *Narratologie* (Paris: Klincksieck, 1977), p. 6. Bal may be correct in terms of the reasoned distinction of narrative levels—*narration* is asymmetrical to *récit* and *histoire*—yet the isolation of *narration* as the moments and ways in which narratives speak of and dramatize the act and the agency of their production seems to me of great importance.

20. Jean Laplanche and J.-B. Pontalis, *Vocabulaire de la psychanalyse* (Paris: Presses Universitaires de France, 1971), "Désir," p. 122.

21. Jacques Lacan, "L'Instance de la lettre dans l'inconscient ou la raison depuis Freud," in *Ecrits* (Paris: Editions du Seuil, 1966), p. 518; English trans. Alan Sheridan, *Ecrits* (New York: Norton, 1977). My exposition of Lacanian thought here is based mainly on this essay, where Lacan rethinks the Freudian concepts of "condensation" and "displacement" (two important operations of the dream work) in rhetorical terms, as metaphor and metonymy, using these terms in the senses made current by Roman Jakobson's influential essay "Two Poles of Language and Two Types of Aphasic Disturbance" (in Jakobson and Morris Halle, *Fundamentals of Language* [The Hague: Mouton, 1956]). For Jakobson, metaphor is typical of lyric poetry, whereas metonymy characterizes narrative, particularly in its nineteenth-century "realist" phase, since narrative proceeds via the synecdochic detail, in the movement from one detail to another. Lacan can thus say that symptom, whereby unconscious desire inscribes itself on the body, *is* metaphor (and indeed, Freud virtually said so himself), whereas desire, insisting in the signifying chain, *is* metonymy.

22. See Freud, "Medusa's Head" [*Das Medusenhaupt*] (1940 [1922]), in *Standard Edition*, vol. 18, pp. 273–74. On this scene as a representation of castration, see Samuel Weber, *Unwrapping Balzac: A Reading of "La Peau de chagrin"* (Toronto: Univ. of Toronto Press, 1979), pp. 99–103.

23. The oedipal conflict, represented as parricide and its punishment,

can be found in latent form throughout Balzac's work and has been well studied by Janet L. Beizer in "The Narrative of Generation and the Generation of Narrative in Balzac" (Doctoral dissertation, Yale Univ., 1981). My next chapter, on Stendhal, may serve to suggest that the oedipal conflict was particularly intense in France during the first half of the nineteenth century, a period marked by an intense political and cultural struggle between youth and gerontocracy.

3. *The Novel and the Guillotine,* or *Fathers and Sons in* Le Rouge et le noir

1. Harry Levin, *The Gates of Horn* (New York: Oxford Univ. Press, 1963), p. 149. The classic exposition of how representation in Stendhal is pervaded by historical perspective may be found in Erich Auerbach, *Mimesis*, trans. Willard Trask (Garden City, N.Y.: Anchor Books, 1957), pp. 400–413.

2. James Joyce, *Ulysses* (New York: Modern Library, 1961), p. 207.

3. See "Family Romances" [*Der Familienroman der Neurotiker*] (1908), in *The Standard Edition of the Complete Psychological Works of Sigmund Freud*, ed. James Strachey (London: Hogarth Press, 1953–74), vol. 9, pp. 237–41; see Roland Barthes, "Introduction à l'analyse structurale des récits," *Communications* 8 (1966), p. 27. The "family romance" as an underlying structure of the modern novel has been well discussed by Marthe Robert in *Roman des origines, origines du roman* (Paris: Grasset, 1972).

4. *Hernani* itself, curiously, stages the eventual victory of the paternal generation over the son, as the aged Don Ruy Gomez reappears on Hernani's wedding night to reclaim Hernani's life, which he previously saved. Hernani has throughout expressed guilt toward his own father, whose memory he was to avenge in killing the king, Don Carlos. Accepting death from the hand of Don Ruy Gomez, he may at the last succumb to the burden of oedipal guilt—as if in token of Victor Hugo's act of compensation for his own oedipal transgression. On Stendhal's attitudes toward the Restoration, see, among others, Geneviève Mouillaud, *"Le Rouge et le noir" de Stendhal: Le roman possible* (Paris: Larousse, 1973).

5. Stendhal, *Le Rouge et le noir*, in *Romans et nouvelles*, ed. Henri Martineau (Paris: Bibliothèque de la Pléiade, 1963), vol. 1, p. 697. Subsequent references are to this edition, and will be given in parentheses in the text. Translations from Stendhal are my own.

6. Henri Martineau summarizes critical objections to the end of the

novel and offers his own psychological interpretation in *L'Oeuvre de Stendhal* (Paris: Le Divan, 1945), pp. 343–51. For another useful summary of critical commentaries on the dénouement, and an attempt to remotivate Julien's acts on a rational basis, see P.-G. Castex, *"Le Rouge et le noir" de Stendhal* (Paris: SEDES, 1967), pp. 124–55.

7. Martineau establishes a careful fictional chronology of the novel in the Garnier edition (Paris: Garnier, 1957), pp. 533–37. On the problem of chronology, see also Charles J. Stivale, "Le Vraisemblable temporel dans *Le Rouge et le noir,*" *Stendhal Club* 84 (1979), pp. 299–313. Concerning revolution and the guillotine, see Stendhal's account of his joy—at age ten—on learning of the execution of Louis XVI, an event he explicitly contrasts with the failure of the July monarchy to execute the Comte de Peyronnet and the other ministers who signed the "ordonnances de Juillet," which touched off the Revolution of 1830. *La Vie de Henry Brulard*, in *Oeuvres intimes*, ed. Henri Martineau (Paris: Bibliothèque de la Pléiade, 1955), p. 94.

8. See Stendhal, "La Comédie est impossible en 1836," in *Mélanges de littérature*, ed. Henri Martineau (Paris: Le Divan, 1933), vol. 3; and the fuller discussion of the question of social comedy and novel of manners in Peter Brooks, *The Novel of Worldliness* (Princeton, N.J.: Princeton Univ. Press, 1969), pp. 219–26. Stendhal's argument is already largely adumbrated in *Racine et Shakespeare* (1823; 1825).

9. Rereading the "Bucci copy" of his novel in 1835, Stendhal noted in the margins of book 1, chapter 21—where Mme de Rênal has been maneuvering her husband to the conclusion that the anonymous letters come from Valenod—"Here is a scene of comedy," after which he goes on to lament that it cannot be put on the stage, and to explain why. See Pléiade edition, p. 1465.

10. See F. W. J. Hemmings's discussion of Julien as a "dreamer" in *Stendhal, A Study of His Novels* (Oxford: Clarendon Press, 1964).

11. Julien states: "Je ne me plaindrai plus du hasard, j'ai retrouvé un père en vous, monsieur." And the Abbé replies: "Il ne faut jamais dire le hasard, mon enfant, dites toujours la Providence"—"Never say fortune, my child, always say Providence." Substituting "Providence" for "fortune," of course, indicates a belief in an overall direction to human plots—that of the Father—which the novel as a whole tends to discredit.

12. The trace of the Duc de Chaulnes in the novel presents many curiosities. The Marquis dubs Julien "the younger brother of the Comte de Chaulnes, that is, the son of my friend the old Duc" (p. 477). Julien dispels his remorse at seducing his benefactor's daughter by recalling with anger

that the Duc de Chaulnes has called him a "domestique" (p. 509), a remark that Julien recalls again upon receiving Mathilde's declaration of love (p. 524): to be put in the role of Julien's father, even fictively, is to assume the burden of oedipal hatred. Mathilde, reflecting on the dishonor she is courting, mentions the Duc de Chaulnes as father of her official fiancé, the Marquis de Croisenois (p. 529). Yet elsewhere in the novel the Duc de Chaulnes is given as the Marquis de la Mole's father-in-law, and after Mathilde announces her pregnancy and her determination to marry Julien, the Marquis thinks of passing on his peerage to Julien, since the Duc de Chaulnes has "several times, since his only son was killed in Spain, spoken of his desire to transmit his title to Norbert [de la Mole] . . ." (p. 637). One is tempted to conclude that the shadowy Duc de Chaulnes, representative of the Ancien Régime and of legitimate authority, is par excellence the figure of paternity in the novel, pressed into service whenever Stendhal needs a reference to paternity. As a figure of legitimation for Julien, he is also alienating, perhaps inevitably; and he may be guilty of putting his biological son to death. And as a figure of paternal authority, he is curiously absent and trivial. The more one probes the mystery of paternity in this novel, the more it appears mysterious.

13. See Victor Brombert, *Stendhal et la voie oblique* (Paris and New Haven: Yale Univ. Press, 1954).

14. The remark occurs, I believe, in Stendhal's *Filosofia Nova*. On these questions, see also Jean Starobinski, "Stendhal pseudonyme," in *L'Oeil vivant* (Paris: Gallimard, 1963), pp. 191–240. Robert André, *Ecriture et pulsions dans le roman stendhalien* (Paris: Klincksieck, 1977), gives a detailed account of Beyle's oedipal conflict and the forms of hatred for the father presented in the novels, especially *La Chartreuse de Parme*. See also Micheline Levowitz-Treu, *L'Amour et la mort chez Stendhal* (Aran: Editions du Grand Chêne, 1978). The relation of Julien's search for a father to political questions is perceptively discussed by Henri-François Imbert in *Les Métamorphoses de la liberté* (Paris: Corti, 1967).

15. "Oui, mon père est comme tous les pères, ce que je n'avais pas su voir jusqu'ici; avec infiniment plus d'esprit et même de sentiment qu'un autre, il n'en veut pas moins me rendre heureux *à sa façon* et non à la mienne." *Lucien Leuwen*, in *Romans et nouvelles*, vol. 1, p. 1355.

16. See Jean Prévost, *La Création chez Stendhal* (Marseilles: Editions du Sagittaire, 1942); and the remarkable essay—touching on a number of the questions that interest me here—by Gérard Genette, " 'Stendhal,' " in *Figures II* (Paris: Editions du Seuil, 1969), pp. 155–93.

17. Gustave Flaubert, *L'Education sentimentale*, in *Oeuvres* (Paris: Bibliothèque de la Pléïade, 1952), vol. 2, p. 352.

18. See Georg Lukács, *The Theory of the Novel*, trans. Anna Bostock (Cambridge: MIT Press, 1971), pp. 124–25. On the nature of Stendhalian temporality, see also Genette, " 'Stendhal,' " and Georges Poulet, *Mesure de l'instant* (Paris: Plon, 1968).

19. René Girard, *Mensonge romantique et vérité romanesque* (Paris: Grasset, 1961).

20. Some examples of the use of "monster" in the novel: When Julien enters his post at the Hôtel de la Mole, the Abbé Pirard notes the magnitude of what the Marquis is doing for him, and says, "Si vous n'êtes pas un monstre, vous aurez pour lui et sa famille une éternelle reconnaissance" ("If you are not a monster, you will be eternally grateful to him and his family") (p. 443); when Julien reflects on the calumny his name will receive if he is killed while climbing to Mathilde's bedroom, he says to himself, "Je serai un monstre dans la posterité" ("I will be a monster for posterity") (p. 537); when the Marquis berates him for seducing Mathilde—and Julien has just cited, in his defense, the words of Tartuffe: "je ne suis pas un ange . . ." ("I'm no angel")—he calls him "Monstre!" (p. 629); when the Abbé Chélan comes to visit Julien in his prison cell, the Abbé addresses him: "Ah! grand Dieu! est-il possible, mon enfant . . . Monstre! devrais-je dire" ("Ah! Lord, is it possible, my child . . . Monster, I should say") (p. 1651). Note also this remark of Stendhal's about his relations with his own father: "J'observai avec remords que je n'avais pas pour lui une *goutte* de tendresse ni d'affection. Je suis donc un monstre me disais-je, et pendant de longues années je n'ai pas trouvé de réponse à cette objection" ("I observed with remorse that I hadn't a *drop* of tenderness or affection for him. I am thus a monster, I said to myself, and for many years I found no answer to this objection"), *La Vie de Henry Brulard*, in *Oeuvres intimes*, pp. 217–18.

21. On the resistance to ending in Stendhal, see the excellent study by D. A. Miller in *Narrative and Its Discontents* (Princeton, N.J.· Princeton Univ. Press, 1981), pp. 195–264.

22. Using the terms of the Russian Formalists, one could say that the *fabula* (the order of event referred to by the narrative) intrudes into the *sjužet* (the order of event in its presentation by the narrative discourse). But to do so would mean reducing the *fabula* to the bare-bones anecdote from which Stendhal worked, whereas the *fabula* is properly understood as the whole of the story to which the narrative discourse refers, the order

of events that a reading of the narrative enables one to construct, an order that, of course, has no existence beyond this construction. What invades the narrative discourse of *Le Rouge et le noir* is distinctly heterogeneous, another order of discourse, another genre, another story. The account of Antoine Berthet's trial in *La Gazette des Tribunaux* is reprinted in the Pléïade edition, pp. 715–30.

23. Some earlier critics of *Le Rouge et le noir*—Léon Blum, Henri Rambaud, Maurice Bardèche—noted that Stendhal seems to insist upon returning to his documentary scenario at the end: see the summary of their comments in Castex, *"Le Rouge et le noir" de Stendhal*, pp. 126–27. Here again, I find the more "traditional" critics closer to the mark: they have noted real problems, though their treatment of them does not fall within the analysis of narrative that interests me here.

24. On the metalepsis of the author, see the discussion by Genette (himself referring to Fontanier) in "Discours du récit," p. 244.

25. Possessing the mother/mistress, Julien may realize a final desired confusion of origins, enacting the oedipal story according to Claude Lévi-Strauss as well as Freud. He has answered the problem of origin by its confusion, "sowing where he was sown": note that not only does Julien want Mme de Rênal to be mother to his unborn child, Mme de Rênal herself earlier expresses the wish that Julien were father to her children—children who curiously are sometimes three in number, and sometimes two, further confusing the question of generation and perhaps thereby further confirming Lévi-Strauss's view that the Oedipus myth tells the story of an insoluble problem: see "The Structural Study of Myth," in *Structural Anthropology* (Garden City, N.Y.: Anchor-Doubleday, 1967), pp. 202–28. As with the postulated paternity of the Duc de Chaulnes, we are here faced with a significant confusion. See also Leo Bersani's remark: "almost the entire story is an immense detour which Julien takes in order to return, in prison, and this time consciously and with full consent, to the happiness of merely being with Mme de Rênal which he had thought himself ready to sacrifice to his ambition." *A Future for Astyanax* (Boston: Little, Brown, 1976), pp. 111–12.

4. Freud's Masterplot: A Model for Narrative

1. Tzvetan Todorov, "Les Transformations narratives," in *Poétique de la prose* (Paris: Editions du Seuil, 1971), p. 240; English trans. Richard Howard, *The Poetics of Prose* (Ithaca, N.Y.: Cornell Univ. Press, 1977). Todorov's

terms *récit* and *histoire* correspond to the Russian formalist distinction between *sjužet* and *fabula*.

2. Todorov in a later article adds to "transformation" the term "succession" and sees the pair as definitional of narrative. He discusses the possible equation of these terms with Jakobson's "metaphor" and "metonymy," to conclude that "the connection is possible but does not seem necessary" (Todorov, "The Two Principles of Narrative," *Diacritics* [Fall 1971], p. 42); but there seem to be good reasons to maintain Jakobson's terms as "master tropes" referring to two aspects of virtually any text.

3. See Barbara Herrnstein Smith, *Poetic Closure* (Chicago: Univ. of Chicago Press, 1968), and Frank Kermode, *The Sense of an Ending* (New York: Oxford Univ. Press, 1967). Kermode's book has been particularly important to my own thinking about endings.

4. Jean-Paul Sartre, *La Nausée* (Paris: Gallimard, 1947), pp. 59–60.

5. Sartre, *Les Mots* (Paris: Gallimard, 1968), p. 171.

6. Kermode, *The Sense of an Ending*, p. 7.

7. Walter Benjamin, "The Storyteller" [*Der Erzähler*], in *Illuminations*, trans. Harry Zohn (New York: Schocken Books, 1969), p. 94.

8. Freud, *Beyond the Pleasure Principle* [*Jenseits des Lustprinzips*] (1920), in *The Standard Edition of the Complete Psychological Works of Sigmund Freud*, ed. James Strachey (London: Hogarth Press, 1953–74), vol. 18, p. 59.

9. J. Hillis Miller has noted that the term *diegesis*, used by Plato to designate the narrative of events—the summary of action, as opposed to its imitative reproduction, or *mimesis*—suggests in its etymology that narrative is the retracing of a line already drawn. See "The Ethics of Reading: Vast Gaps and Parting Hours," in *American Criticism in the Poststructuralist Age*, ed. Ira Konigsberg (Michigan Studies in the Humanities, 1981), p. 25.

10. Freud, "The Theme of the Three Caskets" [*Das Motiv der Kästchenwahl*] (1913), in *Standard Edition*, vol. 12, p. 299.

11. See Freud, "The Dynamics of the Transference" [*Zur Dynamik des Uberträgungs*] (1912), in *Standard Edition*, vol. 12, pp. 99–108; "Remembering, Repeating and Working Through" [*Errinern, Wiederholen, und Durcharbeiten*] (1914), *Standard Edition*, vol. 12, pp. 147–56; "The Uncanny" [*Das Unheimliche*] (1919), *Standard Edition*, vol. 17, pp. 219–52.

12. The dynamic model of psychic life, Freud wrote in 1926, "derives all mental processes . . . from the interplay of forces, which assist or inhibit one another, combine with one another, enter into compromises with one another, etc. All of these forces are originally in the nature of *instincts* . . ." (*Standard Edition*, vol. 20, p. 265). I shall use the term "instinct" since it is

the translation of *Trieb* given throughout the *Standard Edition*. But we should realize that "instinct" is inadequate and somewhat misleading since it loses the sense of "drive" and "force" associated (as the preceding quotation suggests) with Freud's conception of *Trieb*. The currently accepted French translation, *pulsion*, would be more to our purposes: the model that interests me here might indeed be called "pulsional."

13. On the question of the beginning as "intention," see Edward Said, *Beginnings: Intention and Method* (New York: Basic Books, 1975). It occurs to me that the exemplary narrative beginning might be that of Kafka's *Metamorphosis*: waking up to find oneself transformed into a monstrous vermin.

14. See William Empson, "Double Plots," in *Some Versions of Pastoral* (New York: New Directions, 1960), pp. 25–84.

15. Freud, *New Introductory Lectures on Psychoanalysis* [*Neue Folge der Vorlesungen zur Einführung in die Psychoanalyse*] (1933), in *Standard Edition*, vol. 22, p. 95.

16. See Freud, "Analysis Terminable and Interminable" [*Die endliche und die unendliche Analyse*] (1937), in *Standard Edition*, vol. 23, pp. 216–53.

17. Georg Lukács, *The Theory of the Novel*, trans. Anna Bostock (Cambridge: MIT Press, 1971), p. 122.

18. Gérard Genette discusses Proust's "perversion" of time in "Discours du récit," in *Figures III* (Paris: Editions du Seuil, 1972), p. 182.

5. *Repetition, Repression, and Return:*
The Plotting of Great Expectations

1. E. M. Forster's strictures on plot, his refusal of the primacy assigned to plot by Aristotle, in *Aspects of the Novel* (mentioned in chapter 1, herein) are representative of the modernist attitude toward traditional plotting. One finds more extreme dissents later on, for example: Virginia Woolf, *Mr. Bennett and Mrs. Brown* (London: Leonard and Virginia Woolf, 1924); Nathalie Sarraute, *L'Ere du soupçon* (Paris: Gallimard, 1956); Alain Robbe-Grillet, *Pour un nouveau roman* (Paris: Editions de Minuit, 1963).

2. Charles Dickens, *Great Expectations* (London: Oxford Univ. Press, 1975), p. 1. References are to this edition, and will hereafter be given in parentheses in the text. I will include chapter numbers to facilitate reference to other editions.

3. On the theme of reading in the novel, see Max Byrd, " 'Reading' in *Great Expectations*," *PMLA* 91, no. 2 (1976), pp. 259–65.

4. On the archaeological model in Freud, see in particular the use he

makes of Pompeii in "Delusions and Dreams in Jensen's *Gradiva*" [*Der Wahn und die Träume in W. Jensens* Gradiva] (1907), in *The Standard Edition of the Complete Psychological Works of Sigmund Freud*, ed. James Strachey (London: Hogarth Press, 1953–74), vol. 9, pp. 3–95.

5. See *Great Expectations*, chap. 19, p. 149. Miss Havisham is thus seemingly cast in the role of the "Donor," who provides the hero with a magical agent, one of the seven *dramatis personae* of the fairy tale identified by Vladimir Propp in *The Morphology of the Folktale*.

6. On the role of the law as one of the formal orders of the novel, see Moshe Ron, "Autobiographical Narration and Formal Closure in *Great Expectations*," *Hebrew University Studies in Literature* 5, no. 1 (1977), pp. 37–66. The importance of criminality in Dickens has, of course, been noted by many critics, including Edmund Wilson in his seminal essay "Dickens: The Two Scrooges," in *The Wound and the Bow* (Boston: Houghton Mifflin, 1941).

7. Søren Kierkegaard, *Repetition*, trans. Walter Lowrie (Princeton, N.J.: Princeton Univ. Press, 1941), pp. 3–4. For other discussions of repetition in literature, see Gilles Deleuze, *Logique du sens* (Paris: Editions de Minuit, 1969); and J. Hillis Miller, *Fiction and Repetition* (Cambridge: Harvard Univ. Press, 1982).

8. See Freud, "The Dynamics of the Transference" and "Remembering, Repeating and Working Through," in *Standard Edition*, vol. 12; and Jacques Lacan, *Le Séminaire, Livre XI: Les Quatre Concepts fondamentaux de la psychanalyse* (Paris: Editions du Seuil, 1973), pp. 49–50.

9. This scene with Orlick brings to the surface much of the aggressivity latent in the novel, aggressivity that is attributed to Orlick, but may in some sense emanate from Pip himself, as Orlick seems to imply when he repeatedly calls Pip "wolf" and argues that Pip was really responsible for Orlick's bludgeoning of Mrs. Joe. One could make a case for conferring greater interpretive importance on this scene, as is done by Teresa Grant in her excellent essay "Story vs. Discourse: A Dialectical Perspective" (unpublished MS, Univ. of Texas, Austin), which in part takes issue with some of the emphases of an earlier version of the present chapter, published in *New Literary History* 11, no. 3 (1980). Yet I am not convinced that Orlick "works" as a character: his evil appears so total and gratuitous that he at times appears too easy a device for deflecting our attention from Pip's more hostile impulses.

10. The pattern of the incestuous couple, where the implication of the brother-sister relation serves as both attraction and prohibition, has been noted by several critics. See especially Harry Stone, "The Love Pattern in

Dickens' Novels," in *Dickens the Craftsman*, ed. Robert B. Partlow, Jr. (Carbondale: Southern Illinois Univ. Press, 1970); and Albert J. Guerard, *The Triumph of the Novel* (New York: Oxford Univ. Press, 1976), p. 70. *Great Expectations* gives particular weight to the figure of the father as source of the law: Magwitch, assuming in different registers the role of father both to Estella and to Pip, becomes not a figure of authority so much as a principle of interdiction, of prohibition.

6. The Mark of the Beast: Prostitution, Serialization, and Narrative

1. See Peter Brooks, "Virtue-Tripping: Notes on *Le Lys dans la vallée*," *Yale French Studies* 50 (1975), pp. 150–62; and on the "presence" of the body in a number of modern novels, see the interesting study by Roger Kempf, *Sur le corps romanesque* (Paris: Editions du Seuil, 1968).

2. Emile Zola, *Nana*, in *Oeuvres complètes* (Paris: Cercle du Livre Précieux, 1967), vol. 4, p. 171. My understanding of this scene has been enhanced by a fine essay, as yet unpublished, by Janet L. Beizer, "Unwrapping *Nana*: The Courtesan's New Clothes."

3. On the *roman-feuilleton* and Sue's relation to it, see: René Guise, "Balzac et le roman-feuilleton," *L'Année balzacienne* (Paris: Garnier, 1964), pp. 283–328; R. Guise, Marcel Graner, and Liliane Durand-Dessert, "Des *Mystères de Paris* aux *Mystères du peuple*," *Europe* (March-April 1977), pp. 152–67; H. Avenel, *Histoire de la presse française depuis 1789* (Paris: E. Flammarion, 1900); J. André Faucher, *Le Quatrième Pouvoir: la presse, de 1830 à 1930* (Paris: Les Editions Jacquemart, 1957); David Owen Evans, *Le Roman social sous la monarchie de juillet* (Paris: Presses Universitaires de France, 1936); and the issue of *Europe* devoted to Sue, November–December 1982.

4. Eugène Sue, *Les Mystères de Paris* (Paris: Charles Gosselin, 1843), vol. 10, p. 149. Subsequent references are to this text, and will be given in parentheses in the text. *Les Mystères* has been reissued in a four-volume edition by the Editions Libres Hallier, Paris, 1978.

5. For a classic example of Freud's analysis of the displacement upward, see "Fragment of an Analysis of a Case of Hysteria" ("Dora") [*Bruchstück einer Hysterie-Analyse*] (1905), in *The Standard Edition of the Complete Psychological Works of Sigmund Freud*, ed. James Strachey (London: Hogarth Press, 1953–74), vol. 7, p. 30.

6. E. Faure, "*Les Mystères de Paris*, par M. Eugène Sue," book review in

La Revue Indépendante 8 (1843), reprinted in Helga Grubitzsch, ed., *Materialien zur Kritik des Feuilleton-Romans* (Wiesbaden: Akademische Verlagsgesellschaft Athenaion, 1977), pp. 40–41. This useful collection of contemporary responses to *Les Mystères* contains as well the relevant passages from Karl Marx and Friedrich Engels, *Die heilige Familie*—passages composed essentially by Marx.

7. C. A. Sainte-Beuve, "M. Eugène Sue," from *Portraits contemporains* (1846), reprinted Grubitzsch, *Materialien*, p. 71.

8. On these questions, and all others concerning Sue's life and career, see the excellent biography by Jean-Louis Bory, *Eugène Sue: Dandy mais socialiste* (Paris: Hachette, 1962). See also Umberto Eco, "Rhetoric and Ideology in Sue's *Les Mystères de Paris*," in *The Role of the Reader* (Bloomington: Indiana Univ. Press, 1979), pp. 125–41.

9. See Albert Béguin, *Balzac visionnaire* (Geneva: Skira, 1946), pp. 151–79.

10. Balzac, *Splendeurs et misères des courtisanes*, in *La Comédie humaine* (Paris: Bibliothèque de la Pléiade, 1976–81), vol. 6, p. 617. The four parts of Balzac's novel were published over the period 1838 to 1847, and the first part, originally entitled "La Torpille" ("The Torpedo"—Esther's nickname), was offered to Emile de Girardin for publication in *La Presse*. Girardin refused to publish the story of a prostitute for fear of scandalizing his readers.

11. Louis Chevalier, *Classes laborieuses et classes dangereuses* (Paris: Plon, 1958), p. 334; English trans. Frank Jellinek, *Labouring Classes and Dangerous Classes* (London: Routledge and Kegan Paul, 1973).

12. See A.-J.-B. Parent-Duchatelet, *De la prostitution dans la ville de Paris*, 2 vols. (2nd ed.; Paris: J.-B. Baillère, 1837). I have also consulted the edition of 1857, "Complétée par des documents nouveaux . . . par Adolphe Trébuchet et Poiret-Duval."

13. Other notable reports were by Dr. Louis-René Villermé, on workers in the textile industries (1840) and on workers' living quarters (1850), and by Eugène Buret, on working-class misery in France and England (1840).

14. On "policing" as theme and structuring force in the nineteenth-century novel (with particular reference to Wilkie Collins), see D. A. Miller, "The Novel and the Police," in *Glyph* 8 (1981), pp. 127–47.

15. Parent-Duchatelet, *De la prostitution*, vol. 1, p. 7. For an example of Parent-Duchatelet's rhetorical blend of observation and veiling of the evidence, physiology and morality, consider these remarks, concerning sodomy: "Ces malheureuses, livrées à la brutalité d'une foule d'hommes blasées

sur les jouissances que permet la nature, ne refusent pas toujours ces communications illicites qui, pour avoir lieu entre des individus de sexe différent, n'en sont pas moins révoltantes. . . . Je dois avouer qu'il n'est pas un point de la vie et des habitudes des filles plus obscur que celui-ci; on peut dire, à leur louange, qu'elles sont sur ce sujet d'une réserve complète, qu'elles repoussent avec horreur les questions qu'on leur adresse, et qu'elles affectent une certaine indignation lorsqu'on paraît les soupçonner de s'être prêtées à des communications de cette nature" (*De la prostitution*, vol. 1, pp. 225–26).

16. See Michel Foucault, *Surveiller et punir* (Paris: Gallimard, 1975), English trans. Alan Sheridan, *Discipline and Punish* (New York: Pantheon, 1977).

17. See Alain Corbin, *Les Filles de noces: misère sexuelle et prostitution (19e et 20e siècles)* (Paris: Aubier-Montaigne, 1978). Corbin makes clear the connections between Parent-Duchatelet's enterprise and Foucault's notion of "surveillance"—which is not surprising, since he appears to be deeply influenced by Foucault. Corbin's book is enormously useful and illuminating, yet I wonder about the accuracy of the portrait of bourgeois female sexuality he presents: was female sexuality so entirely foreclosed to the middle and upper classes as the official and medical literature Corbin examines may suggest? Surely the novelists—Balzac, Flaubert, Zola, Barbey d'Aurevilly—constantly suggest otherwise. We need a thorough study of the status of female sexuality in nineteenth-century France.

18. Balzac, *Illusions perdues*, in *La Comédie humaine*, vol. 5, p. 493.

19. See Georg Lukács, "*Illusions perdues*," in *Studies in European Realism*, trans. Edith Bone (London: Hillway Publishing Co., 1950). It is worth noting that in part 3 of *Illusions perdues*, Balzac invents an elaborate plot simply from the circulation of a *compte de retour*, or unpaid letter of credit, commenting: "Calembour à part, jamais les romanciers n'ont inventé de conte plus invraisemblable que celui-là . . ." (*La Comédie humaine*, vol. 5, p. 591).

20. These letters are preserved in the Fonds Eugène Sue of the Bibliothèque Historique de la Ville de Paris: see "Correspondance d'Eugène Sue relative aux *Mystères de Paris*," MSS. CP3935. I am most grateful to the director and staff of the Bibliothèque Historique de la Ville de Paris for their help and cooperation when I was studying this correspondence.

21. The letter is without date. The writer is evidently highly intelligent and of some literary talent (she sends Sue some "petits livres," not otherwise identified, written before she was employed at Saint-Lazare); her rhetoric has an effective simplicity, notable after one has spent many hours with

the melodramatic grandiloquence that seemed to come naturally to many of Sue's readers, at least when writing to their idol. I quote Louise Crombach in the original: "Pauvre et obscure comme la plus pauvre et la plus obscure de nos prisonnières, élevée comme elles par des parens indigens et ignorans, comme elles ayant eu faim et froid dans la rue, pendant toute mon enfance, j'ai dû me sentir attirée vers elles! ne pouvant vivre et faire vivre deux vieillards, consacrant tout mon tems comme *dame de l'oeuvre des prisons*, j'ai dû, après deux années passées au service gratuit de cette oeuvre, demander un emploi, qui me donne du pain, et me laisse au milieu de mes pauvres soeurs captives. . . . Si vous saviez, Monsieur, quelle richesse de coeur! que de resources cachées, au fond de ces âmes *paralysées* seulement. Et puis, elles sont du peuple comme moi. Je parle la même langue, et surtout, je la comprends et je l'aime car c'est celle de ma mère!"

22. See Nuel Pharr Davis, *The Life of Wilkie Collins* (Urbana: Univ. of Illinois Press, 1956), p. 228.

7. *Retrospective Lust, or Flaubert's Perversities*

1. Jonathan Culler, in *Flaubert: The Uses of Uncertainty* (Ithaca, N.Y.: Cornell Univ. Press, 1974), discusses at length and very perceptively how Flaubert's texts must be read in terms of their resistance to the ways one "normally" reads novels. I shall discuss later on the ways in which I diverge from Culler's critical project.

2. Gustave Flaubert, *L'Education sentimentale*, in *Oeuvres*, ed. Albert Thibaudet and René Dumesnil (Paris: Bibliothèque de la Pléïade, 1952), vol. 2, p. 49. All references are to this edition, and will hereafter be indicated in parentheses in the text. A word on translation: translations from the novel are my own, and I have sought fidelity more than elegance. Given Flaubert's stylistic peculiarities, I refer to the French original more here than in other chapters, and have tried above all to make my translations a guide to the structure and meaning of the original. I have consulted with profit the translation by Robert Baldick (Harmondsworth, Md.: Penguin Books, 1964), the best English version of which I am aware.

3. One could suggest multiple specific allusions to novels of *La Comédie humaine* here. Most important, no doubt, is the evocation of Vautrin ("the genius of jailbirds"), master-plotter of Balzac's world and paternal counsellor to young men, Rastignac and then Lucien de Rubempré, who takes on himself the role of providence and in particular works to arrange Lucien's marriage to a Faubourg Saint-Germain heiress.

4. For a more detailed discussion of this scene, see Peter Brooks *The Melodramatic Imagination* (New Haven: Yale Univ. Press, 1976), pp. 139–41.

5. Already, this example shows the problems raised when one attempts to view *style indirect libre* as an essentially mimetic technique designed to record a character's (Frédéric's) consciousness. The essential point is made by Roland Barthes, when he notes that "in wielding an irony deeply marked by incertitude," Flaubert creates a "salutary malaise" of writing, whereby one can never tell if he is "responsible" for what he writes, and one is prevented from answering the question: *"Who is speaking?"* See *S/Z* (Paris: Editions du Seuil, 1970), p. 146; English trans. Richard Miller (New York: Hill and Wang, 1974).

6. André Malraux, "Laclos," in *Tableau de la littérature française, XVIIᵉ–XVIIIᵉ siècles* (Paris: Gallimard, 1939), pp. 420–21.

7. On Frédéric's trancelike and hallucinated states, see Victor Brombert, *The Novels of Flaubert* (Princeton, N.J.: Princeton Univ. Press, 1966), pp. 141–42. Brombert's chapter on *L'Education sentimentale* captures superbly the themes and the tonality of Flaubert's *imaginaire*, and I am indebted to him on many points.

8. Proust writes, for instance: *"L'Education sentimentale* est un long rapport de toute une vie, sans que les personnages prennent pour ainsi dire une part active à l'action." See "A propos du 'style' de Flaubert," in *Contre Sainte-Beuve précédé de Pastiches et mélanges et suivi de Essais et articles*, ed. Pierre Clarac and Yves Sandre (Paris: Bibliothèque de la Pléiade, 1971), p. 590. De-dramatization and de-novelization are discussed in more detail by Gérard Genette, "Silences de Flaubert," in *Figures* (Paris: Editions du Seuil, 1966), pp. 223–43—one of the very best essays on Flaubert.

9. Culler, *Flaubert*, p. 85. The difference between Culler and myself is one of emphasis: where he is interested in models of intelligibility and interpretive operations, I am more specifically concerned with narrative organization and the "novelistic." The problem of Culler's analysis, from my perspective, is that his central interest in the "allegory of interpretation and understanding"—how Flaubert prevents classic interpretive moves of "recuperation," rationalization in terms of thematic meanings and messages—tends to make him read Flaubert's demoralizations as ever reaching toward a zero result, virtually a philosophical nihilism, whereas I believe that creative interplay with the novelistic context is of prime importance.

10. Balzac, *Illusions perdues*, in *La Comédie humaine* (Paris: Bibliothèque de la Pléiade, 1976–81), vol. 5, p. 287.

11. The charcoal brazier (*réchaud de charbon*) was used—frequently, if

one trusts literary evidence—to commit suicide. For instance, the attempted suicide of Esther, an important moment in Balzac's *Splendeurs et misères des courtisanes*, uses this method. Frédéric's hallucinated vision is introduced in an *if* clause with a pluperfect verb ("comme s'il avait aperçu . . ."), which would normally demand that *couler* be in the imperfect. Running water was, of course, used to preserve the corpses. For Genette's comments on this sentence, see "Silences de Flaubert," p. 230.

12. Henry James, "Gustave Flaubert," in *Notes on Novelists* (New York: Scribner's, 1914), pp. 86–87.

13. The best case for the love story is made by Brombert, who is aware of what complicates and threatens such an interpretation; Culler demonstrates the negative reading.

14. Proust, "A propos du 'style' de Flaubert," p. 587.

15. In a recent study of Flaubert, "Strategies of Representation: A Study of Flaubert's Works" (forthcoming, Stanford Univ. Press), Michal Peled Ginsburg demonstrates that one can think of Flaubert's narrative as metonymically generated, generated from an arbitrary play of substitutions rather than from thematic coherence, or from the ambitions and choices of the characters.

16. Culler provides a good discussion of some of the effects of *style indirect libre*, especially in *Flaubert*, pp. 112–22, where he is criticizing the view of R. J. Sherrington (in *Three Novels by Flaubert* [Oxford: Oxford Univ. Press, 1970]) that Flaubert's shifting narrators are identifiable and that 70 percent of *L'Education* is narrated from Frédéric's point of view: an attempt at "recuperation" of meaning and coherence which an attentive reading of the text invalidates. See also Barthes on Flaubert's "salutary malaise" (*S/Z*, p. 146) and on "le *fading* des voix," the effect of hearing two radio signals that interfere with one another (pp. 48–49). The best discussion of Flaubert's uses of *style indirect libre* is Michal Peled Ginsburg, "Free Indirect Discourse: Theme and Narrative Voice in Flaubert, George Eliot, and Verga" (Doctoral dissertation, Yale Univ., 1970).

Flaubert's use of *style indirect libre* makes *L'Education sentimentale* a good instance of what Mikhaïl Bakhtin calls "polyphony" and "heteroglossia" in the novel: see "Discourse in the Novel," in *The Dialogic Imagination*, ed. Michael Holquist, trans. Holquist and Caryl Emerson (Austin: Univ. of Texas Press, 1981), pp. 259–422. Flaubert is not one of Bakhtin's preferred examples (and is not mentioned in this major essay), perhaps because—as Holquist has suggested to me—Flaubert appeared ideologically to Bakhtin a major representative of the monologic bourgeois tradition; and perhaps also because Bakhtin would be suspicious of Flaubert's ultimate privilege of the artist, the teller.

17. See Flaubert, *Correspondance* (Paris: Club de l'Honnête Homme, 1974), vol. 2, pp. 268 and 76.

18. For a study of the "narratological" implications of these terms, see Gérard Genette, "Discours du récit," in *Figures III* (Paris: Editions du Seuil, 1972), especially pp. 186 ff. The whole effect of Flaubert's style, especially the use of *style indirect libre* and the avoidance of dramatic "scenes" rendered in dialogue, erases any sharp distinction between mimesis and diegesis.

19. On Flaubert's political stance, see Brombert, *The Novels of Flaubert*, pp. 156–61; Edmund Wilson, "Flaubert's Politics," in *The Triple Thinkers* (New York: Harcourt, Brace, 1938), pp. 100–121; and Jean-Paul Sartre, *L'Idiot de la famille* (Paris: Gallimard, 1971–78), *passim*.

20. See Karl Marx, *The Eighteenth Brumaire of Louis Bonaparte* (New York: International Publishers, 1963), which was first published in 1852.

21. See Brombert's fine discussion of the "double sense of History" created by the Fontainebleau episode, *The Novels of Flaubert*, p. 177.

22. Flaubert's good friend Maxime Du Camp (himself a virulent anti-Communard) reports this remark—uttered as the two viewed the ruins of the Tuileries Palace, burned by the Communards—in his *Souvenirs littéraires* (Paris: Hachette, 1883), vol. 2, p. 474.

23. See Flaubert, *Oeuvres*, vol. 1, p. 622.

24. This little box—which goes back in Frédéric's memories to his first visit to the Arnoux apartment—may recall the glove box which the Vicomtesse de Beauséant presents to Eugène de Rastignac in token of farewell during her last evening in Paris, before she goes to bury herself in Normandy: of this *coffret* Mme de Beauséant herself says, "Il y a beaucoup de moi là-dedans." See *Le Père Goriot*, in *La Comédie humaine*, vol. 3, pp. 265–66.

25. Culler, *Flaubert*, pp. 152–56. See also Brombert, who stresses a vital point when he notes that "Frédéric and Mme Arnoux, during their final encounter, become poets of the past" (*The Novels of Flaubert*, p. 153)—though I read this "poetry" as conferring greater significance on the act of memory and recounting than on the past love. See also Brombert's more recent discussion of this scene in *"L'Education sentimentale*: Articulations et polyvalence," in *La Production du sens chez Flaubert*, ed. Claudine Gothot-Mersch (Paris: Union Générale des Editions, 1975), pp. 55–69.

26. On the importance of the prostitute in Flaubert's imagination, see Brombert, *The Novels of Flaubert*, especially pp. 137–38; and my own com-

ments on the obsessive presence of the prostitute in Flaubert's letters, "Bedbugs and Sandalwood," *The Nation* 230, no. 12 (1980), pp. 375–76.

27. A recent study of the outlines and drafts of *L'Education sentimentale* by Peter Michael Wetherill notes that Flaubert initially intended to supply his readers with an explicit reminder that this episode was alluded to near the start of the novel: "anecdote à laquelle il est fait allusion au premier chapitre," he writes in one version; and in another, "rappeler qu'il en a été question au premier chapitre." See "C'est là ce que nous avons eu de meilleur," *Flaubert à l'oeuvre*, ed. Raymonde Debray-Genette (Paris: Flammarion, 1980), p. 59. Wetherill observes that the elimination of such explicit aids to the reader is part of a general process of what he calls the deliberate suppression of the "Balzacian resonances" of the text, its "obscurcissement" (p. 61)—which, of course, has the effect of making the reader work in new ways to structure his experience of the text.

28. Northrop Frye, *Anatomy of Criticism* (Princeton, N.J.: Princeton Univ. Press, 1957), p. 214.

29. Georg Lukács, *The Theory of the Novel*, trans. Anna Bostock (Cambridge: MIT Press, 1971), p. 126.

8. *Narrative Transaction and Transference*

1. See Roland Barthes, *S/Z* (Paris: Editions du Seuil, 1970), pp. 95–96; English trans. Richard Miller (New York: Hill and Wang, 1974).

2. Guy de Maupassant, "Une Ruse," in *Oeuvres complètes* (Paris: Conard, 1908), vol. 4, p. 139. This tale was first brought to my attention by Angela S. Moger in her fine doctoral dissertation, "Working out (of) Frame(d) Works: A Study of the Structural Frame in Stories by Maupassant, Balzac, Barbey, and Conrad" (Yale University, 1980), which is in general most helpful in thinking about relations of frame to framed. On "Une Ruse," see pp. 43 ff.; and also Moger, "That Obscure Object of Narrative," *Yale French Studies* 63 (1983), pp. 129–38. On the questions that interest me in this chapter, see also Ross Chambers, *Story and Situation* (Minneapolis: Univ. of Minnesota Press, 1984).

3. Honoré de Balzac, *Sarrasine*, in *La Comédie humaine* (Paris: Bibliothèque de la Pléiade, 1976–81), vol. 6, p. 1075.

4. On these and other tales, see Léo Mazet, "Récit(s) dans le récit: l'échange du récit chez Balzac," *L'Année balzacienne*, 1976 (Paris: Garnier, 1976), pp. 129–61. On *Honorine*, see Moger, "Working Out," pp. 76–112. On *Le Lys dans la vallée*, see Peter Brooks, "Virtue-Tripping: Notes on *Le Lys dans la vallée*," *Yale French Studies* 50 (1975).

5. Balzac, "Facino Cane," in *La Comédie humaine*, vol. 6, p. 1019.

6. Balzac, *Le Colonel Chabert*, in *La Comédie humaine*, vol. 3, p. 316.

7. I. A. Richards, *The Philosophy of Rhetoric* (New York: Oxford Univ. Press, 1936), p. 94.

8. On Chabert's discourse, see the interesting analysis by Marcelle Marini, "Chabert mort ou vif," *Littérature* 13 (1974), pp. 92–112.

9. Sigmund Freud, "The Dynamics of the Transference" (1912), in *The Standard Edition of the Complete Psychological Works of Sigmund Freud*, ed. James Strachey (London: Hogarth Press, 1953–74), vol. 12, p. 108.

10. On literature as rhetorical exchange and transaction, see, among other recent studies: Louise M. Rosenblatt, *The Reader, the Text, the Poem* (Carbondale: Southern Illinois Univ. Press, 1978), and Barbara Herrnstein Smith, *On the Margins of Discourse* (Chicago: Univ. of Chicago Press, 1978). Other work generally characterized as "reader-response criticism"—by Stanley Fish and Wolfgang Iser, for instance—at least implicitly refers to a transactional model. Despite its title, Meredith Anne Skura's chapter "Literature as Transference: Rhetorical Function" in her useful book *The Literary Use of the Psychoanalytic Process* (New Haven: Yale Univ. Press, 1981), has little to say about transference and its rhetorical properties and equivalences, since it is mainly devoted to the issue of "transitional spaces" (as derived from D. W. Winnicott) and to the refinement of Skura's phantasy model of the literary text.

11. See Mikhaïl Bakhtin, *Problems of Dostoevsky's Poetics*, trans. R. W. Rotsel (Ann Arbor, Mich.: Ardis, 1973).

12. See William Labov and Joshua Waletsky, "Natural Narrative," in *Essays on the Verbal and Visual Arts* (Proceedings of the 1966 Annual Spring Meeting of the American Ethnological Society), ed. June Helm (Seattle: Univ. of Washington Press, 1967).

9. *An Unreadable Report: Conrad's* Heart of Darkness

1. These "narratological" questions have not been much discussed in the extensive critical literature on Conrad, and I shall thus not make much reference to other interpretations of *Heart of Darkness*. Let me, however, acknowledge a debt to James Guetti's argument in *The Limits of Metaphor* (Ithaca, N.Y.: Cornell Univ. Press, 1967), which has similarities to my own. Guetti is concerned with the failure of Marlow's search for a meaning postulated as at the end of the journey and in the heart of darkness. But Guetti conceives this failure as essentially linguistic—the failure of metaphor—rather than as a problem in narrative. Another study touching on

some of the same issues as mine is the fine essay by Garrett Stewart, "Lying as Dying in *Heart of Darkness*," *PMLA* 95, no. 3 (1980), pp. 319–31—an essay published at nearly the same time as a first version of the present chapter, in an interesting convergence of perspectives. I have also learned from Tzvetan Todorov, "Cœur des ténèbres," in *Les Genres du discours* (Paris: Editions du Seuil, 1978); and Albert J. Guerard, *Conrad the Novelist* (Cambridge: Harvard Univ. Press, 1958).

2. Joseph Conrad, *Heart of Darkness*, in *Youth and Two Other Stories* (Garden City, N.Y.: Doubleday, Page and Co., 1924), p. 142. Subsequent references are to this edition, and will be given in parentheses in the text. Properly, this quotation should be in *double* quotation marks, since everything said by Marlow is already presented in quotation marks, as a report by the first narrator, while everything cited by Marlow is already in double quotes, and ought properly to be in triple quotation marks in my text. For the sake of simplicity, I shall eliminate the first set of quotation marks when I cite Marlow. But it is not without pertinence to my subject that we are always made aware that Marlow is being cited by another.

3. See Tzvetan Todorov, "Typologie du roman policier," in *Poétique de la prose* (Paris: Editions du Seuil, 1971), pp. 55–65; English trans. Richard Howard, *The Poetics of Prose* (Ithaca, N.Y.: Cornell Univ. Press, 1977). The existence of these two time strands in the detective story is lucidly expounded, and played with, by Michel Butor in his novel *L'Emploi du temps* (Paris: Editions de Minuit, 1957).

4. On the "dialogic" and "double-voicedness," see in particular Mikhaïl Bakhtin, "Discourse in the Novel," in *The Dialogic Imagination*, ed. Michael Holquist, trans. Holquist and Caryl Emerson (Austin: Univ. of Texas Press, 1981), pp. 259–422; and *Problems of Dostoevsky's Poetics*, trans. R. W. Rotsel (Ann Arbor, Mich.: Ardis, 1973).

5. F. R. Leavis succinctly states a common critical position when, in reference to another passage from *Heart of Darkness*, he says: "He [Conrad] is intent on making a virtue out of not knowing what he means." *The Great Tradition* (Garden City, N.Y.: Anchor-Doubleday, 1954), p. 219. Among other failures of perception, this remark fails to take account of the fact that it is Marlow, not Conrad, who is speaking.

6. See Guetti: "But 'Heart of Darkness' goes beyond *Moby-Dick*, for the suggestion that the ineffable may simply be an emptiness is present throughout the story." *The Limits of Metaphor*, p. 66.

7. *Lord Jim* (Garden City, N.Y.: Doubleday, Page and Co., 1924), p. 225. Conrad broke off work on *Lord Jim* to write *Heart of Darkness*, returning

to the former when the latter was finished. There is thus a particularly close relation between these two Marlows, though one does not want to call them the same.

8. That is, a classic framed tale would present a set of nested boxes, a set of brackets within brackets: an instance would be Mary Shelley's *Frankenstein*, where Walton's narrative encloses Frankenstein's narrative which encloses the Monster's narrative: when the Monster has finished his narrative, Frankenstein then finishes his, then Walton concludes. If we diagram *Heart of Darkness* as a framed tale, thus:

First Narrator [Marlow [Kurtz [ ] K's death] end M's narrative] First Narrator final paragraph

we realize that the diagram is false: the inner frame of Kurtz's narrative has no such shapely coherence, and—perhaps as consequence—neither Marlow's narrative nor the first narrator's appears to "close" in satisfactory fashion.

9. The question of who is listening to Marlow's narrative is an interesting one that is not susceptible of ultimate resolution. " 'Try to be civil, Marlow,' growled a voice, and I knew that there was at least one listener awake besides myself" (*Heart of Darkness*, p. 94). But whose voice is it? And are the others asleep, or absorbed?

10. On these "functions" of language, see Roman Jakobson, "Closing Statement: Linguistics and Poetics," in *Style in Language*, ed. Thomas Sebeok (Cambridge: MIT Press, 1960). A fuller exposition of the functions is given in chapter eleven, note 8. On dialogue, see Bakhtin, *Problems of Dostoevsky's Poetics*.

11. On the interdependence of "I" and "thou" in discourse, see Emile Benveniste, "De la subjectivité dans le langage," in *Problèmes de linguistique générale* (Paris: Gallimard, 1967), pp. 258–66. For one example of storytelling as "contamination," see Peter Brooks, "Godlike Science/Unhallowed Arts: Language and Monstrosity in *Frankenstein*," *New Literary History* 9, no. 3 (1978).

12. Conrad, "Henry James," in *Notes on Life and Letters* (London: Dent, 1924), pp. 18–19.

10. Fictions of the Wolf Man:
Freud and Narrative Understanding

1. See *The Wolf-Man by the Wolf-Man*, ed. Muriel Gardiner (New York: Basic Books, 1971). This extraordinarily rich, interesting, and well edited volume contains the Wolf Man's memoirs, his "Recollections of Sigmund Freud," as well as further biographical material by Muriel Gardiner and the case histories by Freud and Ruth Mack Brunswick. On the last years of the Wolf Man, see Karin Obholzer, *The Wolf-Man: Conversations with Freud's Patient—Sixty Years Later*, trans. Michael Shaw (New York: Continuum, 1982). A reinterpretation of the Wolf Man's case has been presented by Pierre Abraham and Maria Torok in *Cryptonymie: Le Verbier de l'homme aux loups*, with an important preface by Jacques Derrida (Paris: Editions du Galilée, 1977).

My own quotations from the case history, properly titled *From the History of an Infantile Neurosis* [*Aus der Geschichte einer infantilen Neurose*] (1918), are taken from *The Standard Edition of the Complete Psychological Works of Sigmund Freud*, ed. James Strachey (London: Hogarth Press, 1953–74), vol. 17, pp. 7–122.

2. For evidence of the Wolf Man's mental condition in old age, see the conversations recorded by Obholzer in *The Wolf-Man: Conversations with Freud's Patient*. I find Obholzer's own judgments unreliable, since she apparently wants to discredit psychoanalysis, or at least score points against Freud's claims that his patient was "cured." While it is evident that the Wolf Man remained a compulsive personality who was never entirely free from obsessions and delusions, whose erotic life remained marked by his "sister complex" (determining that his choice of women involve the need to degrade), and who never completely resolved the transference relation to Freud, it also seems clear that he managed to negotiate a reasonably normal existence.

3. Sir Arthur Conan Doyle, "The Adventure of the Cardboard Box," in *The Complete Sherlock Holmes* (Garden City, N.Y.: Doubleday, 1953), vol. 2, p. 1059.

4. *The Wolf-Man by the Wolf-Man*, p. 146.

5. Freud, *From the History of an Infantile Neurosis*, in *Standard Edition*, vol. 17, p. 17. Subsequent references will be given in the text.

6. *Oedipus the King*, trans. Bernard Knox (New York: Pocket Books, 1972), p. 8. Freud was of course fully aware of the possible, and desired, analogy between Oedipus and himself as riddle-answerers. His disciples

realized a youthful aspiration of Freud's when, on his fiftieth birthday (1906), they presented him with a medal with his profile on one side, and on the other a representation of Oedipus with the line: "Who divined the famed riddle [that is, of the Sphinx] and was a man most mighty." See Ernest Jones, *The Life and Work of Sigmund Freud* (New York: Basic Books, 1953), vol. 2, p. 14.

7. Diagrammatically—using Freud's analogy of archaeological layering—we should have a structure that looks like this: $^{4/}1/_{3/_2}$. But the construction of the narrative makes the relation of the layers far more complex, and subverts any simple geological model.

8. It may be helpful to remind the reader of the final chronology of major events and/or phantasies that Freud constructs and appends as a later footnote (1923) to the case history:

> I will once more set out here the chronology of the events mentioned in this case history.
>
> *Born* on Christmas Day.
>
> *1^1/2 years old*: Malaria. Observation of his parents' coitus or of the interview between them into which he later introduced his coitus phantasy.
>
> *Just before 2^1/2*: Scene with Grusha.
>
> *2^1/2*: Screen memory of his parents' departure with his sister. This showed him alone with his Nanya and so disowned Grusha and his sister.
>
> *Before 3^1/4*: His mother's laments to the doctor.
>
> *3^1/4*: Beginning of his seduction by his sister. Soon afterward the threat of castration from his Nanya.
>
> *3^1/2*: The English governess. Beginning of the change in his character.
>
> *4*: The wolf dream. Origin of the phobia.
>
> *4^1/2*: Influence of the Bible story. Appearance of the obsessional symptoms.
>
> *Just before 5*: Hallucination of the loss of his finger.
>
> *5*: Departure from the first estate.
>
> *After 6*: Visit to his sick father.
>
> $\left.\begin{array}{l} 8: \\ 10: \end{array}\right\}$ Final outbreaks of the obsessional neurosis.
>
>   (p. 121)

This chronology represents the order of the story but not, of course, the way its plot "works."

9. Freud, of course, faced this problem of originating deed versus originating phantasy in other instances of his thought as well, perhaps most famously in the question of "the seduction": the large number of recollections of attempts at seduction by a parent figure produced by his patients finally led him to suspect that seduction might be a primal phantasy—a turn in his thought which has been criticized by some socially oriented psychoanalysts who want to claim a high frequency of such seductions. And in *Totem and Taboo* (1913), *Standard Edition*, vol. 13, Freud admits that the killing of the primal father may have been a phantasy rather than a real event. Though his conception of primitive man makes him argue that it may be assumed that here "in the beginning was the Deed," he also contends that "the heart of the matter"—the effects of the originary murder—remains the same whether it was deed or phantasy.

Jonathan Culler discusses both the Wolf Man (as discussed by myself in an earlier version of this chapter, published in *Diacritics*) and *Totem and Taboo* as examples of the "double logic" of narrative; see "Story and Discourse in the Analysis of Narrative," in *The Pursuit of Signs* (London: Routledge and Kegan Paul, 1981).

10. Jacques Lacan, "L'Instance de la lettre dans l'inconscient," in *Ecrits* (Paris: Editions du Seuil, 1966), p. 518.

11. See Henry James, *The Art of the Novel*, ed. R. P. Blackmur (New York: Scribner's, 1934), p. 5.

12. Steven Marcus, "Freud and Dora: Story, History, Case History," *Partisan Review* 41, no. 1 (1974), p. 92. A longer version of this essay is in Marcus, *Representations: Essays on Literature and Society* (New York: Random House, 1975). Marcus in this fine essay makes a number of interesting points about Freud as narrative historian and "modernist" writer.

13. See Freud, "Constructions in Analysis" (1937), in *Standard Edition*, vol. 23, pp. 257–69, where he notes how a patient's assent to a construction made by the analyst is confirmed by the production of "new memories which complete and extend the construction," and also how analysis may not always bring recollection of what has been repressed, but sometimes rather produces in the patient "an assured conviction of the truth of the construction which achieves the same therapeutic result as a recaptured memory." This essay is discussed in more detail in my Conclusion.

14. Lacan, "Intervention sur le transfert," in *Ecrits*, p. 216.

15. See in particular Mikhaïl Bakhtin, "Discourse in the Novel," in *The Dialogic Imagination*, ed. Michael Holquist, trans. Holquist and Caryl Emerson (Austin: Univ. of Texas Press, 1981). See also Tzvetan Todorov, *Mikhaïl*

Bakhtine et le principe dialogique (Paris: Editions du Seuil, 1981).

16. Lacan argues convincingly against the optimistic interpretation: see "L'Instance de la lettre," p. 524.

11. Incredulous Narration: Absalom, Absalom!

1. William Faulkner, *Absalom, Absalom!* (first published 1936; New York: Modern Library, 1951), p. 292. Subsequent references will be given in parentheses in the text.

Since most of the extensive critical literature on this novel does not bear directly on the "narratological" analysis that interests me here, I shall make little reference to it, though, of course, on a number of points of interpretation I can claim no originality. I owe a general debt to the critical perspectives furnished by: James Guetti, *The Limits of Metaphor* (Ithaca, N.Y.: Cornell Univ. Press, 1967); Joseph W. Reed, Jr., *Faulkner's Narrative* New Haven: Yale Univ. Press, 1973); and Albert J. Guerard, *The Triumph of the Novel* (New York: Oxford Univ. Press, 1976). Also—as mentioned further on—I have found of great interest: Patricia Drechsel Tobin, *Time and the Novel: The Genealogical Imperative* (Princeton, N.J.: Princeton Univ. Press, 1978); and John T. Irwin, *Doubling and Incest / Repetition and Revenge* (Baltimore: Johns Hopkins Univ. Press, 1975). See also John T. Matthews, *The Play of Faulkner's Language* (Ithaca, N.Y.: Cornell Univ. Press, 1982), which reads Faulkner's novels in a perspective derived from the work of Jacques Derrida, but nonetheless seems to me to revert far too much, in its commentaries and interpretations, to questions of psychological motivation, intuited when they are not explicit, which make his study far more conventional than he claims.

2. Gérard Genette offers an important corrective to traditional Anglo-American studies of narrative "point of view" by distinguishing "focalization" (the consciousness that takes in the narrative) from "voice" (the discourse that tells the narrative). See in "Discours du récit," in *Figures III* (Paris: Editions du Seuil, 1972), the chapters on "mode" and "voix."

3. One of Faulkner's foremost interpreters, Cleanth Brooks, argues that during the visit to Sutpen's Hundred, Quentin learns Bon's identity—as Sutpen's son and as part Negro—in his conversation with Henry Sutpen: see *William Faulkner: The Yoknapatawpha Country* (New Haven: Yale Univ. Press, 1963), pp. 314–17 and 436–41. The juxtaposition of the two passages I have just cited suggests otherwise, and the representation of the meeting

with Henry, in chapter 9 (cited further on in this chapter), tends to invalidate Brooks's interpretation, since it suggests that no information is exchanged between Henry and Quentin. Brooks's interpretation appears an unwarranted inference on the part of a reader in search of "hard" information. He indeed takes his hypothesis to extreme lengths in a more recent essay, timing Quentin's interview with Henry to show that it can be spoken aloud in twenty seconds, and thus to demonstrate that during the visit to Sutpen's Hundred further words "could have been" spoken between them—for instance: "If Quentin had merely formed the words 'Charles Bon was your friend—?', it is easy to imagine Henry's replying: 'More than my friend. My brother.' Faulkner has preferred to leave it to his reader to imagine this or something like it." ("The Narrative Structure of *Absalom, Absalom!*," *Georgia Review* 29, no. 2 [1975], p. 387.) Here we have an example of an active interpreter overanxious to fill the gaps and arrest the indeterminacies of the text—to the point of rewriting it. Brooks also cites the theory of Hershel Parker, that Quentin deduces the information from looking at Jim Bond during the visit to Sutpen's Hundred, seeing that he bore the Sutpen face (see "What Quentin Saw 'Out There,' " *The Mississippi Quarterly* 27 [Summer 1974], pp. 323–26). While closer to the kinds of knowing suggested by the text, this is still in the nature of an arbitrary interpretive hypothesis. Whereas to say that Quentin infers his information from seeing Clytie, whom he knows from his father to be Sutpen's daughter (see pp. 61–62) and whose "pigmentation" he cannot fail to witness here, simply restates the textual evidence—what Shreve and Quentin say—and furthermore adheres to the manner in which Clytie is used, as hermeneutic clue, through the novel.

4. Tobin offers an interesting discussion of how Quentin is forced to repeat the father: see *Time and the Novel*, pp. 107–32; and Irwin pursues with tenacity the question of fathers and sons, and its relation to the problem of incest, throughout *Doubling and Incest/Repetition and Revenge*.

5. See Roland Barthes, *S/Z* (Paris: Editions du Seuil, 1970), pp. 157–58; English trans. Richard Miller (New York: Hill and Wang, 1974). I say "nearly a literal realization of Barthes's point" because I cannot conceive of what a literal realization could mean. Faulkner's text creates a rhetorical situation in which the traditional authority of tellers has been surrendered to listeners, which metaphorically invites us as readers to speak in the text. Claudia Brodsky, in "The Working of Narrative in *Absalom, Absalom!*, A Textual Analysis," *American Studies* 23, no. 2 (1979), pp. 240–59, takes a

different approach, speaking of "an omniscience made up of many subjectivities" (p. 253).

6. Irwin chooses this approach, reading the two novels as if they formed one text, which is legitimate given his interest in discovering a psychic patterning common to Faulkner's texts, yet troubling when he occasionally calls upon the one text to "explain" the other. Surely we must remain aware of the problematic and occasionally contradictory relations of the two texts, and the issue of definition of text posed to us. If I have preferred to work within the confines of the textual system labeled *Absalom, Absalom!*, I am conscious that the definition of limits is not without its uncertainties even here: does one, for instance, include within the text the appended Genealogy, which records the death of the narrator, Quentin? Or the Chronology, which contains an error, since it puts Quentin's visit to Sutpen's Hundred with Rosa Coldfield in September, 1910, whereas it took place in September, 1909 (Quentin's suicide occurs on June 2, 1910)? One might consider Genealogy and Chronology as the work of a first reader of *Absalom, Absalom!*—Faulkner himself—who was not wholly able to master the text.

7. Irwin writes: "Of the many levels of meaning in *Absalom*, the deepest level is to be found in the symbolic identification of incest and miscegenation and in the relationship of this symbolic identification both to Quentin Compson's personal history in *The Sound and the Fury* and to the story that Quentin narrates in *Absalom, Absalom!*" (*Doubling and Incest/Repetition and Revenge*, pp. 25–26.) This seems to me exactly wrong, and I do not see that Irwin's interesting arguments concerning both incest and miscegenation ever establish an "identification" of the two, which on the contrary stand in a creative, dynamic—and also tragic—tension.

8. In Roman Jakobson's theory of language, the factors necessarily involved in verbal communication are as follows:

CONTEXT

ADDRESSER   MESSAGE   ADDRESSEE

CONTACT

CODE

As a result, we have the following functions of language:

REFERENTIAL

EMOTIVE   POETIC   CONATIVE

PHATIC

METALINGUAL

See "Closing Statement: Linguistics and Poetics," in *Style in Language*, ed. Thomas Sebeok (Cambridge: MIT Press, 1960), pp. 353–58.

9. Stanley Leavy, *The Psychoanalytic Dialogue* (New Haven: Yale Univ. Press, 1980), p. 80.

In Conclusion: Endgames and the Study of Plot

1. The classic exposition of "spatial form" is Joseph Frank, "Spatial Form in Modern Literature," in *The Widening Gyre* (New Brunswick, N.J.: Rutgers Univ. Press, 1963). The concept has been effectively criticized by Frank Kermode in *The Sense of an Ending* (New York: Oxford Univ. Press, 1967). Following Kermode, the best recent argument for the necessity of narrative understanding is Paul Ricoeur, *Temps et récit* (Paris: Editions du Seuil, 1983).

2. Alain Robbe-Grillet, *La Jalousie* (Paris: Editions de Minuit, 1957), p. 101. My translation.

3. Jorge Luis Borges, "The Garden of Forking Paths," in *Labyrinths*, trans. and ed. Donald A. Yates and James E. Irby (New York: New Directions, 1964), p. 24.

4. Sigmund Freud, "Constructions in Analysis" [*Konstruktionen in der Analyse*] (1937), in *The Standard Edition of the Complete Psychological Works of Sigmund Freud*, ed. James Strachey (London: Hogarth Press, 1953–74), vol. 23, pp. 258–59.

5. Henry James, Preface to *The American*, in *The Art of the Novel*, ed. R. P. Blackmur (New York: Scribner's, 1932), p. 32.

INDEX

About the Author

PETER BROOKS, educated at Harvard, London University, and the Sorbonne, now teaches at Yale, where he is Tripp Professor of the Humanities, Director of the Whitney Humanities Center, and current Chairman of the French Department. A distinguished critic, reviewer, and essayist, Professor Brooks is the author of *The Novel of Worldliness* (Princeton University Press) and *The Melodramatic Imagination* (Yale University Press) and has contributed to *Partisan Review*, *The New York Times Book Review*, *The Nation*, and *The New Republic*, among other periodicals.

... as an erotic (feminine) exp

... as an assertive (masc) impli
exp.

...tell...
...is ... the ego,
...ssertion of power

...) is receptivity, an affirmation
... an embracing
of power

In the productive
exchange, there is a fluidity
betw people   of roles.

Healthy person contains both
"masc" + "fem"

but the use of gendered
terms here is problematic —
points out probs women have w/
assertion of power,
~~women~~ men have w/
receptivity.

If one person wants one role
all the time, it forces
the other person to play
the other role all the
time

my own conflict betw. active +
passive roles in therapy.